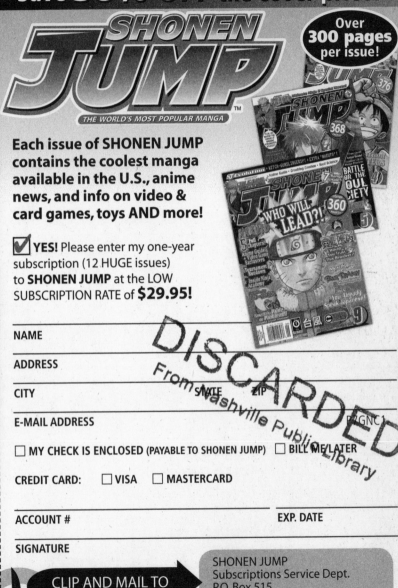

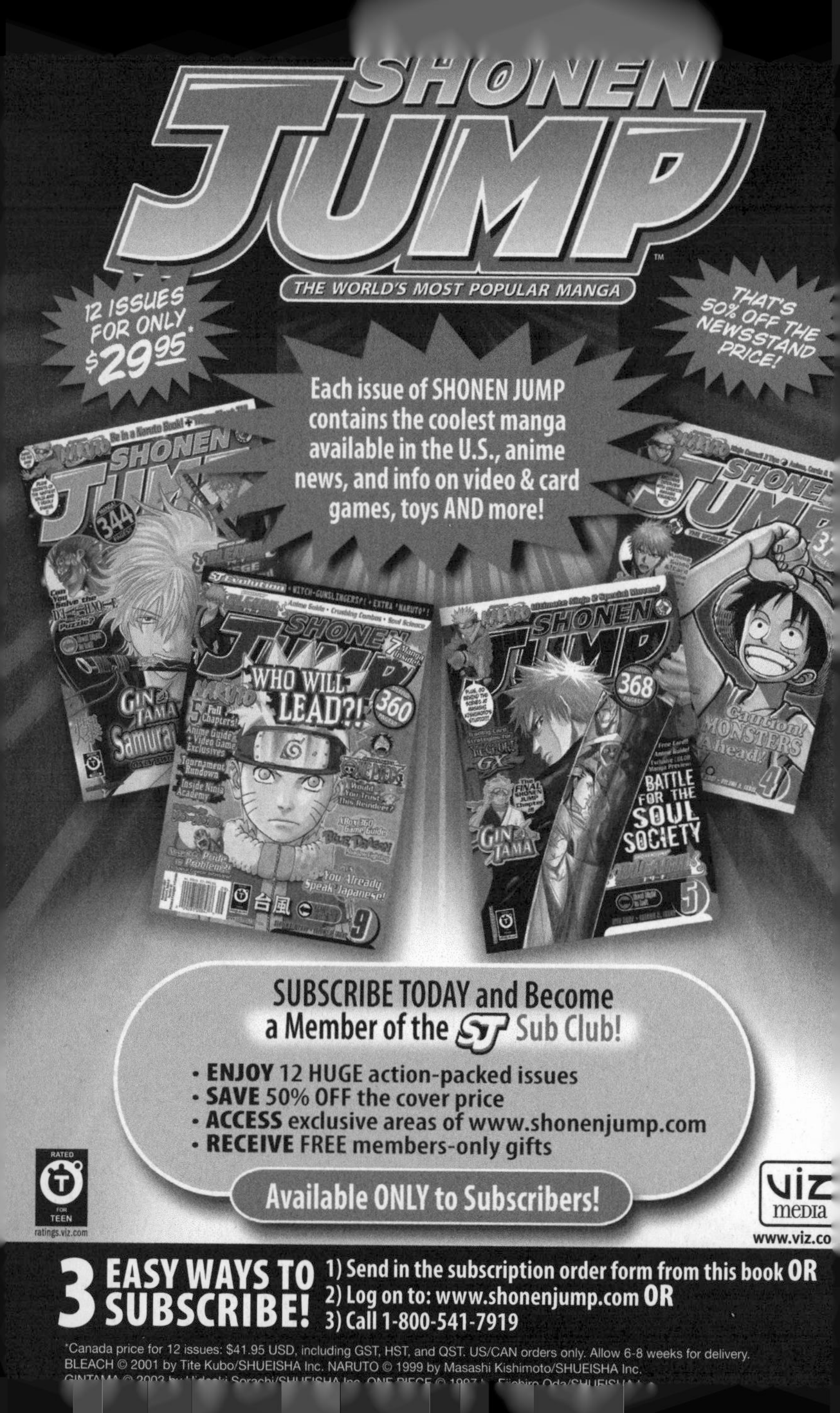
SHONEN JUMP
THE WORLD'S MOST POPULAR MANGA
12 ISSUES FOR ONLY $29.95*
THAT'S 50% OFF THE NEWSSTAND PRICE!
Each issue of SHONEN JUMP contains the coolest manga available in the U.S., anime news, and info on video & card games, toys AND more!
SUBSCRIBE TODAY and Become a Member of the SJ Sub Club!
• ENJOY 12 HUGE action-packed issues
• SAVE 50% OFF the cover price
• ACCESS exclusive areas of www.shonenjump.com
• RECEIVE FREE members-only gifts
Available ONLY to Subscribers!
RATED T FOR TEEN
ratings.viz.com
VIZ media
www.viz.co
3 EASY WAYS TO SUBSCRIBE!
1) Send in the subscription order form from this book OR
2) Log on to: www.shonenjump.com OR
3) Call 1-800-541-7919
*Canada price for 12 issues: $41.95 USD, including GST, HST, and QST. US/CAN orders only. Allow 6-8 weeks for delivery.
BLEACH © 2001 by Tite Kubo/SHUEISHA Inc. NARUTO © 1999 by Masashi Kishimoto/SHUEISHA Inc.

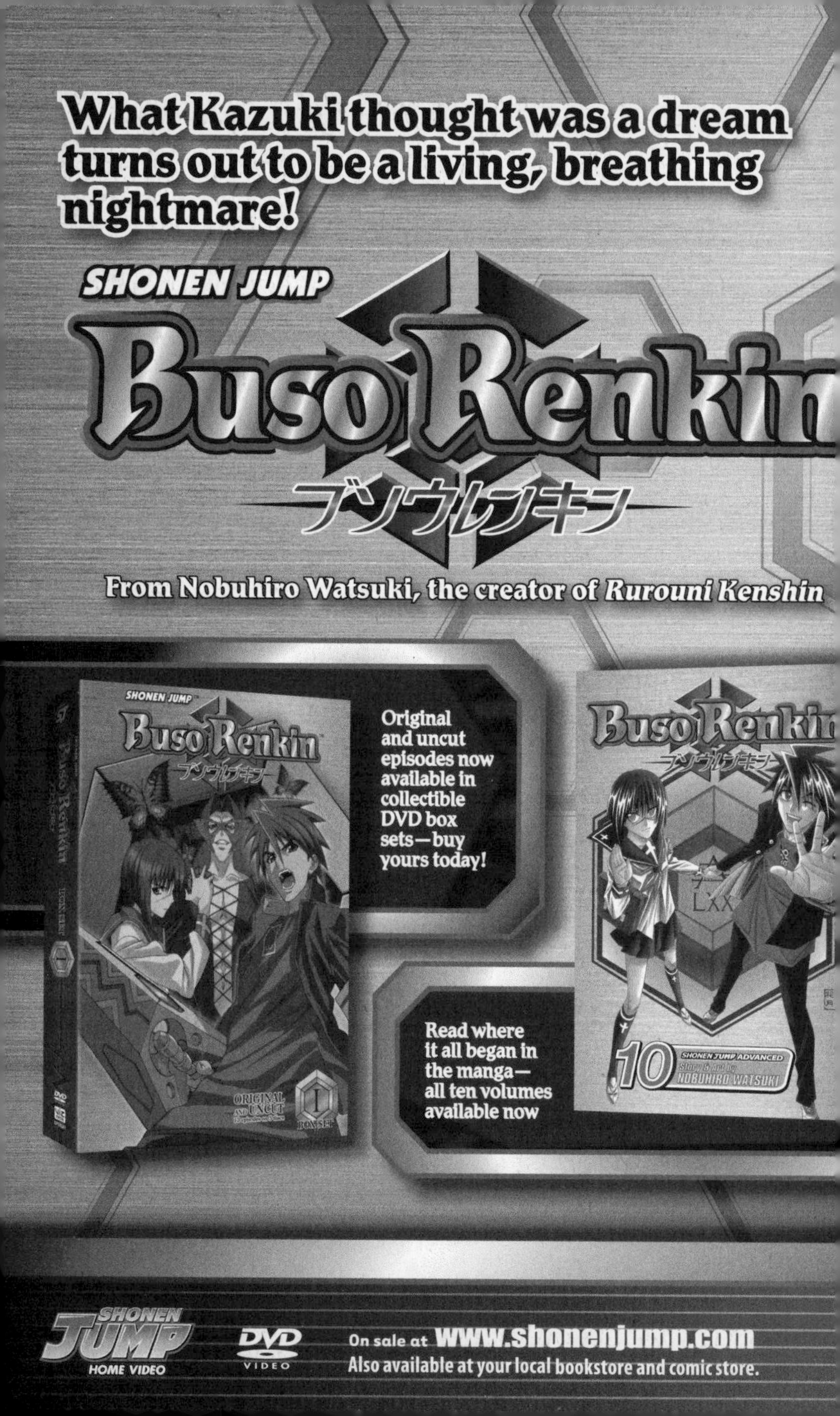
What Kazuki thought was a dream turns out to be a living, breathing nightmare!
SHONEN JUMP
Buso Renkin
ブソウレンキン
From Nobuhiro Watsuki, the creator of *Rurouni Kenshin*
SHONEN JUMP
Buso Renkin
ブソウレンキン
ORIGINAL AND UNCUT
BOX SET
Original and uncut episodes now available in collectible DVD box sets—buy yours today!
Buso Renkin
ブソウレンキン
10
SHONEN JUMP ADVANCED
Story & Art by NOBUHIRO WATSUKI
Read where it all began in the manga—all ten volumes available now
SHONEN JUMP HOME VIDEO
DVD VIDEO
On sale at www.shonenjump.com
Also available at your local bookstore and comic store.

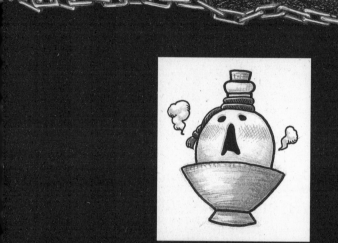

Kazunari Kakei

Due to a report of general good health at my medical checkup, the amount of alcohol I allow myself each day has increased...

NORA: The Last Chronicle of Devildom is Kazunari Kakei's first manga series. It debuted in the April 2004 issue of *Monthly Shonen Jump* and eventually spawned a second series, *SUREBREC: NORA the 2nd*, which premiered in *Monthly Shonen Jump*'s March 2007 issue.

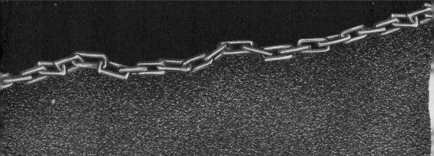

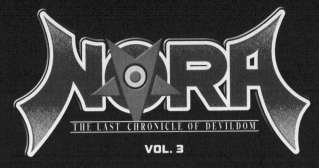

NORA

THE LAST CHRONICLE OF DEVILDOM

VOL. 3

STORY AND ART BY
KAZUNARI KAKEI

English Adaptation/Park Cooper and Barb Lien-Cooper
Translation/Nori Minami
Touch-up Art & Lettering/Annaliese Christman
Design/Sam Elzway
Editor/Carol Fox

Editor in Chief, Books/Alvin Lu
Editor in Chief, Magazines/Marc Weidenbaum
VP, Publishing Licensing/Rika Inouye
VP, Sales & Product Marketing/Gonzalo Ferreyra
VP, Creative/Linda Espinosa
Publisher/Hyoe Narita

Printed in the U.S.A.

Published by VIZ Media, LLC
P.O. Box 77010
San Francisco, CA 94107

10 9 8 7 6 5 4 3 2 1
First printing, February 2009

THE WORLD'S MOST
CUTTING-EDGE MANGA

SHONEN
JUMP
ADVANCED

www.shonenjump.com

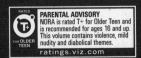

SHONEN JUMP ADVANCED
Manga Edition

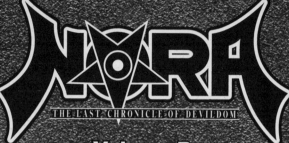

NORA

THE LAST CHRONICLE OF DEVILDOM

Volume 3:
The Soul Stones

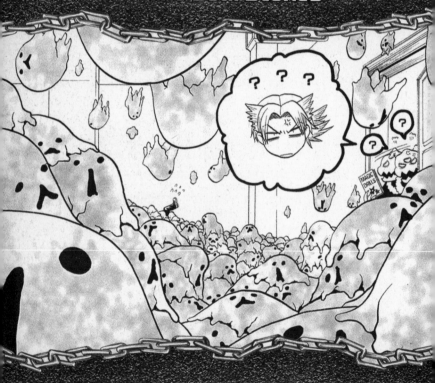

Kazunari Kakei

OUR FIENDISH CAST

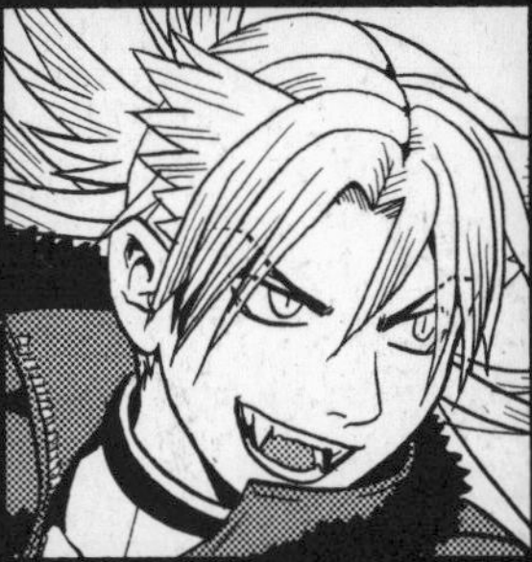

NORA

THE DEMON WORLD'S PROBLEM CHILD, NORA'S FOUL TEMPER IS SURPASSED ONLY BY HIS STUPIDITY. NORA IS BETTER KNOWN AS THE VICIOUS DOG OF DISASTER, THE LEGENDARY DEMON CERBERUS. HIS POWER IS SAID TO SURPASS THAT OF THE DARK LIEGE HERSELF.

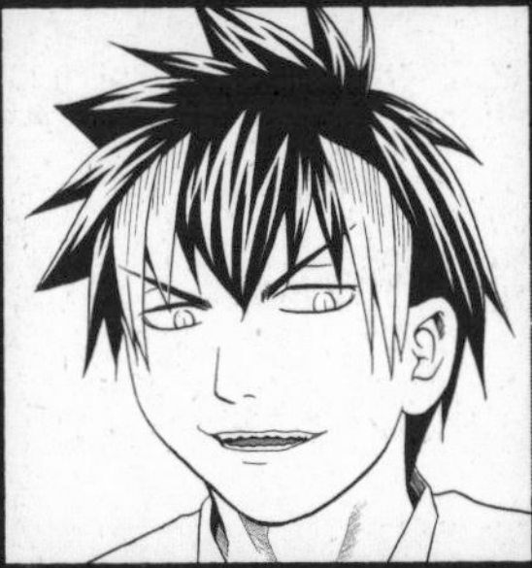

KAZUMA

KAZUMA SEEMS TO HAVE IT ALL. HE'S THE PRESIDENT OF THE STUDENT COUNCIL, AS WELL AS A CLEVER GUY WHO'S GOOD AT SPORTS. HE'S ALSO NORA'S MASTER. DESPITE SEEMING CALM AND COMPOSED, KAZUMA'S GOT QUITE A TEMPER. AS A RESULT, OTHER STUDENTS FEAR HIM. VERDICT: HE'S MORE DEVILISH THAN ANY DEMON.

TENRYO ACADEMY MIDDLE SCHOOL STUDENT COUNCIL

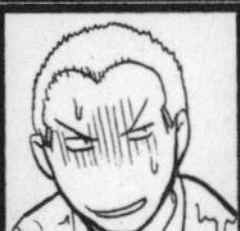

FUJIMOTO

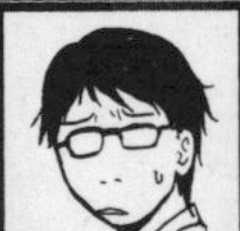

YANO

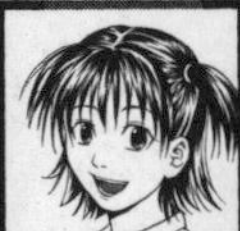

KOYUKI HIRASAKA

DARK LIEGE ARMY

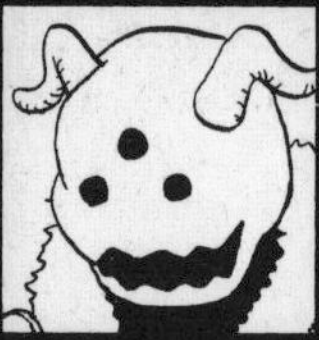

HER INFERNAL MAJESTY, THE DARK LIEGE

THE COMMANDER-IN-CHIEF OF THE DARK LIEGE ARMY, AND THE ONE WHO EXILED NORA TO THE HUMAN WORLD. WHEN SHE WEARS HER GLAMOUR SPELL, SHE'S ONE SMOKIN' HOTTIE.

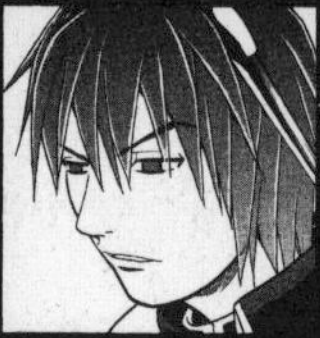

NAVAL FLEET GENERAL

RIVAN

LAID BACK AND SEEMINGLY LAZY, ONCE RIVAN SNAPS, NOBODY CAN HOLD HIM DOWN. FISHING IS HIS HOBBY.

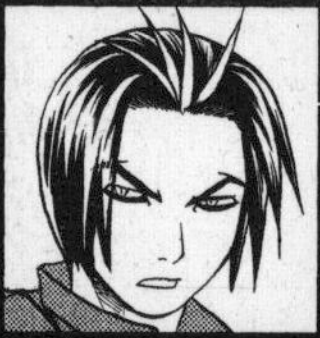

NAVAL FLEET LIEUTENANT GENERAL

BARIK

BARIK IS SURLY, INFLEXIBLE, AND DOES NOT LIKE NORA IN THE LEAST. BAD LUCK SEEMS TO PLAGUE HIM WHEREVER HE GOES.

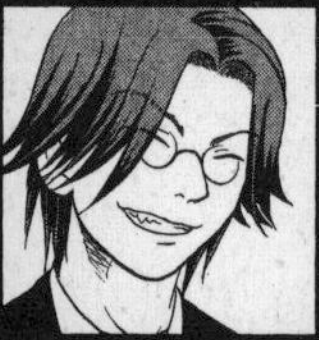

KNELL

A MEMBER OF THE DEMON RESISTANCE WHO MAY HAVE HIS OWN SECRET AGENDA. OR MAYBE HE'D JUST RATHER PICK UP GIRLS. HE'S POWERFUL AND IGUNISU MAGIA HAS NO EFFECT ON HIM—INSTEAD, THE *LADIES* SEEM TO BE HIS WEAKNESS.

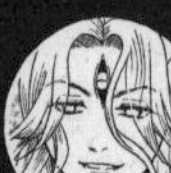

LISTEN TO TEACHER! ♥

THE DARK LIEGE EXPLAINS IT ALL

HELLO DARLINGS! DARK LIEGE HERE. ♥

GOSH, MY LITTLE DEMON PUP NORA HAS BEEN A BOTHER! DON'T I HAVE ENOUGH TROUBLE WITH THE RESISTANCE AND OUTLAW DEMONS REBELLING AGAINST MY DARK LIEGE ARMY WITHOUT NORA CAUSING ME PROBLEMS?

THAT'S WHY I SENT MY STRAY DOGGIE TO THE HUMAN WORLD, TELLING HIM HE SIMPLY MUST LEARN TO BEHAVE. AND IF HE ALSO HELPS BY BATTLING THE OUTLAW DEMONS THAT HAVE TRESPASSED INTO THE HUMAN WORLD, SO MUCH THE BETTER.♥

OH, I'M SO WICKED! THE HUMAN I CHOSE TO HOUSEBREAK MY LITTLE CUR IS KAZUMA MAGARI.

BY ENTERING INTO A MASTER AND SERVANT CONTRACT WITH KAZUMA, NORA BECAME KAZUMA'S "FAMILIAR SPIRIT." AS SUCH, NORA CAN'T USE HIS MAGIC OR RELEASE HIS SEAL SPELL TO RETURN TO HIS REGULAR APPEARANCE WITHOUT HIS NEW MASTER'S "APPROVAL."

TO COMPLICATE MATTERS, A RESISTANCE MEMBER HEARD THAT THE LEGENDARY CERBERUS IS NOW IN THE HUMAN WORLD. HE STARTED A FIGHT WITH OUR HEROES!

BUT AS A CONSEQUENCE OF HIS PREVIOUS BATTLE WITH RIVAN, NORA STARTED TO GRASP THE FLOW OF HIS MAGICAL POWER, AND AMAZINGLY HE DEFEATED HIS ENEMY WITH AN INCREDIBLY POWERFUL BLOW. HOORAY!

AND WHEN SILLY OLD KAZUMA FOUND OUT THAT SOME IN THE RESISTANCE WERE ATTACKING HUMANS JUST FOR SPORT, HE BECAME SIMPLY *FURIOUS* AND VOWED TO *DESTROY* THE RESISTANCE *COMPLETELY!!* ISN'T THAT SWEET OF HIM?!

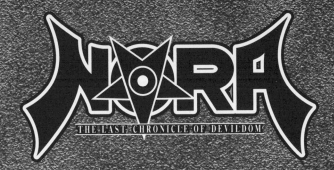

CONTENTS

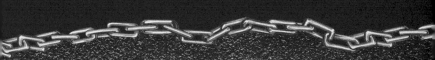

The Outbreak 7

The Soul Stones............................ 53

Cognition 97

Do Your Business........................ 139

Volume 3:
The Soul Stones

Story 9: The Outbreak

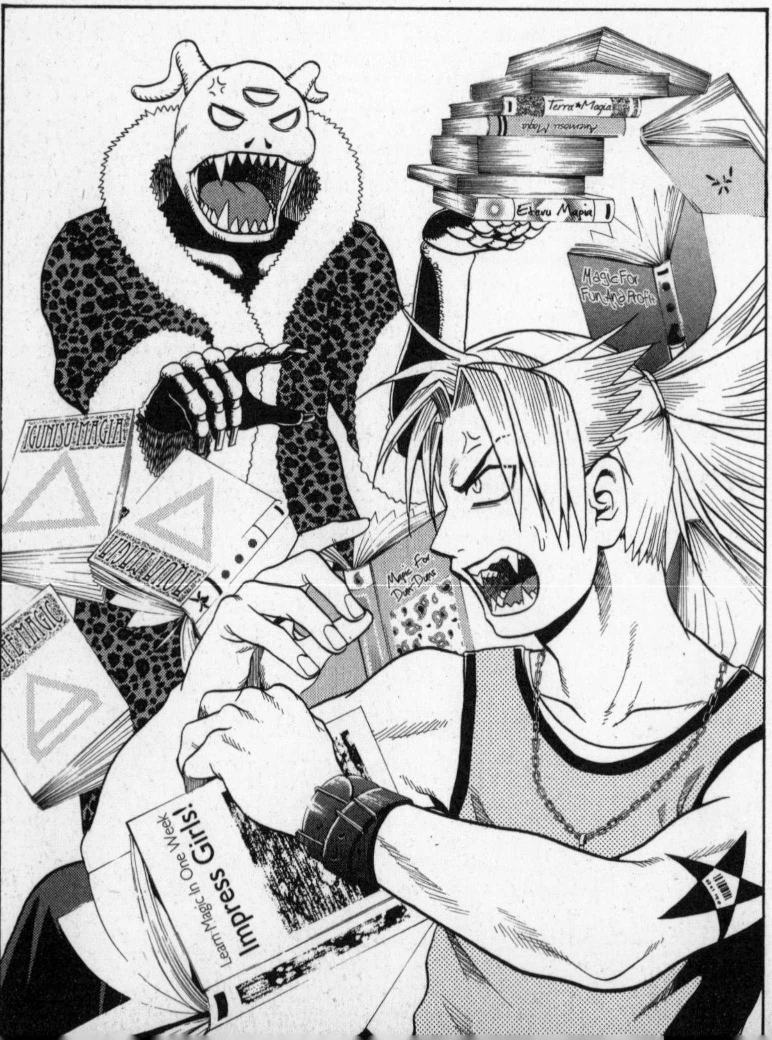
Terra*Magia
Eteru Magia
Magic For Fun And Profit
IGUNISU MAGIA
AQUA MAGIA
Magic For Dum-Dums
Learn Magic In One Week
Impress Girls!

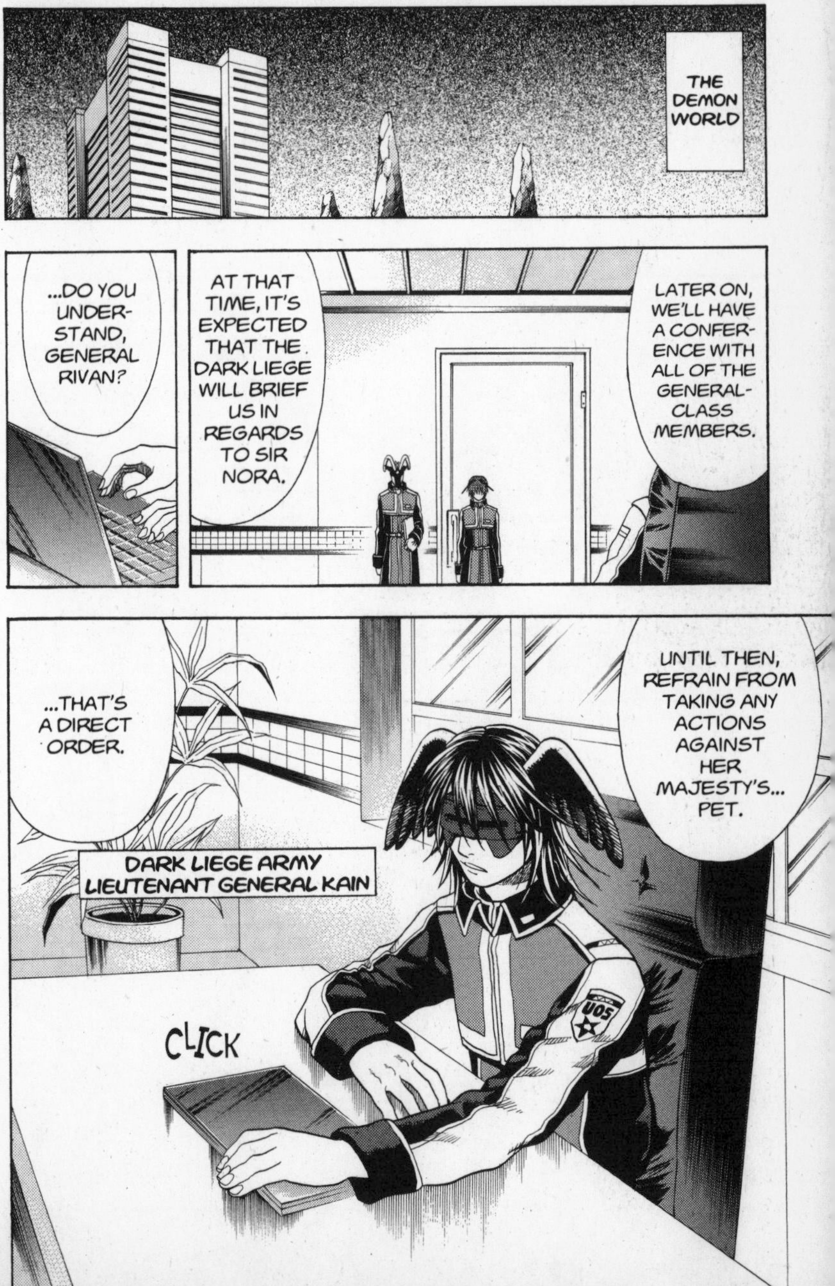
THE DEMON WORLD
LATER ON, WE'LL HAVE A CONFERENCE WITH ALL OF THE GENERAL-CLASS MEMBERS.
AT THAT TIME, IT'S EXPECTED THAT THE DARK LIEGE WILL BRIEF US IN REGARDS TO SIR NORA.
...DO YOU UNDERSTAND, GENERAL RIVAN?
UNTIL THEN, REFRAIN FROM TAKING ANY ACTIONS AGAINST HER MAJESTY'S... PET.
...THAT'S A DIRECT ORDER.
DARK LIEGE ARMY LIEUTENANT GENERAL KAIN
CLICK

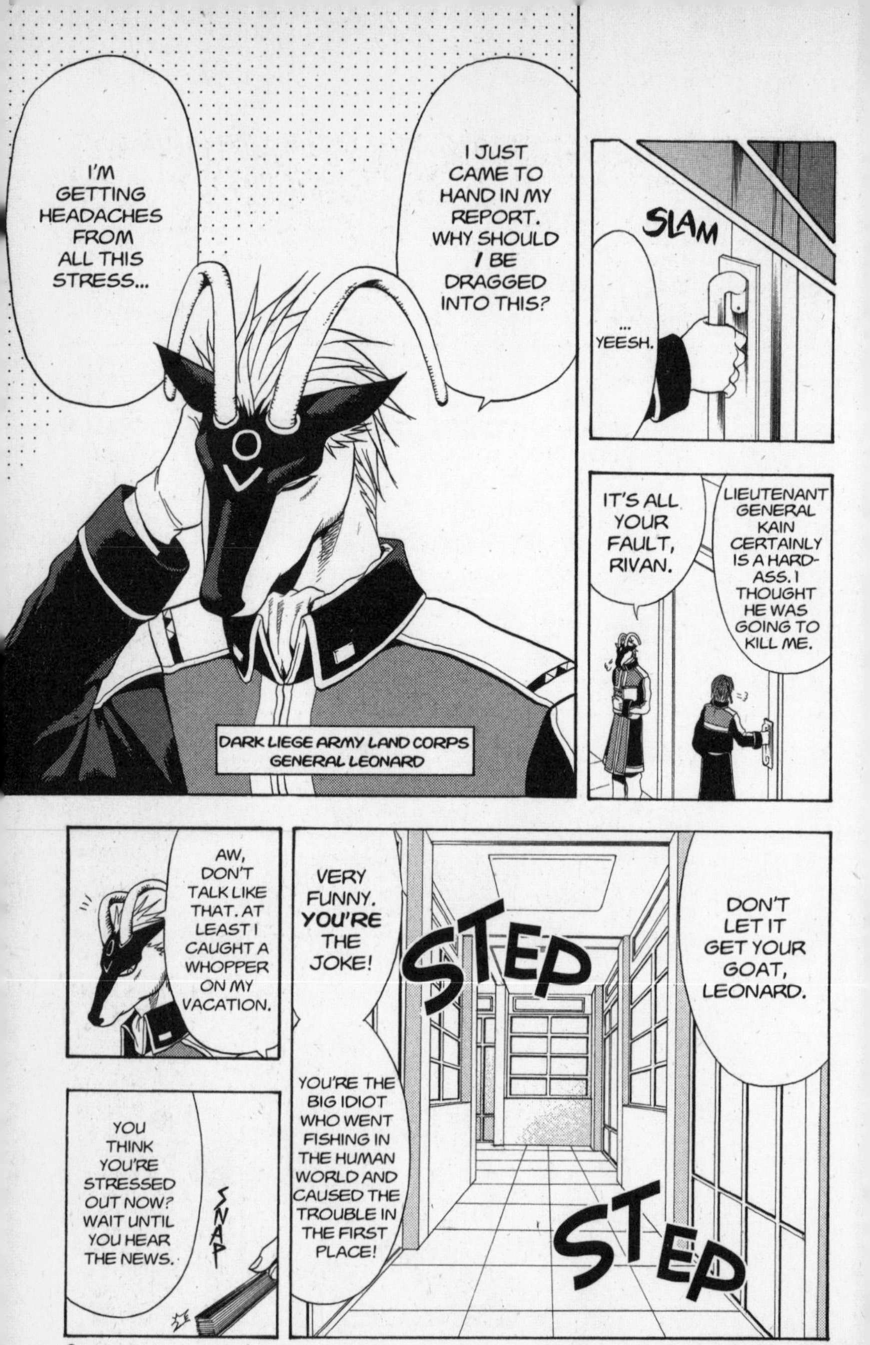
SLAM
... YEESH.
LIEUTENANT GENERAL KAIN CERTAINLY IS A HARD-ASS. I THOUGHT HE WAS GOING TO KILL ME.
IT'S ALL YOUR FAULT, RIVAN.
I JUST CAME TO HAND IN MY REPORT. WHY SHOULD *I* BE DRAGGED INTO THIS?
I'M GETTING HEADACHES FROM ALL THIS STRESS...
DARK LIEGE ARMY LAND CORPS GENERAL LEONARD
DON'T LET IT GET YOUR GOAT, LEONARD.
VERY FUNNY. **YOU'RE** THE JOKE!
STEP
YOU'RE THE BIG IDIOT WHO WENT FISHING IN THE HUMAN WORLD AND CAUSED THE TROUBLE IN THE FIRST PLACE!
STEP
AW, DON'T TALK LIKE THAT. AT LEAST I CAUGHT A WHOPPER ON MY VACATION.
YOU THINK YOU'RE STRESSED OUT NOW? WAIT UNTIL YOU HEAR THE NEWS.
SNAP

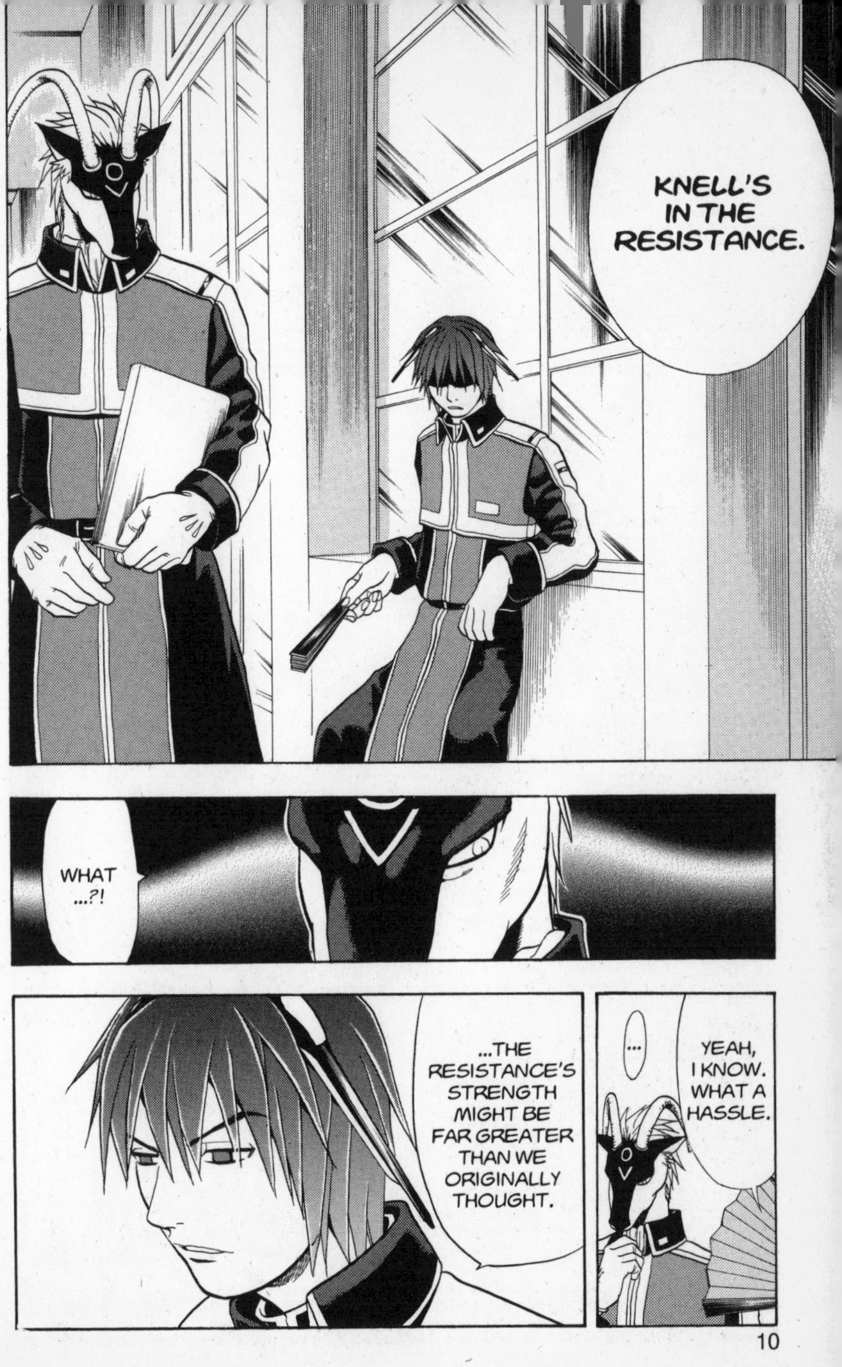
KNELL'S IN THE RESISTANCE.
WHAT ...?!
...
YEAH, I KNOW. WHAT A HASSLE.
...THE RESISTANCE'S STRENGTH MIGHT BE FAR GREATER THAN WE ORIGINALLY THOUGHT.

READ THIS WAY

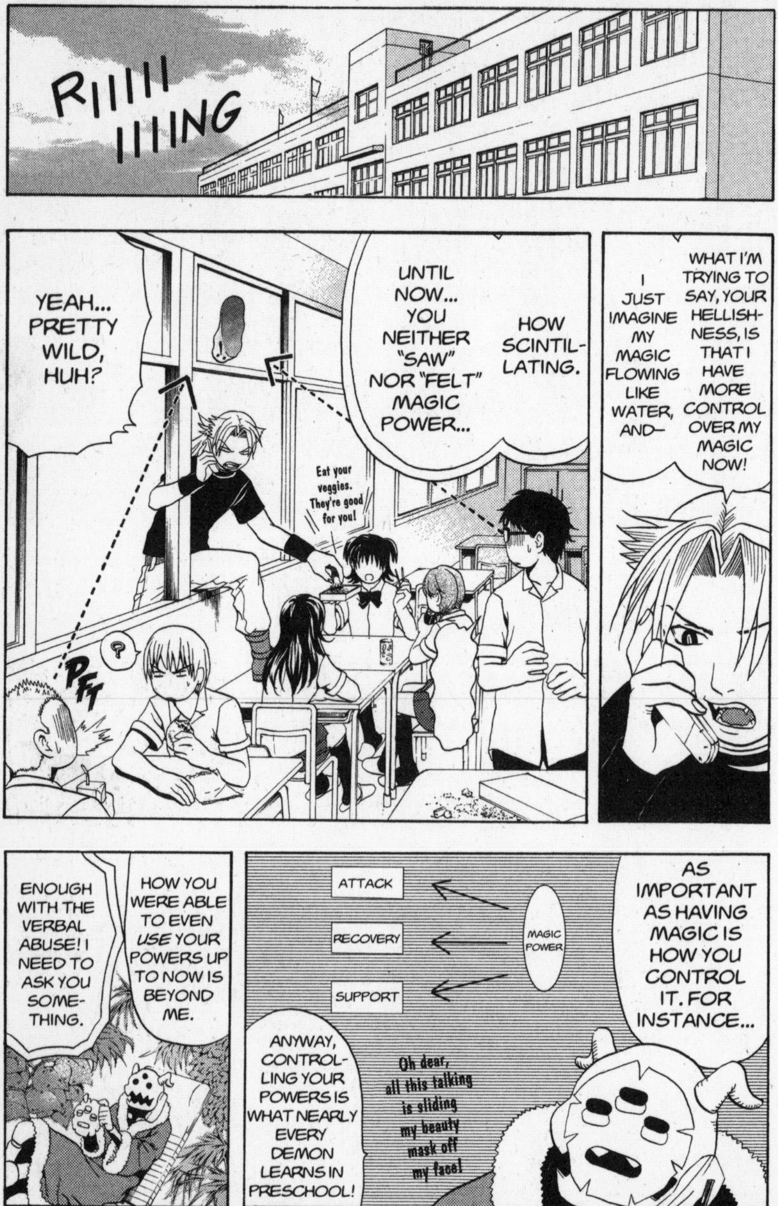
RIIIII IIIING
WHAT I'M TRYING TO SAY, YOUR HELLISHNESS, IS THAT I HAVE MORE CONTROL OVER MY MAGIC NOW!
I JUST IMAGINE MY MAGIC FLOWING LIKE WATER, AND—
HOW SCINTILLATING.
UNTIL NOW... YOU NEITHER "SAW" NOR "FELT" MAGIC POWER...
YEAH... PRETTY WILD, HUH?
Eat your veggies. They're good for you!
?
PFT
AS IMPORTANT AS HAVING MAGIC IS HOW YOU CONTROL IT. FOR INSTANCE...
MAGIC POWER
ATTACK
RECOVERY
SUPPORT
Oh dear, all this talking is sliding my beauty mask off my face!
ANYWAY, CONTROLLING YOUR POWERS IS WHAT NEARLY EVERY DEMON LEARNS IN PRESCHOOL!
HOW YOU WERE ABLE TO EVEN USE YOUR POWERS UP TO NOW IS BEYOND ME.
ENOUGH WITH THE VERBAL ABUSE! I NEED TO ASK YOU SOMETHING.

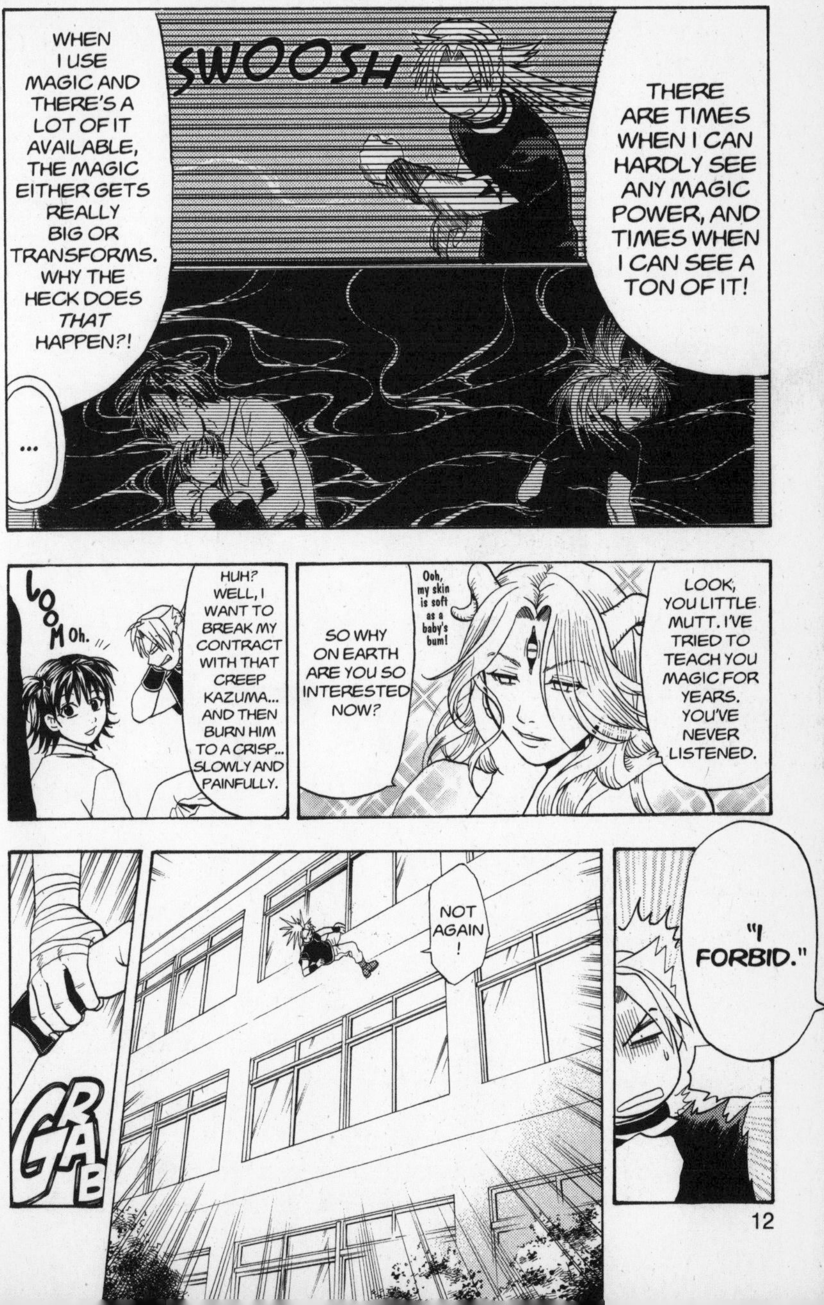
THERE ARE TIMES WHEN I CAN HARDLY SEE ANY MAGIC POWER, AND TIMES WHEN I CAN SEE A TON OF IT!
SWOOSH
WHEN I USE MAGIC AND THERE'S A LOT OF IT AVAILABLE, THE MAGIC EITHER GETS REALLY BIG OR TRANSFORMS. WHY THE HECK DOES *THAT* HAPPEN?!
...
LOOK, YOU LITTLE MUTT. I'VE TRIED TO TEACH YOU MAGIC FOR YEARS. YOU'VE NEVER LISTENED.
Ooh, my skin is soft as a baby's bum!
SO WHY ON EARTH ARE YOU SO INTERESTED NOW?
HUH? WELL, I WANT TO BREAK MY CONTRACT WITH THAT CREEP KAZUMA... AND THEN BURN HIM TO A CRISP... SLOWLY AND PAINFULLY.
Oh.
LOOM
"I FORBID."
NOT AGAIN!
GRAB

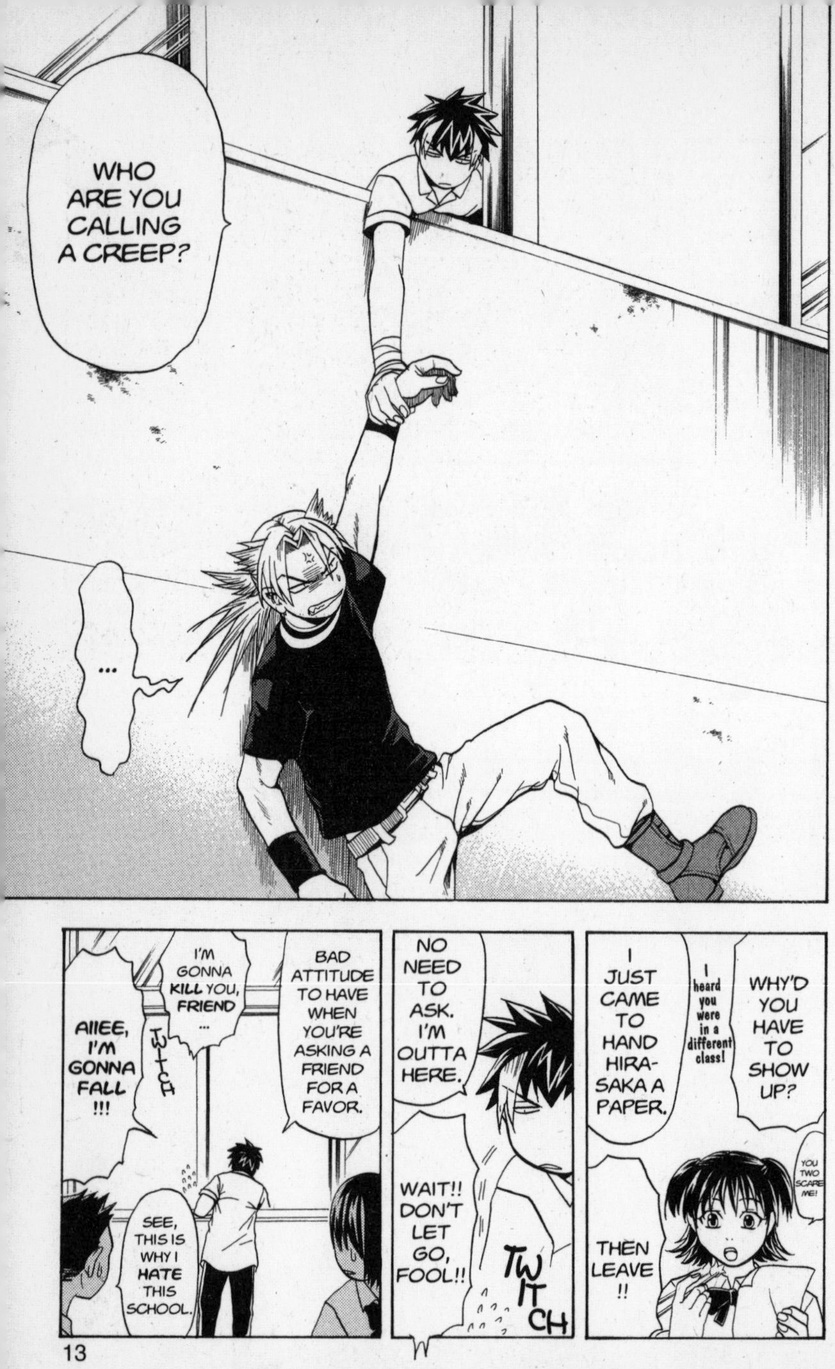
WHO ARE YOU CALLING A CREEP?
...
WHY'D YOU HAVE TO SHOW UP?
I heard you were in a different class!
I JUST CAME TO HAND HIRA-SAKA A PAPER.
YOU TWO SCARE ME!
THEN LEAVE!!
NO NEED TO ASK. I'M OUTTA HERE.
WAIT!! DON'T LET GO, FOOL!!
TWITCH
BAD ATTITUDE TO HAVE WHEN YOU'RE ASKING A FRIEND FOR A FAVOR.
I'M GONNA KILL YOU, FRIEND...
TWITCH
AIIEE, I'M GONNA FALL!!!
SEE, THIS IS WHY I HATE THIS SCHOOL.

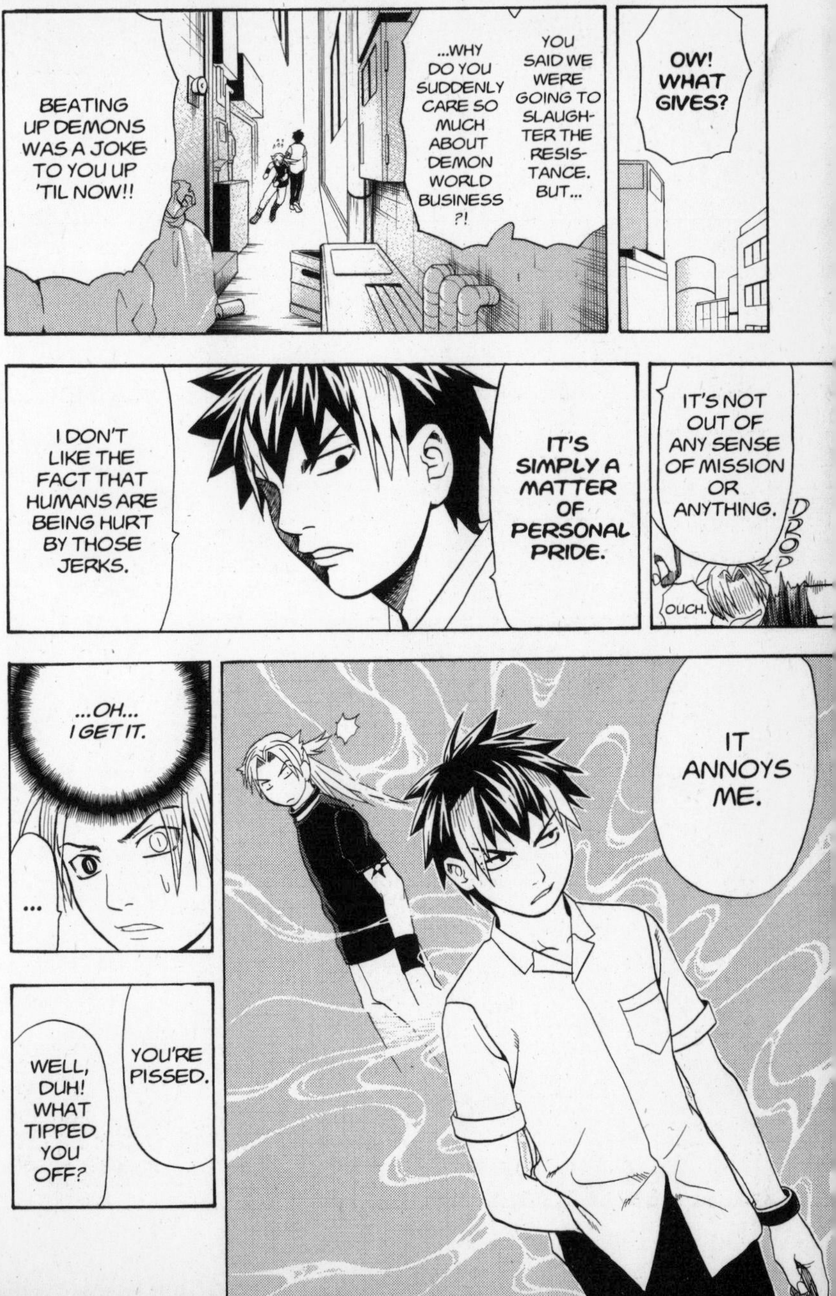
OW! WHAT GIVES?
YOU SAID WE WERE GOING TO SLAUGHTER THE RESISTANCE. BUT...
...WHY DO YOU SUDDENLY CARE SO MUCH ABOUT DEMON WORLD BUSINESS?!
BEATING UP DEMONS WAS A JOKE TO YOU UP 'TIL NOW!!
IT'S NOT OUT OF ANY SENSE OF MISSION OR ANYTHING.
DROP
OUCH.
IT'S SIMPLY A MATTER OF PERSONAL PRIDE.
I DON'T LIKE THE FACT THAT HUMANS ARE BEING HURT BY THOSE JERKS.
IT ANNOYS ME.
...OH... I GET IT.
...
YOU'RE PISSED.
WELL, DUH! WHAT TIPPED YOU OFF?

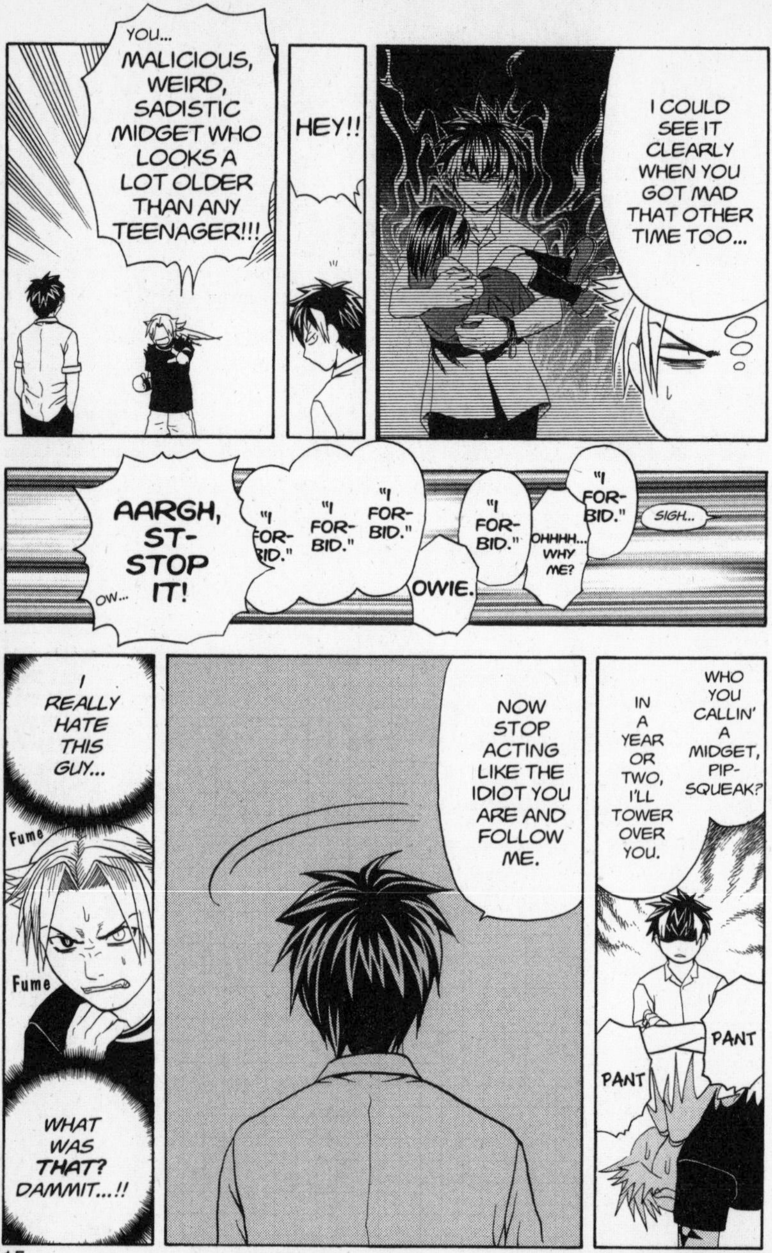
I COULD SEE IT CLEARLY WHEN YOU GOT MAD THAT OTHER TIME TOO...
HEY!!
YOU... MALICIOUS, WEIRD, SADISTIC MIDGET WHO LOOKS A LOT OLDER THAN ANY TEENAGER!!!
SIGH...
"I FOR-BID."
"I FOR-BID."
OHHHH... WHY ME?
"I FOR-BID."
"I FOR-BID."
"I FOR-BID."
OWIE.
AARGH, ST-STOP IT!
OW...
WHO YOU CALLIN' A MIDGET, PIP-SQUEAK?
IN A YEAR OR TWO, I'LL TOWER OVER YOU.
PANT
PANT
NOW STOP ACTING LIKE THE IDIOT YOU ARE AND FOLLOW ME.
I REALLY HATE THIS GUY...
Fume
Fume
WHAT WAS THAT? DAMMIT...!!

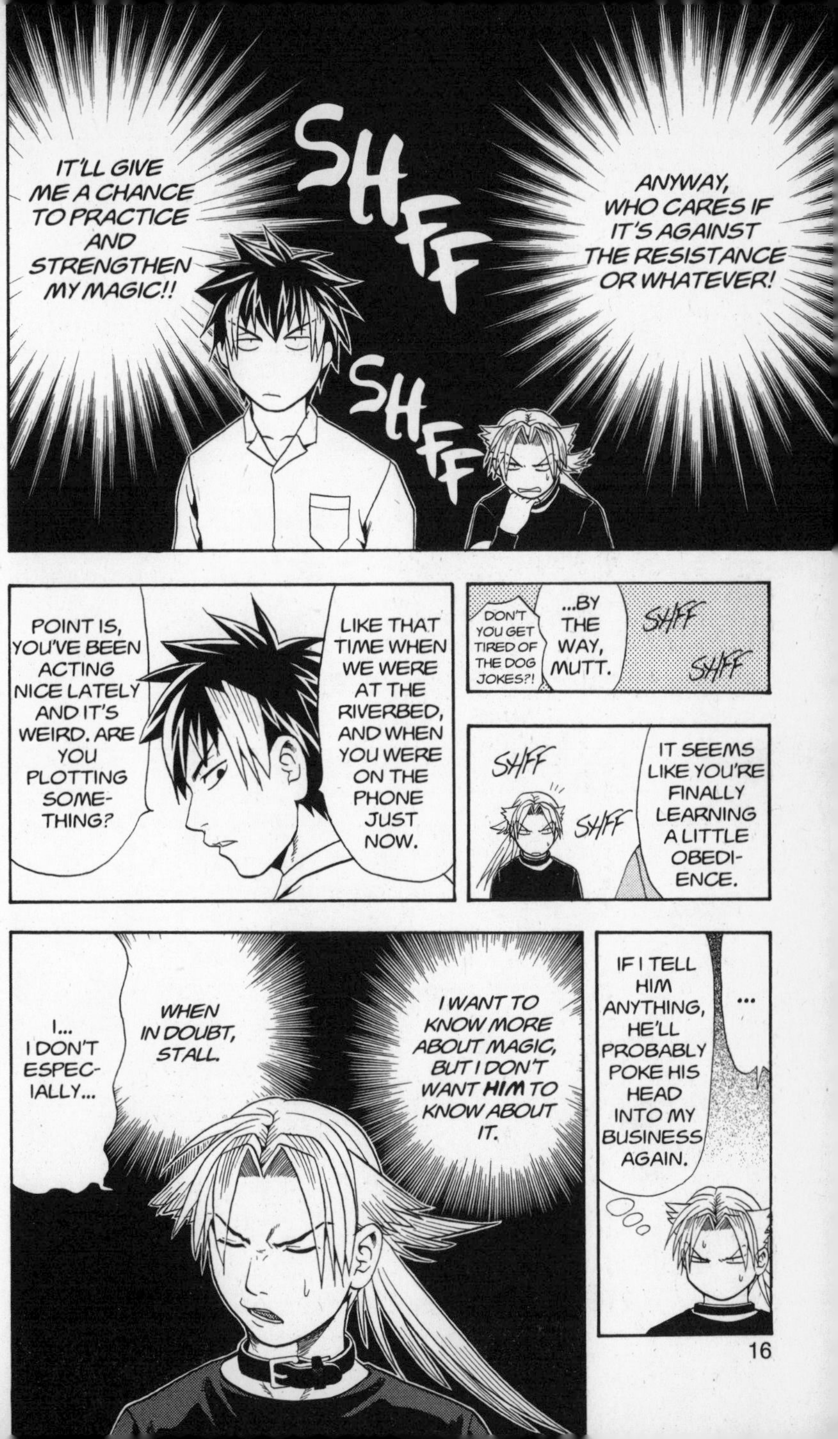
ANYWAY, WHO CARES IF IT'S AGAINST THE RESISTANCE OR WHATEVER!
SHFF
IT'LL GIVE ME A CHANCE TO PRACTICE AND STRENGTHEN MY MAGIC!!
SHFF
SHFF
SHFF
...BY THE WAY, MUTT.
DON'T YOU GET TIRED OF THE DOG JOKES?!
IT SEEMS LIKE YOU'RE FINALLY LEARNING A LITTLE OBEDI- ENCE.
SHFF
SHFF
LIKE THAT TIME WHEN WE WERE AT THE RIVERBED, AND WHEN YOU WERE ON THE PHONE JUST NOW.
POINT IS, YOU'VE BEEN ACTING NICE LATELY AND IT'S WEIRD. ARE YOU PLOTTING SOME- THING?
...
IF I TELL HIM ANYTHING, HE'LL PROBABLY POKE HIS HEAD INTO MY BUSINESS AGAIN.
I WANT TO KNOW MORE ABOUT MAGIC, BUT I DON'T WANT **HIM** TO KNOW ABOUT IT.
WHEN IN DOUBT, STALL.
I... I DON'T ESPEC- IALLY...

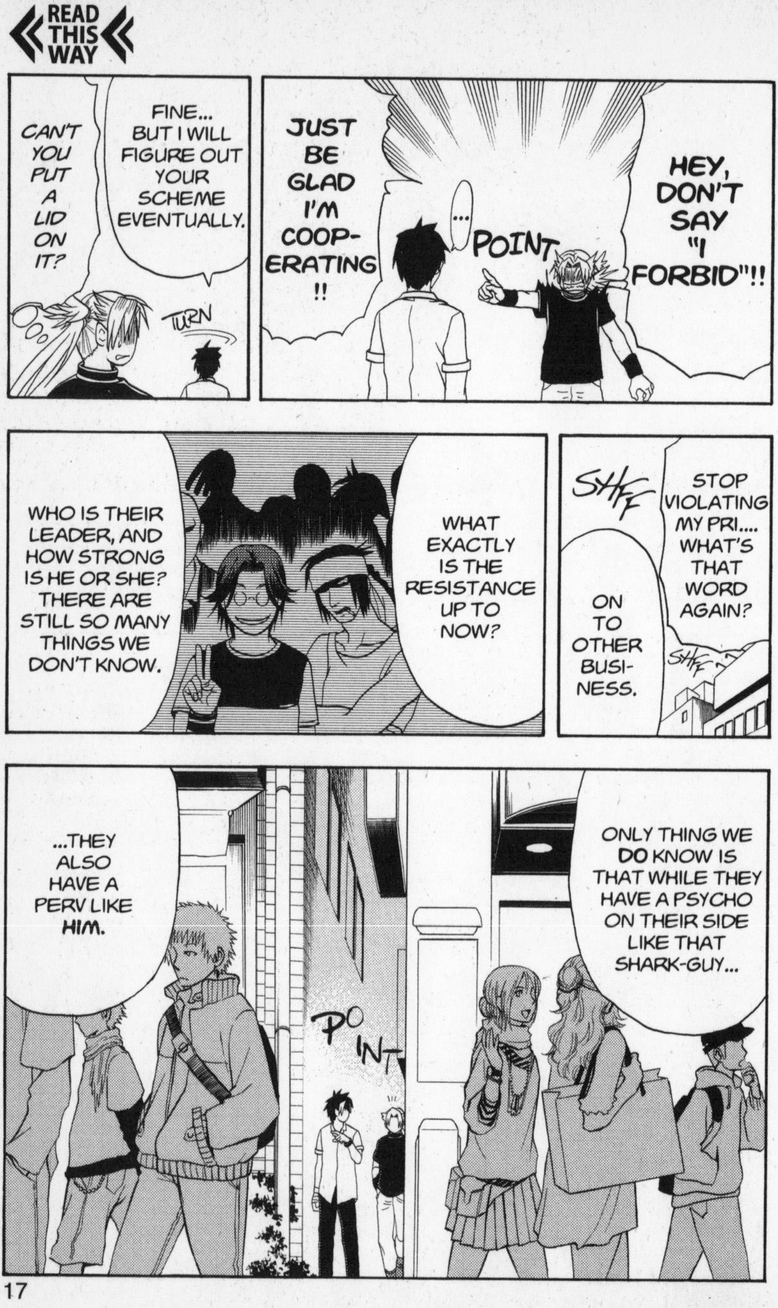
READ THIS WAY
HEY, DON'T SAY "I FORBID"!!
JUST BE GLAD I'M COOPERATING!!
POINT
...
FINE... BUT I WILL FIGURE OUT YOUR SCHEME EVENTUALLY.
CAN'T YOU PUT A LID ON IT?
TURN
STOP VIOLATING MY PRI.... WHAT'S THAT WORD AGAIN?
SHFF
ON TO OTHER BUSINESS.
SHFF
WHAT EXACTLY IS THE RESISTANCE UP TO NOW?
WHO IS THEIR LEADER, AND HOW STRONG IS HE OR SHE? THERE ARE STILL SO MANY THINGS WE DON'T KNOW.
ONLY THING WE DO KNOW IS THAT WHILE THEY HAVE A PSYCHO ON THEIR SIDE LIKE THAT SHARK-GUY...
...THEY ALSO HAVE A PERV LIKE HIM.
POINT

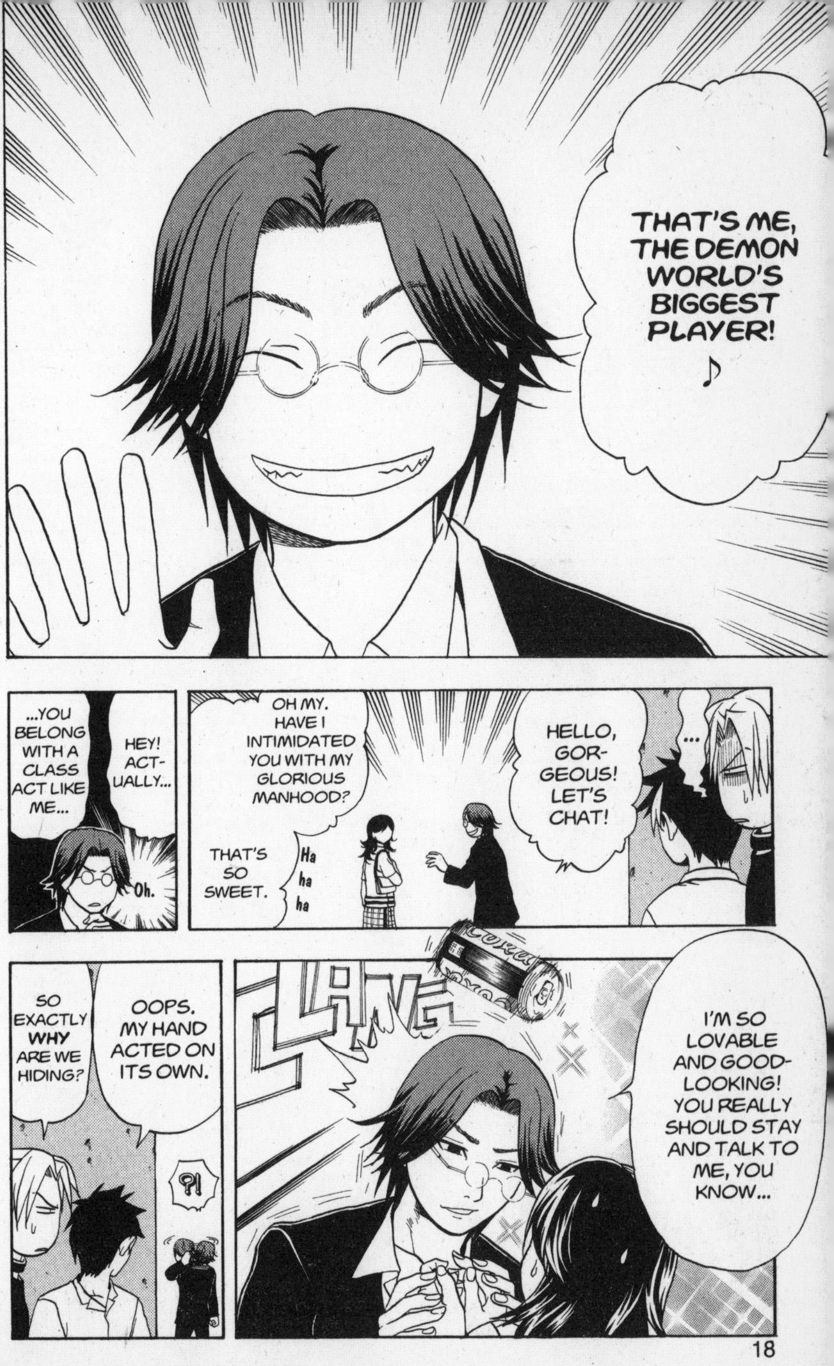

THAT'S ME, THE DEMON WORLD'S BIGGEST PLAYER! ♪
...
HELLO, GOR-GEOUS! LET'S CHAT!
OH MY. HAVE I INTIMIDATED YOU WITH MY GLORIOUS MANHOOD?
Ha ha ha
THAT'S SO SWEET.
HEY! ACT-UALLY...
...YOU BELONG WITH A CLASS ACT LIKE ME...
Oh.
CLANG
I'M SO LOVABLE AND GOOD-LOOKING! YOU REALLY SHOULD STAY AND TALK TO ME, YOU KNOW...
OOPS. MY HAND ACTED ON ITS OWN.
SO EXACTLY **WHY** ARE WE HIDING?
?!

READ THIS WAY

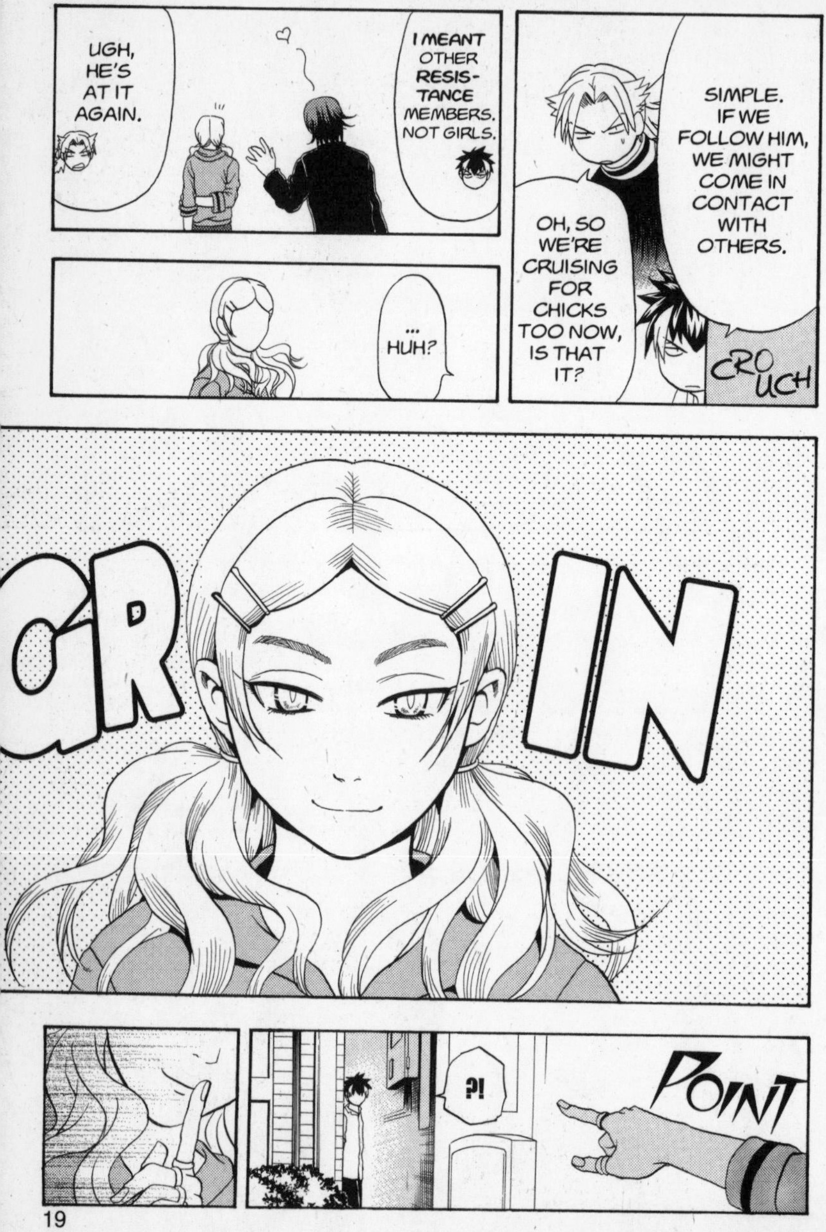
SIMPLE. IF WE FOLLOW HIM, WE MIGHT COME IN CONTACT WITH OTHERS.
OH, SO WE'RE CRUISING FOR CHICKS TOO NOW, IS THAT IT?
CROUCH
I MEANT OTHER RESISTANCE MEMBERS. NOT GIRLS.
UGH, HE'S AT IT AGAIN.
... HUH?
GRIN
POINT
?!

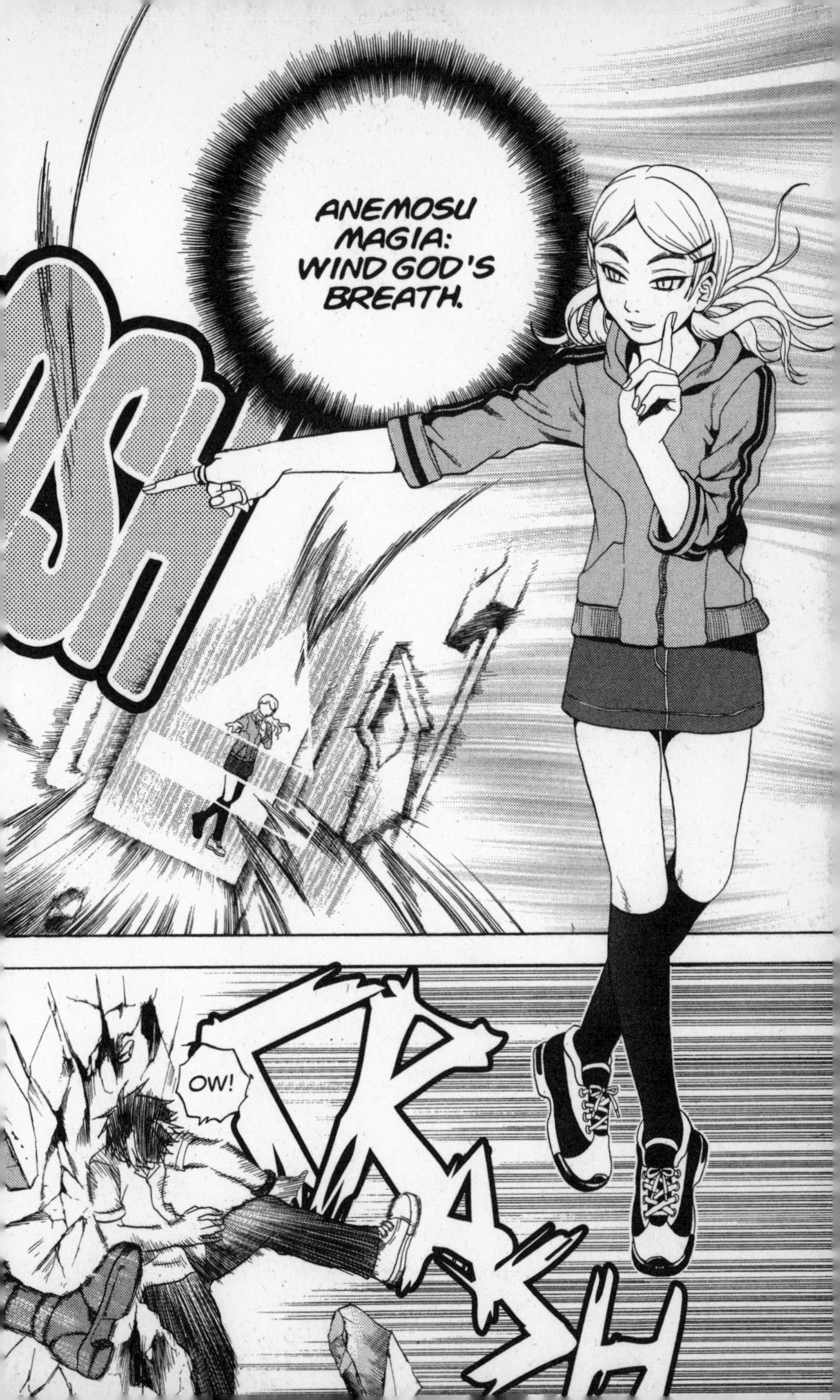
ANEMOSU MAGIA: WIND GOD'S BREATH.
OW!

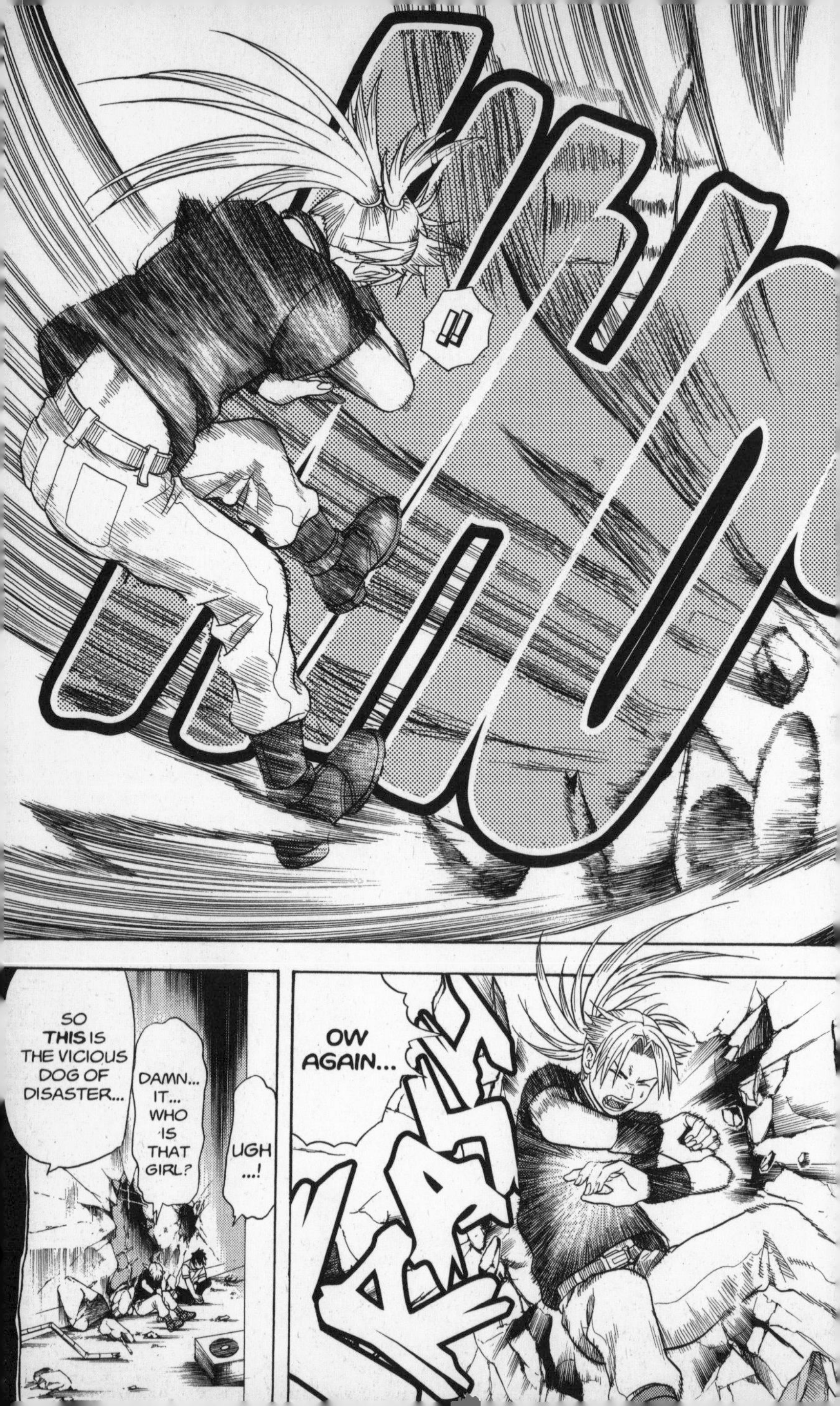
!!
OW AGAIN...
UGH ...!
DAMN... IT... WHO IS THAT GIRL?
SO THIS IS THE VICIOUS DOG OF DISASTER...

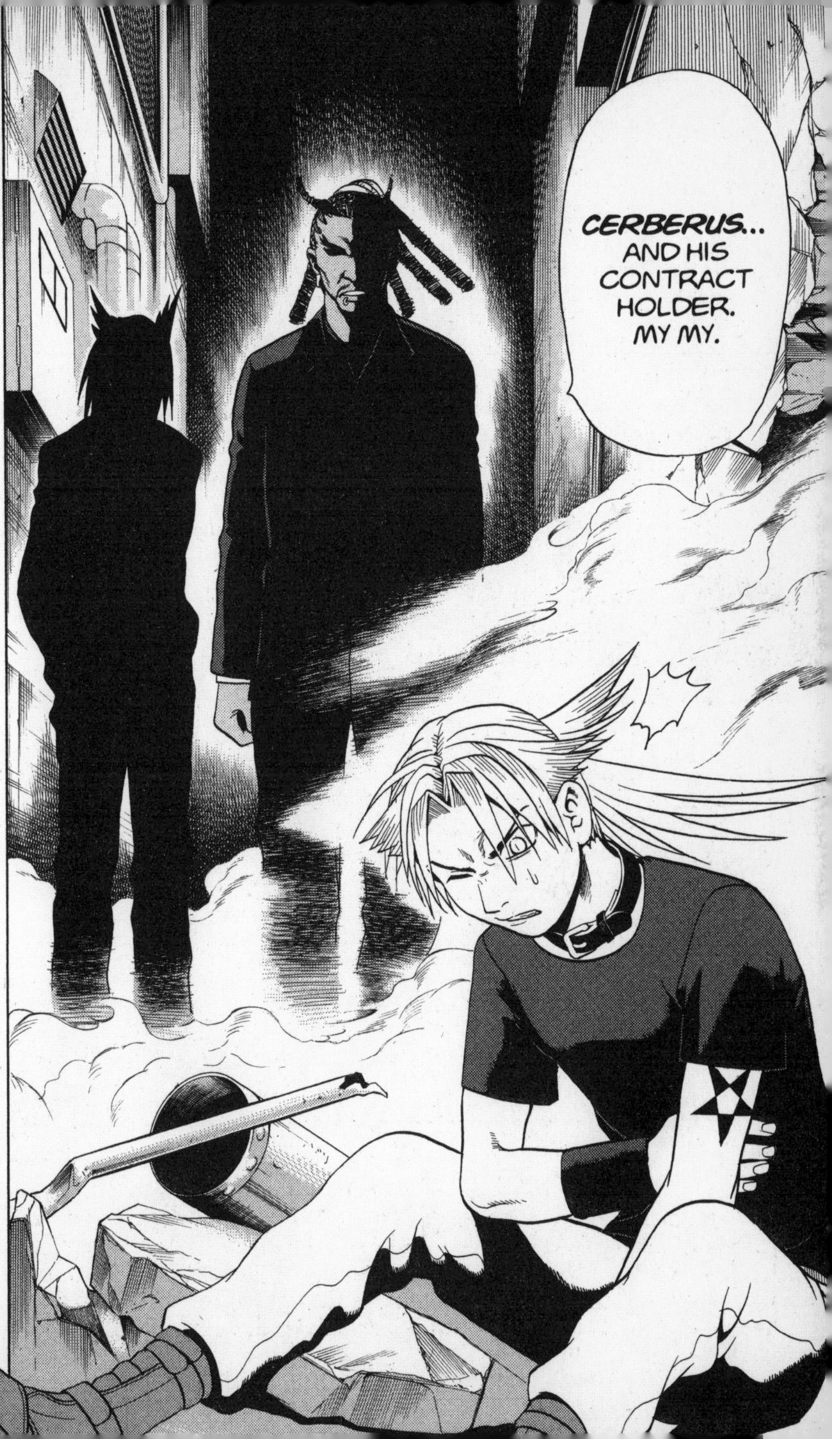
CERBERUS... AND HIS CONTRACT HOLDER. MY MY.

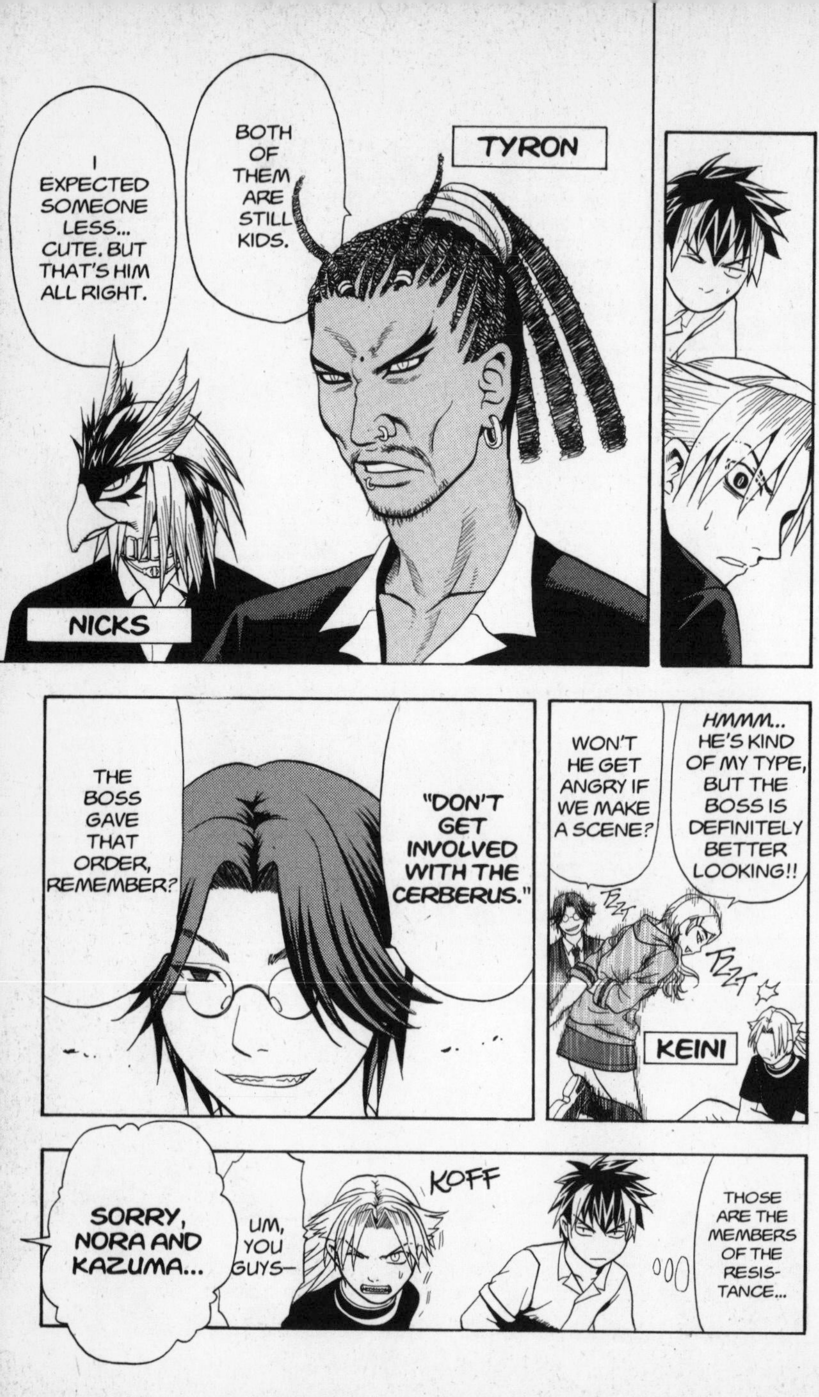
TYRON
BOTH OF THEM ARE STILL KIDS.
I EXPECTED SOMEONE LESS... CUTE. BUT THAT'S HIM ALL RIGHT.
NICKS
HMMM... HE'S KIND OF MY TYPE, BUT THE BOSS IS DEFINITELY BETTER LOOKING!!
WON'T HE GET ANGRY IF WE MAKE A SCENE?
FZZT
FZZT
KEINI
"DON'T GET INVOLVED WITH THE CERBERUS."
THE BOSS GAVE THAT ORDER, REMEMBER?
THOSE ARE THE MEMBERS OF THE RESISTANCE...
KOFF
UM, YOU GUYS—
SORRY, NORA AND KAZUMA...

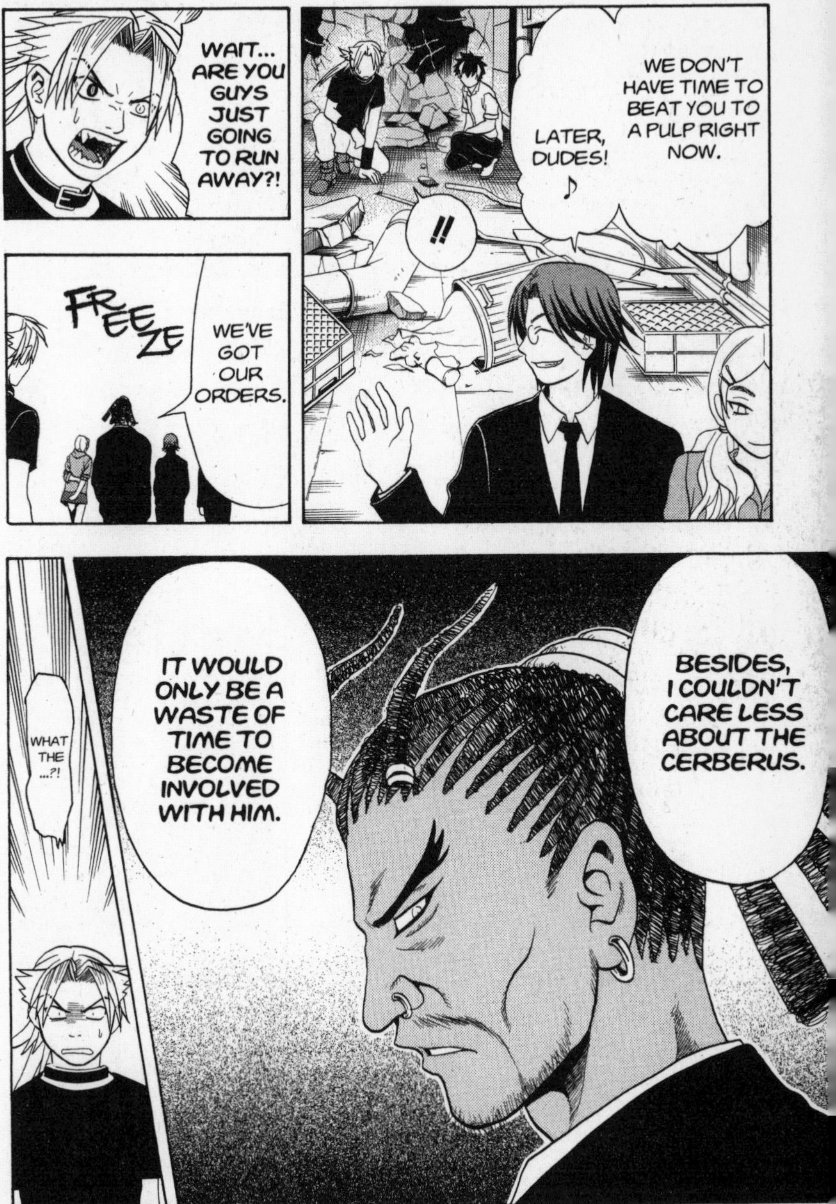
WE DON'T HAVE TIME TO BEAT YOU TO A PULP RIGHT NOW.
LATER, DUDES! ♪
!!
WAIT... ARE YOU GUYS JUST GOING TO RUN AWAY?!
WE'VE GOT OUR ORDERS.
FREEZE
BESIDES, I COULDN'T CARE LESS ABOUT THE CERBERUS.
IT WOULD ONLY BE A WASTE OF TIME TO BECOME INVOLVED WITH HIM.
WHAT THE ...?!

READ THIS WAY

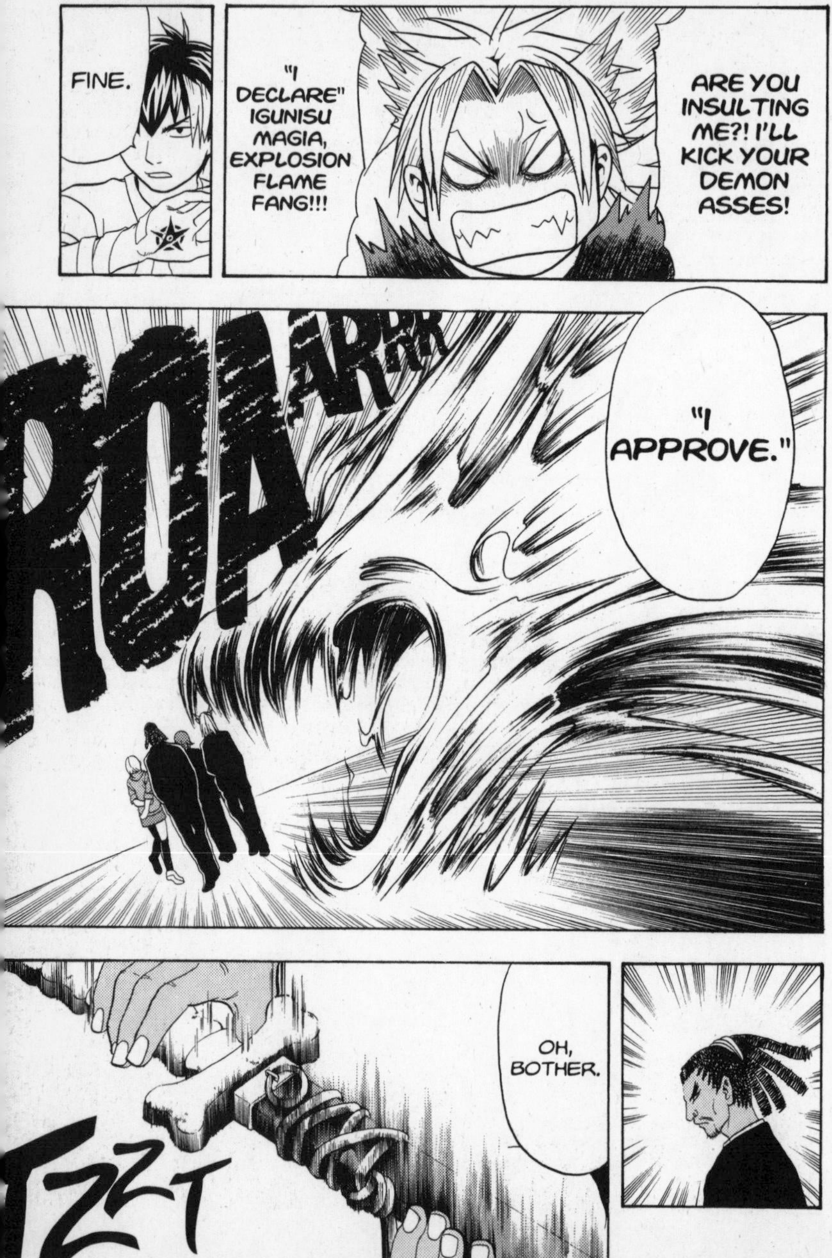
ARE YOU INSULTING ME?! I'LL KICK YOUR DEMON ASSES!
"I DECLARE" IGUNISU MAGIA, EXPLOSION FLAME FANG!!!
FINE.
"I APPROVE."
ROAARRR
OH, BOTHER.
TZZT

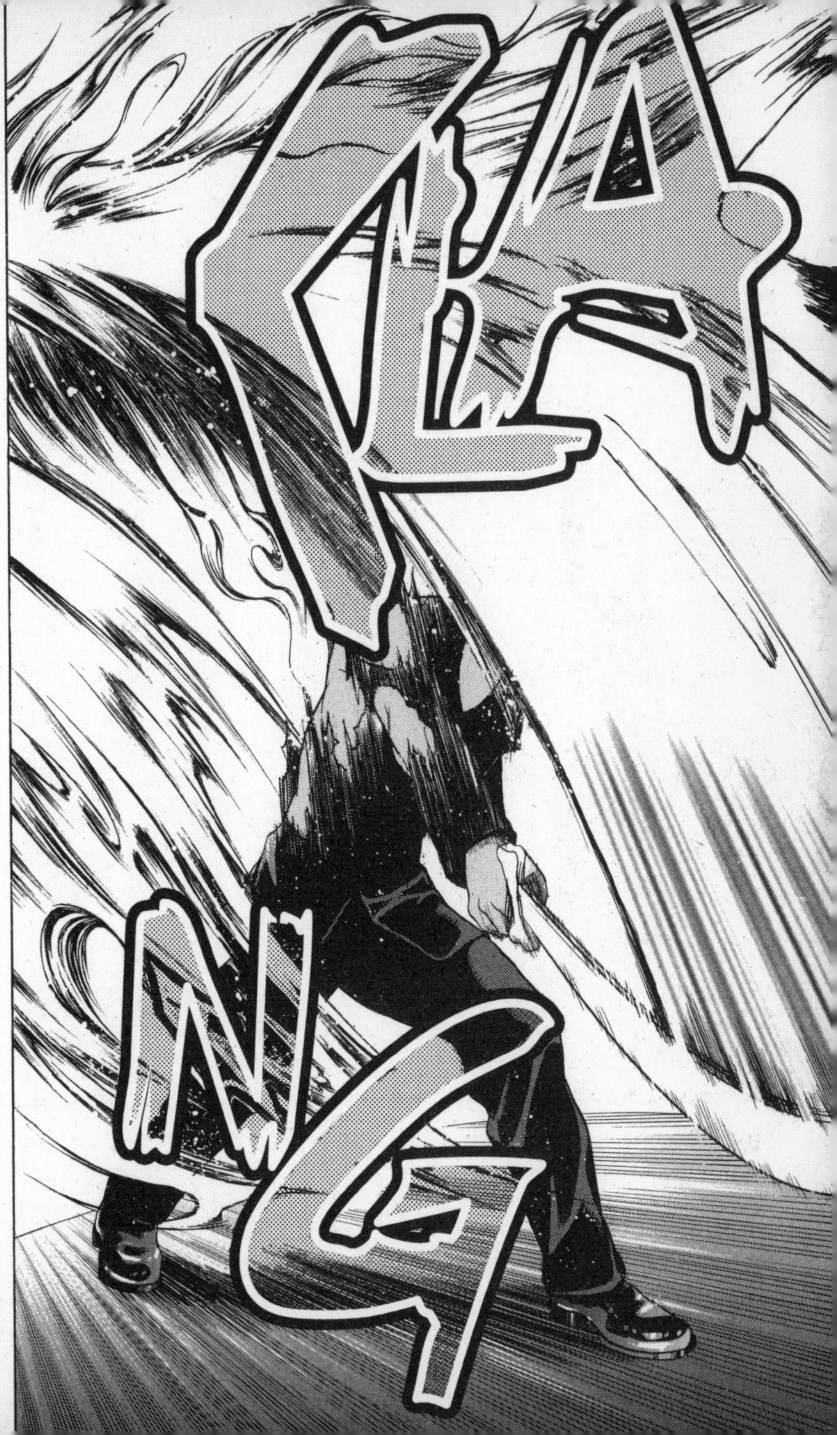
CLANG

READ THIS WAY

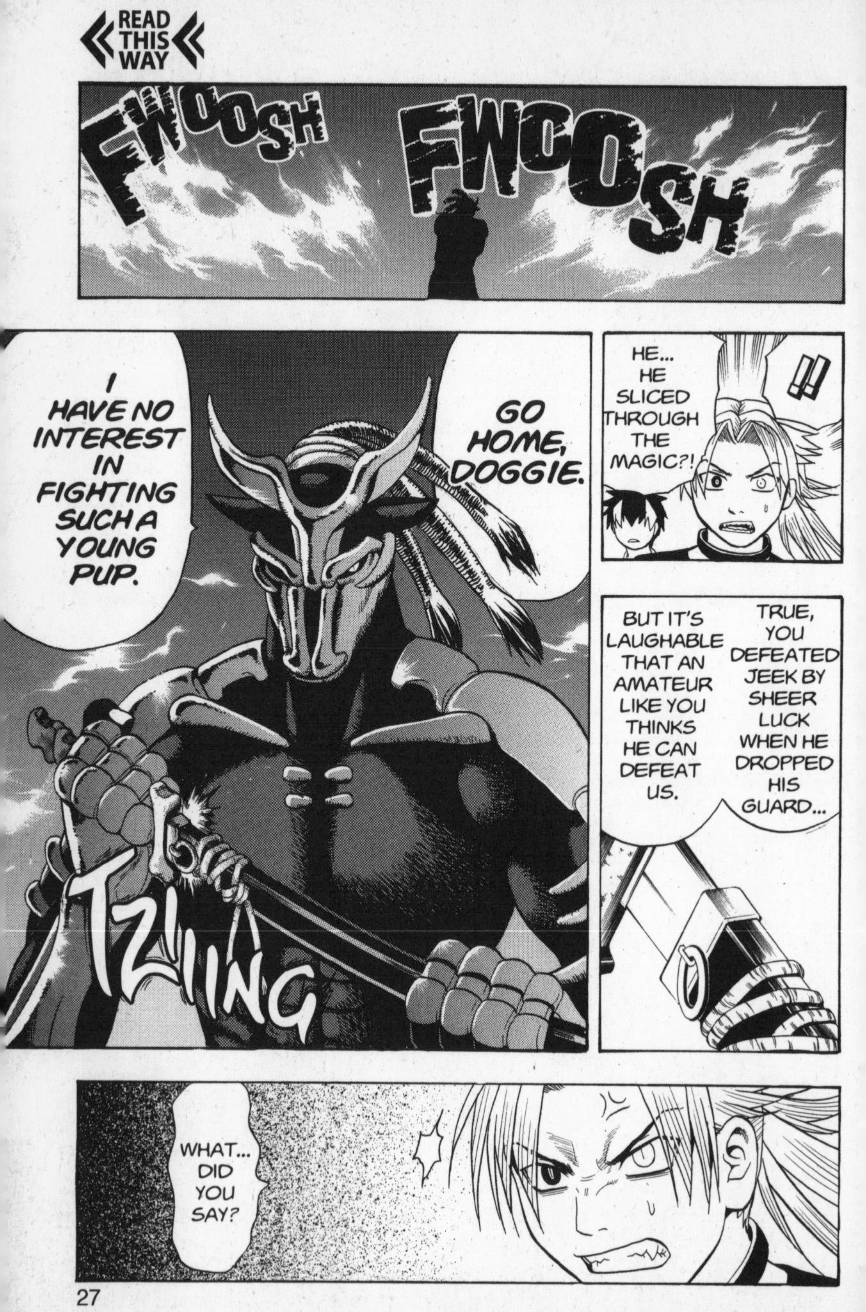
FWOOSH
FWOOSH
HE... HE SLICED THROUGH THE MAGIC?!
!!
TRUE, YOU DEFEATED JEEK BY SHEER LUCK WHEN HE DROPPED HIS GUARD...
BUT IT'S LAUGHABLE THAT AN AMATEUR LIKE YOU THINKS HE CAN DEFEAT US.
GO HOME, DOGGIE.
I HAVE NO INTEREST IN FIGHTING SUCH A YOUNG PUP.
TZIING
WHAT... DID YOU SAY?

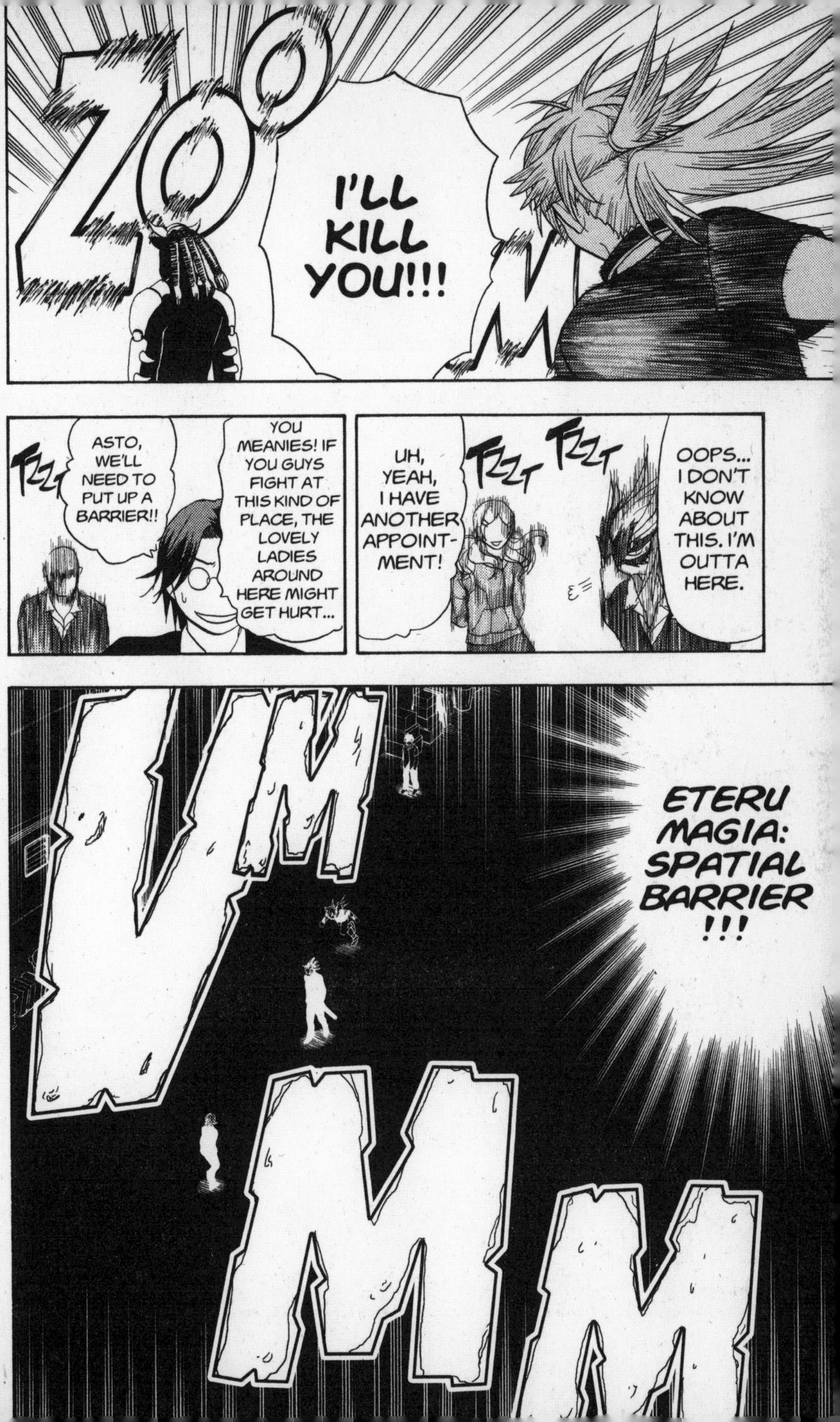
ZOOOM
I'LL KILL YOU!!!
TZZZT
OOPS... I DON'T KNOW ABOUT THIS. I'M OUTTA HERE.
TZZZT
UH, YEAH, I HAVE ANOTHER APPOINT-MENT!
YOU MEANIES! IF YOU GUYS FIGHT AT THIS KIND OF PLACE, THE LOVELY LADIES AROUND HERE MIGHT GET HURT...
TZZZT
ASTO, WE'LL NEED TO PUT UP A BARRIER!!
ETERU MAGIA: SPATIAL BARRIER!!!
VMMM

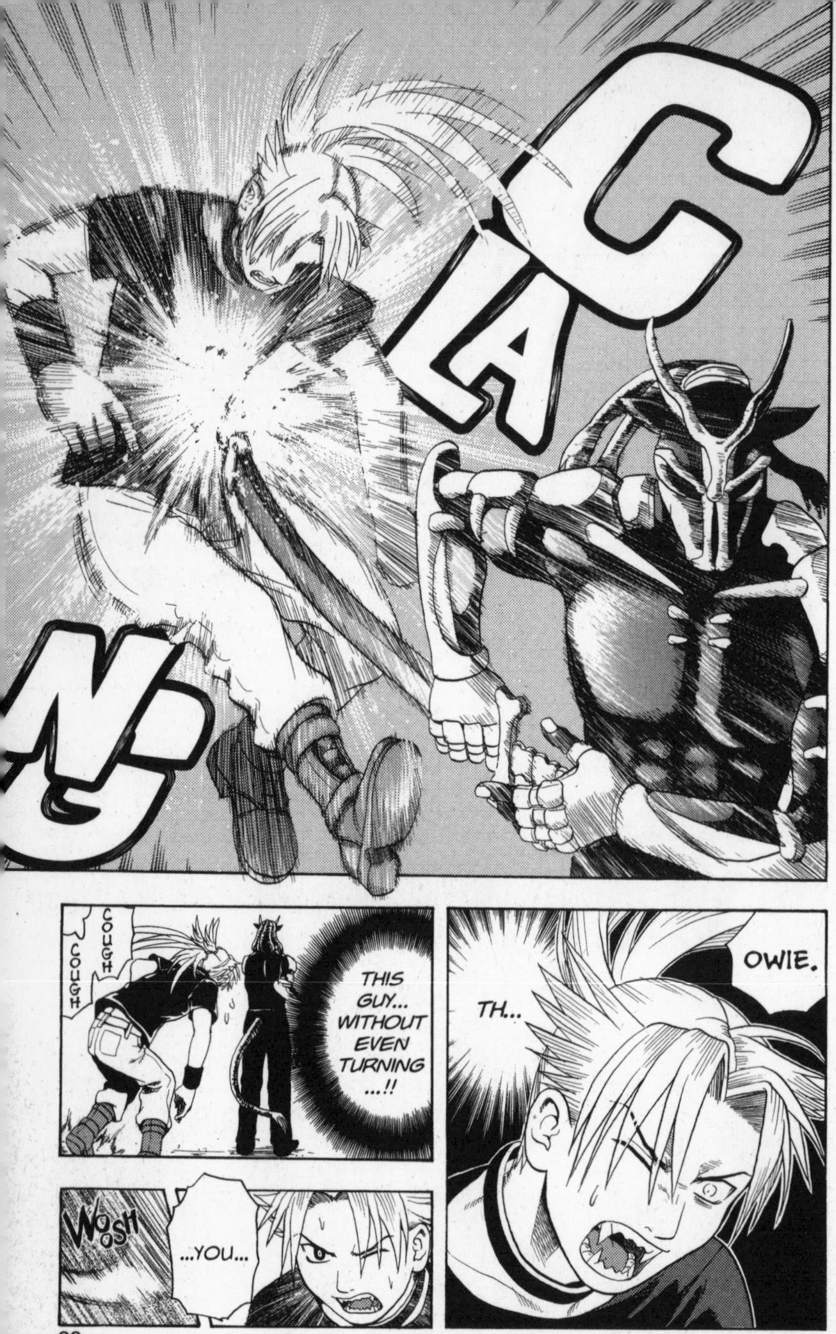

OWIE.
TH...
THIS GUY... WITHOUT EVEN TURNING ...!!
COUGH
COUGH
WOOSH
...YOU...

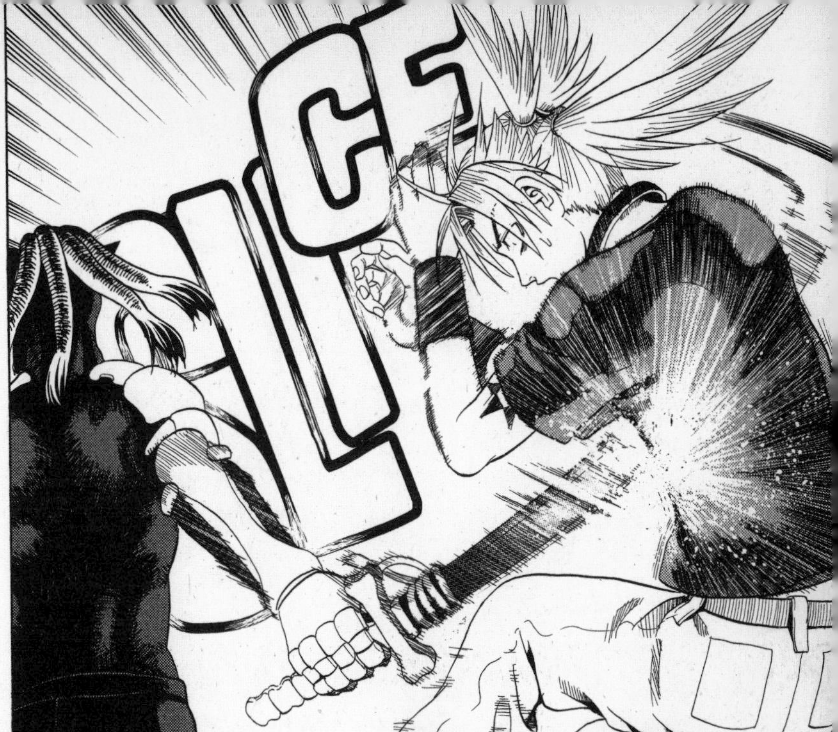
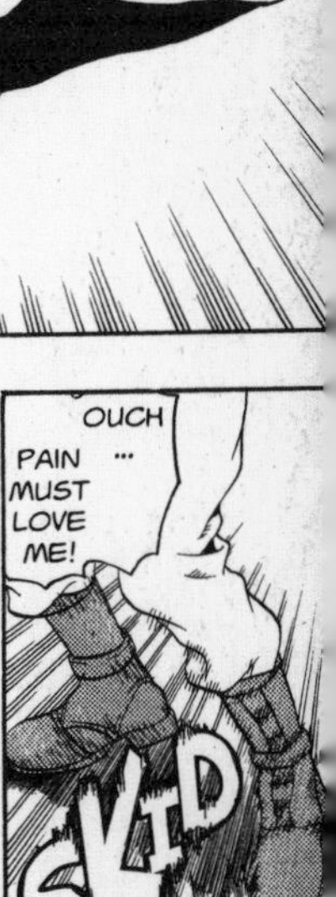
OUCH ...
PAIN MUST LOVE ME!
SKID
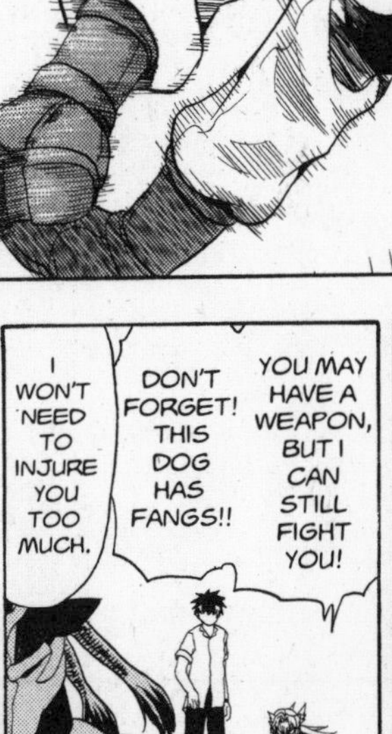
YOU MAY HAVE A WEAPON, BUT I CAN STILL FIGHT YOU!
DON'T FORGET! THIS DOG HAS FANGS!!
I WON'T NEED TO INJURE YOU TOO MUCH.
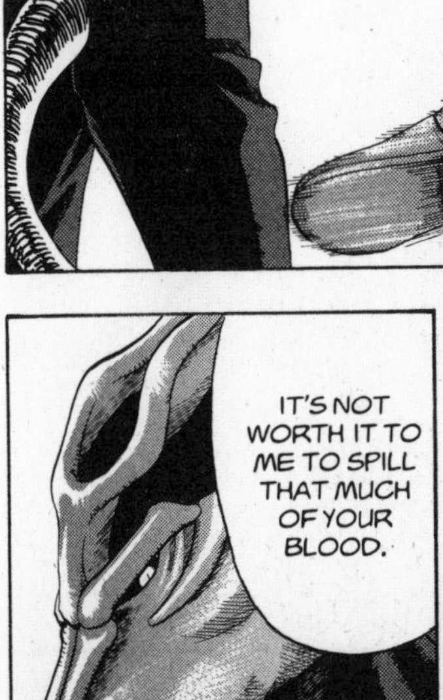
IT'S NOT WORTH IT TO ME TO SPILL THAT MUCH OF YOUR BLOOD.

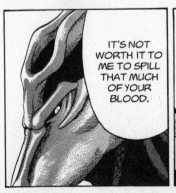

READ THIS WAY

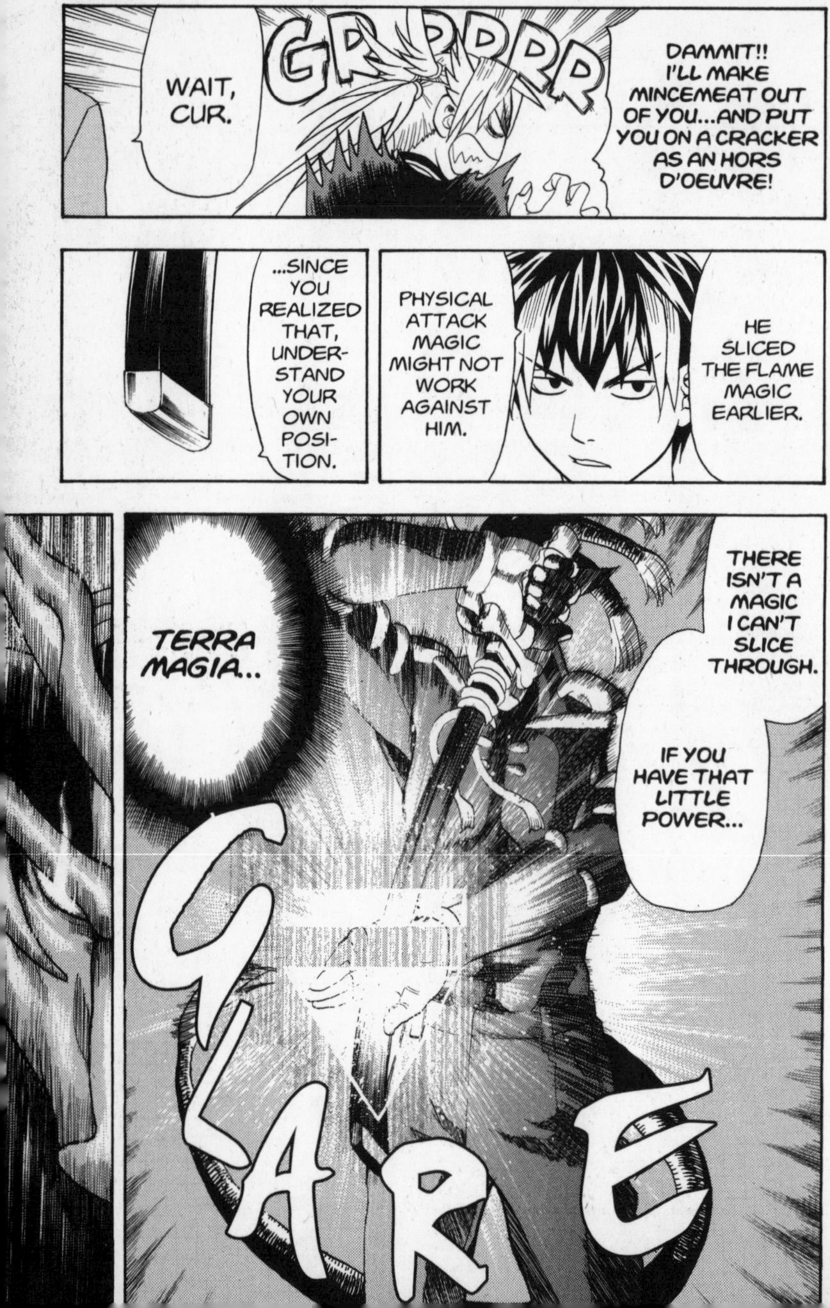
DAMMIT!! I'LL MAKE MINCEMEAT OUT OF YOU...AND PUT YOU ON A CRACKER AS AN HORS D'OEUVRE!
GRRRR
WAIT, CUR.
HE SLICED THE FLAME MAGIC EARLIER.
PHYSICAL ATTACK MAGIC MIGHT NOT WORK AGAINST HIM.
...SINCE YOU REALIZED THAT, UNDER-STAND YOUR OWN POSI-TION.
THERE ISN'T A MAGIC I CAN'T SLICE THROUGH.
IF YOU HAVE THAT LITTLE POWER...
TERRA MAGIA...
GLARE

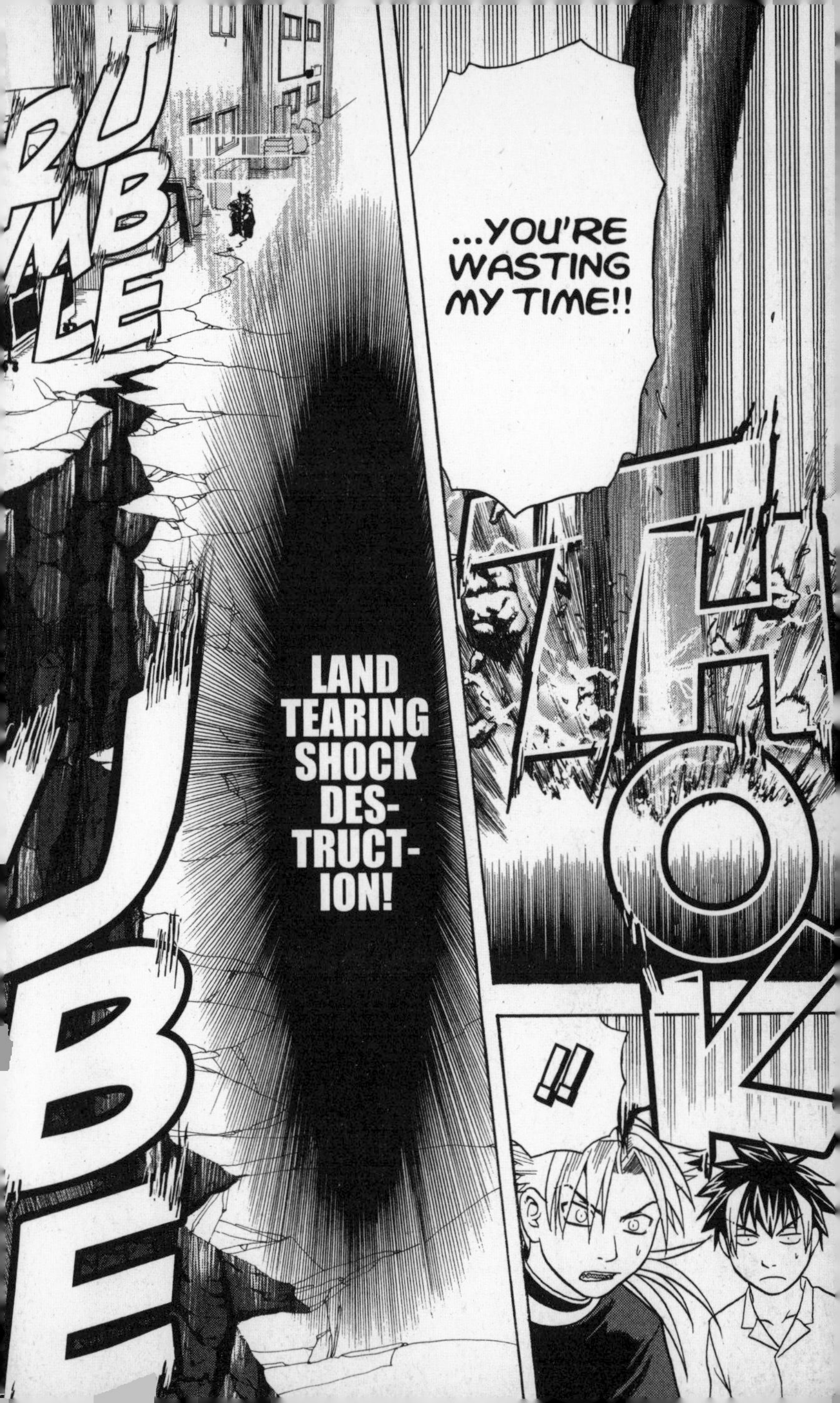
...YOU'RE WASTING MY TIME!!
!!
LAND TEARING SHOCK DES-TRUCT-ION!

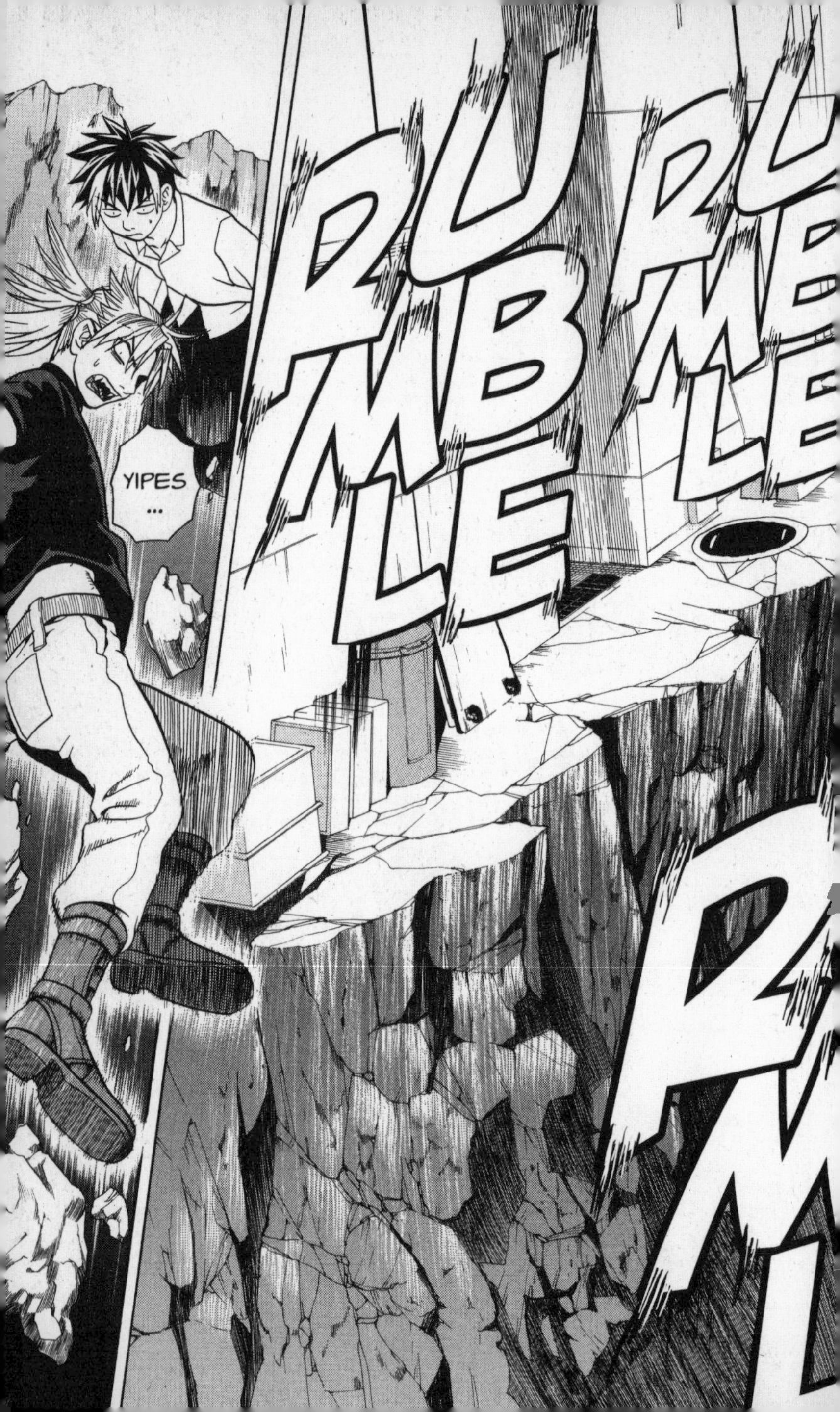
RUMBLE
YIPES ...

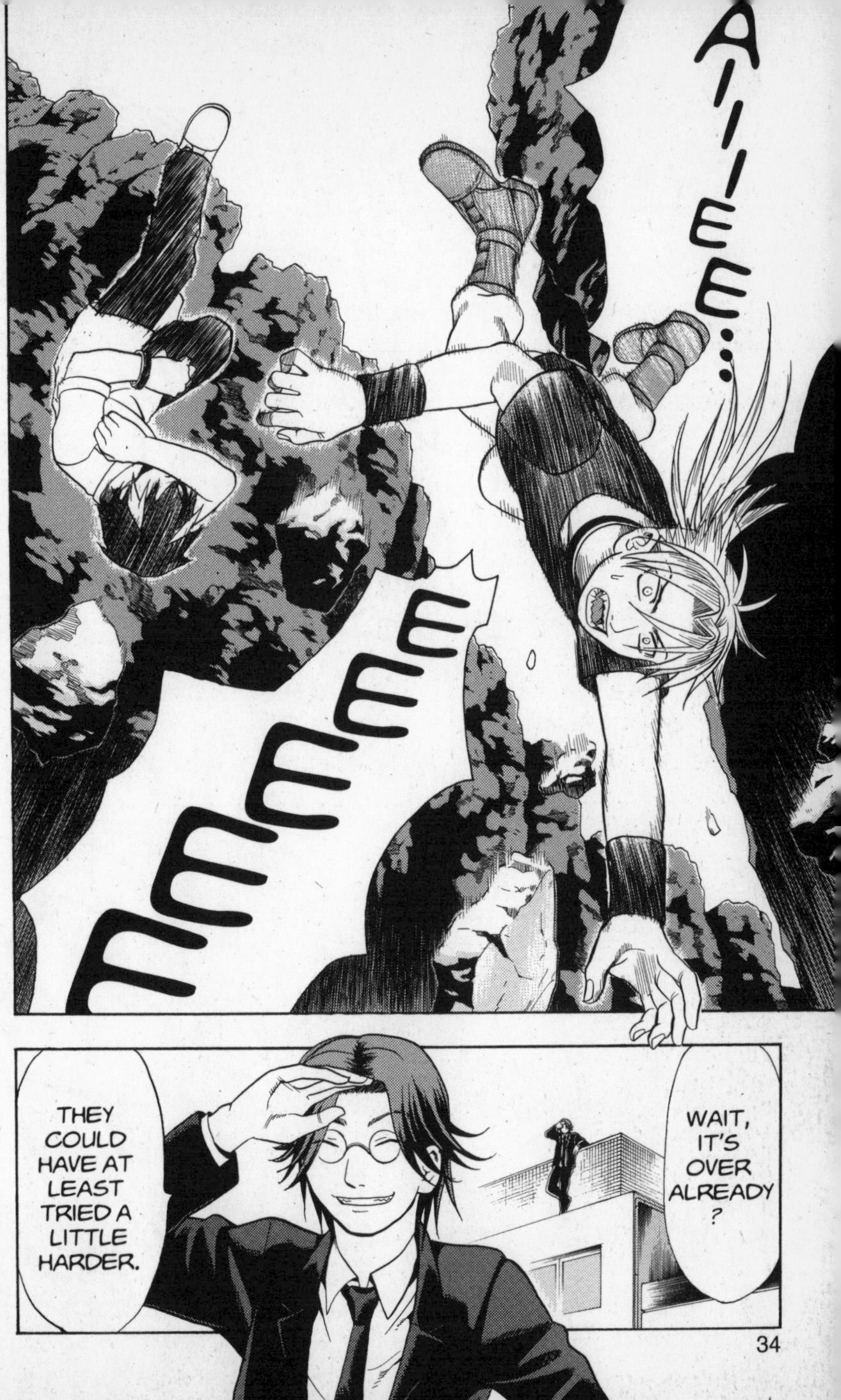
AIIIEE...
EEEEEE
WAIT, IT'S OVER ALREADY?
THEY COULD HAVE AT LEAST TRIED A LITTLE HARDER.

READ THIS WAY

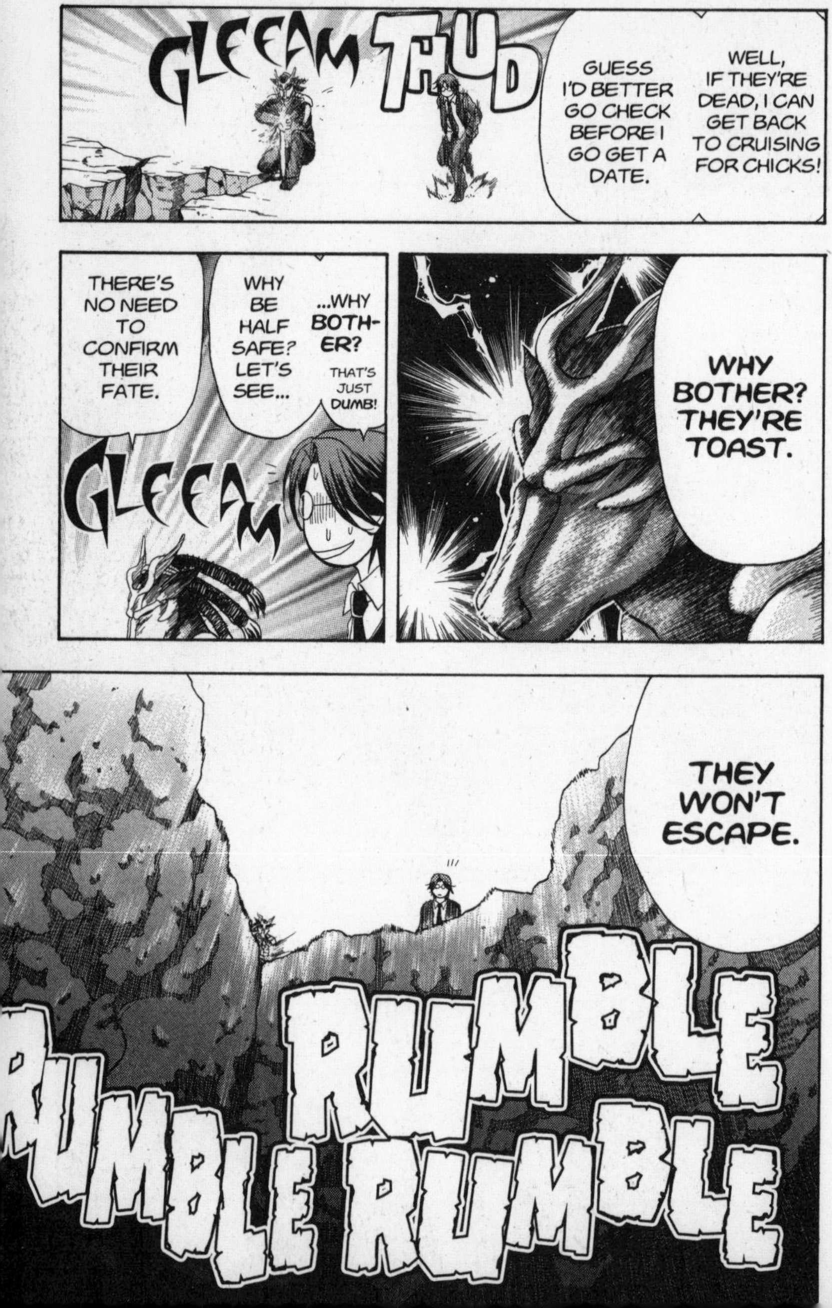
WELL, IF THEY'RE DEAD, I CAN GET BACK TO CRUISING FOR CHICKS!
GUESS I'D BETTER GO CHECK BEFORE I GO GET A DATE.
THUD
GLEEAM
WHY BOTHER? THEY'RE TOAST.
...WHY BOTHER?
THAT'S JUST DUMB!
WHY BE HALF SAFE? LET'S SEE...
THERE'S NO NEED TO CONFIRM THEIR FATE.
GLEEAM
THEY WON'T ESCAPE.
RUMBLE
RUMBLE
RUMBLE

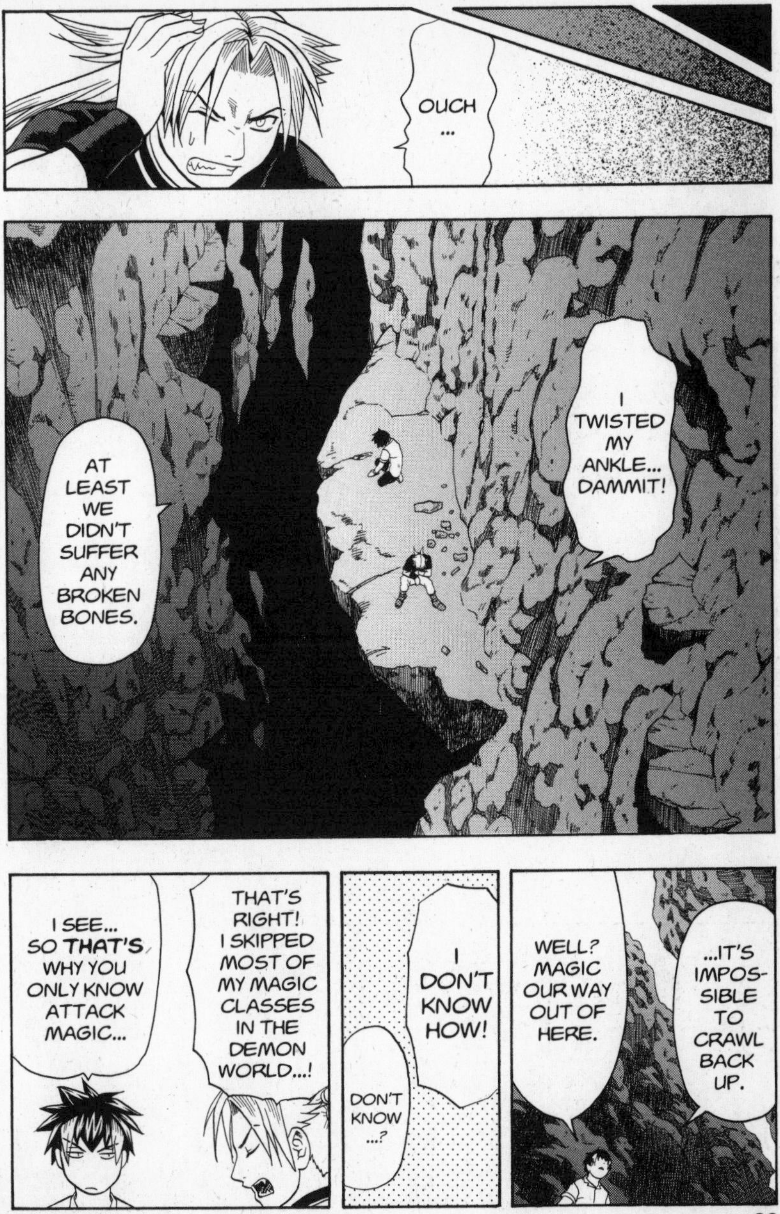
OUCH ...
I TWISTED MY ANKLE... DAMMIT!
AT LEAST WE DIDN'T SUFFER ANY BROKEN BONES.
...IT'S IMPOSSIBLE TO CRAWL BACK UP.
WELL? MAGIC OUR WAY OUT OF HERE.
I DON'T KNOW HOW!
DON'T KNOW ...?
THAT'S RIGHT! I SKIPPED MOST OF MY MAGIC CLASSES IN THE DEMON WORLD...!
I SEE... SO **THAT'S** WHY YOU ONLY KNOW ATTACK MAGIC...

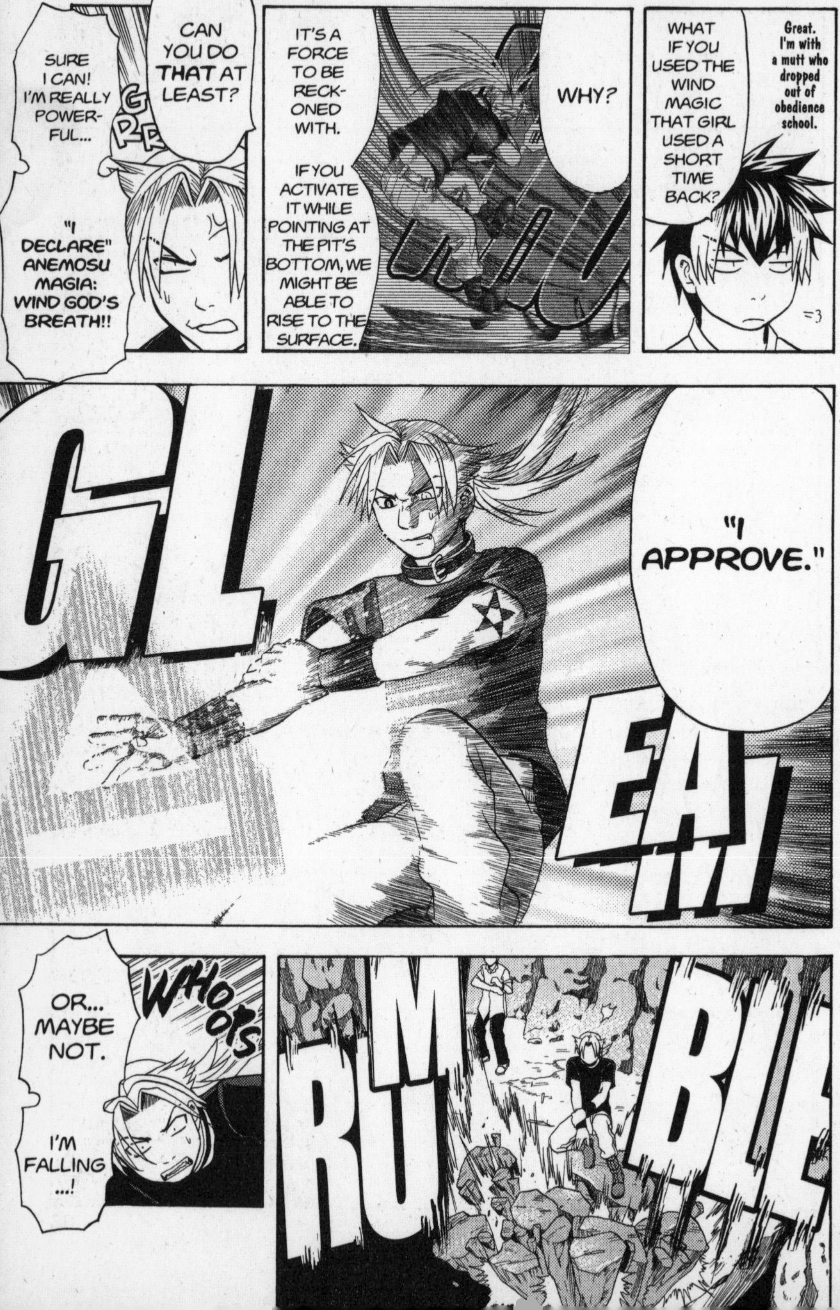
Great. I'm with a mutt who dropped out of obedience school.
WHAT IF YOU USED THE WIND MAGIC THAT GIRL USED A SHORT TIME BACK?
WHY?
IT'S A FORCE TO BE RECKONED WITH.
IF YOU ACTIVATE IT WHILE POINTING AT THE PIT'S BOTTOM, WE MIGHT BE ABLE TO RISE TO THE SURFACE.
CAN YOU DO THAT AT LEAST?
SURE I CAN! I'M REALLY POWERFUL...
GRR
"I DECLARE" ANEMOSU MAGIA: WIND GOD'S BREATH!!
"I APPROVE."
EAT
GL
RUMBLE
WHOOPS
OR... MAYBE NOT.
I'M FALLING ...!

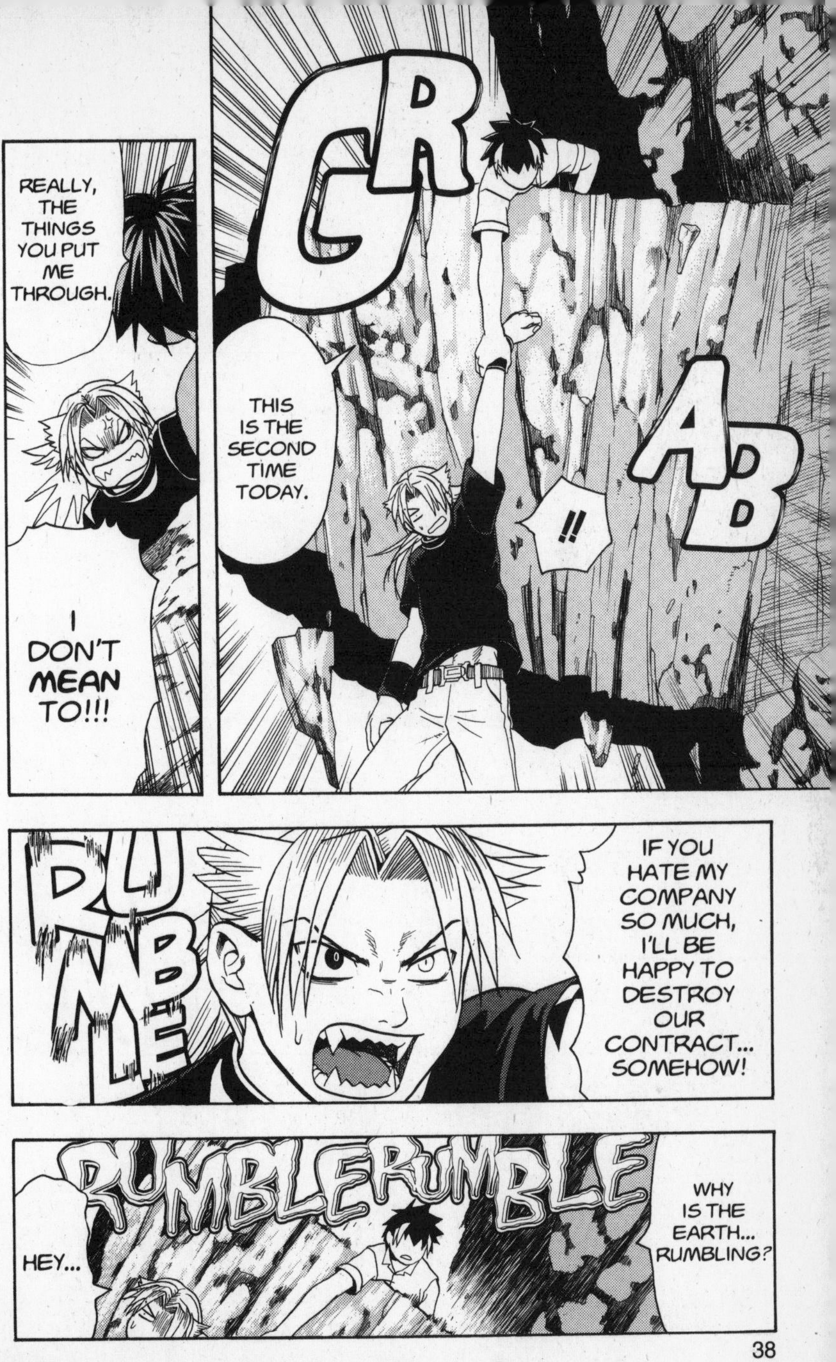
CRAB
THIS IS THE SECOND TIME TODAY.
!!
REALLY, THE THINGS YOU PUT ME THROUGH.
I DON'T MEAN TO!!!
IF YOU HATE MY COMPANY SO MUCH, I'LL BE HAPPY TO DESTROY OUR CONTRACT... SOMEHOW!
RUMBLE
WHY IS THE EARTH... RUMBLING?
RUMBLERUMBLE
HEY...

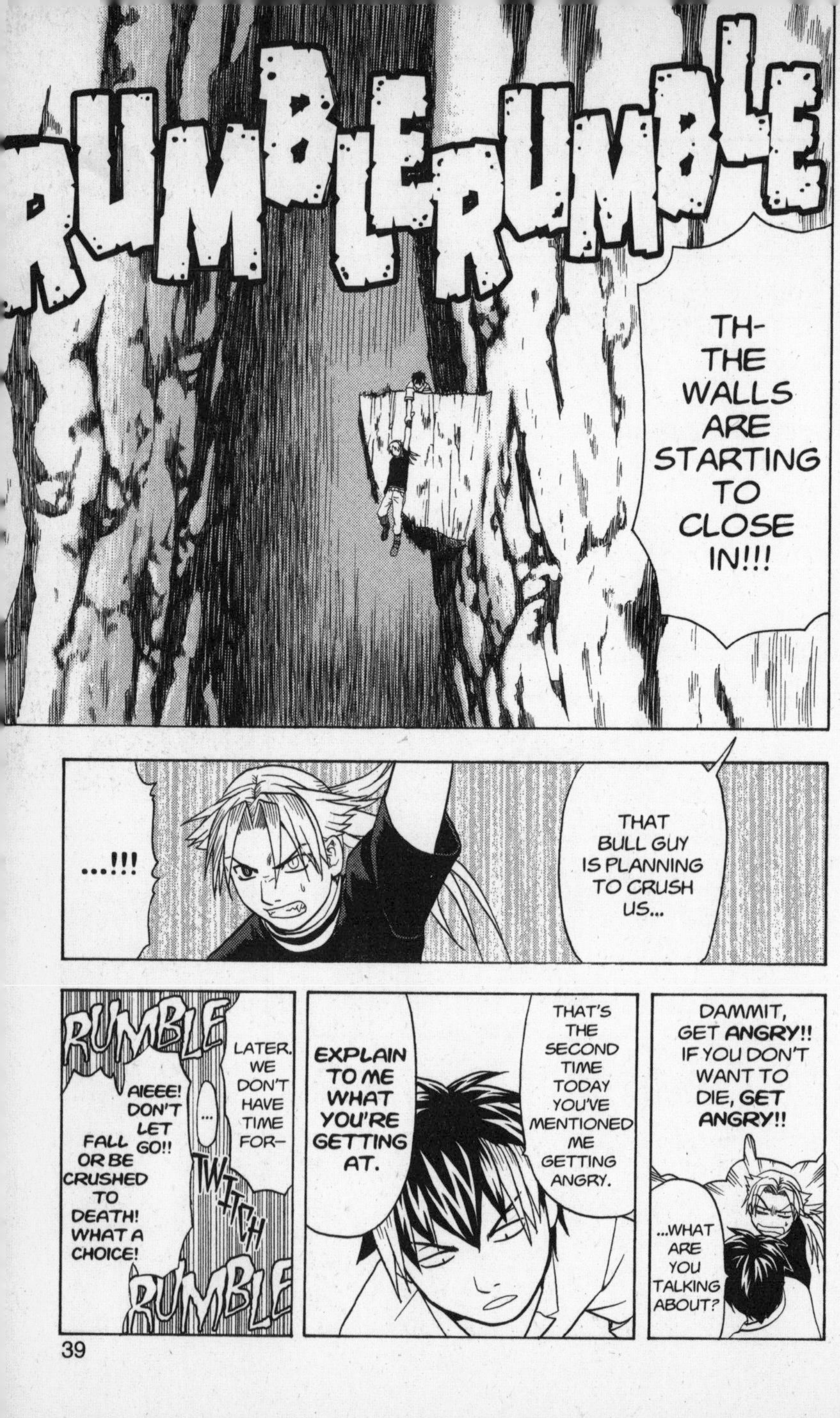
RUMBLE RUMBLE
TH- THE WALLS ARE STARTING TO CLOSE IN!!!
THAT BULL GUY IS PLANNING TO CRUSH US...
...!!!
DAMMIT, GET ANGRY!! IF YOU DON'T WANT TO DIE, GET ANGRY!!
...WHAT ARE YOU TALKING ABOUT?
THAT'S THE SECOND TIME TODAY YOU'VE MENTIONED ME GETTING ANGRY.
EXPLAIN TO ME WHAT YOU'RE GETTING AT.
LATER. WE DON'T HAVE TIME FOR–
RUMBLE
...
TWITCH
AIEEE! DON'T LET GO!! FALL OR BE CRUSHED TO DEATH! WHAT A CHOICE!
RUMBLE

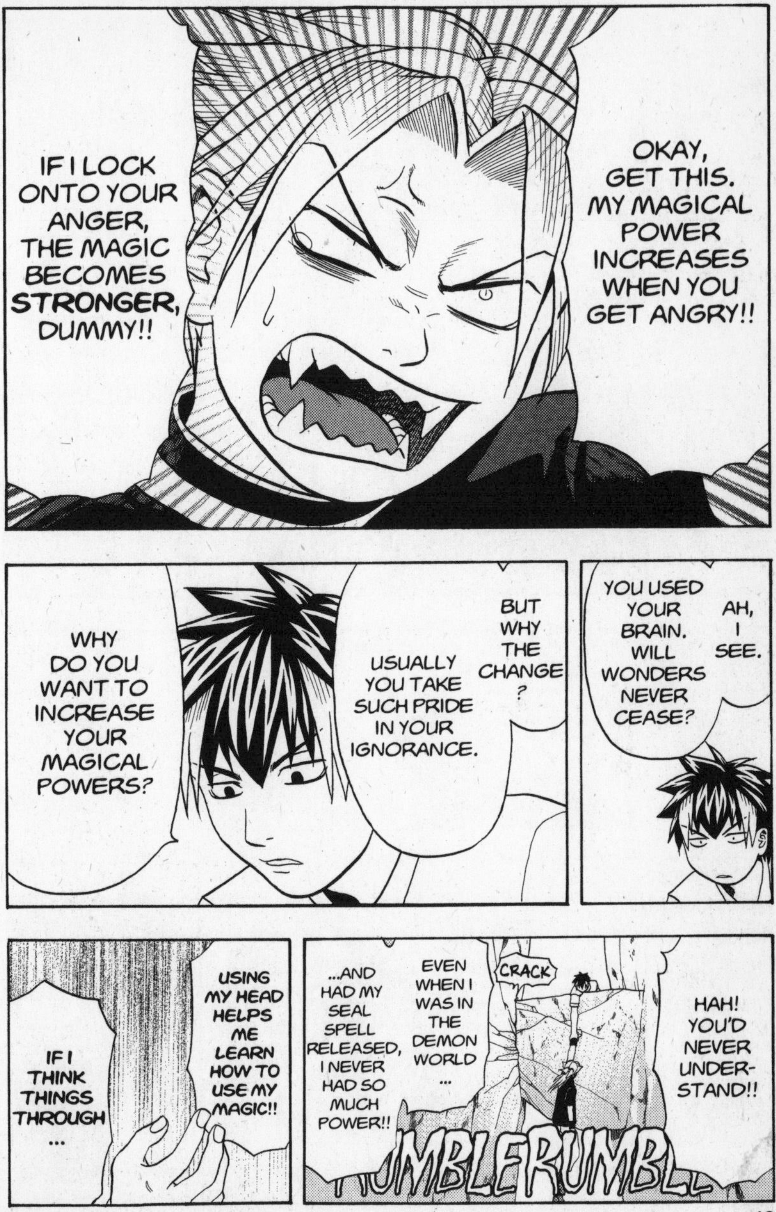
OKAY, GET THIS. MY MAGICAL POWER INCREASES WHEN YOU GET ANGRY!!
IF I LOCK ONTO YOUR ANGER, THE MAGIC BECOMES STRONGER, DUMMY!!
AH, I SEE.
YOU USED YOUR BRAIN. WILL WONDERS NEVER CEASE?
BUT WHY THE CHANGE?
USUALLY YOU TAKE SUCH PRIDE IN YOUR IGNORANCE.
WHY DO YOU WANT TO INCREASE YOUR MAGICAL POWERS?
HAH! YOU'D NEVER UNDER-STAND!!
CRACK
EVEN WHEN I WAS IN THE DEMON WORLD...
...AND HAD MY SEAL SPELL RELEASED, I NEVER HAD SO MUCH POWER!!
UMBLERUMBL
USING MY HEAD HELPS ME LEARN HOW TO USE MY MAGIC!!
IF I THINK THINGS THROUGH...

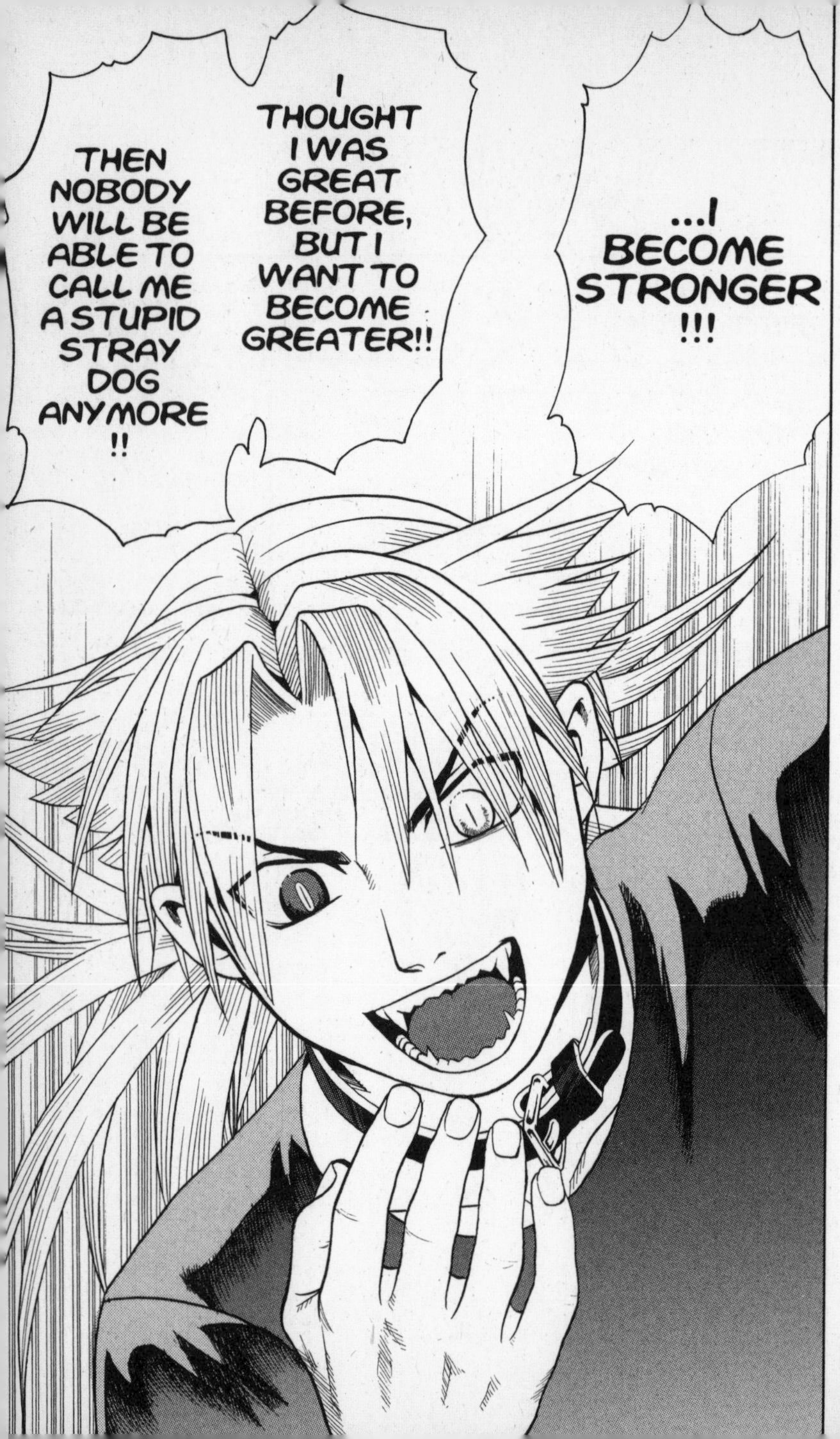
...I BECOME STRONGER!!!
I THOUGHT I WAS GREAT BEFORE, BUT I WANT TO BECOME GREATER!!
THEN NOBODY WILL BE ABLE TO CALL ME A STUPID STRAY DOG ANYMORE!!

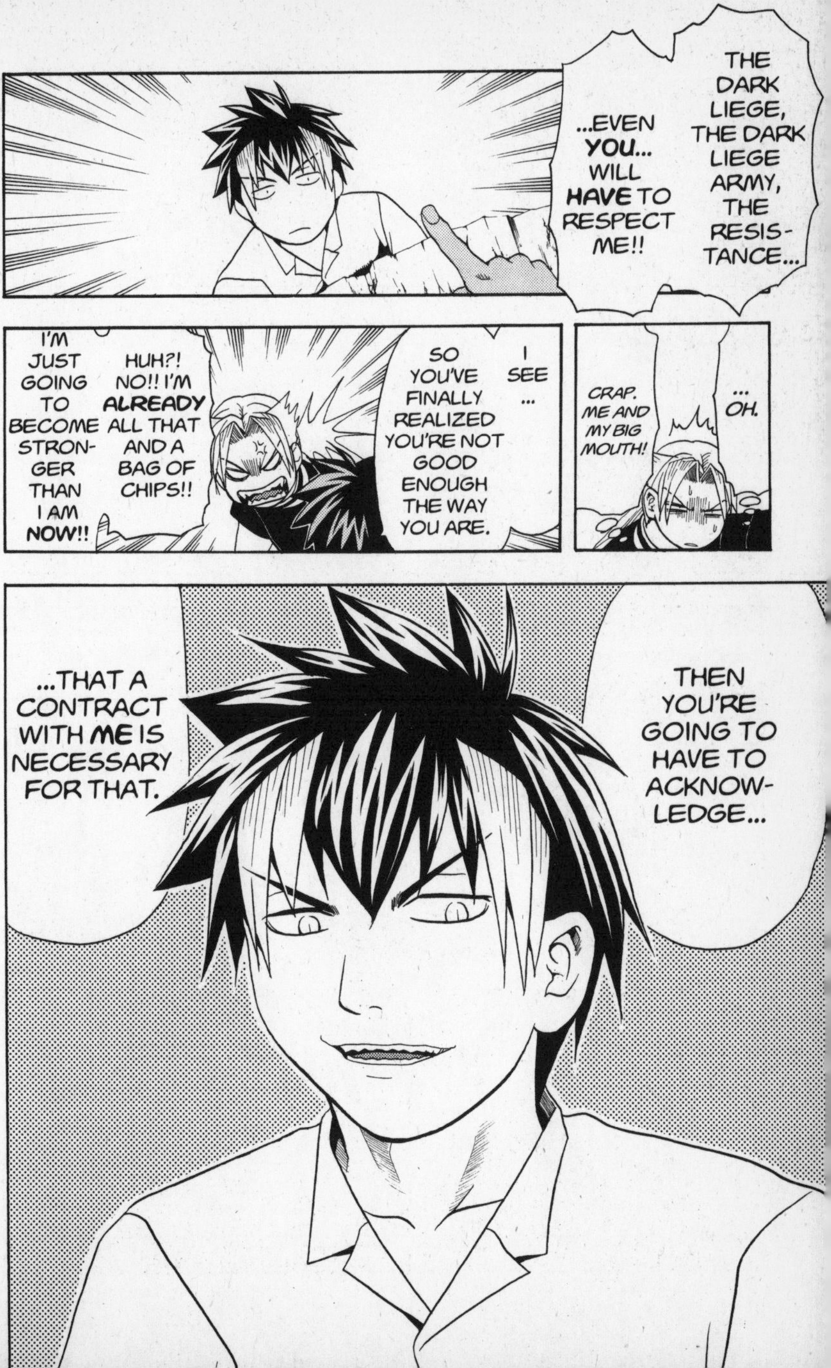
THE DARK LIEGE, THE DARK LIEGE ARMY, THE RESISTANCE...
...EVEN YOU... WILL HAVE TO RESPECT ME!!
...OH.
CRAP. ME AND MY BIG MOUTH!
I SEE...
SO YOU'VE FINALLY REALIZED YOU'RE NOT GOOD ENOUGH THE WAY YOU ARE.
HUH?! NO!! I'M ALREADY ALL THAT AND A BAG OF CHIPS!!
I'M JUST GOING TO BECOME STRONGER THAN I AM NOW!!
THEN YOU'RE GOING TO HAVE TO ACKNOWLEDGE...
...THAT A CONTRACT WITH ME IS NECESSARY FOR THAT.

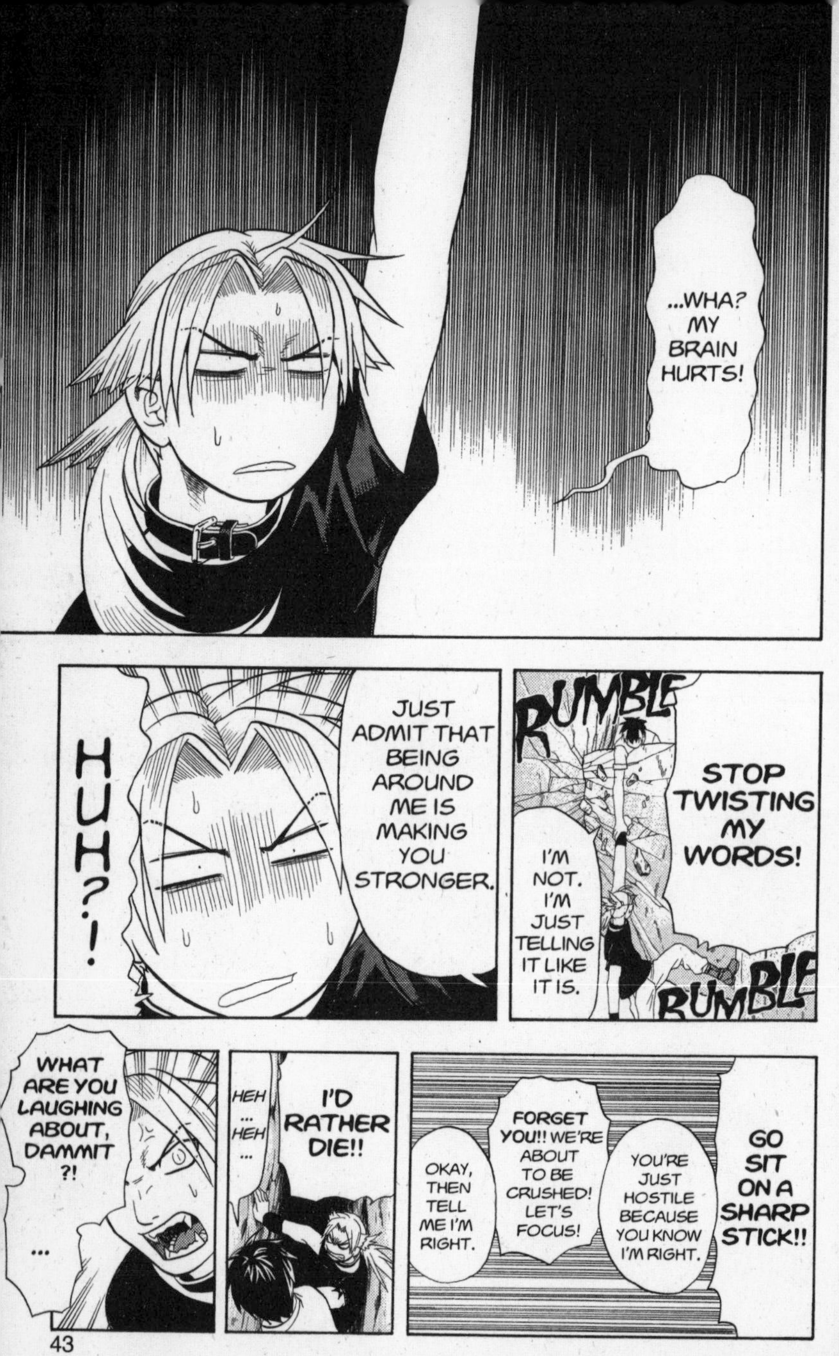
...WHA? MY BRAIN HURTS!
RUMBLE
STOP TWISTING MY WORDS!
I'M NOT. I'M JUST TELLING IT LIKE IT IS.
RUMBLE
JUST ADMIT THAT BEING AROUND ME IS MAKING YOU STRONGER.
HUH?!
GO SIT ON A SHARP STICK!!
YOU'RE JUST HOSTILE BECAUSE YOU KNOW I'M RIGHT.
FORGET YOU!! WE'RE ABOUT TO BE CRUSHED! LET'S FOCUS!
OKAY, THEN TELL ME I'M RIGHT.
I'D RATHER DIE!!
HEH ... HEH ...
WHAT ARE YOU LAUGHING ABOUT, DAMMIT ?!
...

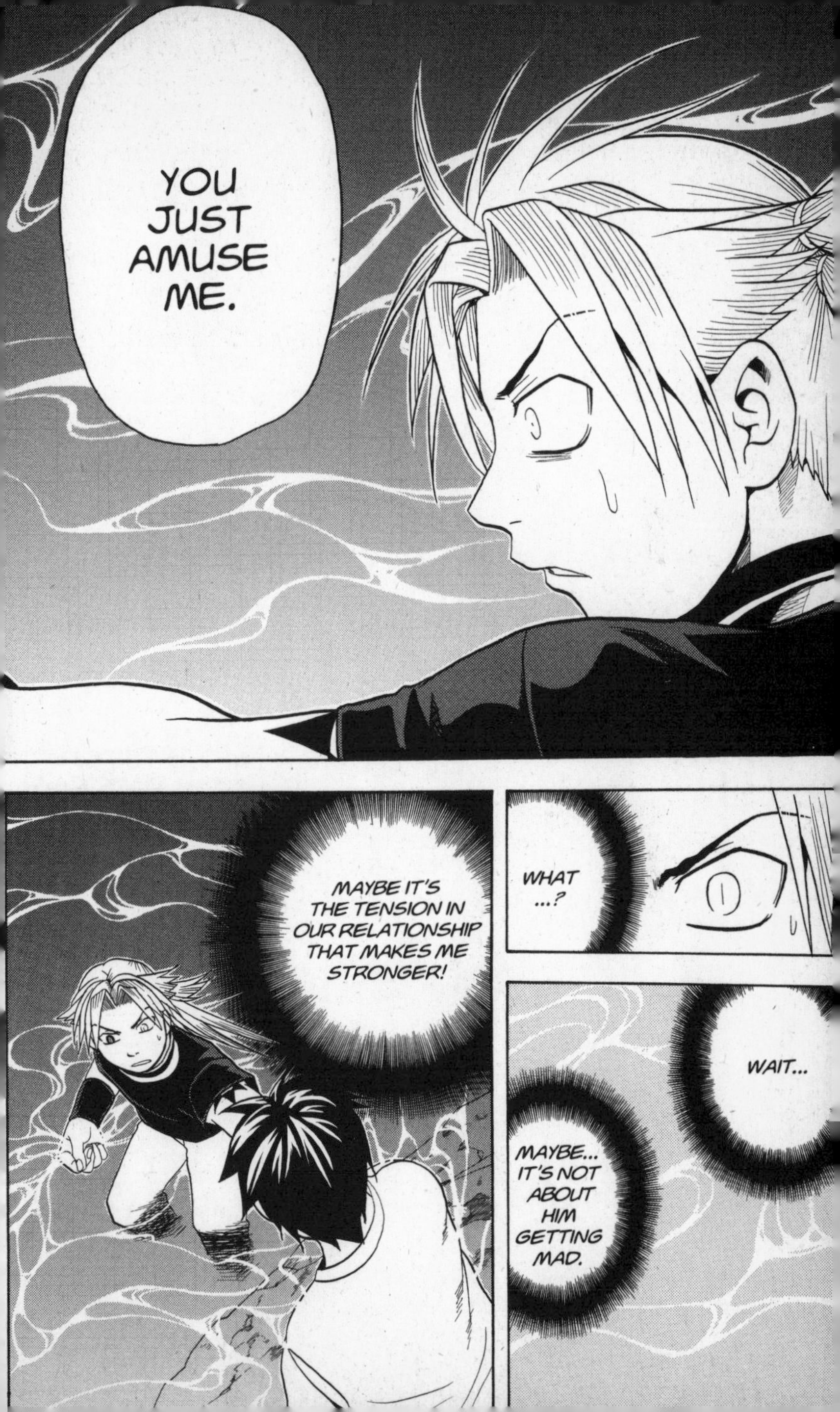
YOU JUST AMUSE ME.
WHAT ...?
WAIT...
MAYBE... IT'S NOT ABOUT HIM GETTING MAD.
MAYBE IT'S THE TENSION IN OUR RELATIONSHIP THAT MAKES ME STRONGER!

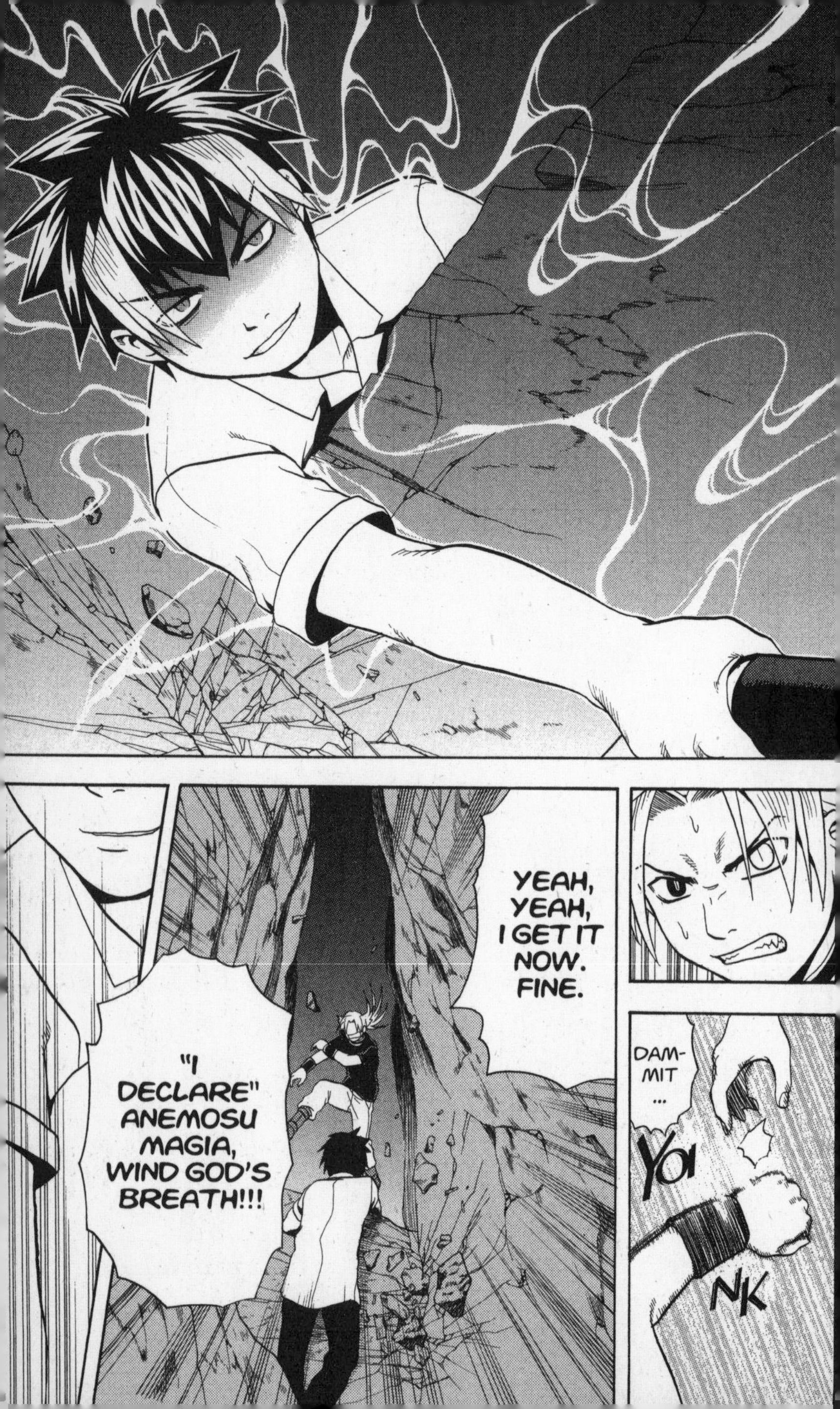
DAM-MIT ...
YOINK
YEAH, YEAH, I GET IT NOW. FINE.
"I DECLARE" ANEMOSU MAGIA, WIND GOD'S BREATH!!!

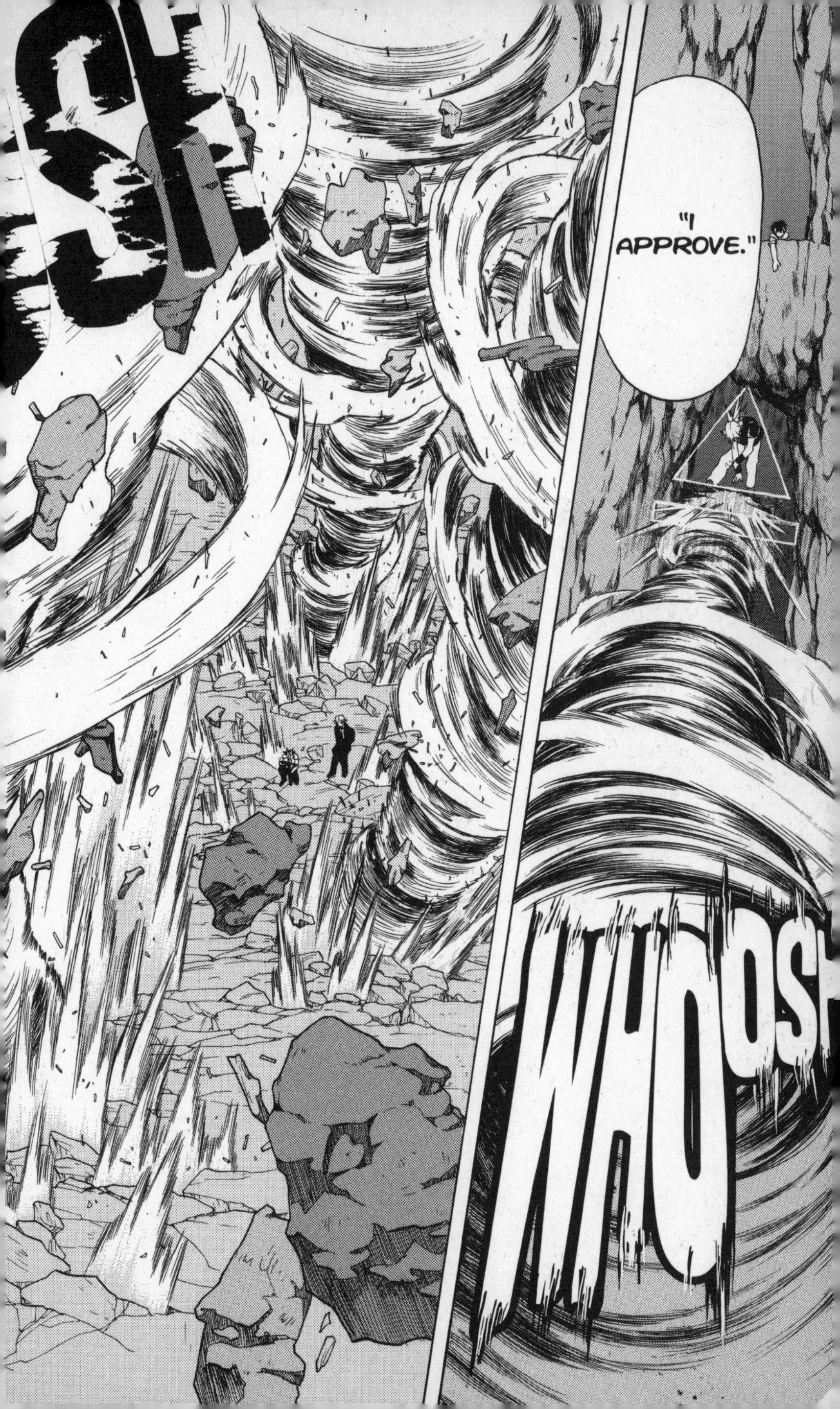

"I APPROVE."
WHOOS
SH

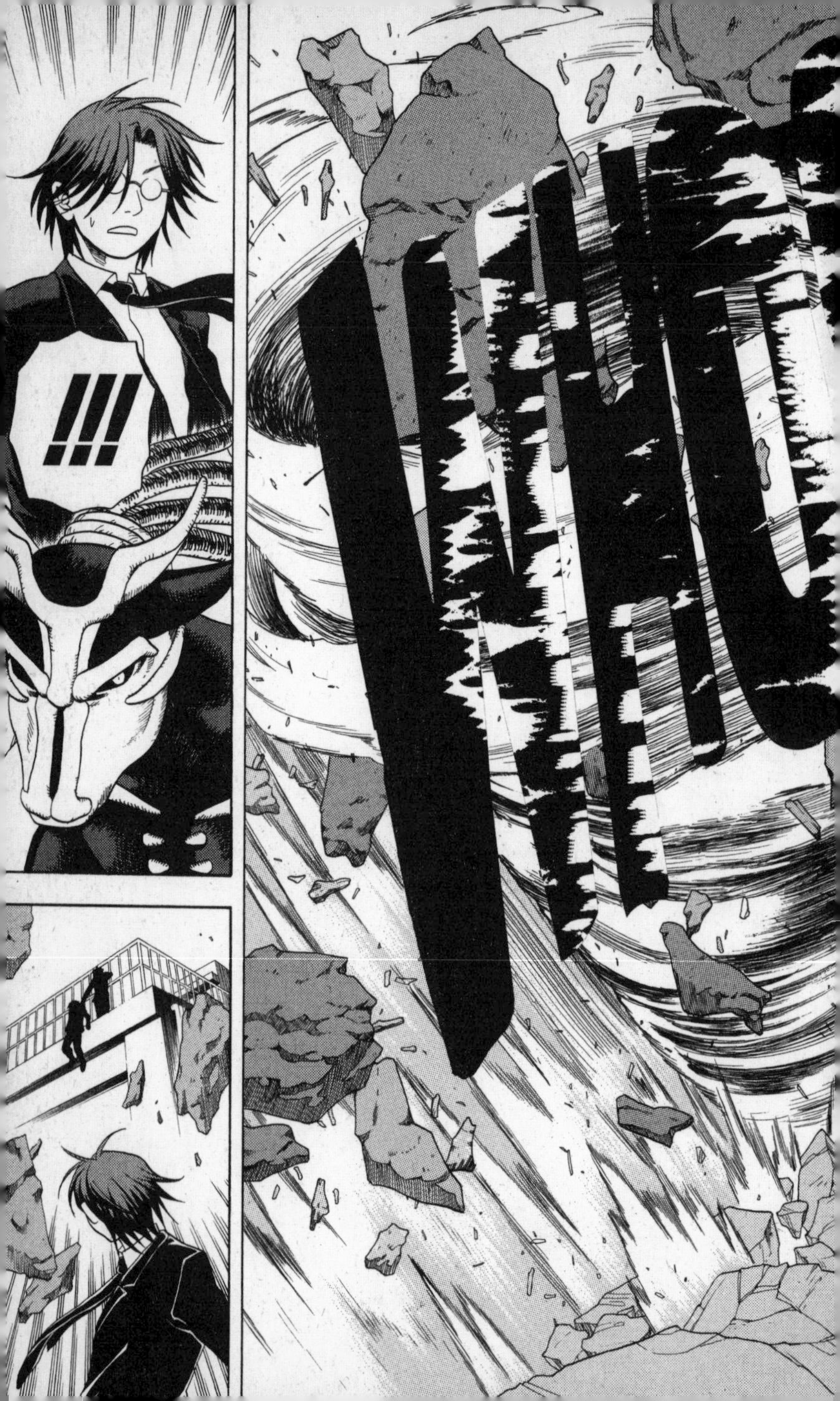
!!!

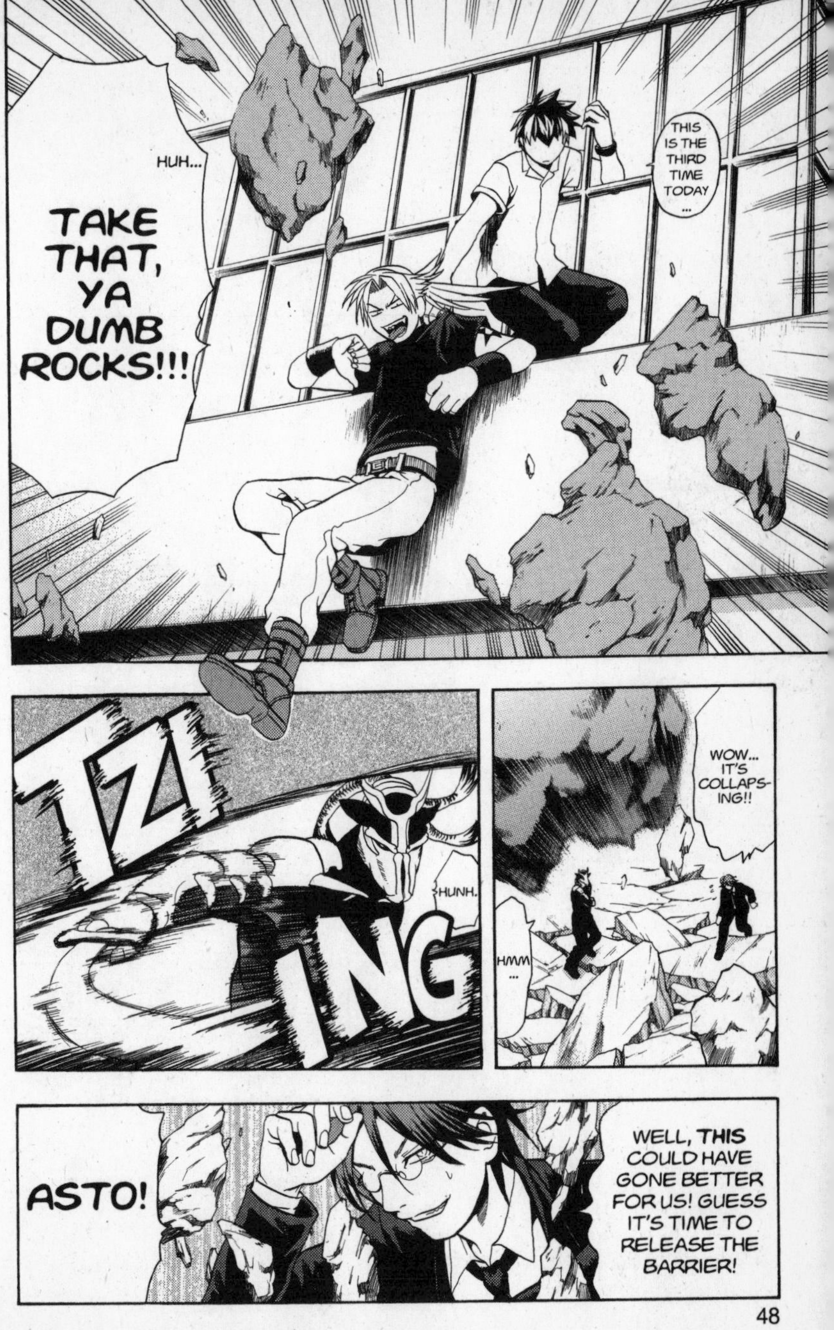
THIS IS THE THIRD TIME TODAY ...
HUH...
TAKE THAT, YA DUMB ROCKS!!!
WOW... IT'S COLLAPS-ING!!
HMM ...
TZI
ING
HUNH.
WELL, THIS COULD HAVE GONE BETTER FOR US! GUESS IT'S TIME TO RELEASE THE BARRIER!
ASTO!

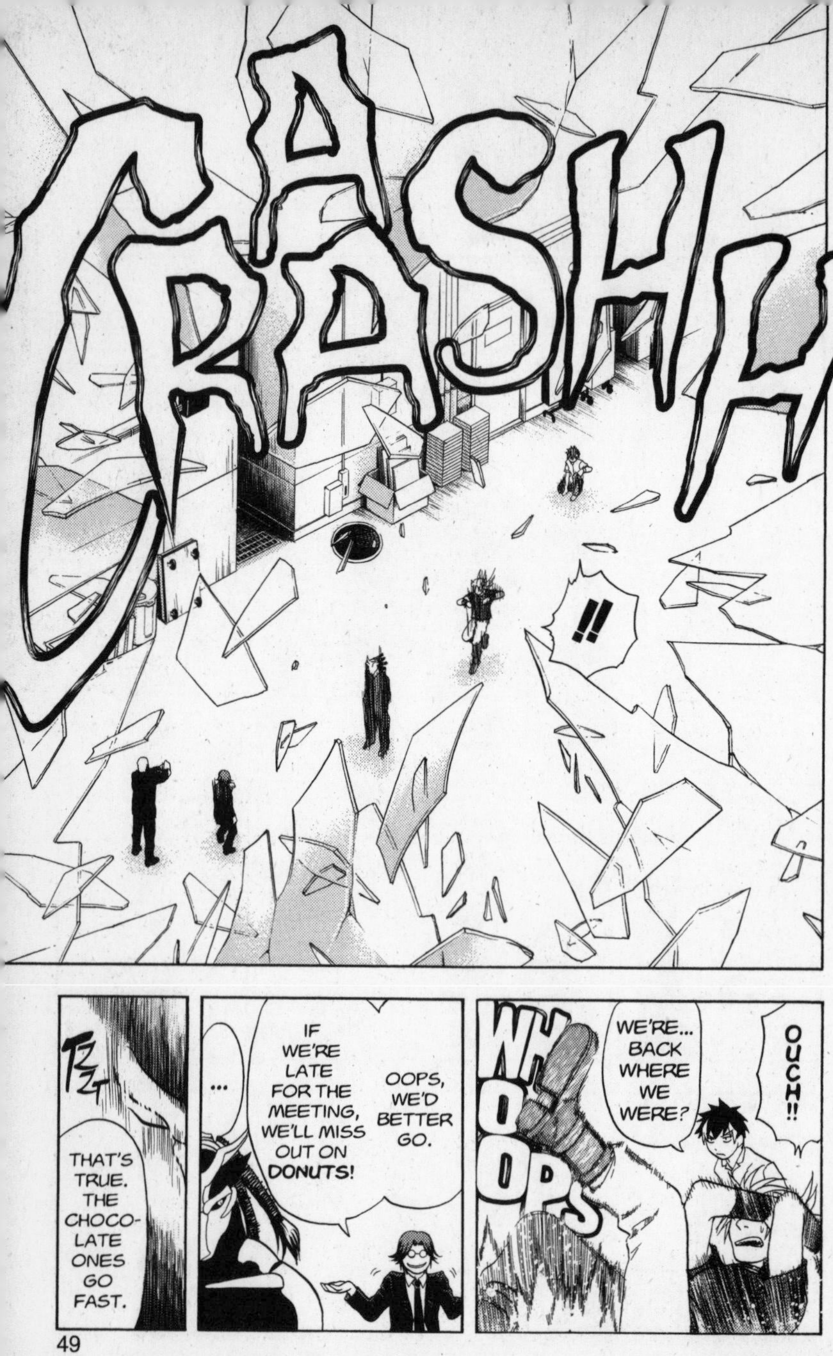
CRASH
!!
OUCH!!
WE'RE... BACK WHERE WE WERE?
WHOOPS
OOPS, WE'D BETTER GO.
IF WE'RE LATE FOR THE MEETING, WE'LL MISS OUT ON **DONUTS!**
...
TZZT
THAT'S TRUE. THE CHOCO-LATE ONES GO FAST.

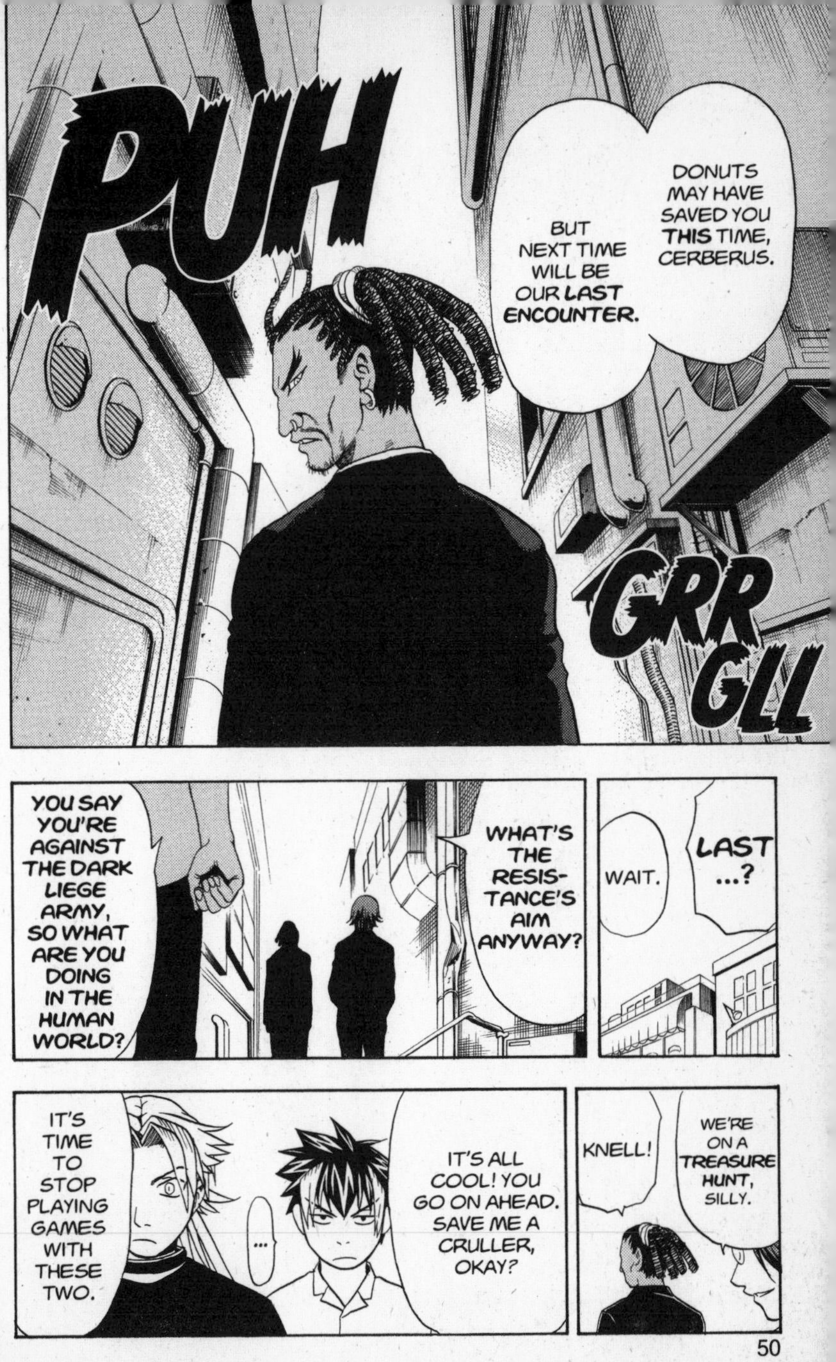
DONUTS MAY HAVE SAVED YOU THIS TIME, CERBERUS.
BUT NEXT TIME WILL BE OUR LAST ENCOUNTER.
PUH
GRR GLL
LAST ...?
WAIT.
WHAT'S THE RESIS-TANCE'S AIM ANYWAY?
YOU SAY YOU'RE AGAINST THE DARK LIEGE ARMY, SO WHAT ARE YOU DOING IN THE HUMAN WORLD?
WE'RE ON A TREASURE HUNT, SILLY.
KNELL!
IT'S ALL COOL! YOU GO ON AHEAD. SAVE ME A CRULLER, OKAY?
...
IT'S TIME TO STOP PLAYING GAMES WITH THESE TWO.

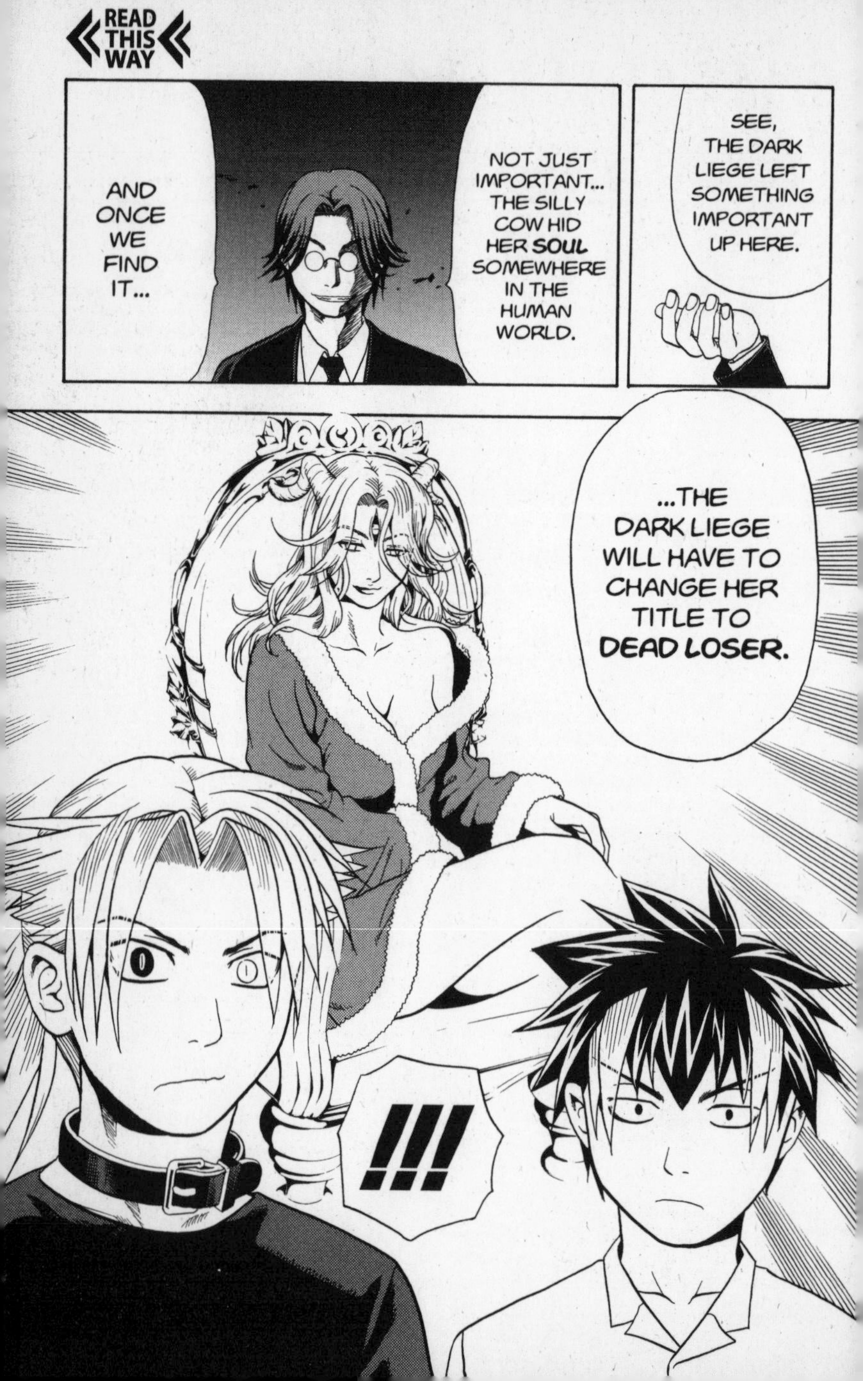
READ THIS WAY
SEE, THE DARK LIEGE LEFT SOMETHING IMPORTANT UP HERE.
NOT JUST IMPORTANT... THE SILLY COW HID HER **SOUL** SOMEWHERE IN THE HUMAN WORLD.
AND ONCE WE FIND IT...
...THE DARK LIEGE WILL HAVE TO CHANGE HER TITLE TO **DEAD LOSER.**
!!!

CHARACTER DATA

HER HELLISHNESS
THE DARK LIEGE
HEIGHT: 178CM
FAVORITE FOOD: **DEVIL'S** FOOD CAKE...AND OTHER SWEETS! ♥
FOOD SHE HATES: THAT'S A SECRET! ♥
INTERESTS AND
SPECIAL TALENTS: MY INTRICATE BEAUTY REGIME, OF COURSE!
NOTES: COMMANDER-IN-CHIEF OF THE DARK LIEGE ARMY. SHE'S THE HEAD HONCHO, THE BOSS LADY— YOU GET THE PICTURE. SHE MIGHT LOOK SWEET AND SEXY, BUT HELL HATH NO FURY...AND YOU KNOW THE REST.

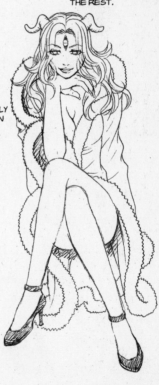

JELLY
HEIGHT: ?
FAVORITE FOOD: ?
FOOD IT HATES: ?
INTERESTS AND
SPECIAL TALENTS: ?
NOTES: LOWER-CLASS DEMONS COMMONLY SEEN IN THE DEMON WORLD. THEY'RE MOSTLY JUST KEPT AS PETS.

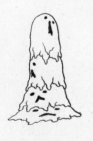

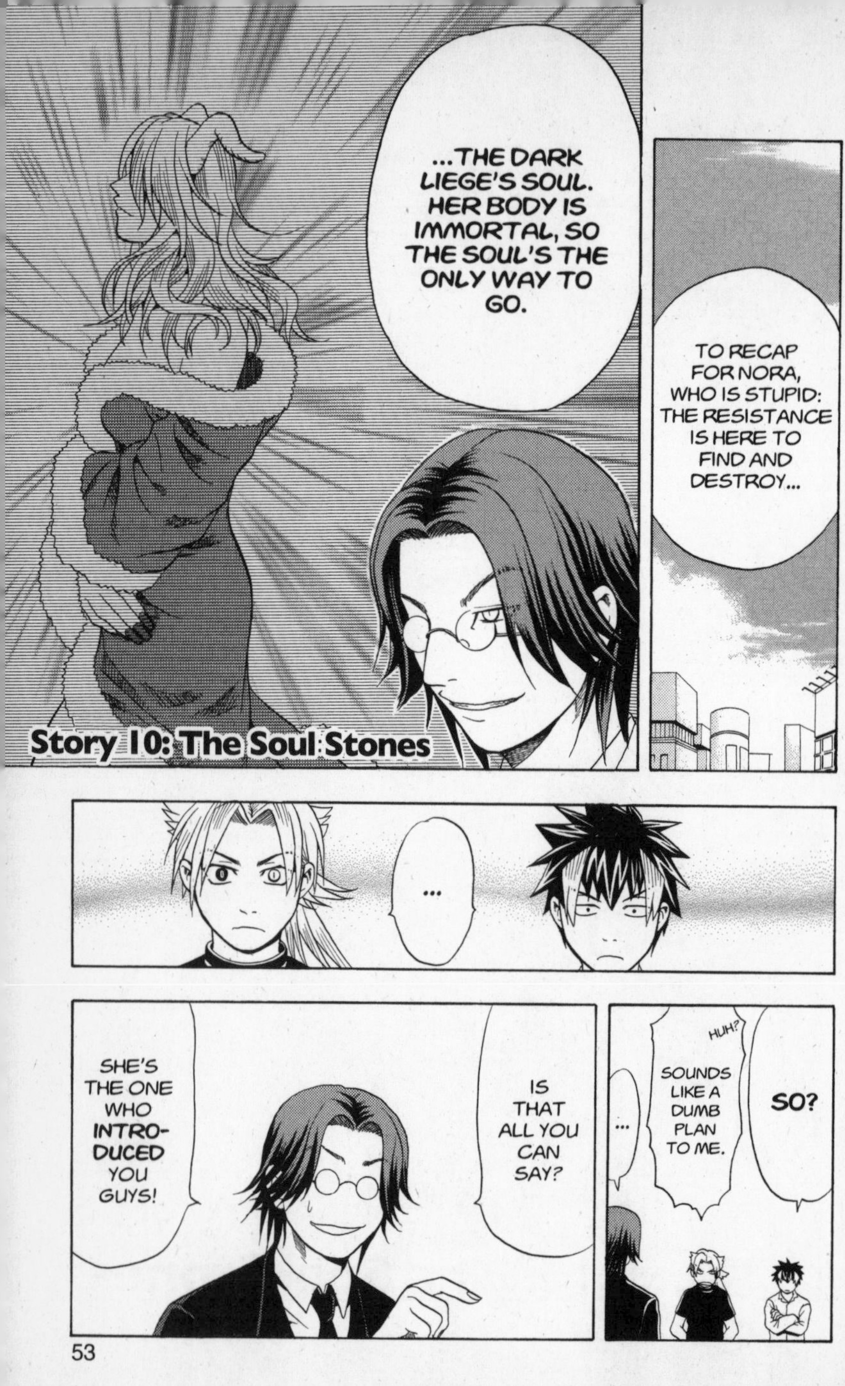
TO RECAP FOR NORA, WHO IS STUPID: THE RESISTANCE IS HERE TO FIND AND DESTROY...
...THE DARK LIEGE'S SOUL. HER BODY IS IMMORTAL, SO THE SOUL'S THE ONLY WAY TO GO.
Story 10: The Soul Stones
...
SO?
HUH?
SOUNDS LIKE A DUMB PLAN TO ME.
...
IS THAT ALL YOU CAN SAY?
SHE'S THE ONE WHO INTRODUCED YOU GUYS!

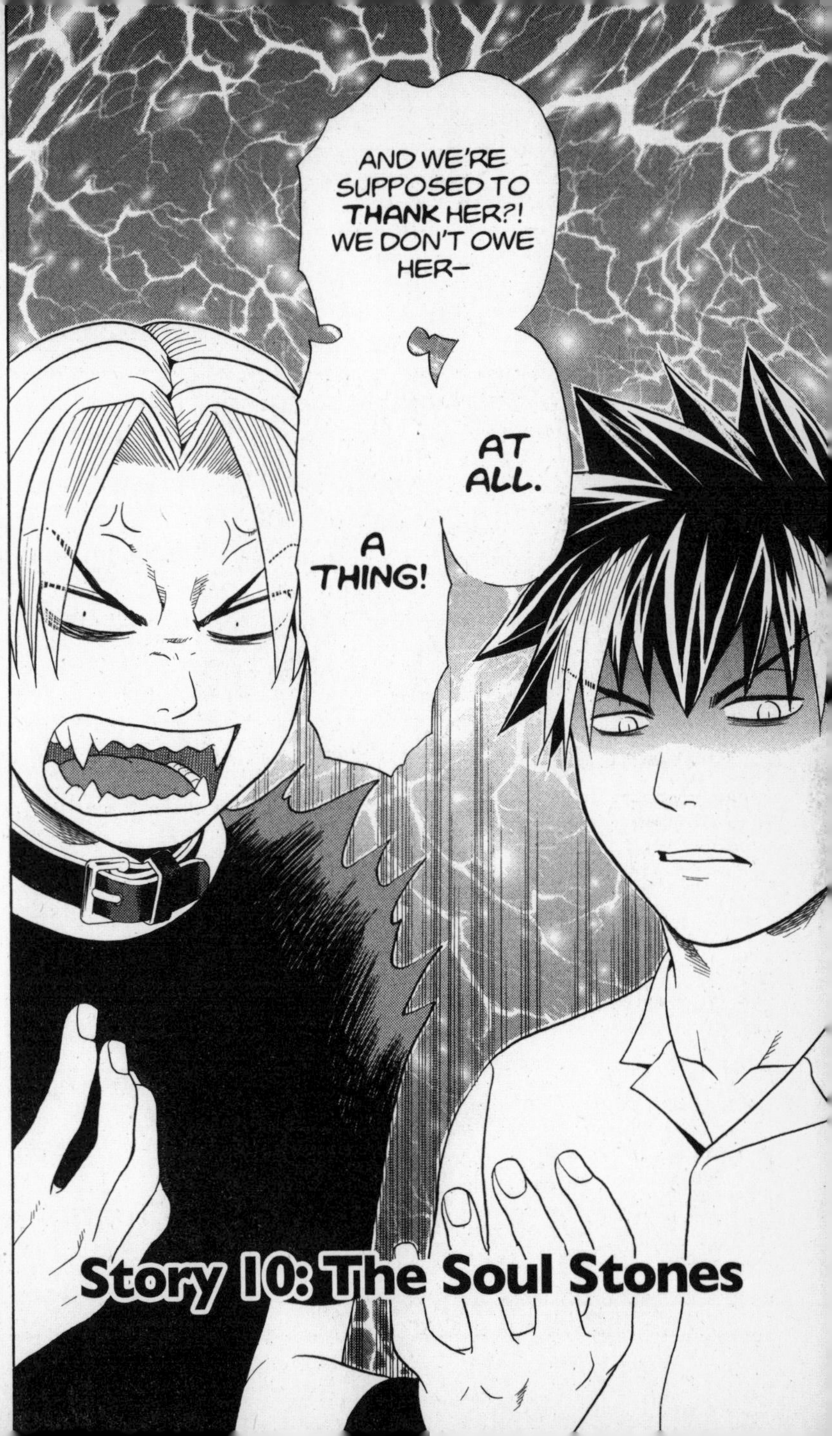
AND WE'RE SUPPOSED TO THANK HER?! WE DON'T OWE HER—
AT ALL.
A THING!

Story 10: The Soul Stones

READ THIS WAY

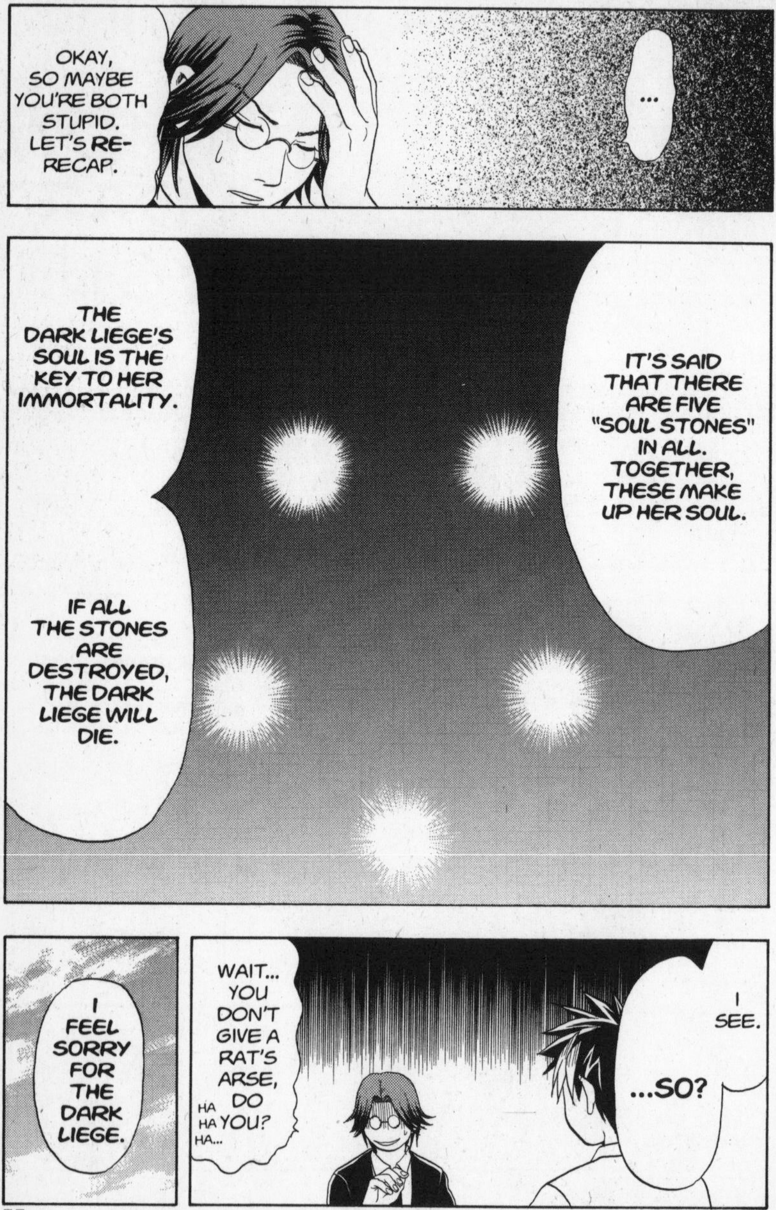

...
OKAY, SO MAYBE YOU'RE BOTH STUPID. LET'S RE-RECAP.
IT'S SAID THAT THERE ARE FIVE "SOUL STONES" IN ALL. TOGETHER, THESE MAKE UP HER SOUL.
THE DARK LIEGE'S SOUL IS THE KEY TO HER IMMORTALITY.
IF ALL THE STONES ARE DESTROYED, THE DARK LIEGE WILL DIE.
I SEE.
...SO?
WAIT... YOU DON'T GIVE A RAT'S ARSE, DO YOU?
HA HA HA...
I FEEL SORRY FOR THE DARK LIEGE.

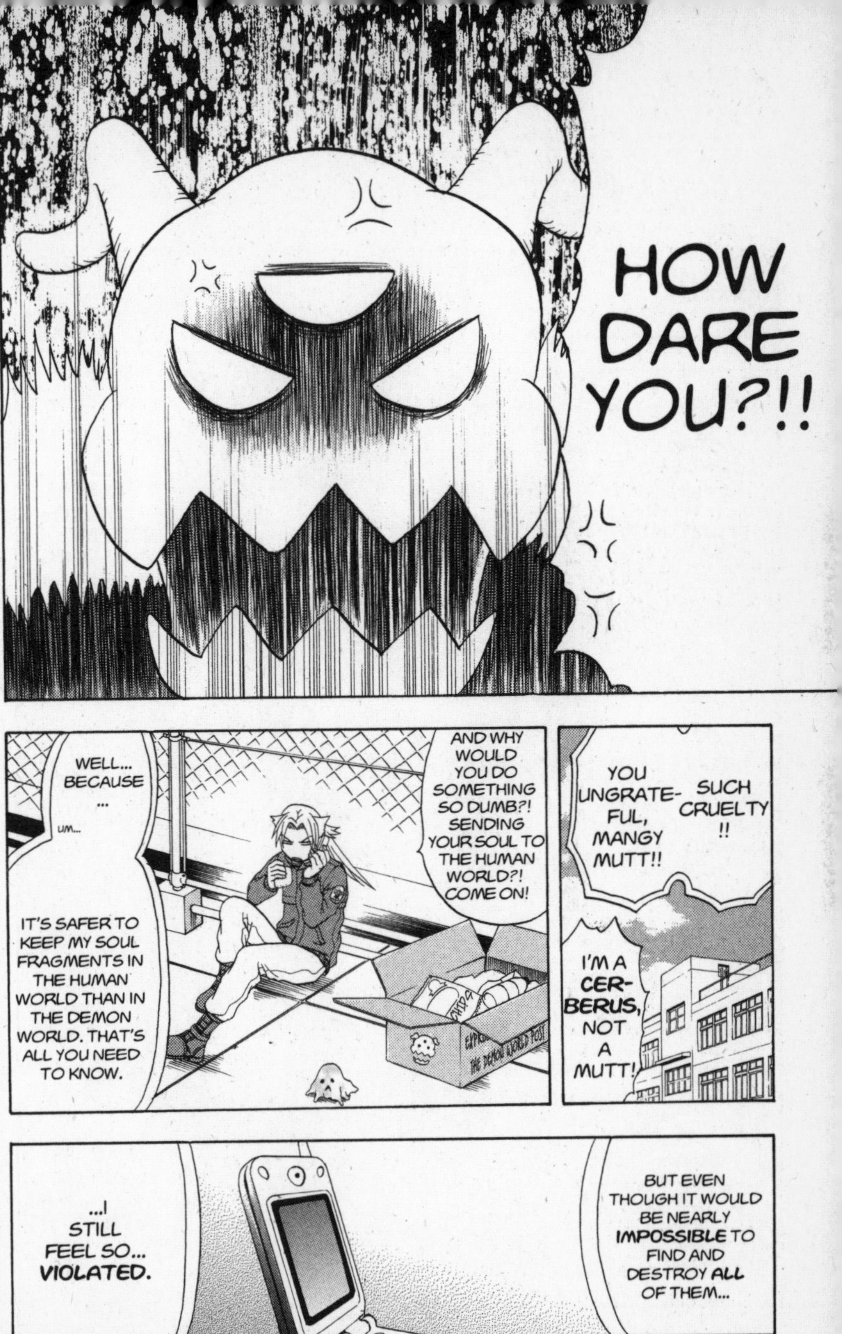
HOW DARE YOU?!!
SUCH CRUELTY!!
YOU UNGRATEFUL, MANGY MUTT!!
I'M A CERBERUS, NOT A MUTT!
AND WHY WOULD YOU DO SOMETHING SO DUMB?! SENDING YOUR SOUL TO THE HUMAN WORLD?! COME ON!
WELL... BECAUSE ...
UM...
IT'S SAFER TO KEEP MY SOUL FRAGMENTS IN THE HUMAN WORLD THAN IN THE DEMON WORLD. THAT'S ALL YOU NEED TO KNOW.
BUT EVEN THOUGH IT WOULD BE NEARLY IMPOSSIBLE TO FIND AND DESTROY ALL OF THEM...
...I STILL FEEL SO... VIOLATED.

READ THIS WAY

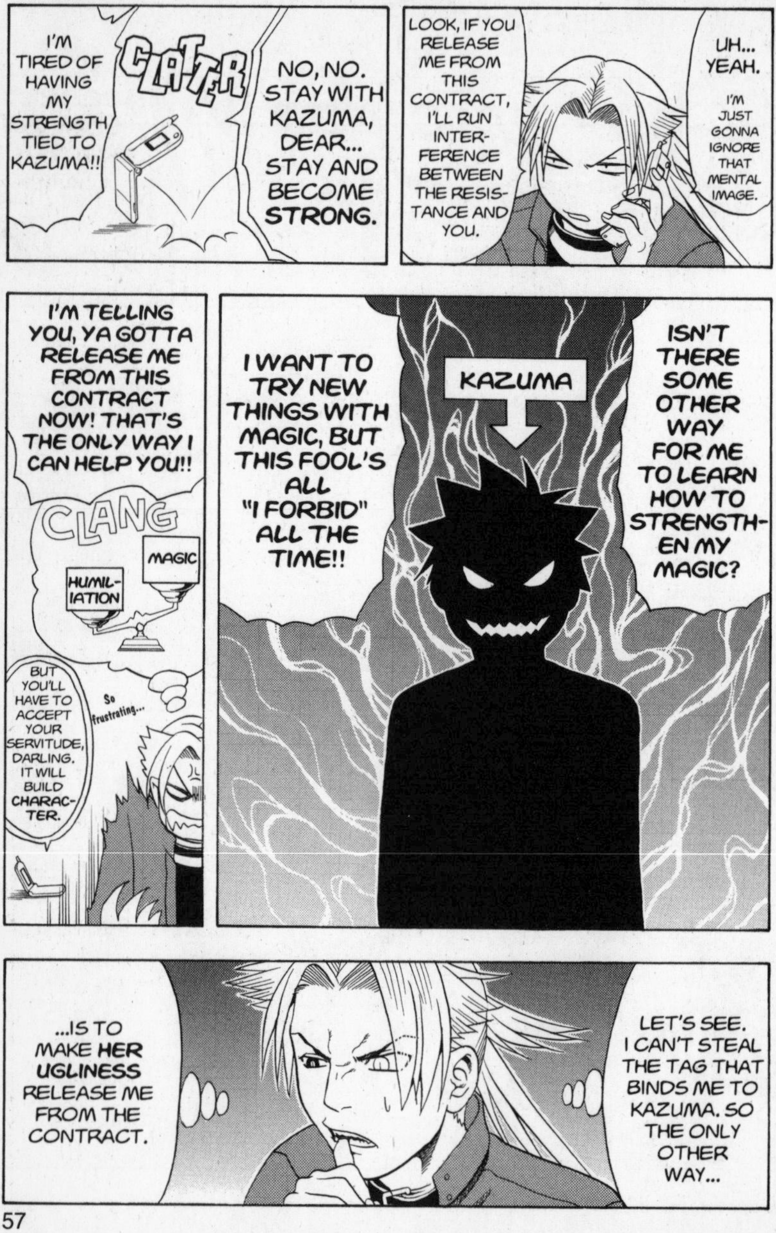
UH... YEAH.
I'M JUST GONNA IGNORE THAT MENTAL IMAGE.
LOOK, IF YOU RELEASE ME FROM THIS CONTRACT, I'LL RUN INTERFERENCE BETWEEN THE RESISTANCE AND YOU.
NO, NO. STAY WITH KAZUMA, DEAR... STAY AND BECOME STRONG.
CLATTER
I'M TIRED OF HAVING MY STRENGTH TIED TO KAZUMA!!
ISN'T THERE SOME OTHER WAY FOR ME TO LEARN HOW TO STRENGTHEN MY MAGIC?
KAZUMA
I WANT TO TRY NEW THINGS WITH MAGIC, BUT THIS FOOL'S ALL "I FORBID" ALL THE TIME!!
I'M TELLING YOU, YA GOTTA RELEASE ME FROM THIS CONTRACT NOW! THAT'S THE ONLY WAY I CAN HELP YOU!!
CLANG
MAGIC
HUMILIATION
So frustrating...
BUT YOU'LL HAVE TO ACCEPT YOUR SERVITUDE, DARLING. IT WILL BUILD CHARACTER.
LET'S SEE. I CAN'T STEAL THE TAG THAT BINDS ME TO KAZUMA. SO THE ONLY OTHER WAY...
...IS TO MAKE HER UGLINESS RELEASE ME FROM THE CONTRACT.

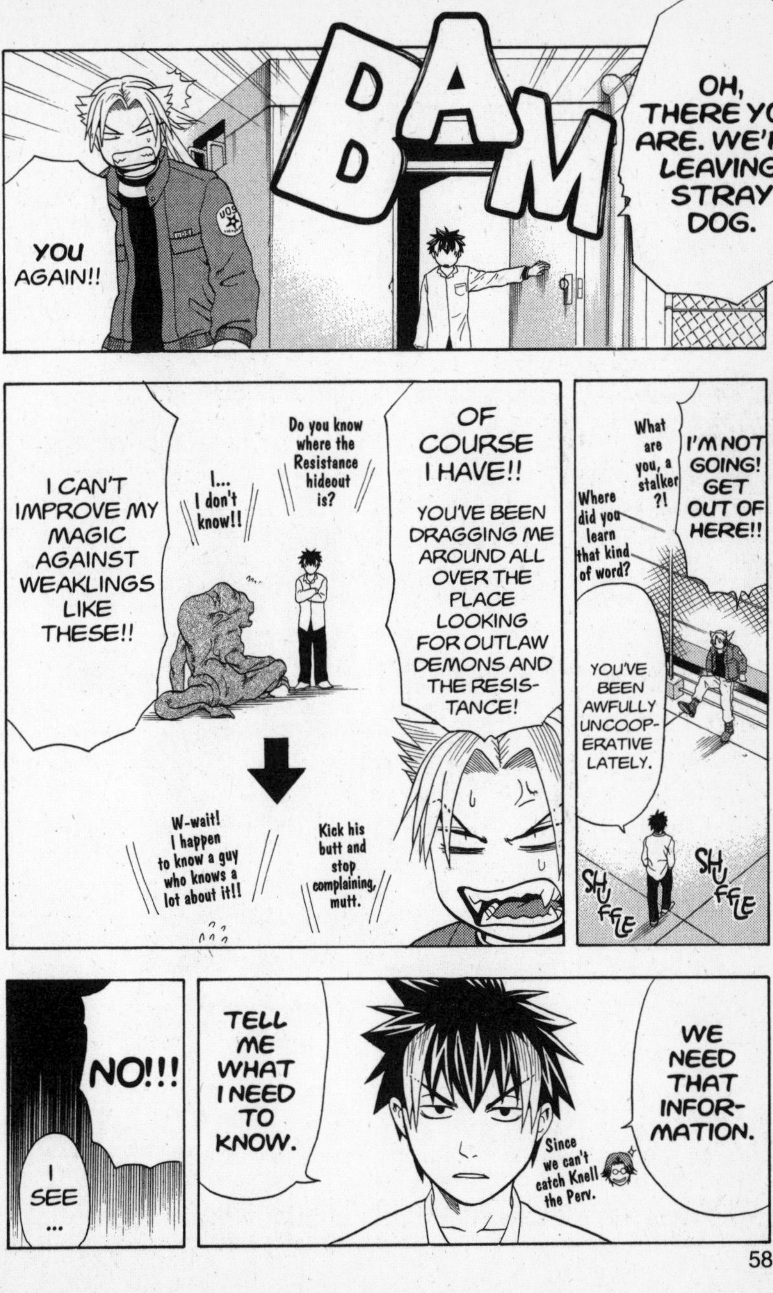
OH, THERE YOU ARE. WE'RE LEAVING, STRAY DOG.
BAM
YOU AGAIN!!
I'M NOT GOING! GET OUT OF HERE!!
What are you, a stalker?!
Where did you learn that kind of word?
YOU'VE BEEN AWFULLY UNCOOPERATIVE LATELY.
SHUFFLE
SHUFFLE
OF COURSE I HAVE!! YOU'VE BEEN DRAGGING ME AROUND ALL OVER THE PLACE LOOKING FOR OUTLAW DEMONS AND THE RESISTANCE!
Do you know where the Resistance hideout is?
I... I don't know!!
I CAN'T IMPROVE MY MAGIC AGAINST WEAKLINGS LIKE THESE!!
Kick his butt and stop complaining, mutt.
W-wait! I happen to know a guy who knows a lot about it!!
WE NEED THAT INFORMATION.
Since we can't catch Knell the Perv.
TELL ME WHAT I NEED TO KNOW.
NO!!!
I SEE...

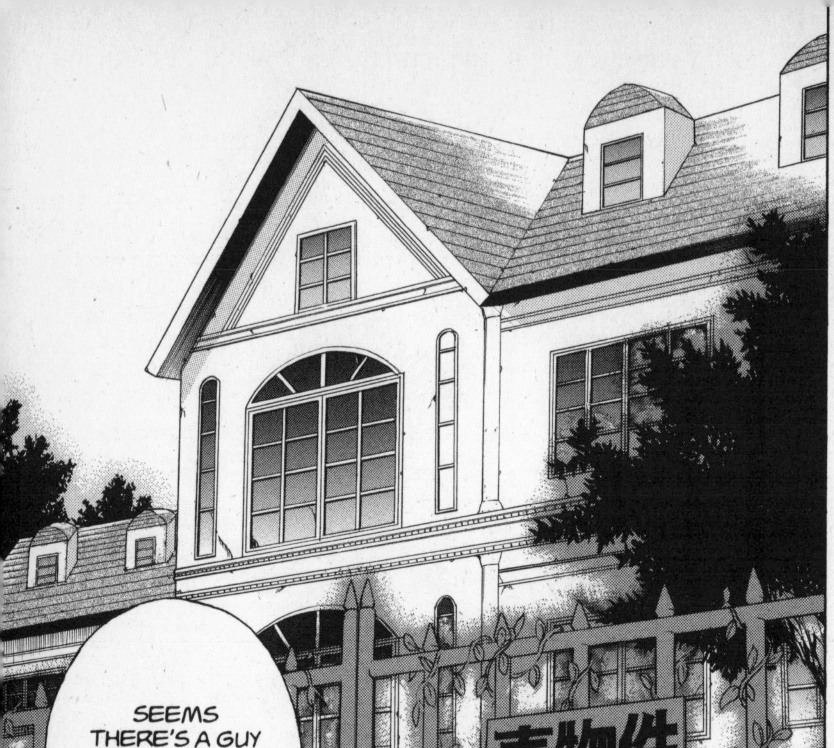
SEEMS THERE'S A GUY HERE WHO DOES BUSINESS WITH OUTLAW DEMONS AND OTHERS FROM THE UNDERWORLD.
売物件

SIGN: PROPERTY FOR SALE

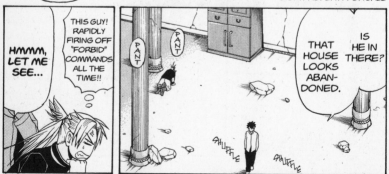

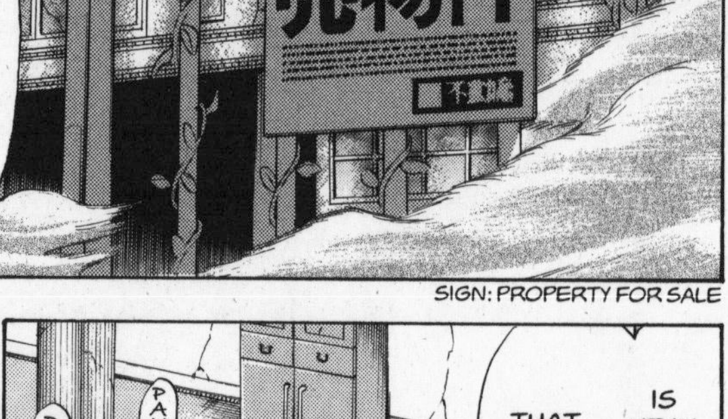
IS HE IN THERE?
THAT HOUSE LOOKS ABAN-DONED.
PANT
PANT
SHUFFLE
SHUFFLE

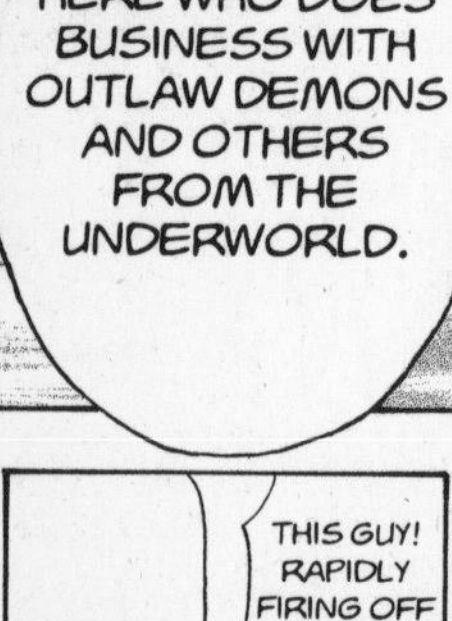
THIS GUY! RAPIDLY FIRING OFF "FORBID" COMMANDS ALL THE TIME!!
HMMM, LET ME SEE...

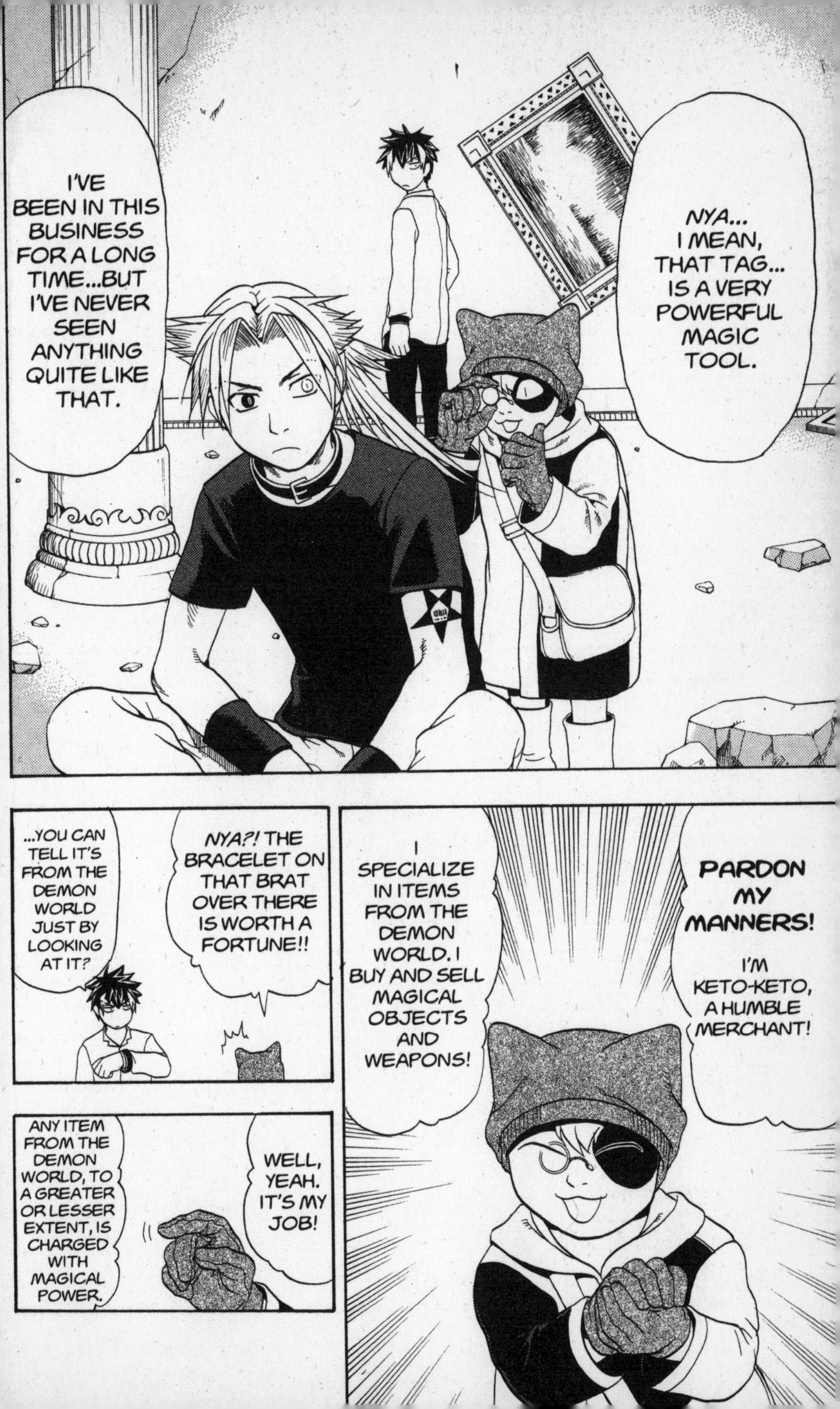

NYA... I MEAN, THAT TAG... IS A VERY POWERFUL MAGIC TOOL.
I'VE BEEN IN THIS BUSINESS FOR A LONG TIME...BUT I'VE NEVER SEEN ANYTHING QUITE LIKE THAT.
PARDON MY MANNERS!
I'M KETO-KETO, A HUMBLE MERCHANT!
I SPECIALIZE IN ITEMS FROM THE DEMON WORLD. I BUY AND SELL MAGICAL OBJECTS AND WEAPONS!
NYA?! THE BRACELET ON THAT BRAT OVER THERE IS WORTH A FORTUNE!!
...YOU CAN TELL IT'S FROM THE DEMON WORLD JUST BY LOOKING AT IT?
WELL, YEAH. IT'S MY JOB!
ANY ITEM FROM THE DEMON WORLD, TO A GREATER OR LESSER EXTENT, IS CHARGED WITH MAGICAL POWER.

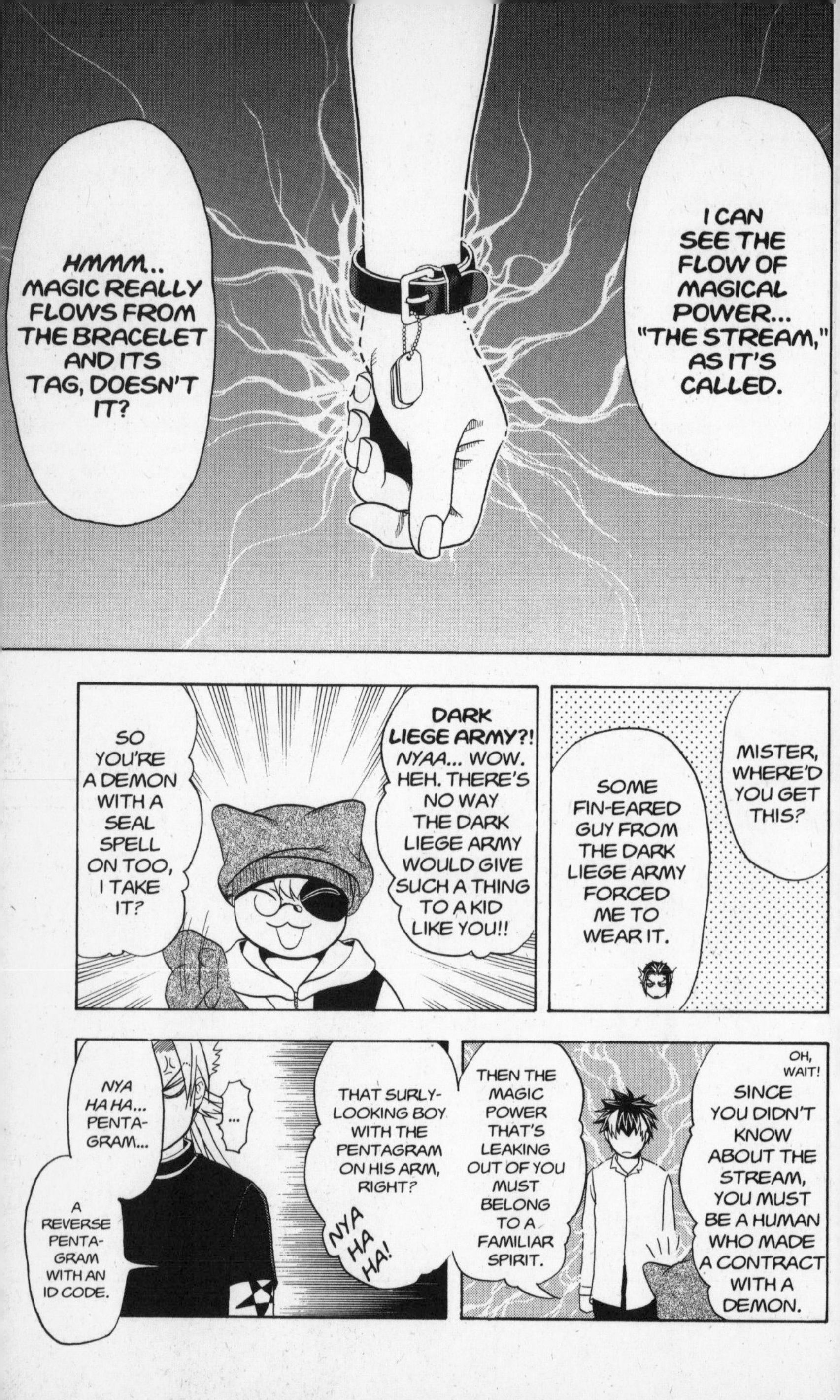
I CAN SEE THE FLOW OF MAGICAL POWER... "THE STREAM," AS IT'S CALLED.
HMMM... MAGIC REALLY FLOWS FROM THE BRACELET AND ITS TAG, DOESN'T IT?
MISTER, WHERE'D YOU GET THIS?
SOME FIN-EARED GUY FROM THE DARK LIEGE ARMY FORCED ME TO WEAR IT.
DARK LIEGE ARMY?! NYAA... WOW. HEH. THERE'S NO WAY THE DARK LIEGE ARMY WOULD GIVE SUCH A THING TO A KID LIKE YOU!!
SO YOU'RE A DEMON WITH A SEAL SPELL ON TOO, I TAKE IT?
OH, WAIT!
SINCE YOU DIDN'T KNOW ABOUT THE STREAM, YOU MUST BE A HUMAN WHO MADE A CONTRACT WITH A DEMON.
THEN THE MAGIC POWER THAT'S LEAKING OUT OF YOU MUST BELONG TO A FAMILIAR SPIRIT.
THAT SURLY-LOOKING BOY WITH THE PENTAGRAM ON HIS ARM, RIGHT?
NYA HA HA!
...
NYA HA HA... PENTA-GRAM...
A REVERSE PENTA-GRAM WITH AN ID CODE.

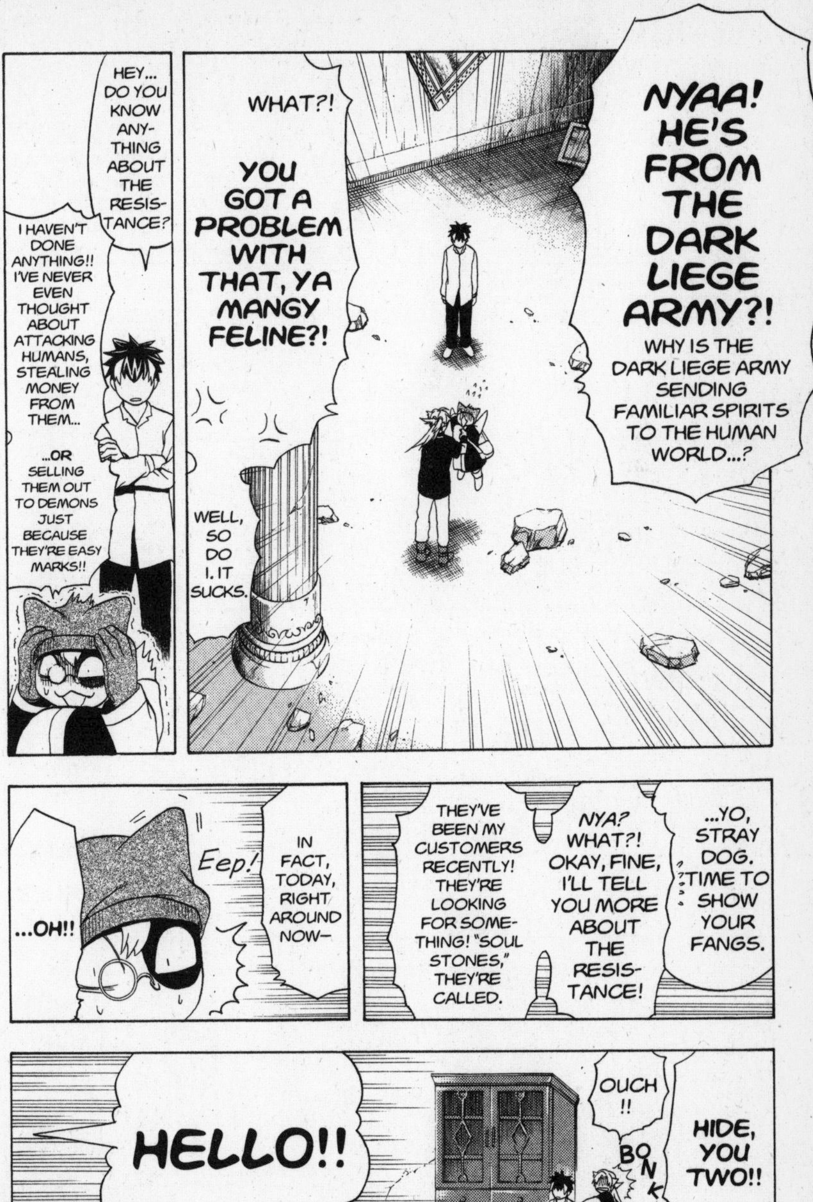
NYAA! HE'S FROM THE DARK LIEGE ARMY?!
WHY IS THE DARK LIEGE ARMY SENDING FAMILIAR SPIRITS TO THE HUMAN WORLD...?
WHAT?!
YOU GOT A PROBLEM WITH THAT, YA MANGY FELINE?!
WELL, SO DO I. IT SUCKS.
HEY... DO YOU KNOW ANYTHING ABOUT THE RESISTANCE?
I HAVEN'T DONE ANYTHING!! I'VE NEVER EVEN THOUGHT ABOUT ATTACKING HUMANS, STEALING MONEY FROM THEM...
...OR SELLING THEM OUT TO DEMONS JUST BECAUSE THEY'RE EASY MARKS!!
...YO, STRAY DOG. TIME TO SHOW YOUR FANGS.
NYA? WHAT?! OKAY, FINE, I'LL TELL YOU MORE ABOUT THE RESISTANCE!
THEY'VE BEEN MY CUSTOMERS RECENTLY! THEY'RE LOOKING FOR SOMETHING! "SOUL STONES," THEY'RE CALLED.
IN FACT, TODAY, RIGHT AROUND NOW—
Eep!
...OH!!
HIDE, YOU TWO!!
OUCH!!
BONK
HELLO!!

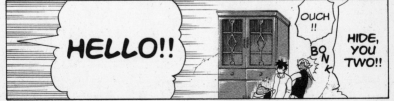

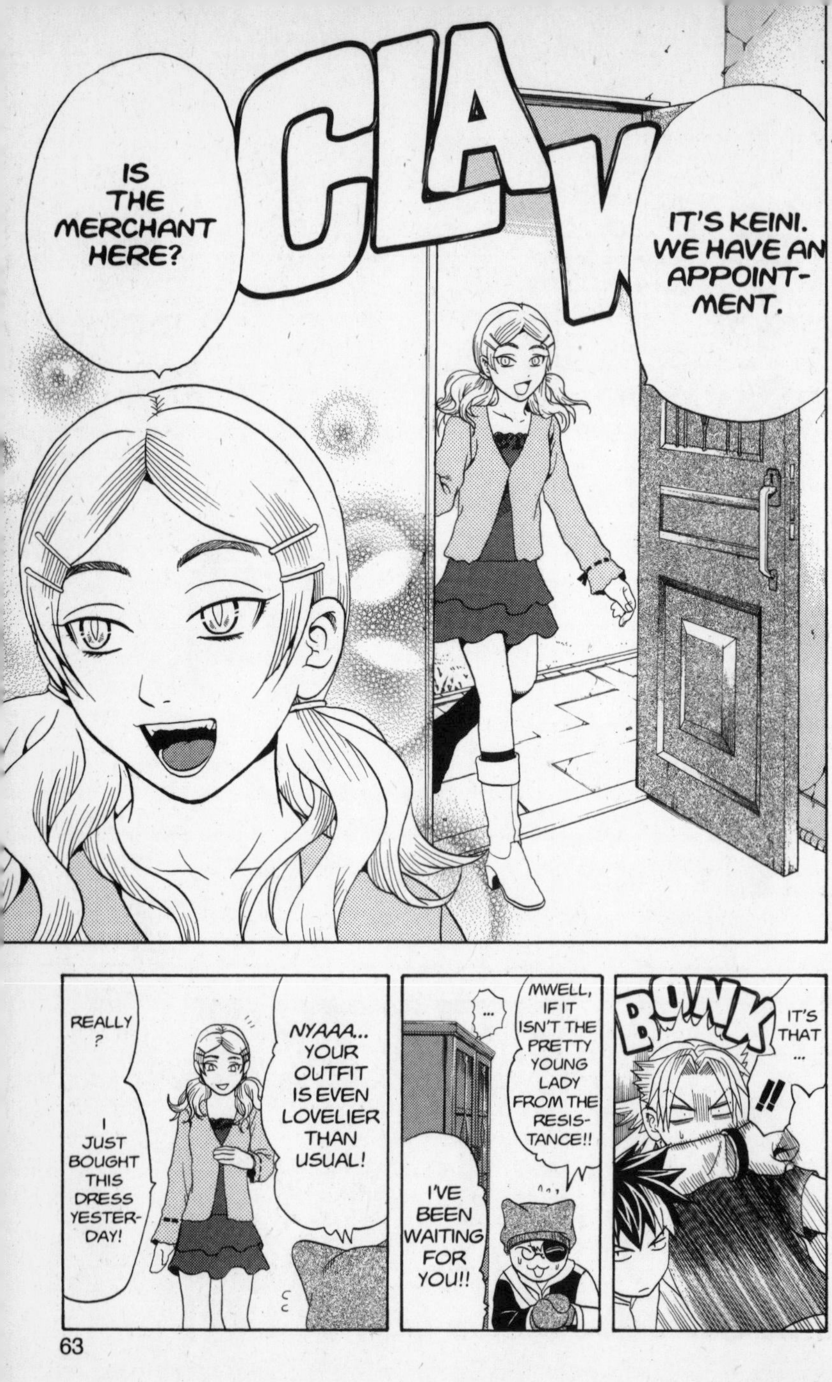
CLAV
IT'S KEINI. WE HAVE AN APPOINT-MENT.
IS THE MERCHANT HERE?
BONK
IT'S THAT ...
!!
MWELL, IF IT ISN'T THE PRETTY YOUNG LADY FROM THE RESIS-TANCE!!
...
I'VE BEEN WAITING FOR YOU!!
NYAAA... YOUR OUTFIT IS EVEN LOVELIER THAN USUAL!
REALLY?
I JUST BOUGHT THIS DRESS YESTER-DAY!

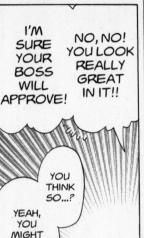

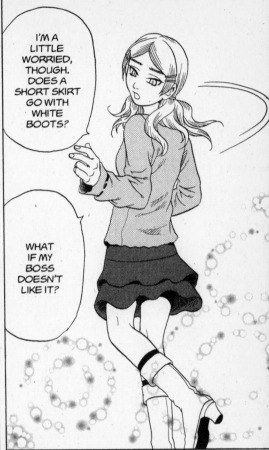

I'M A LITTLE WORRIED, THOUGH. DOES A SHORT SKIRT GO WITH WHITE BOOTS?
WHAT IF MY BOSS DOESN'T LIKE IT?
NO, NO! YOU LOOK REALLY GREAT IN IT!!
I'M SURE YOUR BOSS WILL APPROVE!
YOU THINK SO...?
YEAH, YOU MIGHT BE RIGHT! I HOPE YOU ARE!!
HEY...
Grin Grin
DID YOU GET THAT SPECIAL ITEM READY FOR ME?
OF COURSE.
THE SOUL STONES ARE HERE...
!!
THEY MUST BE CON-NECTED TO... HER SOUL IN SOME WAY!

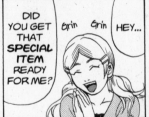

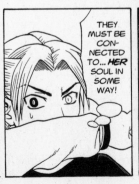

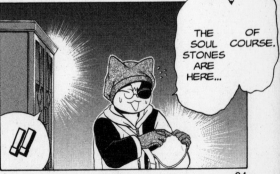

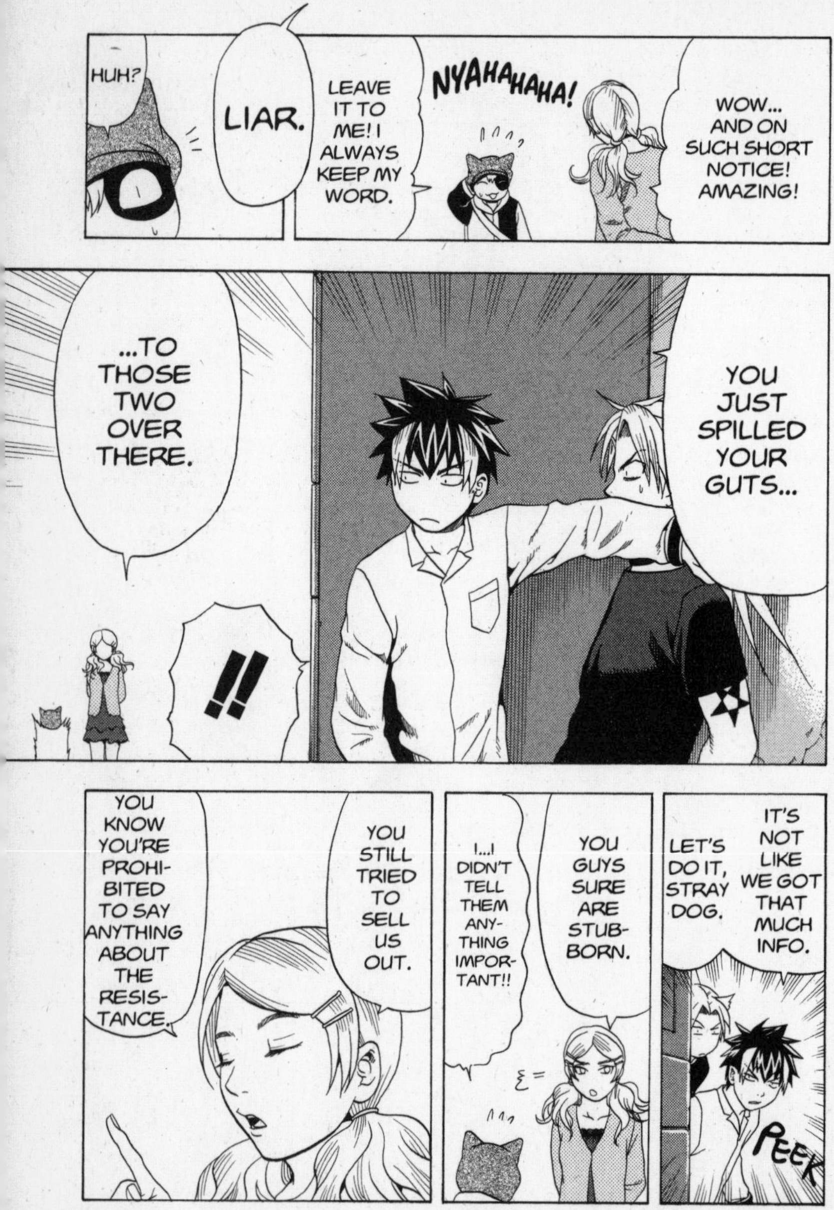
WOW... AND ON SUCH SHORT NOTICE! AMAZING!
NYAHAHAHA!
LEAVE IT TO ME! I ALWAYS KEEP MY WORD.
LIAR.
HUH?
YOU JUST SPILLED YOUR GUTS...
...TO THOSE TWO OVER THERE.
!!
IT'S NOT LIKE WE GOT THAT MUCH INFO.
LET'S DO IT, STRAY DOG.
PEEK
YOU GUYS SURE ARE STUBBORN.
I...I DIDN'T TELL THEM ANYTHING IMPORTANT!!
YOU STILL TRIED TO SELL US OUT.
YOU KNOW YOU'RE PROHIBITED TO SAY ANYTHING ABOUT THE RESISTANCE.

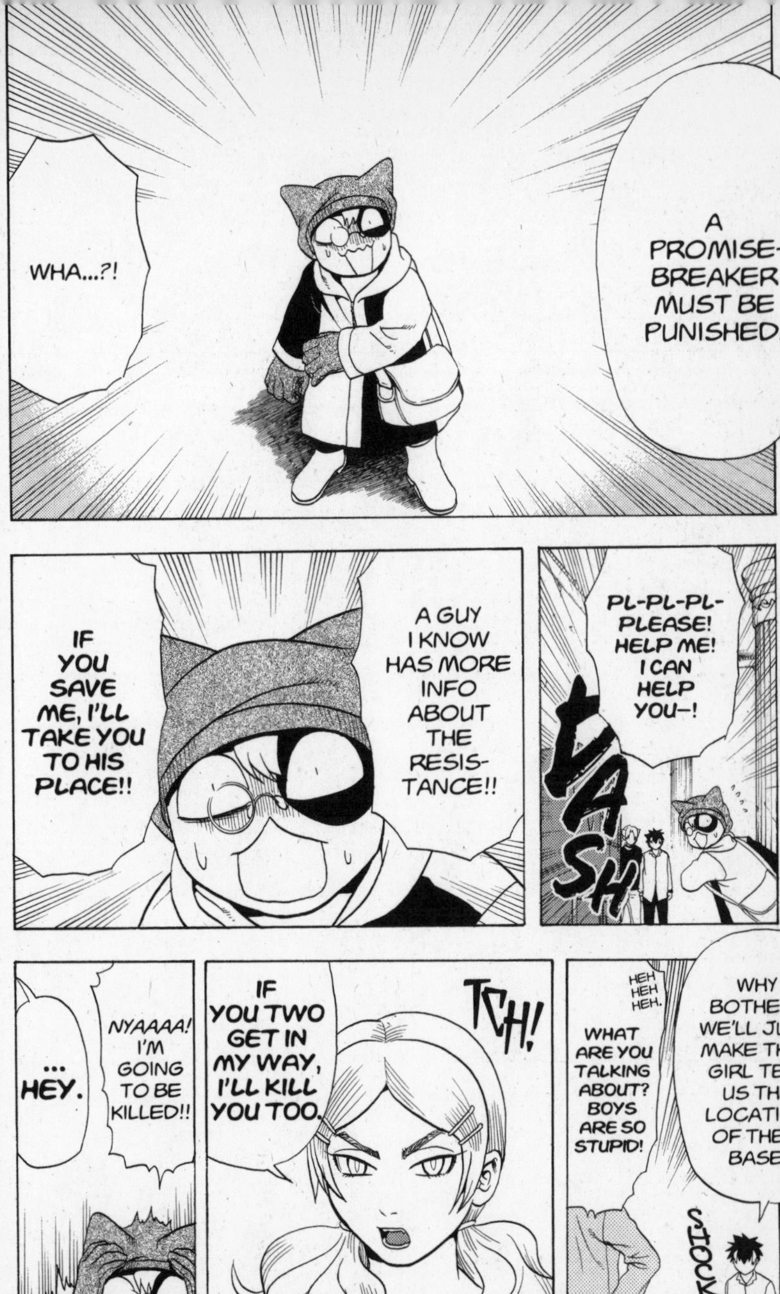
A PROMISE-BREAKER MUST BE PUNISHED.
WHA...?!
PL-PL-PL-PLEASE! HELP ME! I CAN HELP YOU—!
VASH
A GUY I KNOW HAS MORE INFO ABOUT THE RESISTANCE!!
IF YOU SAVE ME, I'LL TAKE YOU TO HIS PLACE!!
WHY BOTHER? WE'LL JUST MAKE THAT GIRL TELL US THE LOCATION OF THEIR BASE.
HEH HEH HEH.
WHAT ARE YOU TALKING ABOUT? BOYS ARE SO STUPID!
SHOCK
TCH!
IF YOU TWO GET IN MY WAY, I'LL KILL YOU TOO.
NYAAAA! I'M GOING TO BE KILLED!!
...HEY.

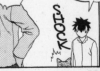

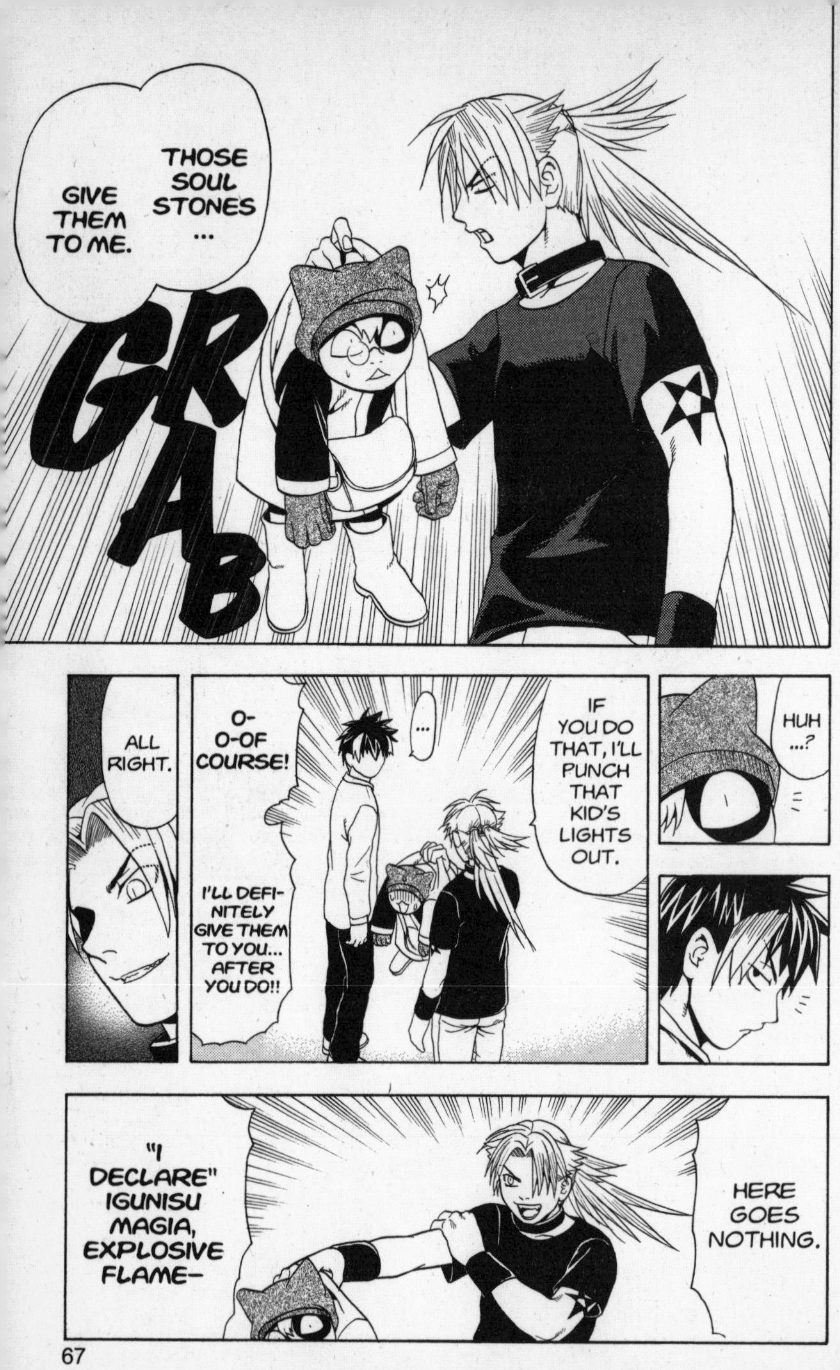
THOSE SOUL STONES... GIVE THEM TO ME.
GRAB
HUH...?
IF YOU DO THAT, I'LL PUNCH THAT KID'S LIGHTS OUT.
...
O-O-OF COURSE!
I'LL DEFINITELY GIVE THEM TO YOU... AFTER YOU DO!!
ALL RIGHT.
HERE GOES NOTHING.
"I DECLARE" IGUNISU MAGIA, EXPLOSIVE FLAME–

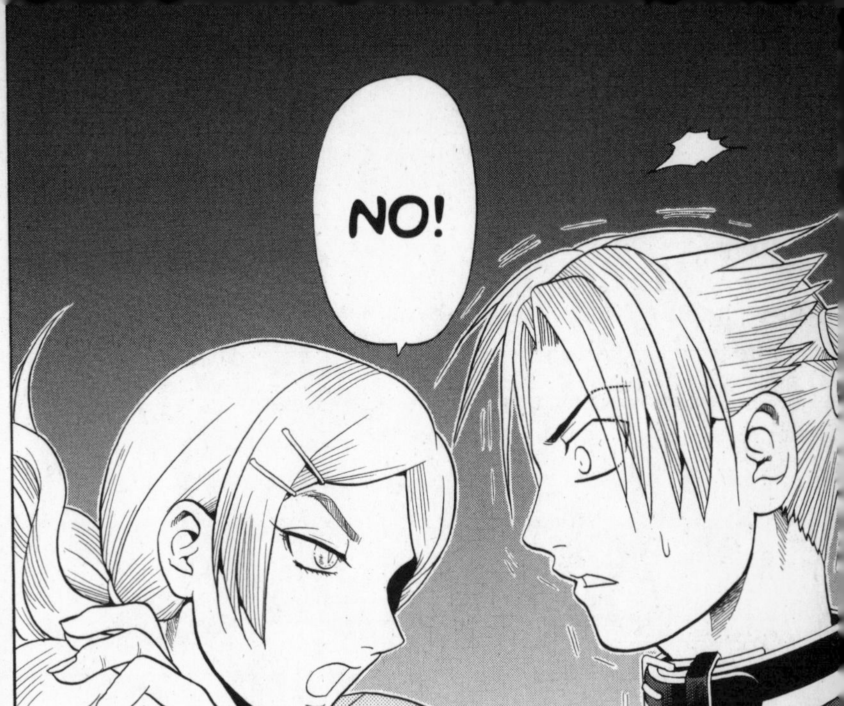
NO!

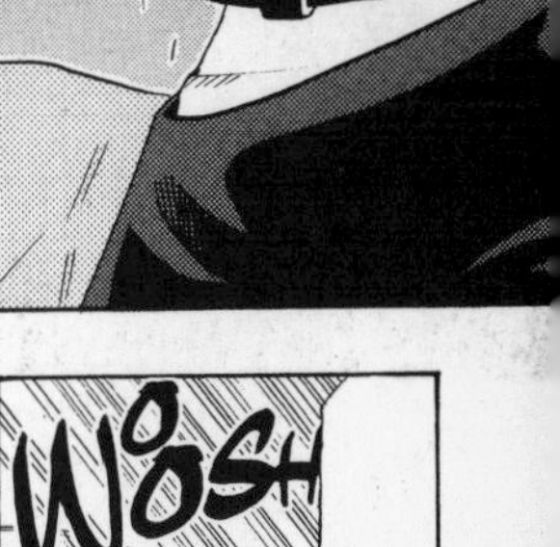
WOOSH
... OOPS.

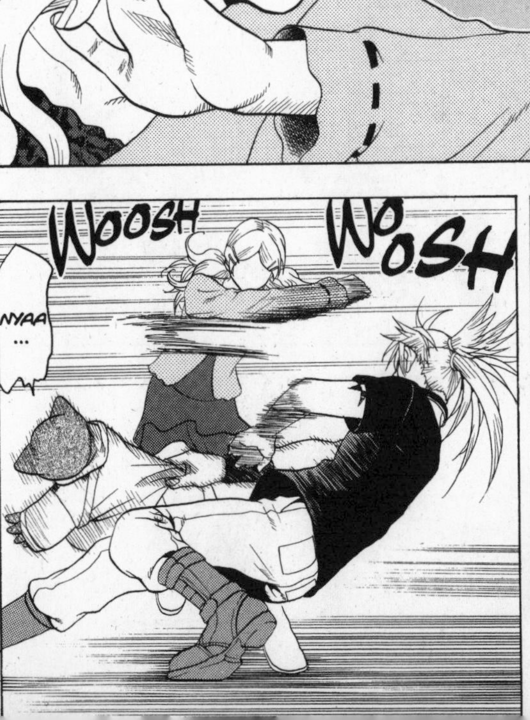
WOOSH
WOOSH
NYAA ...

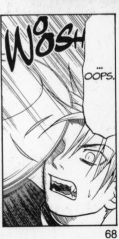

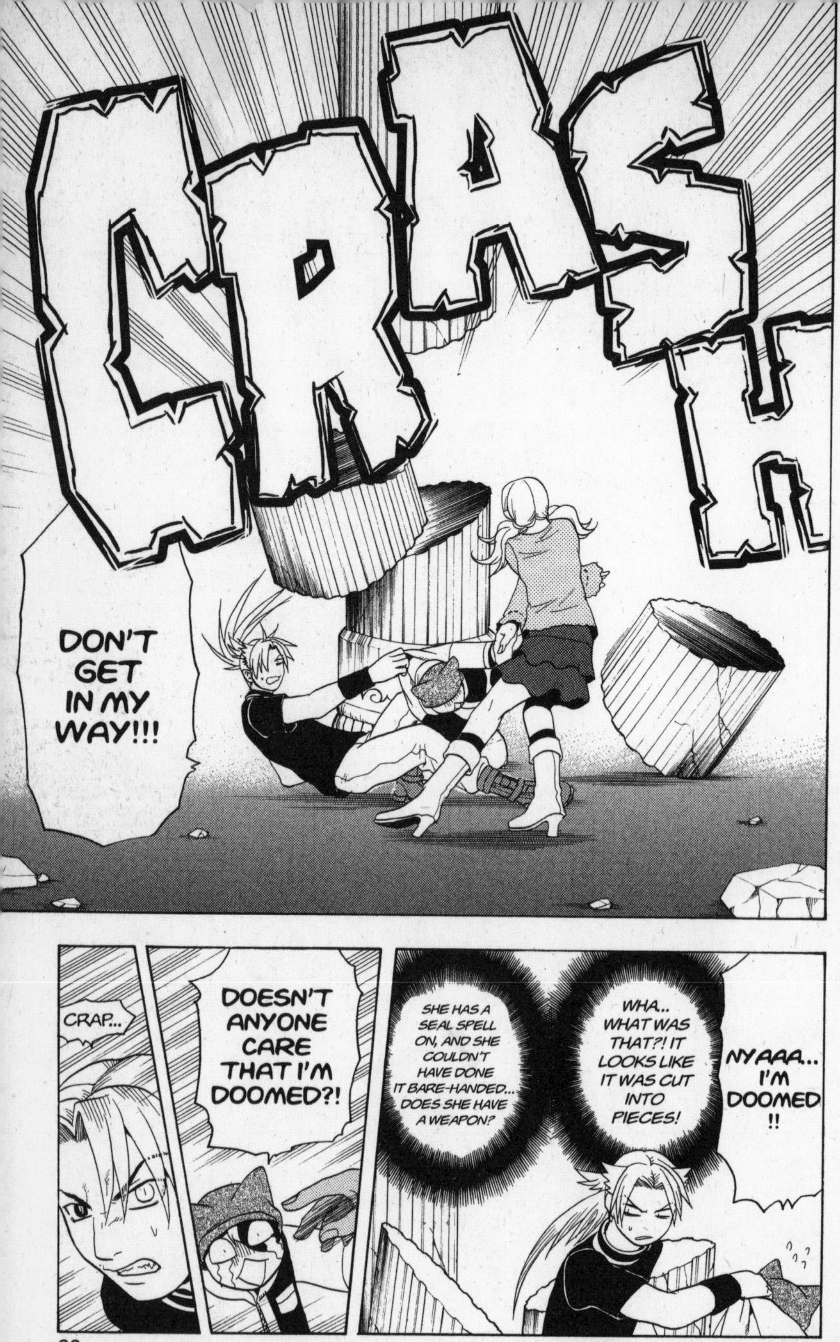
CRASH
DON'T GET IN MY WAY!!!
NYAAA... I'M DOOMED!!
WHA... WHAT WAS THAT?! IT LOOKS LIKE IT WAS CUT INTO PIECES!
SHE HAS A SEAL SPELL ON, AND SHE COULDN'T HAVE DONE IT BARE-HANDED... DOES SHE HAVE A WEAPON?
DOESN'T ANYONE CARE THAT I'M DOOMED?!
CRAP...

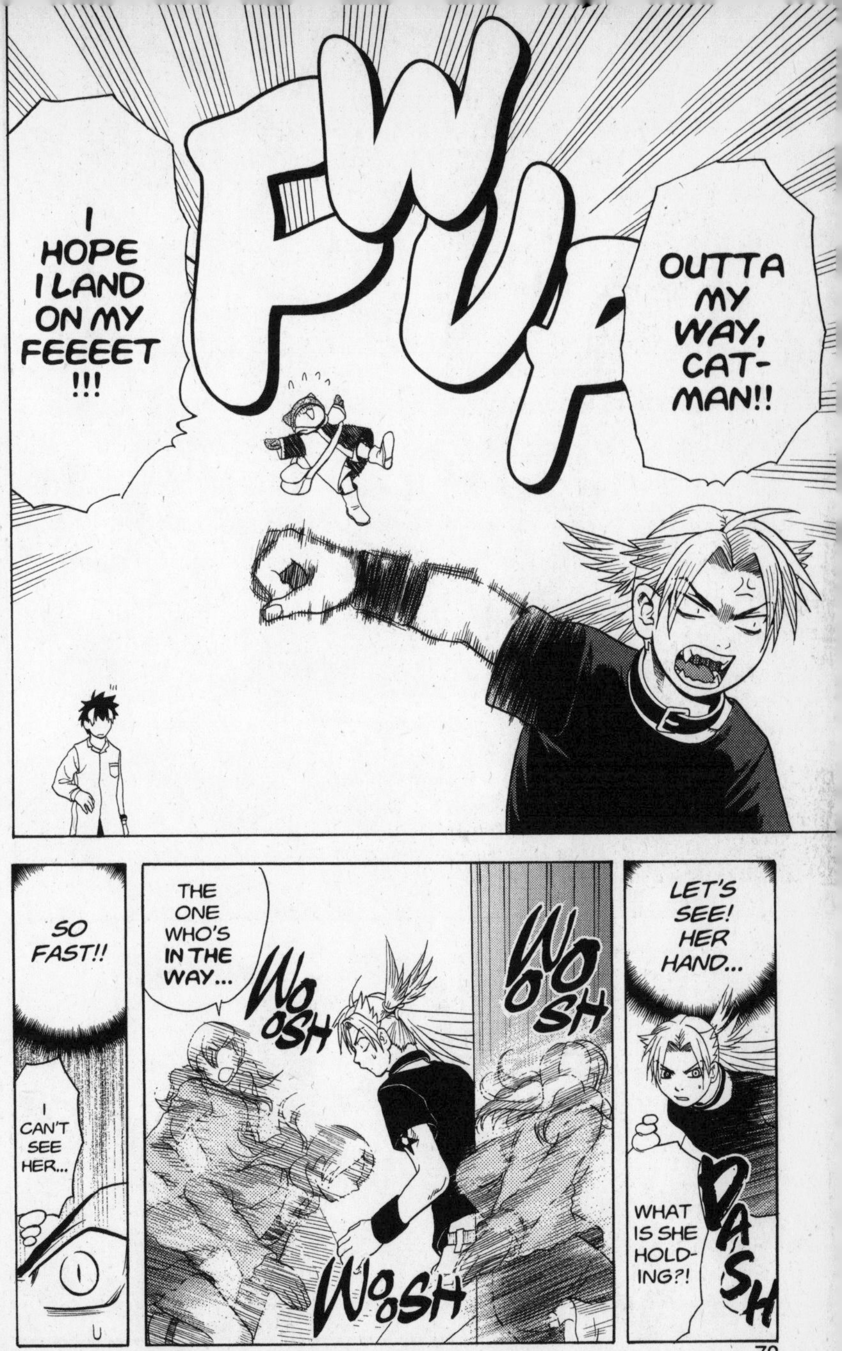
FWUP
OUTTA MY WAY, CAT-MAN!!
I HOPE I LAND ON MY FEEEEET!!!
LET'S SEE! HER HAND...
DASH
WHAT IS SHE HOLDING?!
THE ONE WHO'S IN THE WAY...
WOOSH
WOOSH
WOOSH
SO FAST!!
I CAN'T SEE HER...

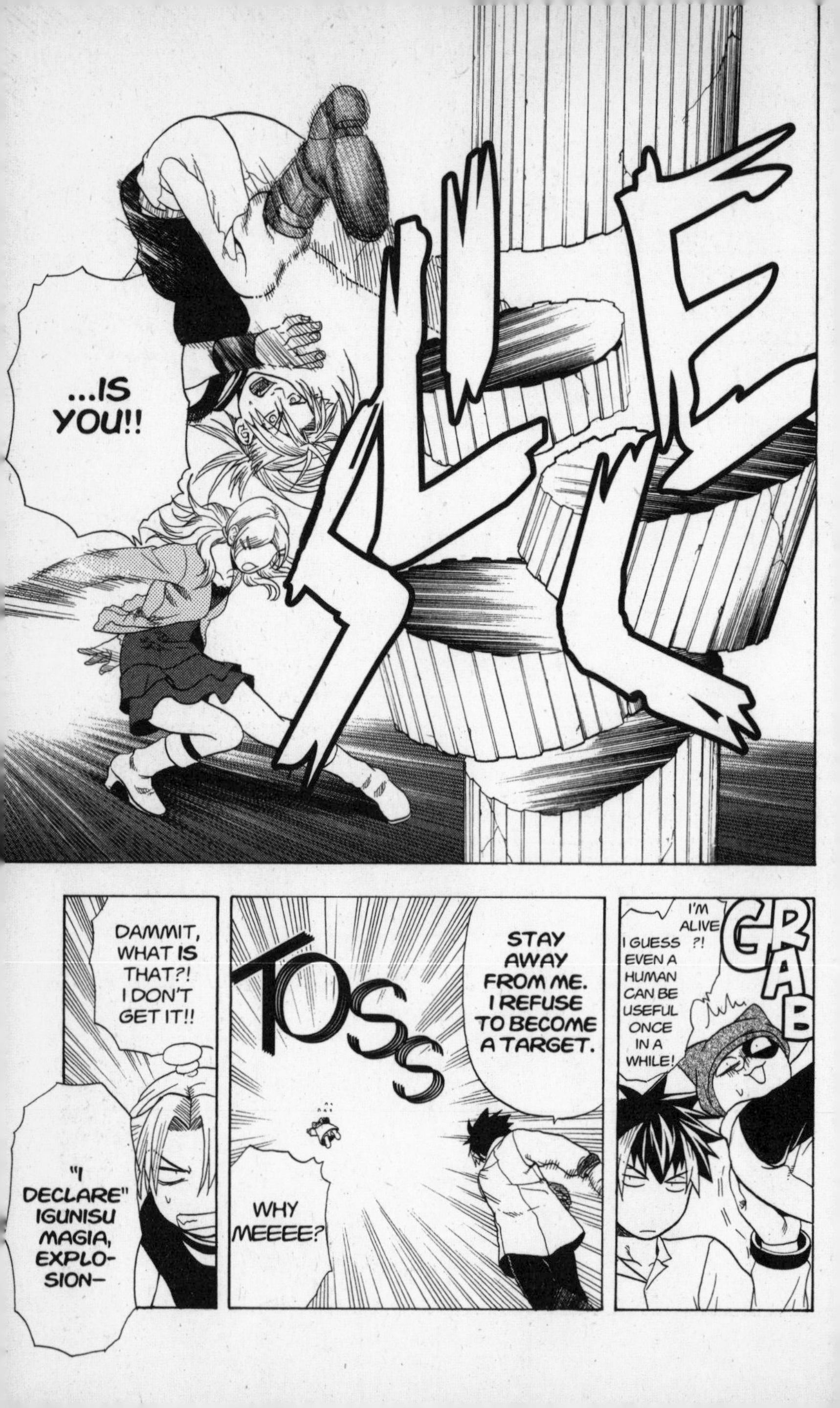
...IS YOU!!
GRAB
I'M ALIVE?!
I GUESS EVEN A HUMAN CAN BE USEFUL ONCE IN A WHILE!
STAY AWAY FROM ME. I REFUSE TO BECOME A TARGET.
TOSS
WHY MEEEE?
DAMMIT, WHAT IS THAT?! I DON'T GET IT!!
"I DECLARE" IGUNISU MAGIA, EXPLOSION–

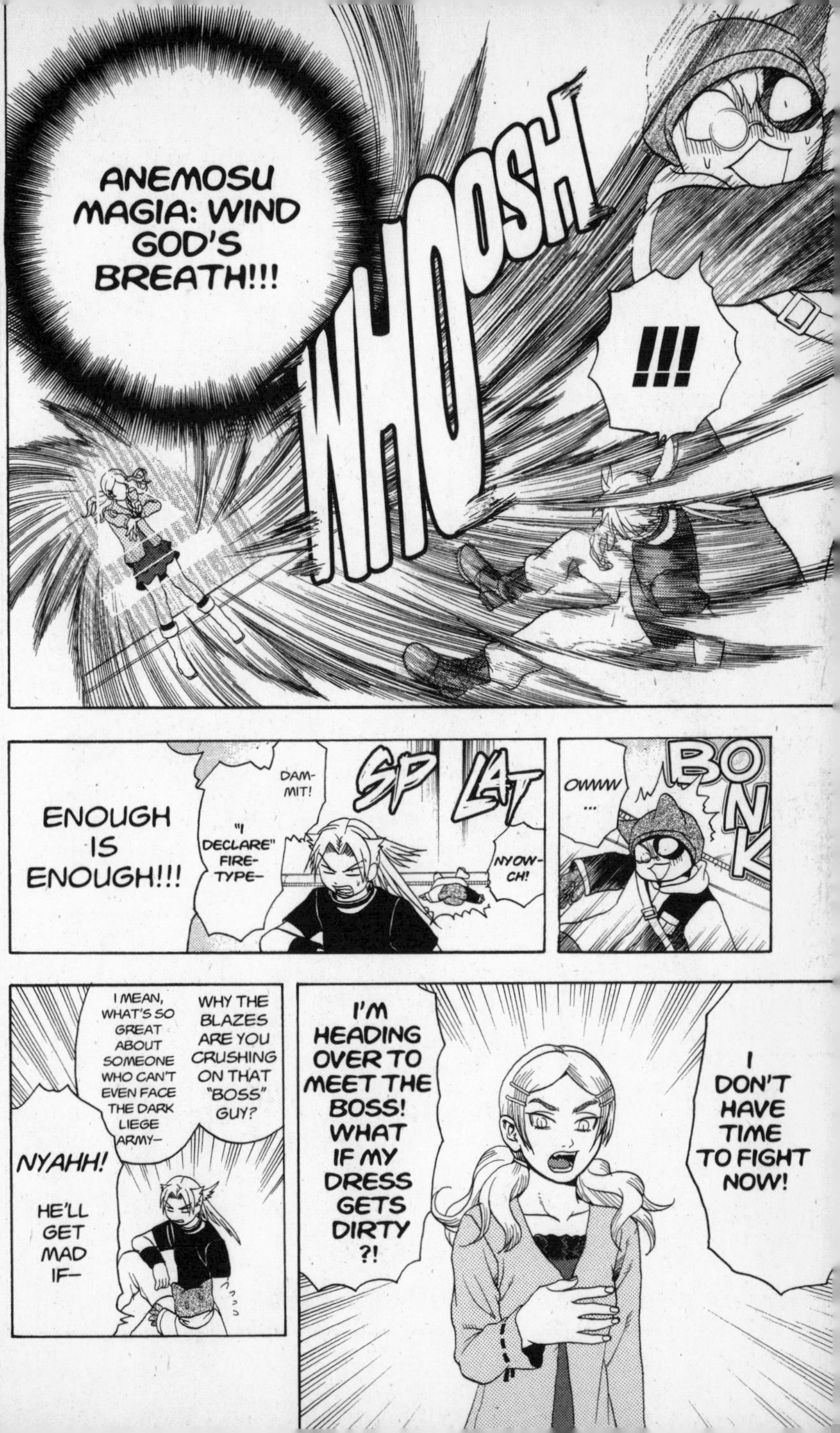
ANEMOSU MAGIA: WIND GOD'S BREATH!!!
WHOOSH
!!!
BONK
OWWW...
NYOW-CH!
SPLAT
DAM-MIT!
"I DECLARE" FIRE-TYPE—
ENOUGH IS ENOUGH!!!
I DON'T HAVE TIME TO FIGHT NOW!
I'M HEADING OVER TO MEET THE BOSS! WHAT IF MY DRESS GETS DIRTY?!
WHY THE BLAZES ARE YOU CRUSHING ON THAT "BOSS" GUY?
I MEAN, WHAT'S SO GREAT ABOUT SOMEONE WHO CAN'T EVEN FACE THE DARK LIEGE ARMY—
NYAHH!
HE'LL GET MAD IF—

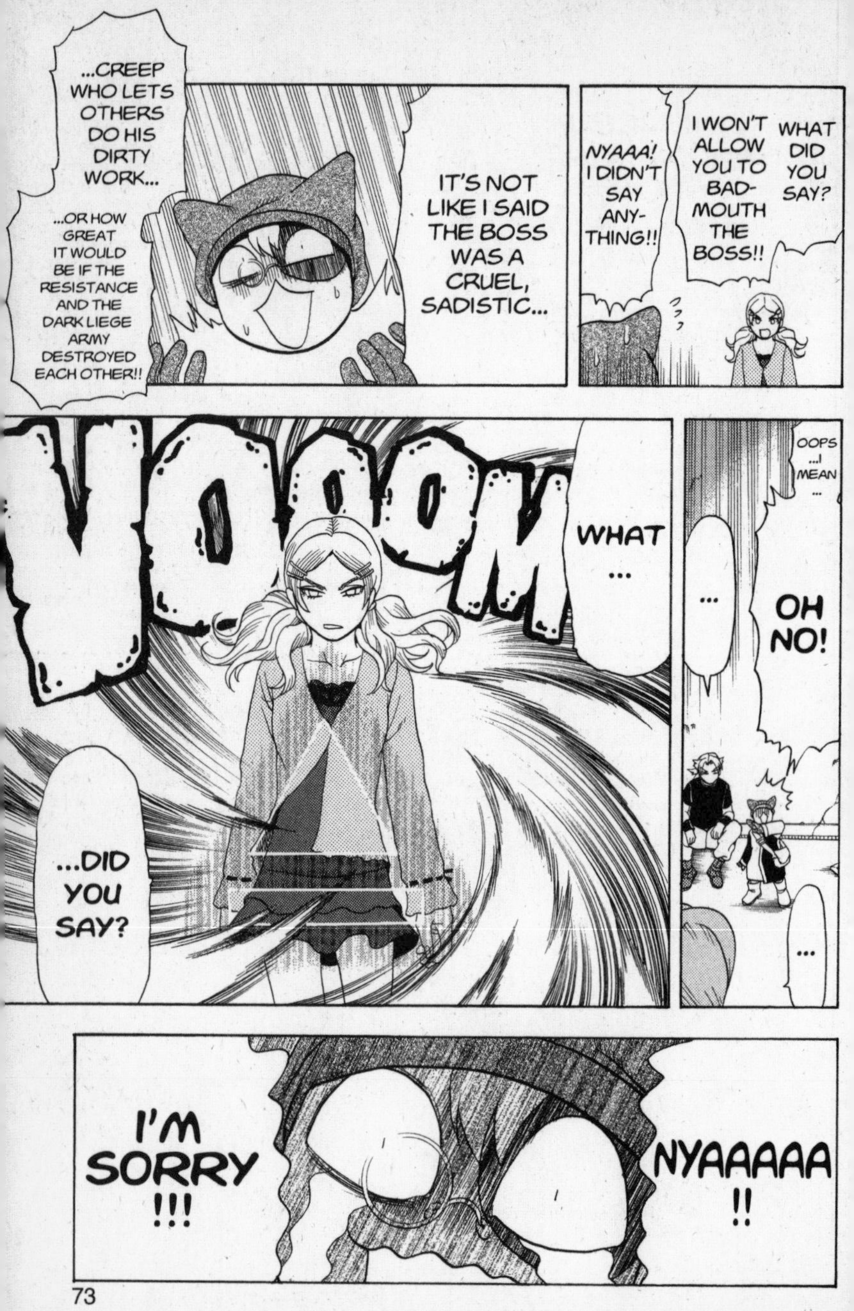
WHAT DID YOU SAY?
I WON'T ALLOW YOU TO BAD-MOUTH THE BOSS!!
NYAAA! I DIDN'T SAY ANYTHING!!
IT'S NOT LIKE I SAID THE BOSS WAS A CRUEL, SADISTIC...
...CREEP WHO LETS OTHERS DO HIS DIRTY WORK...
...OR HOW GREAT IT WOULD BE IF THE RESISTANCE AND THE DARK LIEGE ARMY DESTROYED EACH OTHER!!
OOPS ...I MEAN ...
OH NO!
...
...
WHAT ...
VOOOM
...DID YOU SAY?
NYAAAAA !!
I'M SORRY !!!

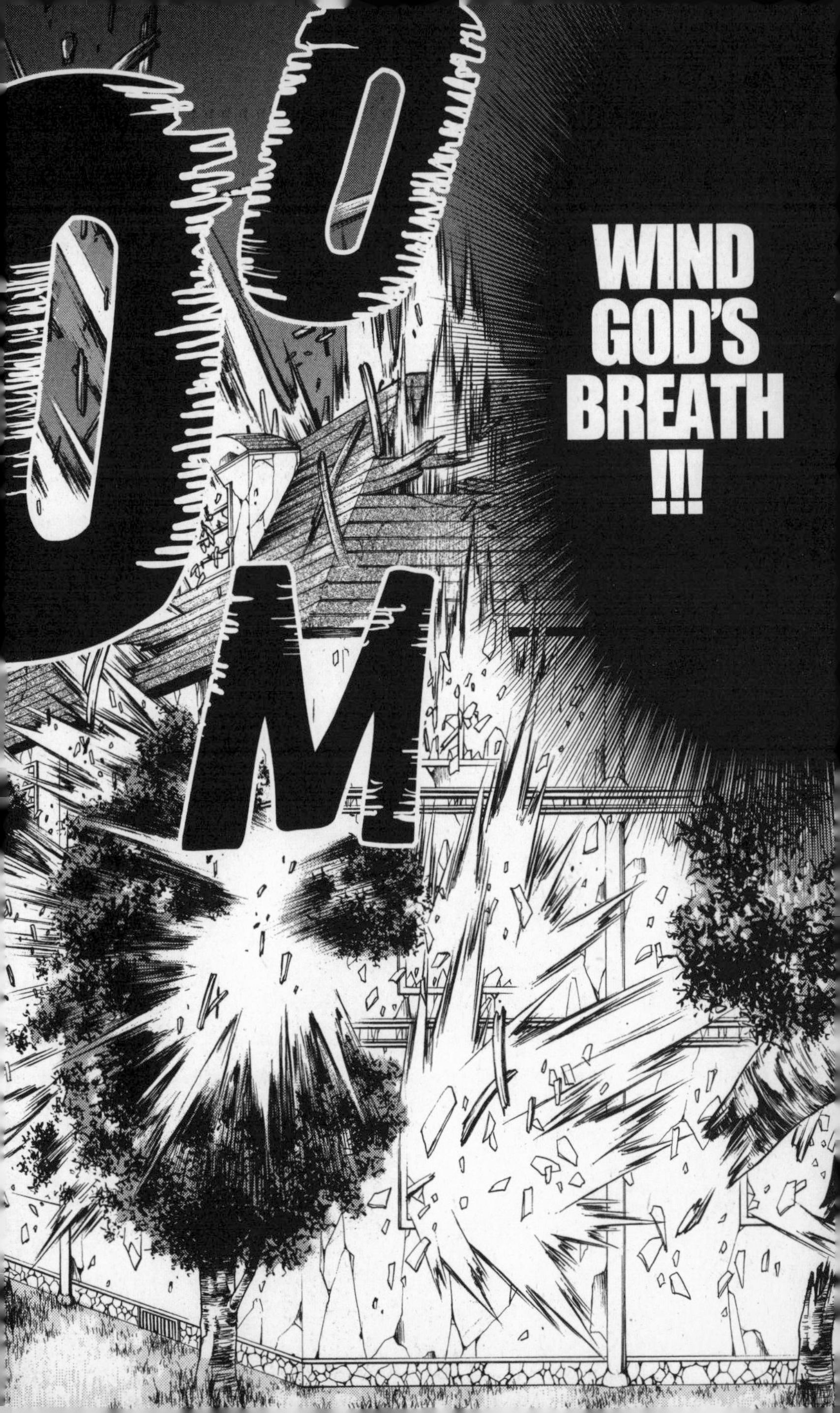
WIND GOD'S BREATH!!!

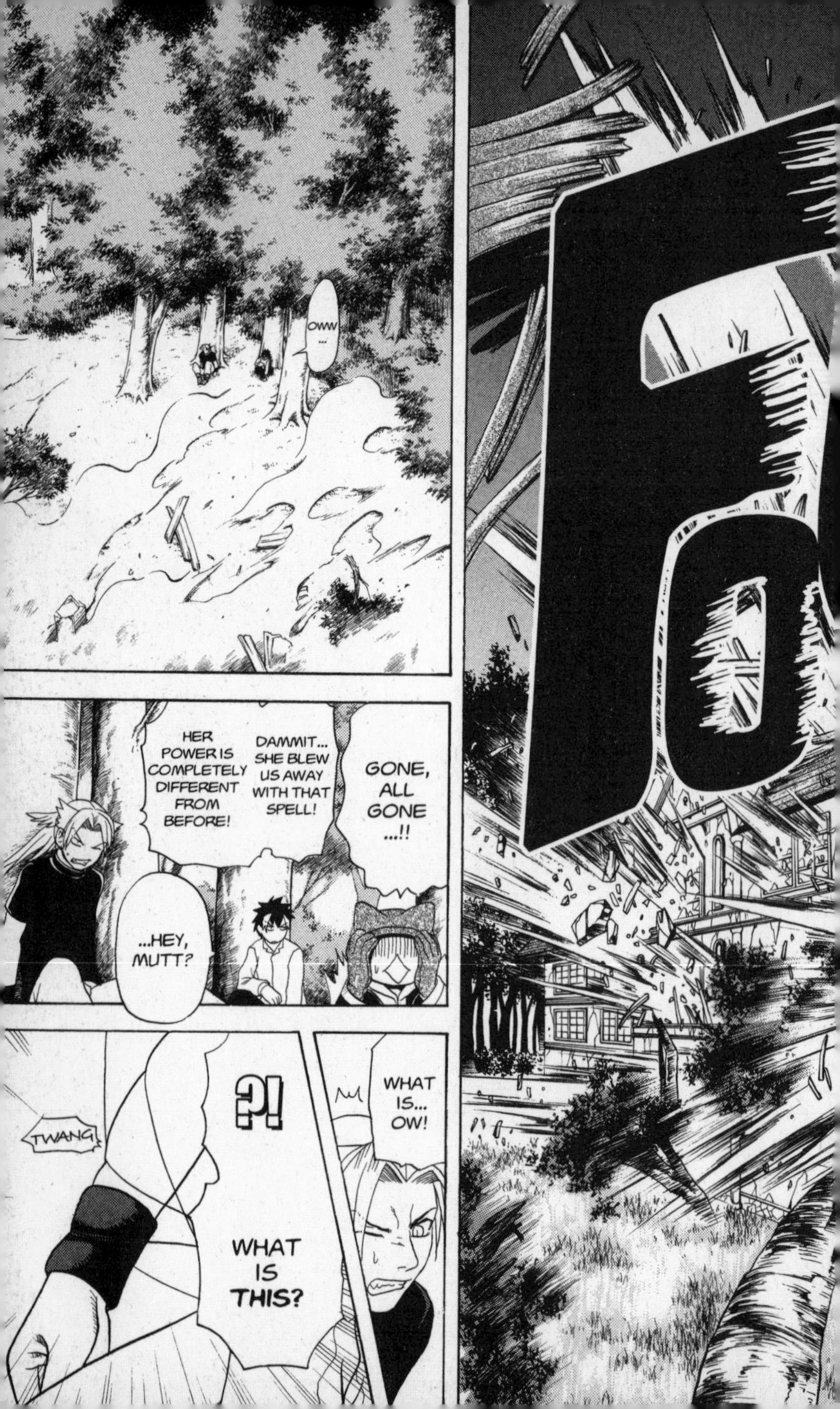
OWW...
GONE, ALL GONE...!!
DAMMIT... SHE BLEW US AWAY WITH THAT SPELL!
HER POWER IS COMPLETELY DIFFERENT FROM BEFORE!
...HEY, MUTT?
WHAT IS... OW!
?!
TWANG
WHAT IS THIS?

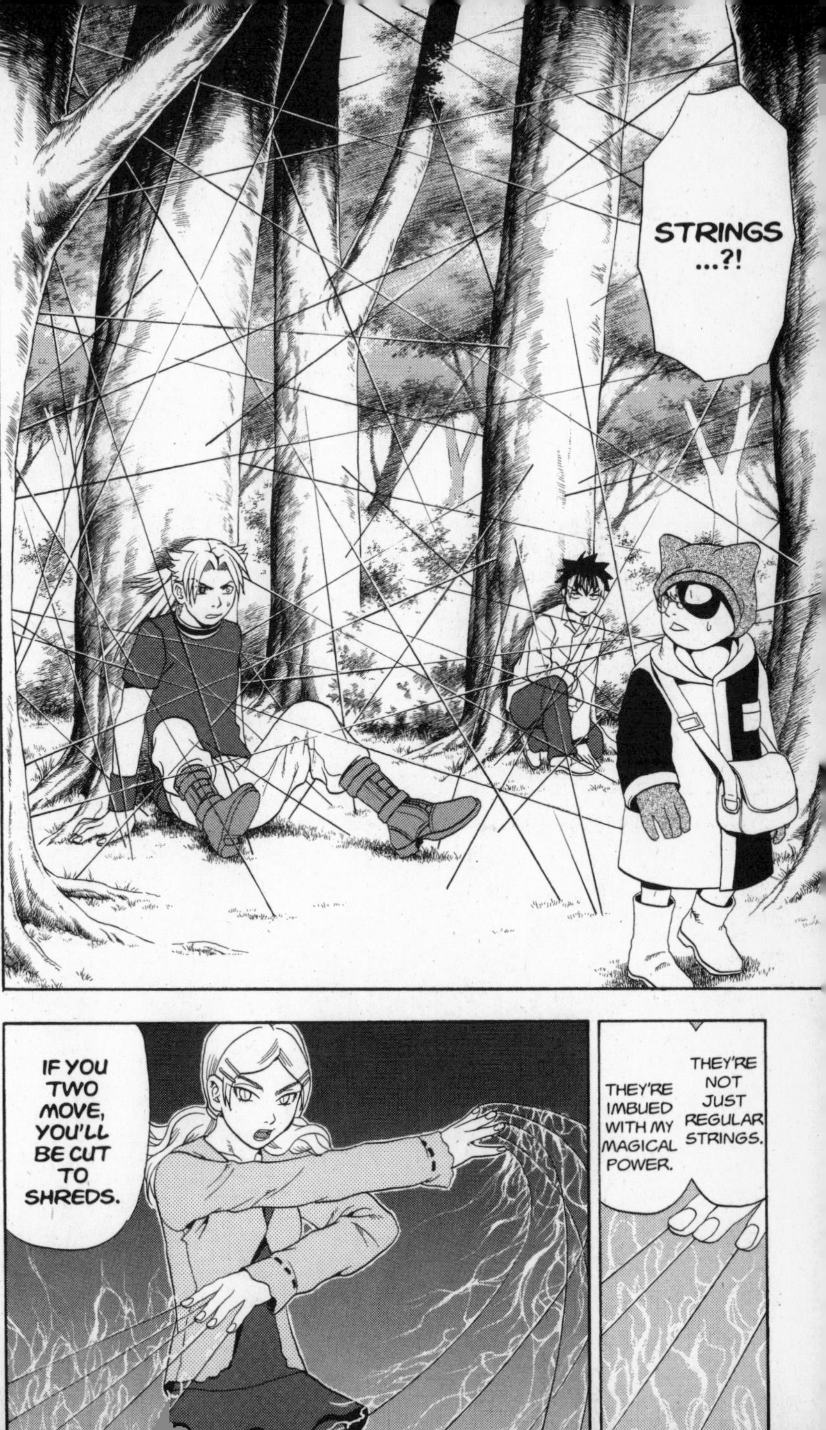
STRINGS ...?!
THEY'RE NOT JUST REGULAR STRINGS.
THEY'RE IMBUED WITH MY MAGICAL POWER.
IF YOU TWO MOVE, YOU'LL BE CUT TO SHREDS.

READ THIS WAY

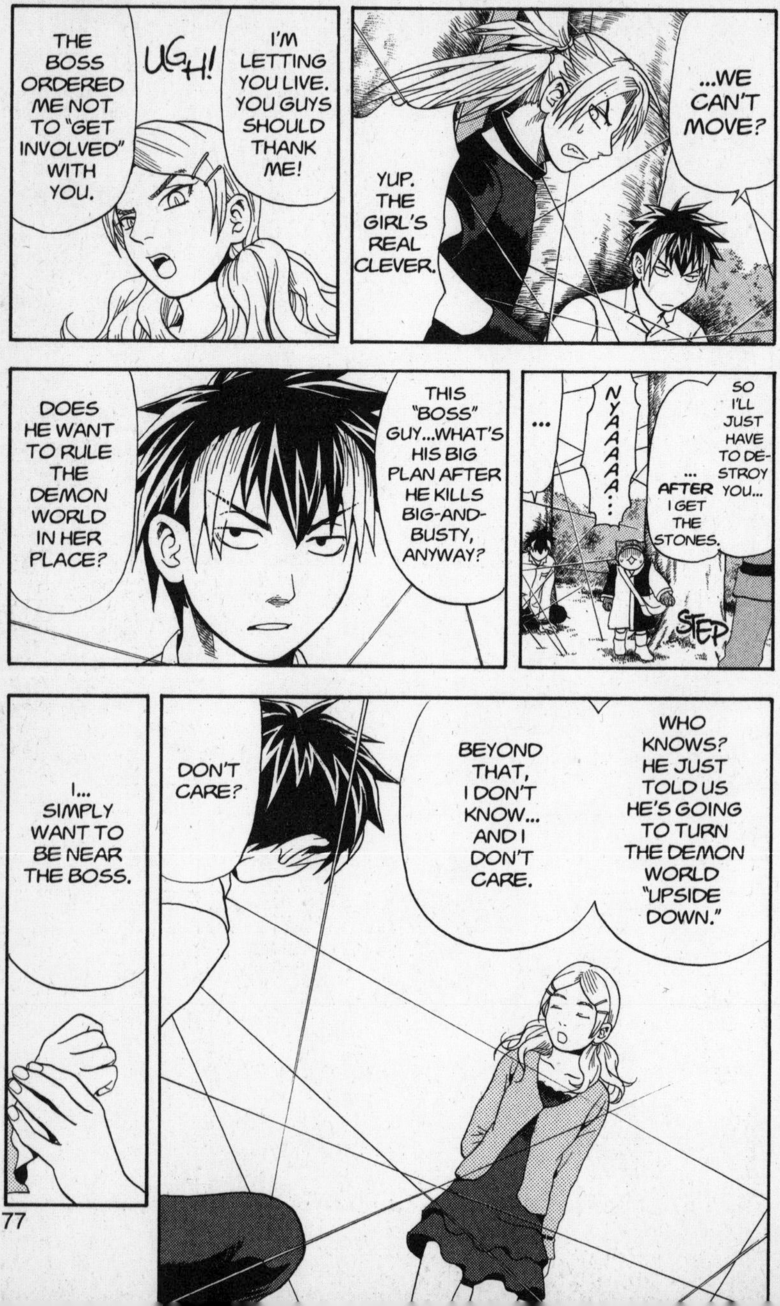
...WE CAN'T MOVE?
YUP. THE GIRL'S REAL CLEVER.
I'M LETTING YOU LIVE. YOU GUYS SHOULD THANK ME!
UGH!
THE BOSS ORDERED ME NOT TO "GET INVOLVED" WITH YOU.
SO I'LL JUST HAVE TO DESTROY YOU...
... AFTER I GET THE STONES.
STEP
NYAAAAAA...
...
THIS "BOSS" GUY...WHAT'S HIS BIG PLAN AFTER HE KILLS BIG-AND-BUSTY, ANYWAY?
DOES HE WANT TO RULE THE DEMON WORLD IN HER PLACE?
WHO KNOWS? HE JUST TOLD US HE'S GOING TO TURN THE DEMON WORLD "UPSIDE DOWN."
BEYOND THAT, I DON'T KNOW... AND I DON'T CARE.
DON'T CARE?
I... SIMPLY WANT TO BE NEAR THE BOSS.

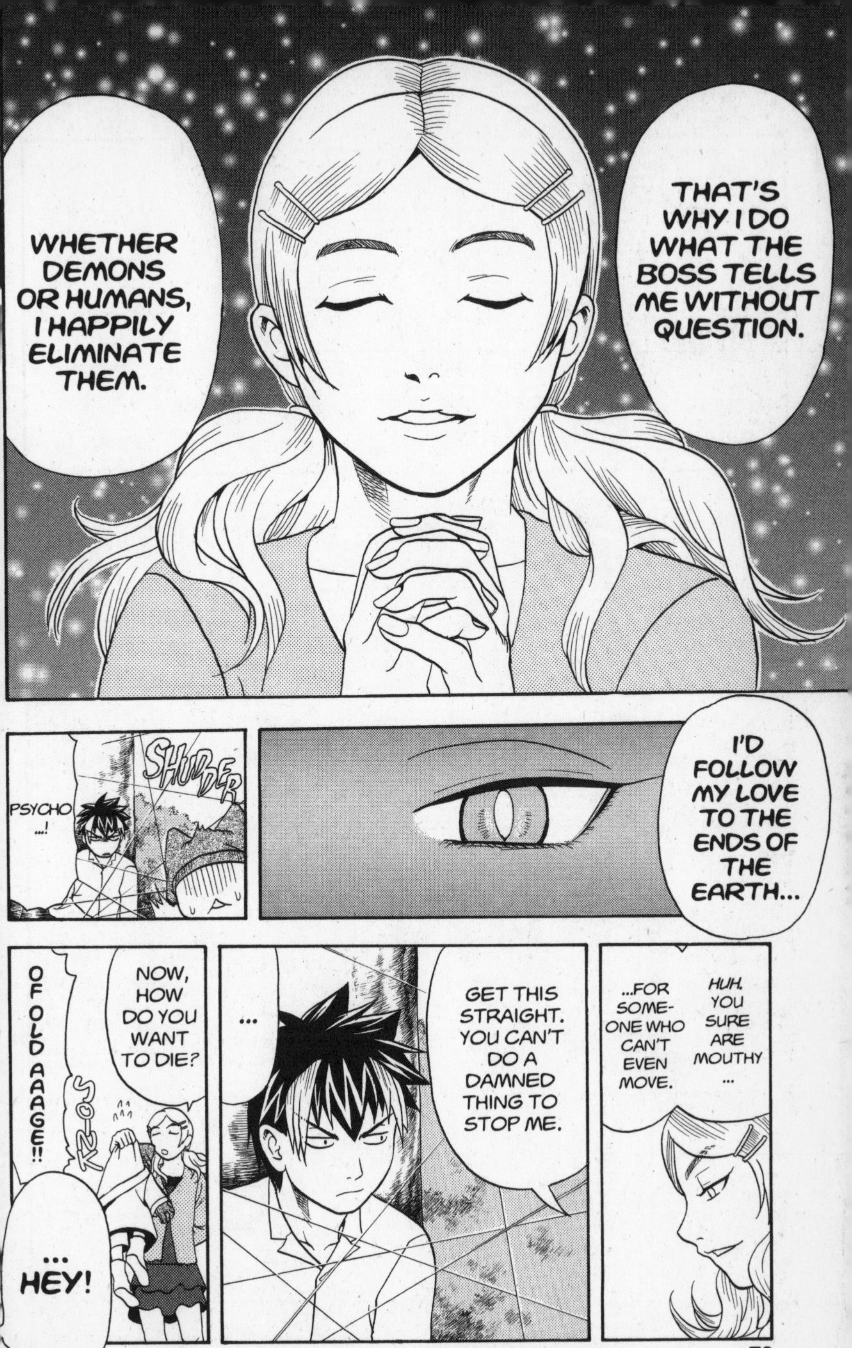
THAT'S WHY I DO WHAT THE BOSS TELLS ME WITHOUT QUESTION.
WHETHER DEMONS OR HUMANS, I HAPPILY ELIMINATE THEM.
I'D FOLLOW MY LOVE TO THE ENDS OF THE EARTH...
SHUDDER
PSYCHO ...!
HUH. YOU SURE ARE MOUTHY ...
...FOR SOME-ONE WHO CAN'T EVEN MOVE.
GET THIS STRAIGHT. YOU CAN'T DO A DAMNED THING TO STOP ME.
...
NOW, HOW DO YOU WANT TO DIE?
OF OLD AAAGE!!
SOINK
... HEY!

READ THIS WAY

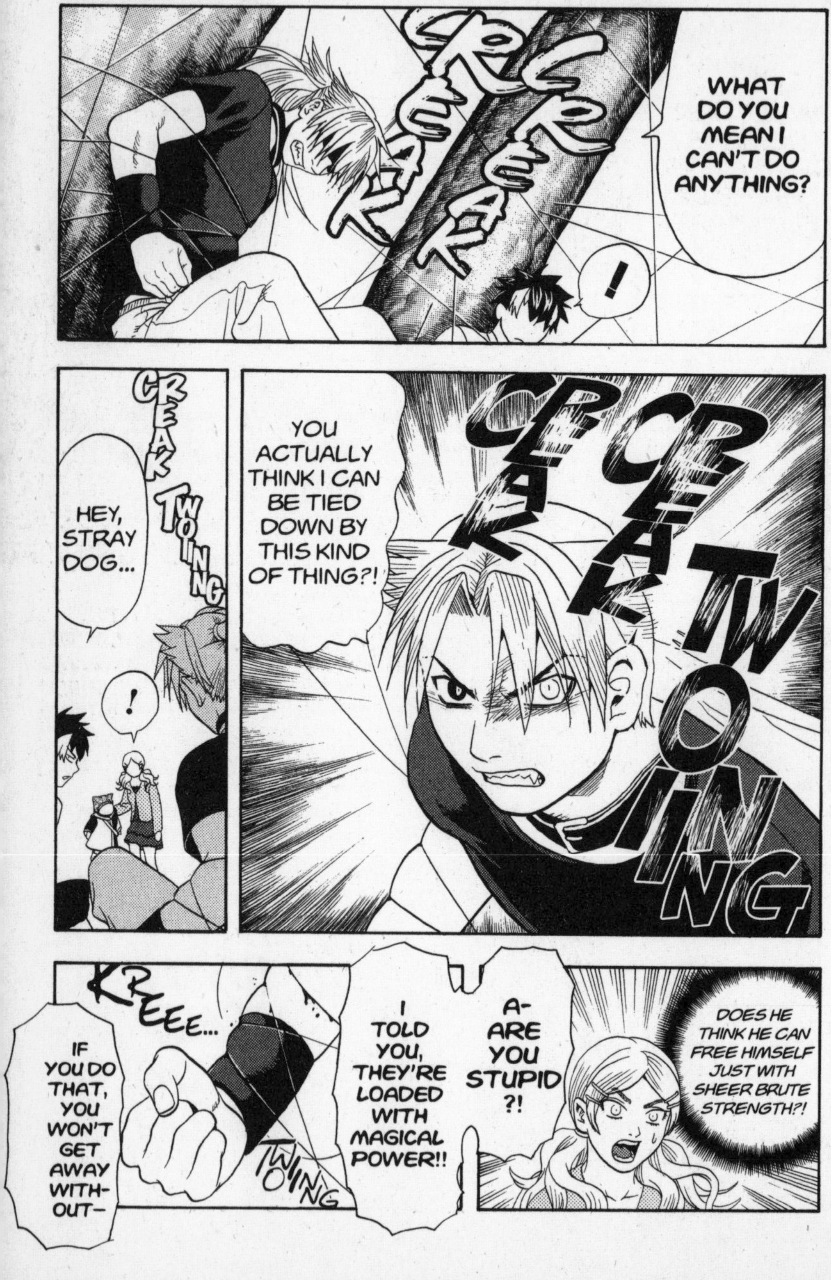

CREAK
CREAK
WHAT DO YOU MEAN I CAN'T DO ANYTHING?
!
YOU ACTUALLY THINK I CAN BE TIED DOWN BY THIS KIND OF THING?!
CREAK
CREAK
TWOING
CREAK
HEY, STRAY DOG...
TWOING
!
DOES HE THINK HE CAN FREE HIMSELF JUST WITH SHEER BRUTE STRENGTH?!
A-ARE YOU STUPID?!
I TOLD YOU, THEY'RE LOADED WITH MAGICAL POWER!!
KREEEE...
IF YOU DO THAT, YOU WON'T GET AWAY WITH-OUT—
TWOING

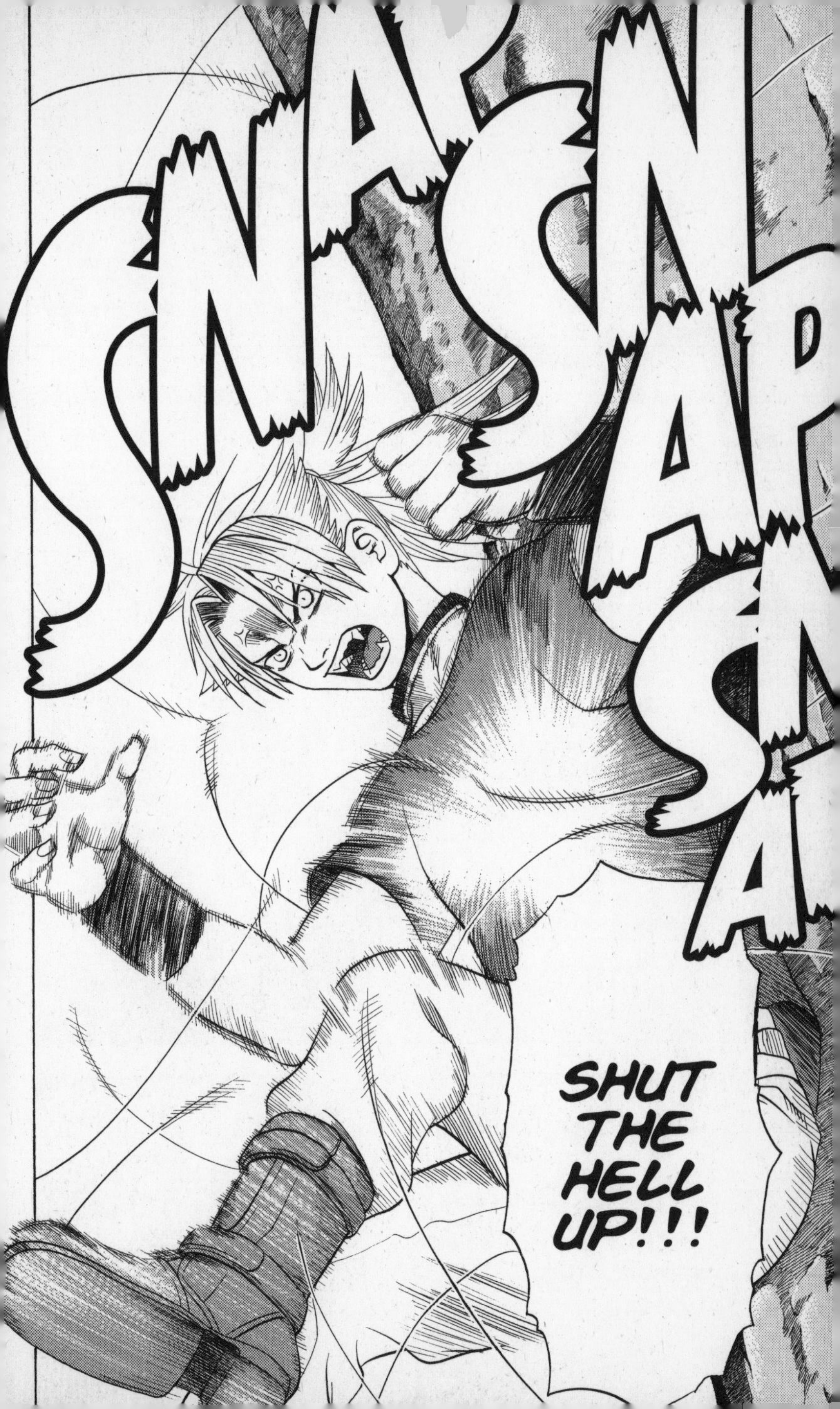
SHUT THE HELL UP!!!

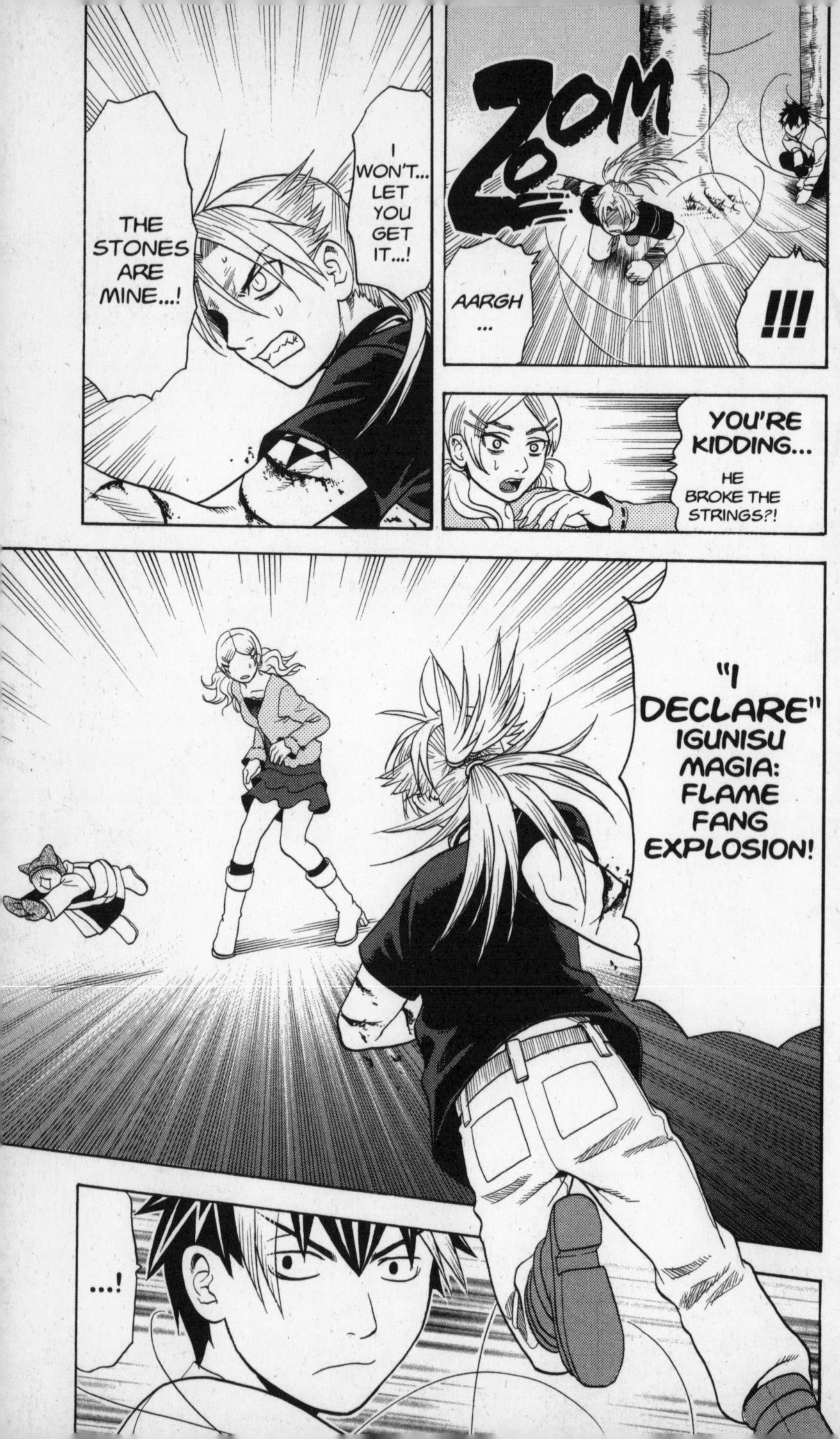
ZOOM
!!!
AARGH ...
YOU'RE KIDDING...
HE BROKE THE STRINGS?!
I WON'T... LET YOU GET IT...!
THE STONES ARE MINE...!
"I DECLARE" IGUNISU MAGIA: FLAME FANG EXPLOSION!
...!

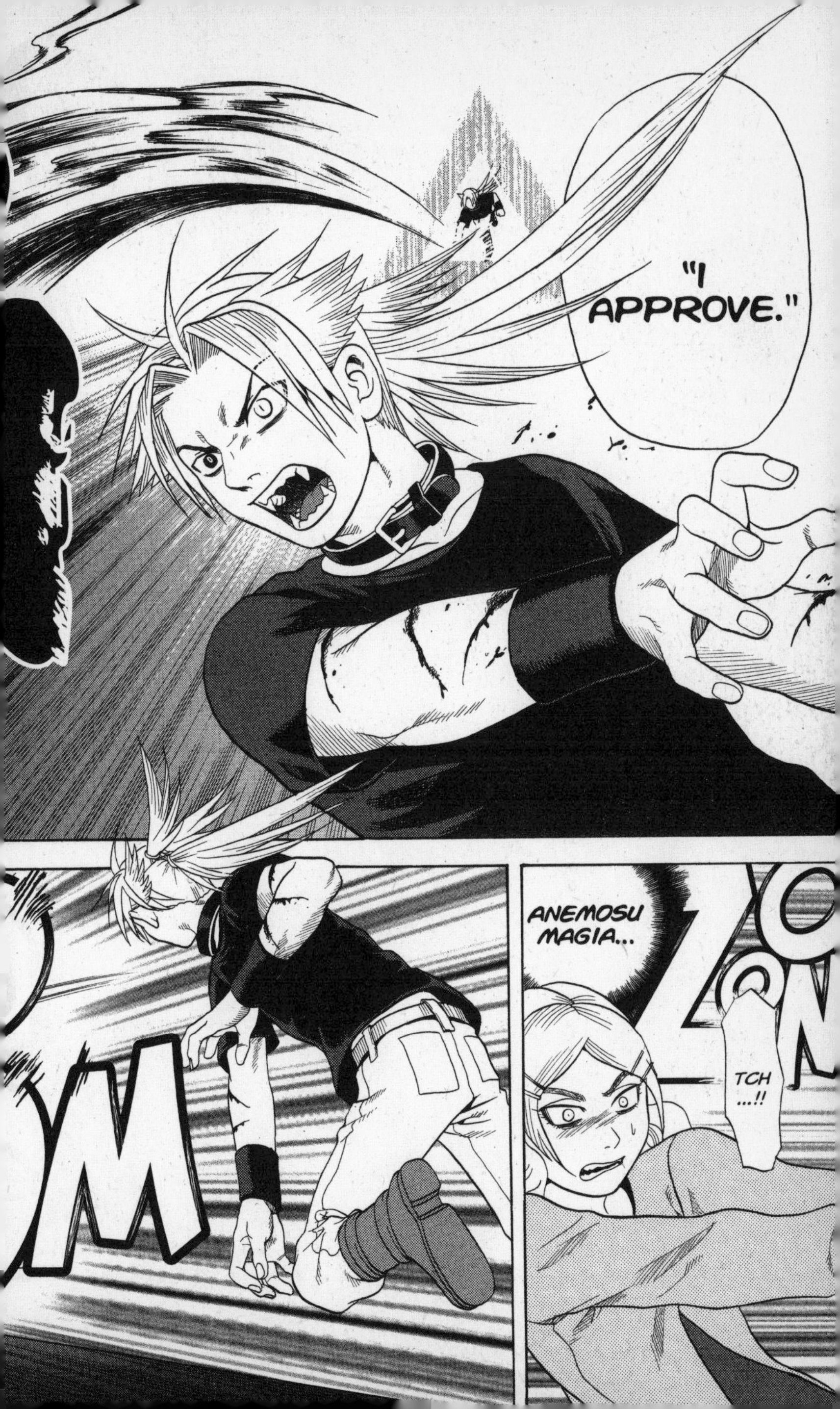
"I APPROVE."
ANEMOSU MAGIA...
TCH ...!!

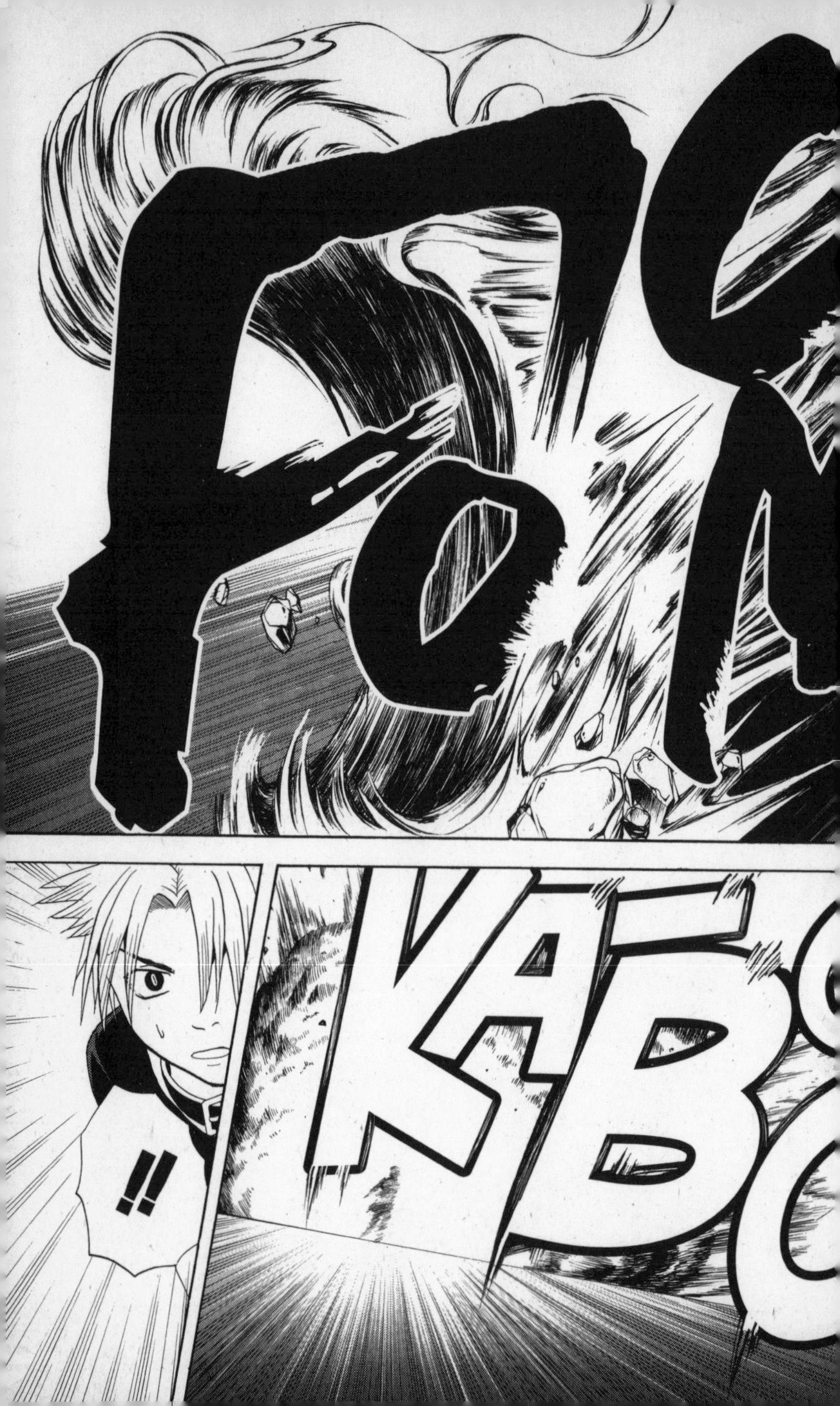
!!

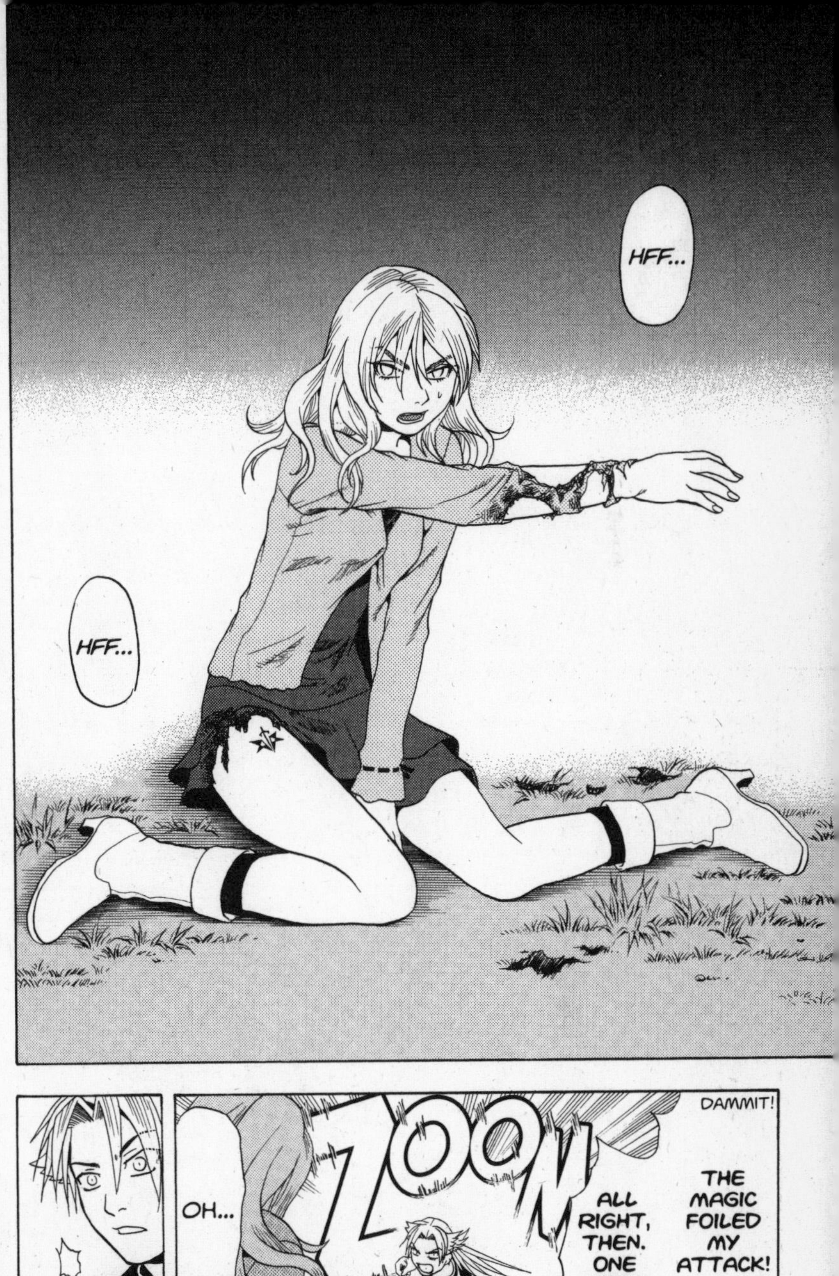
HFF...
HFF...
DAMMIT!
THE MAGIC FOILED MY ATTACK!
ALL RIGHT, THEN. ONE MORE TIME!
ZOOOM
OH...
!

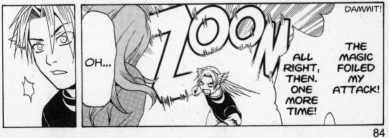

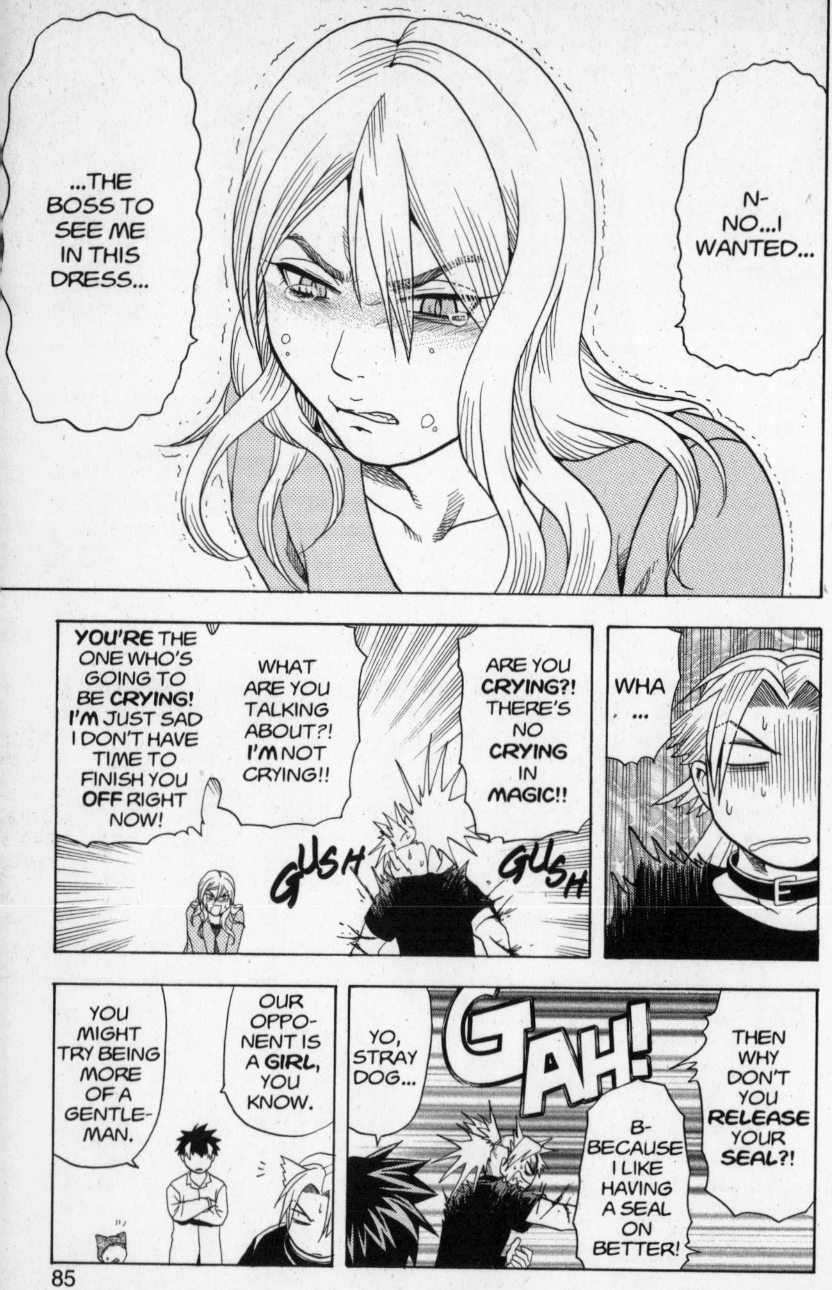
N-NO...I WANTED...
...THE BOSS TO SEE ME IN THIS DRESS...
WHA...
ARE YOU CRYING?! THERE'S NO CRYING IN MAGIC!!
WHAT ARE YOU TALKING ABOUT?! I'M NOT CRYING!!
YOU'RE THE ONE WHO'S GOING TO BE CRYING! I'M JUST SAD I DON'T HAVE TIME TO FINISH YOU OFF RIGHT NOW!
GUSH
GUSH
THEN WHY DON'T YOU RELEASE YOUR SEAL?!
GAH!
B-BECAUSE I LIKE HAVING A SEAL ON BETTER!
YO, STRAY DOG...
OUR OPPONENT IS A GIRL, YOU KNOW.
YOU MIGHT TRY BEING MORE OF A GENTLEMAN.

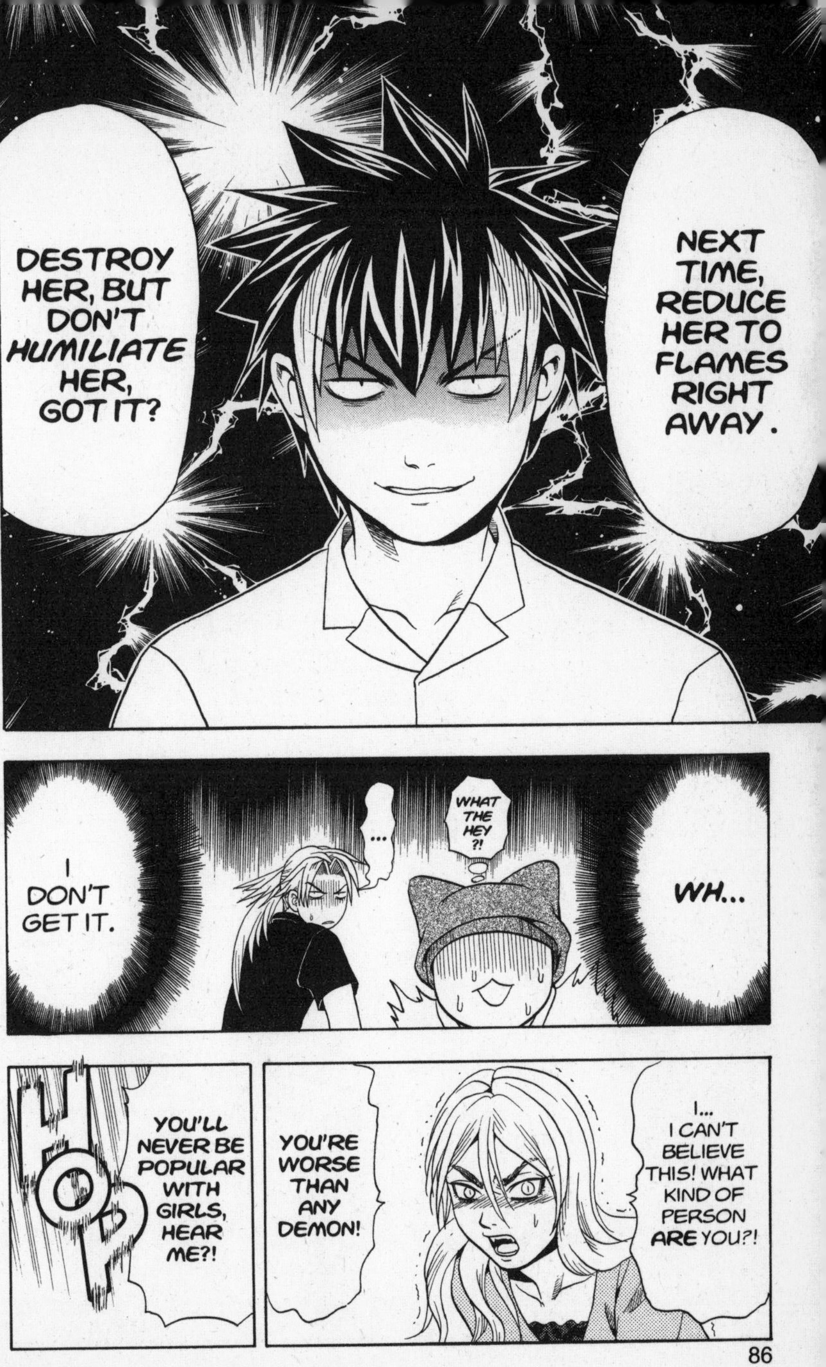
NEXT TIME, REDUCE HER TO FLAMES RIGHT AWAY.
DESTROY HER, BUT DON'T *HUMILIATE* HER, GOT IT?
WH...
WHAT THE HEY?!
...
I DON'T GET IT.
I... I CAN'T BELIEVE THIS! WHAT KIND OF PERSON **ARE** YOU?!
YOU'RE WORSE THAN ANY DEMON!
YOU'LL NEVER BE POPULAR WITH GIRLS, HEAR ME?!

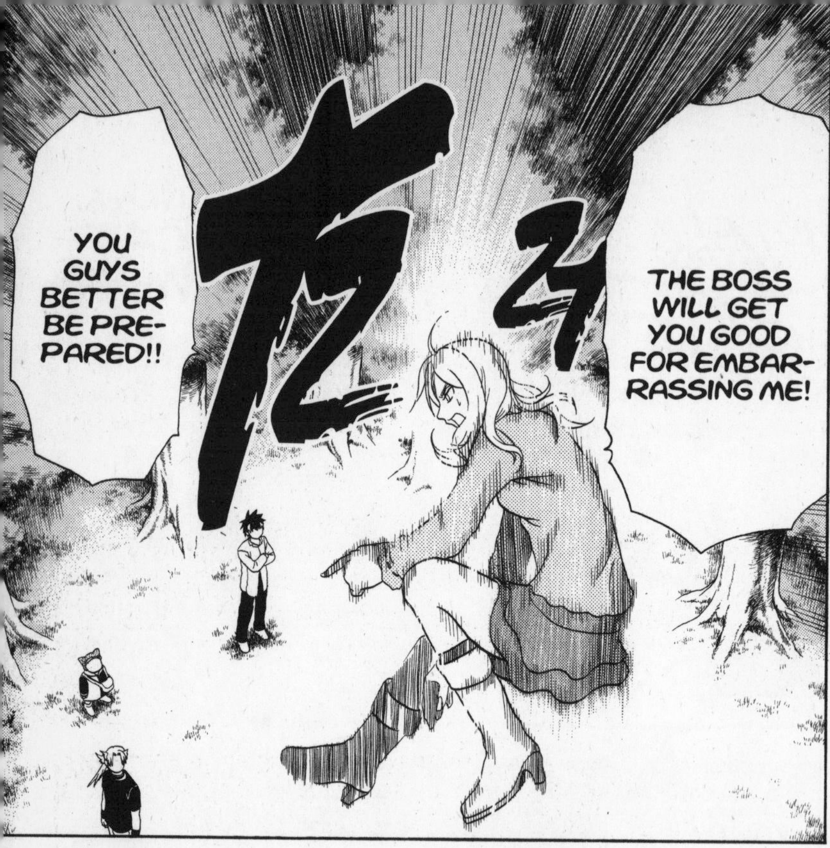
THE BOSS WILL GET YOU GOOD FOR EMBAR-RASSING ME!
YOU GUYS BETTER BE PRE-PARED!!

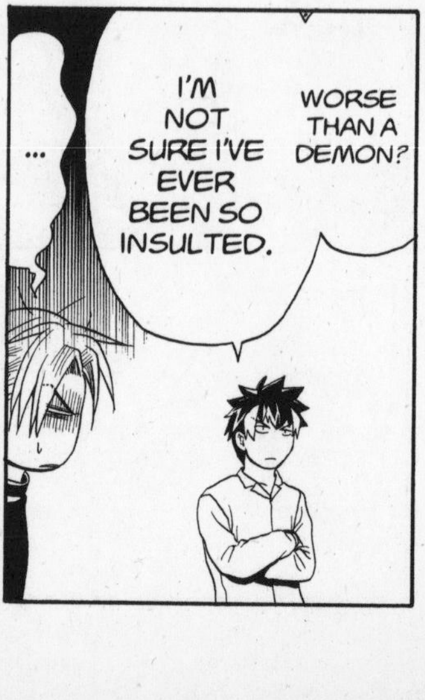
WORSE THAN A DEMON?
I'M NOT SURE I'VE EVER BEEN SO INSULTED.
...

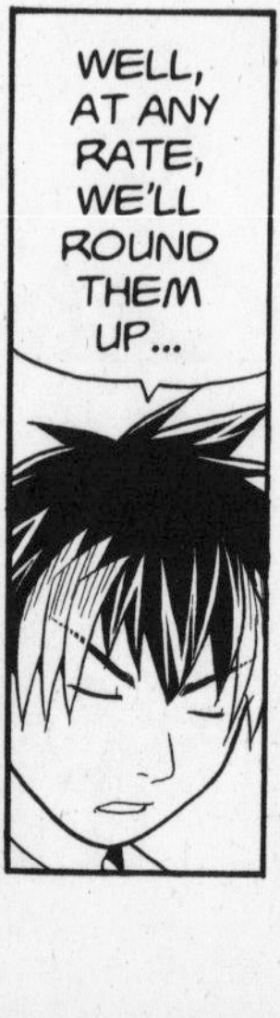
WELL, AT ANY RATE, WE'LL ROUND THEM UP...

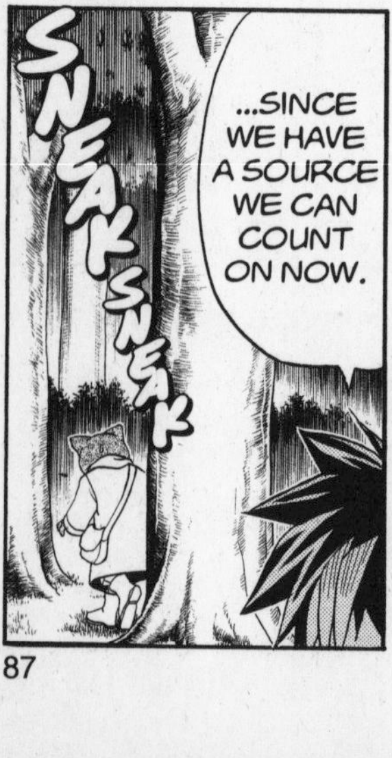
...SINCE WE HAVE A SOURCE WE CAN COUNT ON NOW.
SNEAK SNEAK

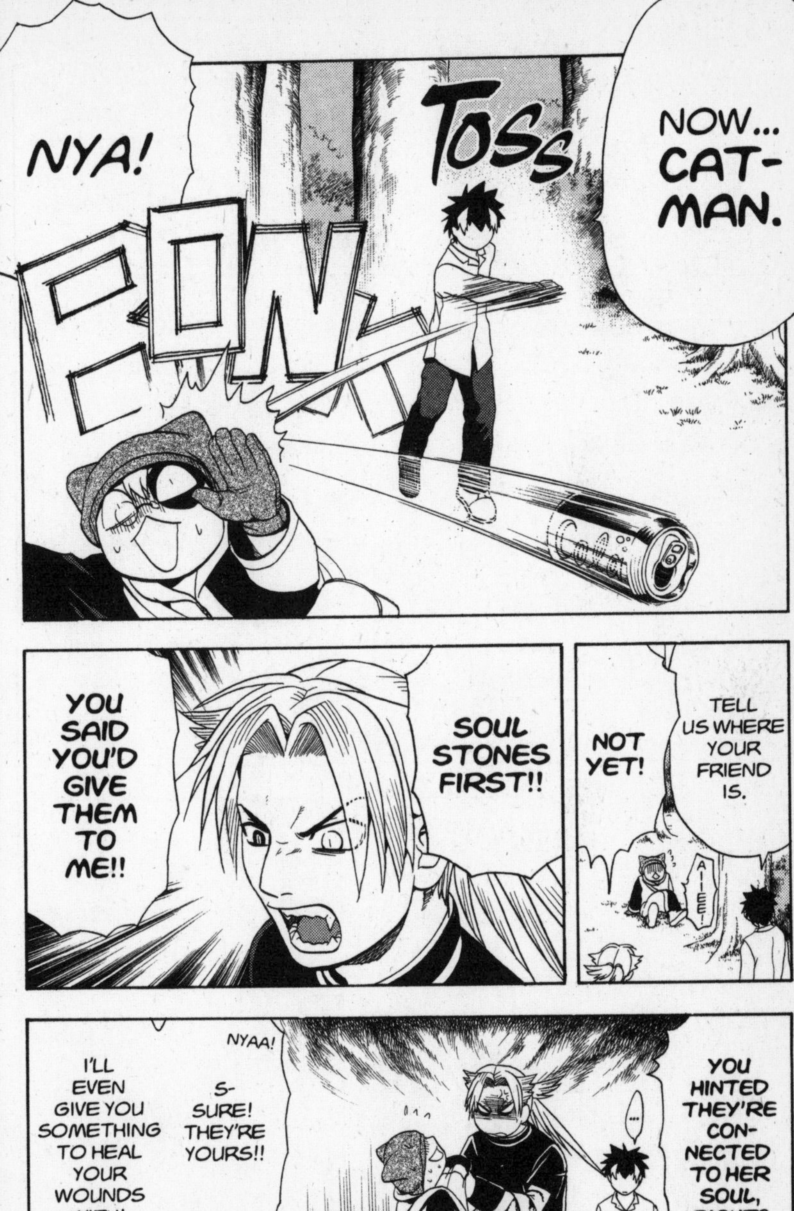
NOW... CAT-MAN.
TOSS
POW
NYA!
TELL US WHERE YOUR FRIEND IS.
NOT YET!
AIEE!
SOUL STONES FIRST!!
YOU SAID YOU'D GIVE THEM TO ME!!
YOU HINTED THEY'RE CON-NECTED TO HER SOUL, RIGHT?
...
NYAA!
S- SURE! THEY'RE YOURS!!
I'LL EVEN GIVE YOU SOMETHING TO HEAL YOUR WOUNDS WITH!

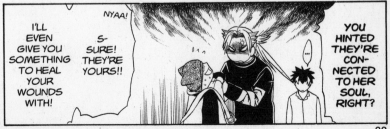

READ THIS WAY

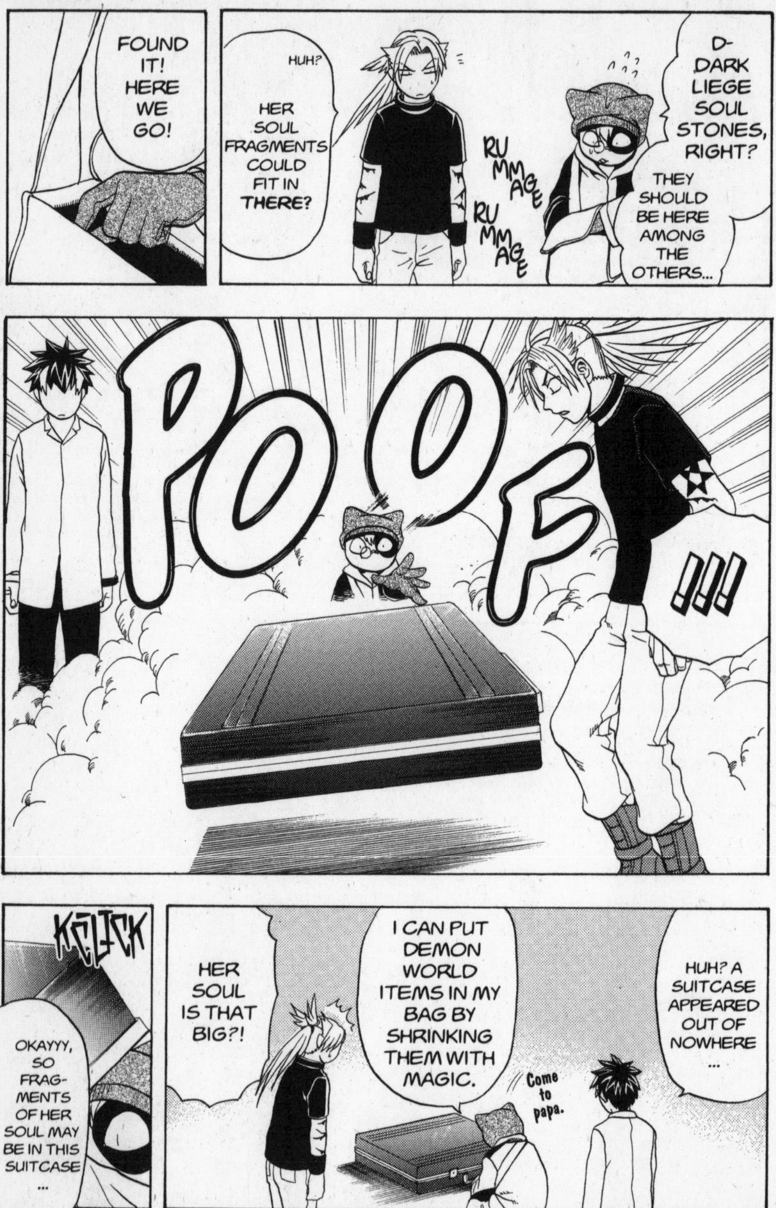
D-DARK LIEGE SOUL STONES, RIGHT?
THEY SHOULD BE HERE AMONG THE OTHERS...
RUMMAGE
RUMMAGE
HUH? HER SOUL FRAGMENTS COULD FIT IN THERE?
FOUND IT! HERE WE GO!
POOF
!!!
HUH? A SUITCASE APPEARED OUT OF NOWHERE...
I CAN PUT DEMON WORLD ITEMS IN MY BAG BY SHRINKING THEM WITH MAGIC.
Come to papa.
HER SOUL IS THAT BIG?!
KCLICK
OKAYYY, SO FRAGMENTS OF HER SOUL MAY BE IN THIS SUITCASE...

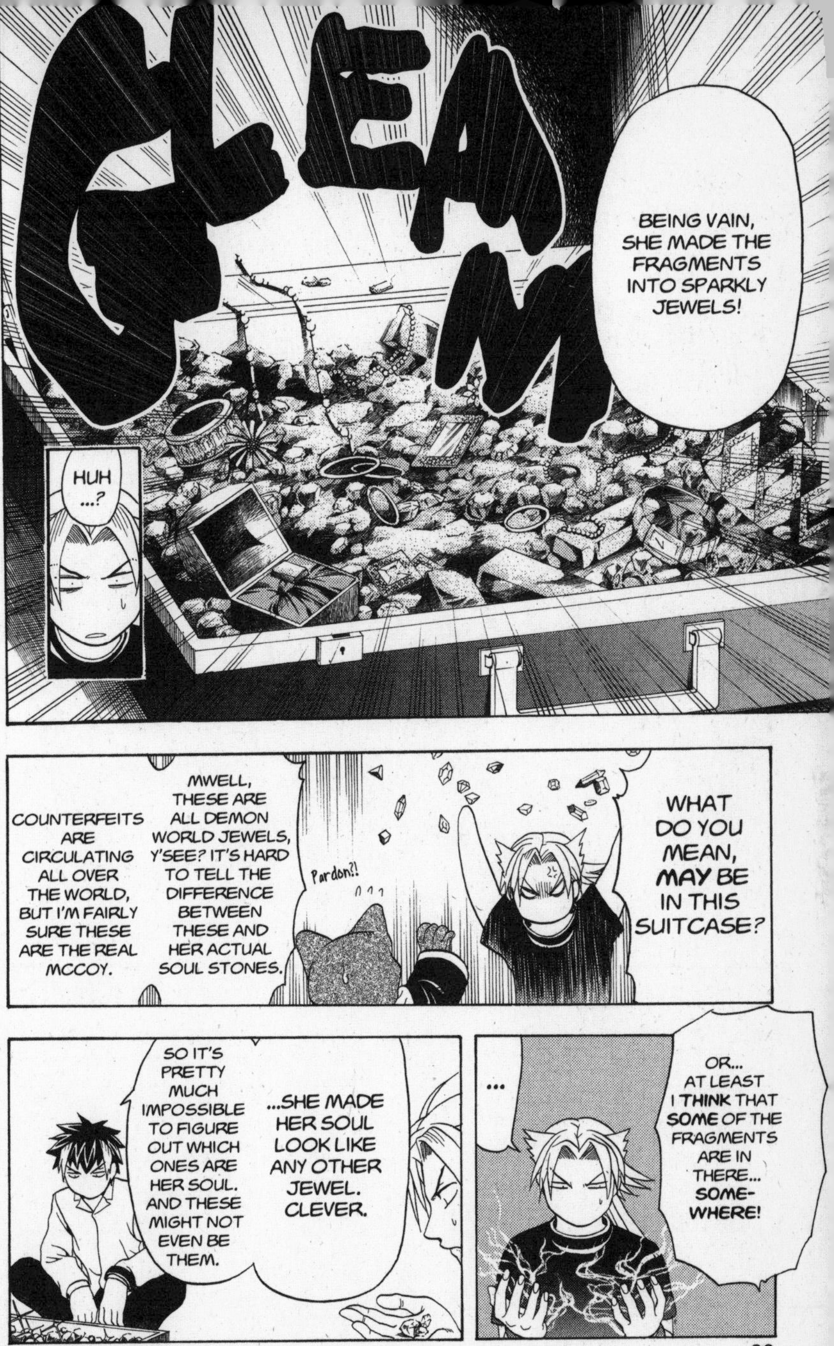
GLEAM
BEING VAIN, SHE MADE THE FRAGMENTS INTO SPARKLY JEWELS!
HUH ...?
WHAT DO YOU MEAN, MAY BE IN THIS SUITCASE?
Pardon?!
MWELL, THESE ARE ALL DEMON WORLD JEWELS, Y'SEE? IT'S HARD TO TELL THE DIFFERENCE BETWEEN THESE AND HER ACTUAL SOUL STONES.
COUNTERFEITS ARE CIRCULATING ALL OVER THE WORLD, BUT I'M FAIRLY SURE THESE ARE THE REAL MCCOY.
OR... AT LEAST I THINK THAT SOME OF THE FRAGMENTS ARE IN THERE... SOME-WHERE!
...
...SHE MADE HER SOUL LOOK LIKE ANY OTHER JEWEL. CLEVER.
SO IT'S PRETTY MUCH IMPOSSIBLE TO FIGURE OUT WHICH ONES ARE HER SOUL. AND THESE MIGHT NOT EVEN BE THEM.

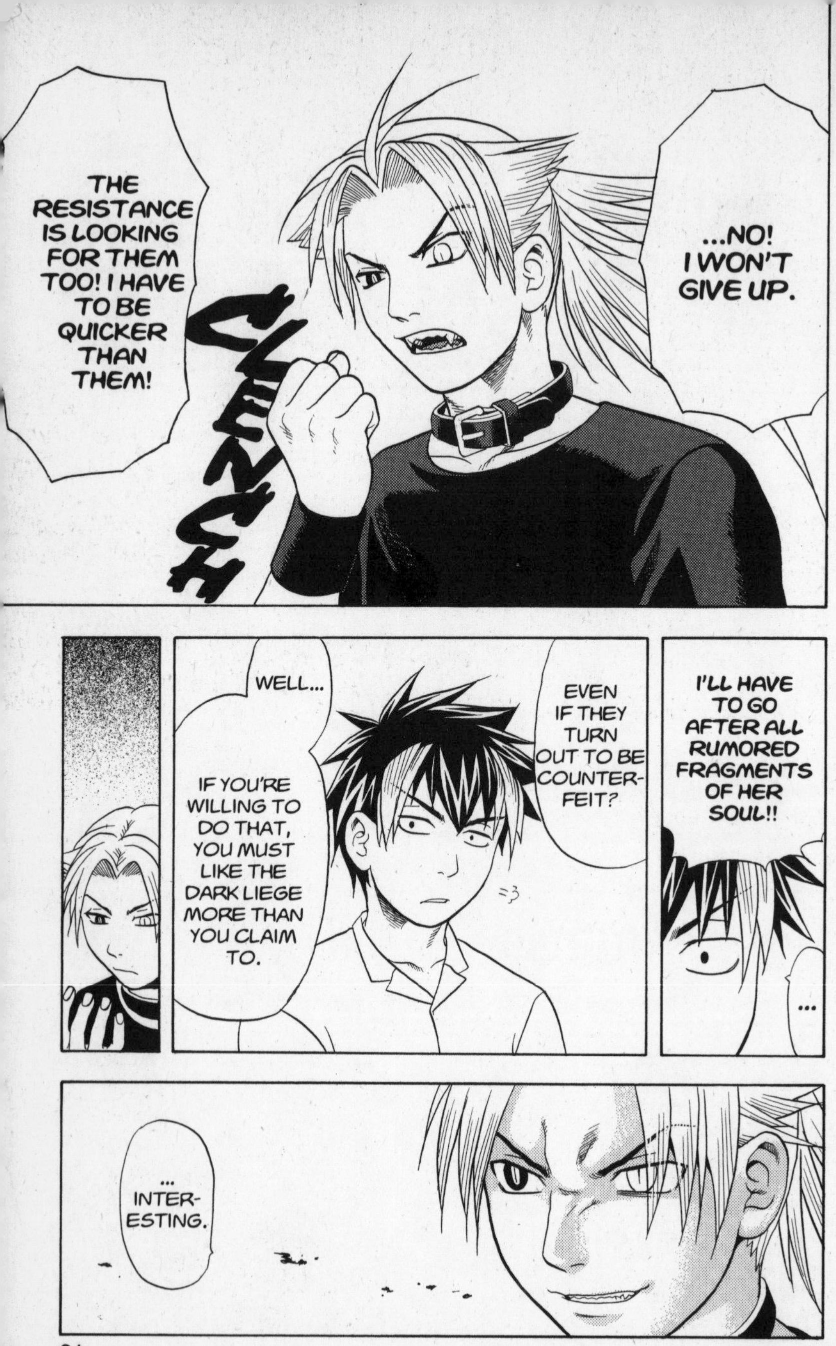
...NO! I WON'T GIVE UP.
THE RESISTANCE IS LOOKING FOR THEM TOO! I HAVE TO BE QUICKER THAN THEM!
CLENCH
I'LL HAVE TO GO AFTER ALL RUMORED FRAGMENTS OF HER SOUL!!
...
EVEN IF THEY TURN OUT TO BE COUNTER-FEIT?
WELL...
IF YOU'RE WILLING TO DO THAT, YOU MUST LIKE THE DARK LIEGE MORE THAN YOU CLAIM TO.
... INTER-ESTING.

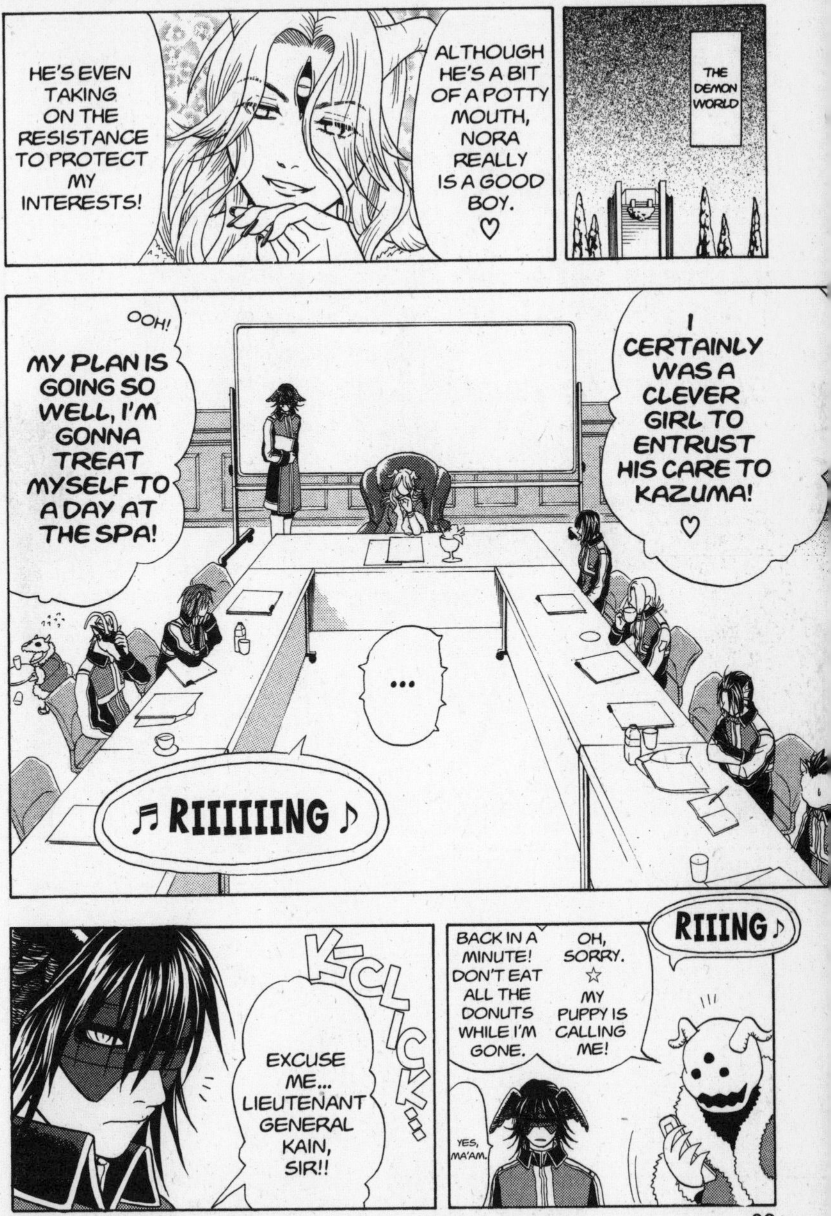
THE DEMON WORLD
ALTHOUGH HE'S A BIT OF A POTTY MOUTH, NORA REALLY IS A GOOD BOY. ♡
HE'S EVEN TAKING ON THE RESISTANCE TO PROTECT MY INTERESTS!
I CERTAINLY WAS A CLEVER GIRL TO ENTRUST HIS CARE TO KAZUMA! ♡
OOH!
MY PLAN IS GOING SO WELL, I'M GONNA TREAT MYSELF TO A DAY AT THE SPA!
...
♬ RIIIIIING ♪
RIIING ♪
OH, SORRY. ☆ MY PUPPY IS CALLING ME!
BACK IN A MINUTE! DON'T EAT ALL THE DONUTS WHILE I'M GONE.
YES, MA'AM.
K-CLICK...
EXCUSE ME... LIEUTENANT GENERAL KAIN, SIR!!

READ THIS WAY

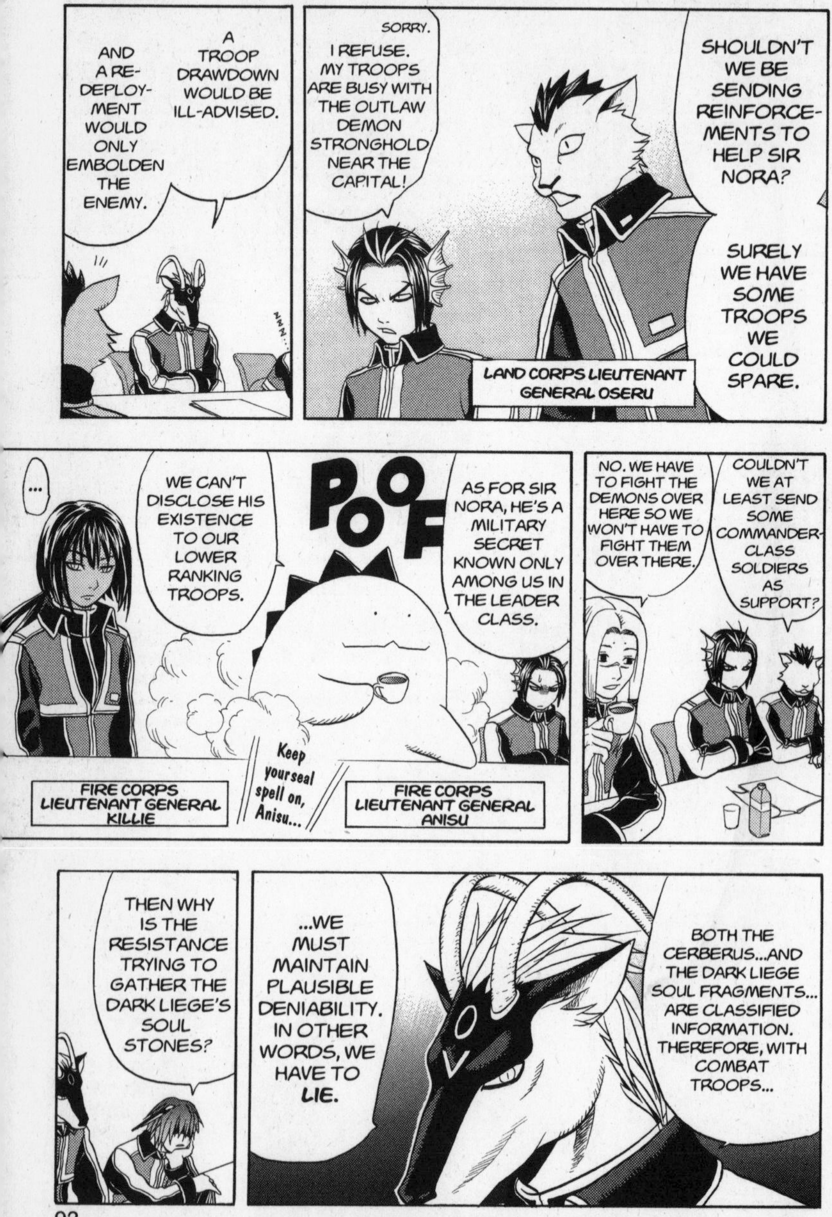
SHOULDN'T WE BE SENDING REINFORCEMENTS TO HELP SIR NORA?
SURELY WE HAVE SOME TROOPS WE COULD SPARE.
LAND CORPS LIEUTENANT GENERAL OSERU
SORRY.
I REFUSE. MY TROOPS ARE BUSY WITH THE OUTLAW DEMON STRONGHOLD NEAR THE CAPITAL!
A TROOP DRAWDOWN WOULD BE ILL-ADVISED.
AND A REDEPLOYMENT WOULD ONLY EMBOLDEN THE ENEMY.
NNN...
COULDN'T WE AT LEAST SEND SOME COMMANDER-CLASS SOLDIERS AS SUPPORT?
NO. WE HAVE TO FIGHT THE DEMONS OVER HERE SO WE WON'T HAVE TO FIGHT THEM OVER THERE.
AS FOR SIR NORA, HE'S A MILITARY SECRET KNOWN ONLY AMONG US IN THE LEADER CLASS.
POOF
FIRE CORPS LIEUTENANT GENERAL ANISU
Keep your seal spell on, Anisu...
WE CAN'T DISCLOSE HIS EXISTENCE TO OUR LOWER RANKING TROOPS.
...
FIRE CORPS LIEUTENANT GENERAL KILLIE
BOTH THE CERBERUS...AND THE DARK LIEGE SOUL FRAGMENTS... ARE CLASSIFIED INFORMATION. THEREFORE, WITH COMBAT TROOPS...
...WE MUST MAINTAIN PLAUSIBLE DENIABILITY. IN OTHER WORDS, WE HAVE TO LIE.
THEN WHY IS THE RESISTANCE TRYING TO GATHER THE DARK LIEGE'S SOUL STONES?

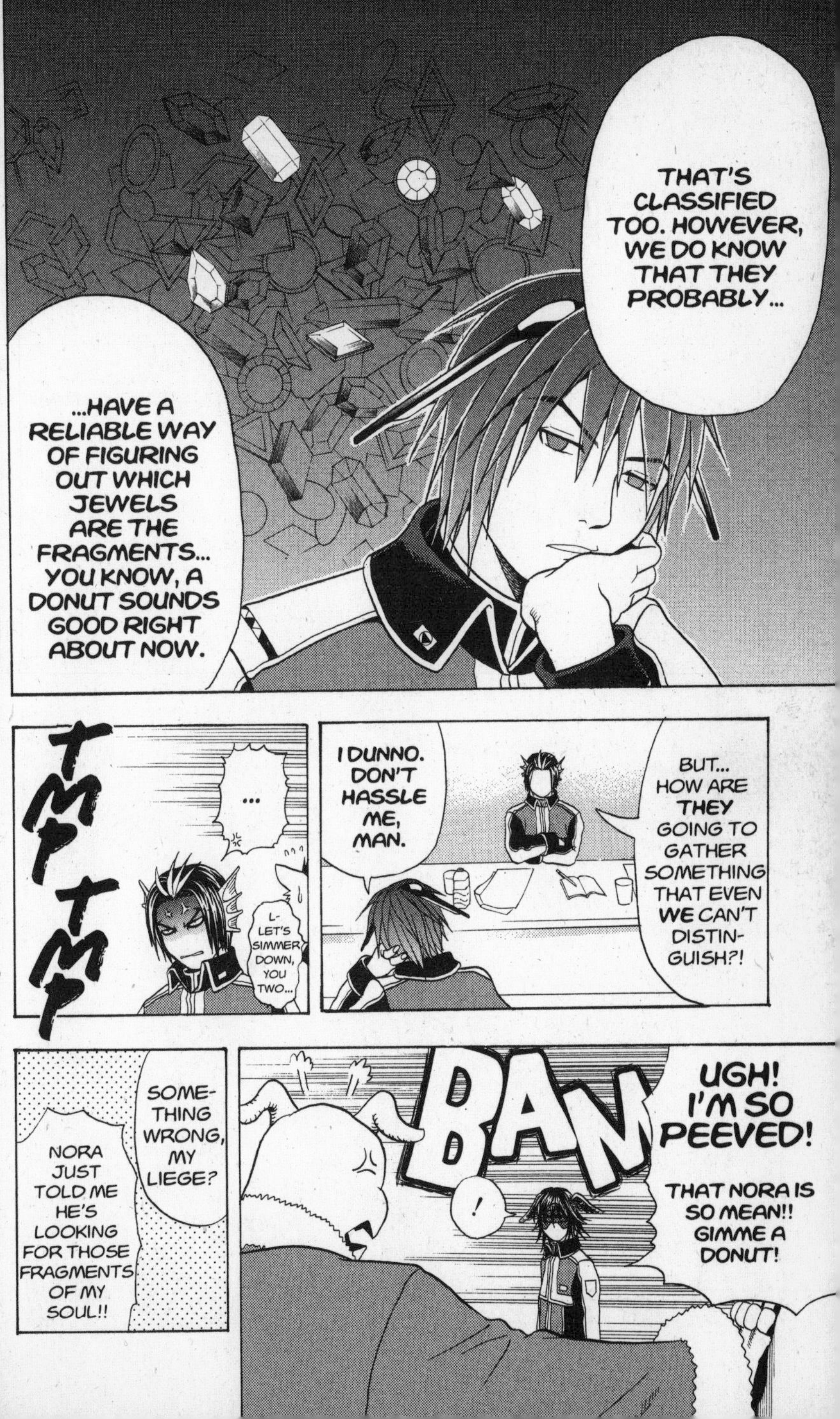
THAT'S CLASSIFIED TOO. HOWEVER, WE DO KNOW THAT THEY PROBABLY...
...HAVE A RELIABLE WAY OF FIGURING OUT WHICH JEWELS ARE THE FRAGMENTS... YOU KNOW, A DONUT SOUNDS GOOD RIGHT ABOUT NOW.
BUT... HOW ARE THEY GOING TO GATHER SOMETHING THAT EVEN WE CAN'T DISTINGUISH?!
I DUNNO. DON'T HASSLE ME, MAN.
...
L-LET'S SIMMER DOWN, YOU TWO...
TMP TMP
UGH! I'M SO PEEVED!
THAT NORA IS SO MEAN!! GIMME A DONUT!
BAM
!
SOMETHING WRONG, MY LIEGE?
NORA JUST TOLD ME HE'S LOOKING FOR THOSE FRAGMENTS OF MY SOUL!!

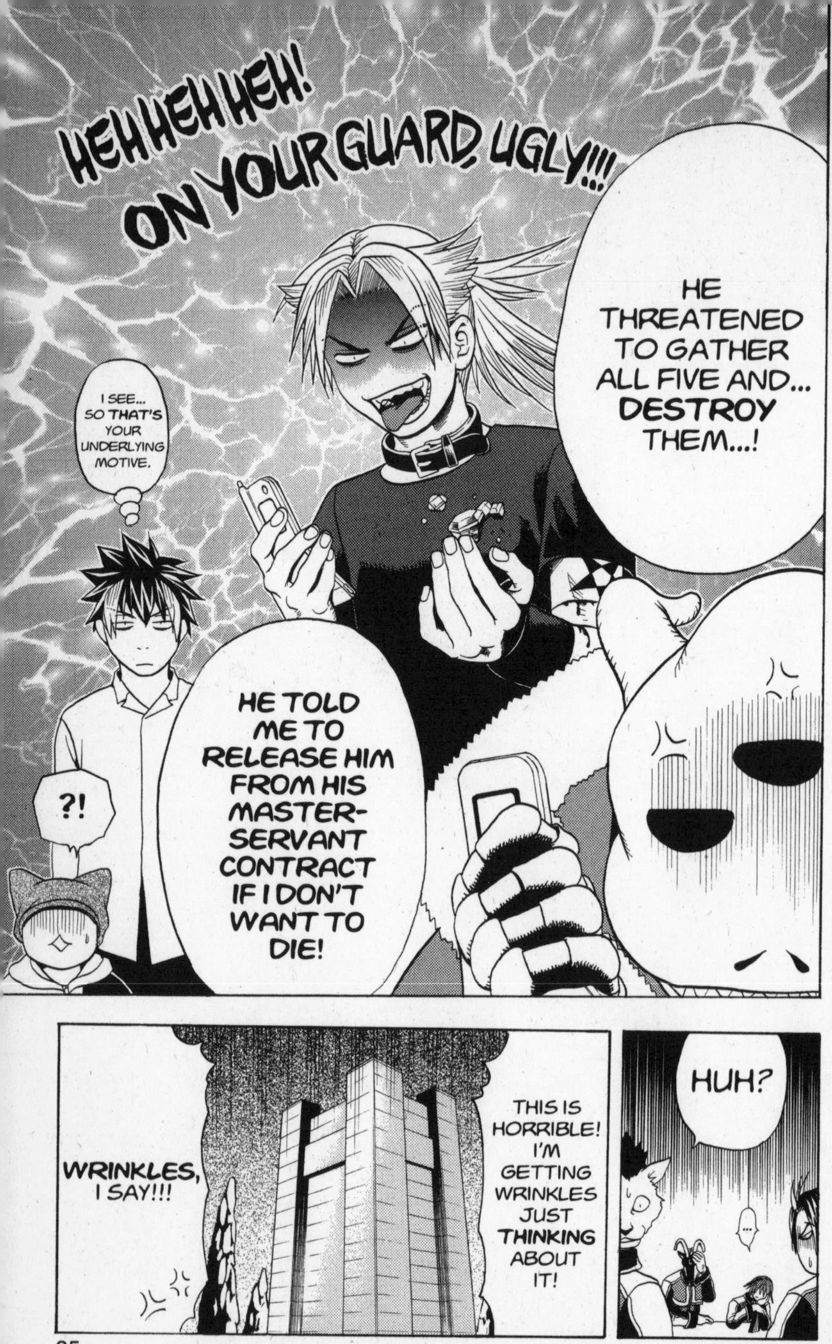
HEH HEH HEH! ON YOUR GUARD, UGLY!!!
HE THREATENED TO GATHER ALL FIVE AND... DESTROY THEM...!
I SEE... SO THAT'S YOUR UNDERLYING MOTIVE.
HE TOLD ME TO RELEASE HIM FROM HIS MASTER-SERVANT CONTRACT IF I DON'T WANT TO DIE!
?!
HUH?
...
THIS IS HORRIBLE! I'M GETTING WRINKLES JUST THINKING ABOUT IT!
WRINKLES, I SAY!!!

CHARACTER DATA

KEINI

HEIGHT: 158 CM
FAVORITE FOOD: MILK CHOCOLATE, SWEETS
FOOD SHE HATES: NATTO BEANS, CELERY
INTERESTS AND
SPECIAL TALENTS: HIGH FASHION
NOTES: A RESISTANCE MEMBER WHO
HOLDS AN UNUSUAL AFFECTION
FOR HER BOSS. WHILE NOT
NORMALLY COMBATIVE, SHE
SHOULDN'T BE MESSED WITH.

KETO-KETO

HEIGHT: 111 CM
FAVORITE FOOD: SASHIMI
FOOD HE HATES: LIVER
INTERESTS AND
SPECIAL TALENTS: BUYING AND SELLING ITEMS FROM
THE DEMON WORLD
NOTES: A FENCE WHO DEALS IN STOLEN
ARTIFACTS. HE HAS THE ABILITY TO
SHRINK MERCHANDISE TO FIT INSIDE
HIS BAG. ALTHOUGH HE LOOKS LIKE A
CAT, HE HAS A SEALING SPELL ON.

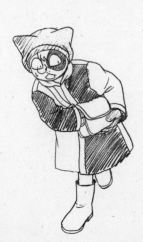

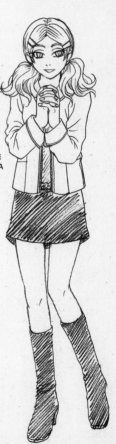

Story 11: Cognition

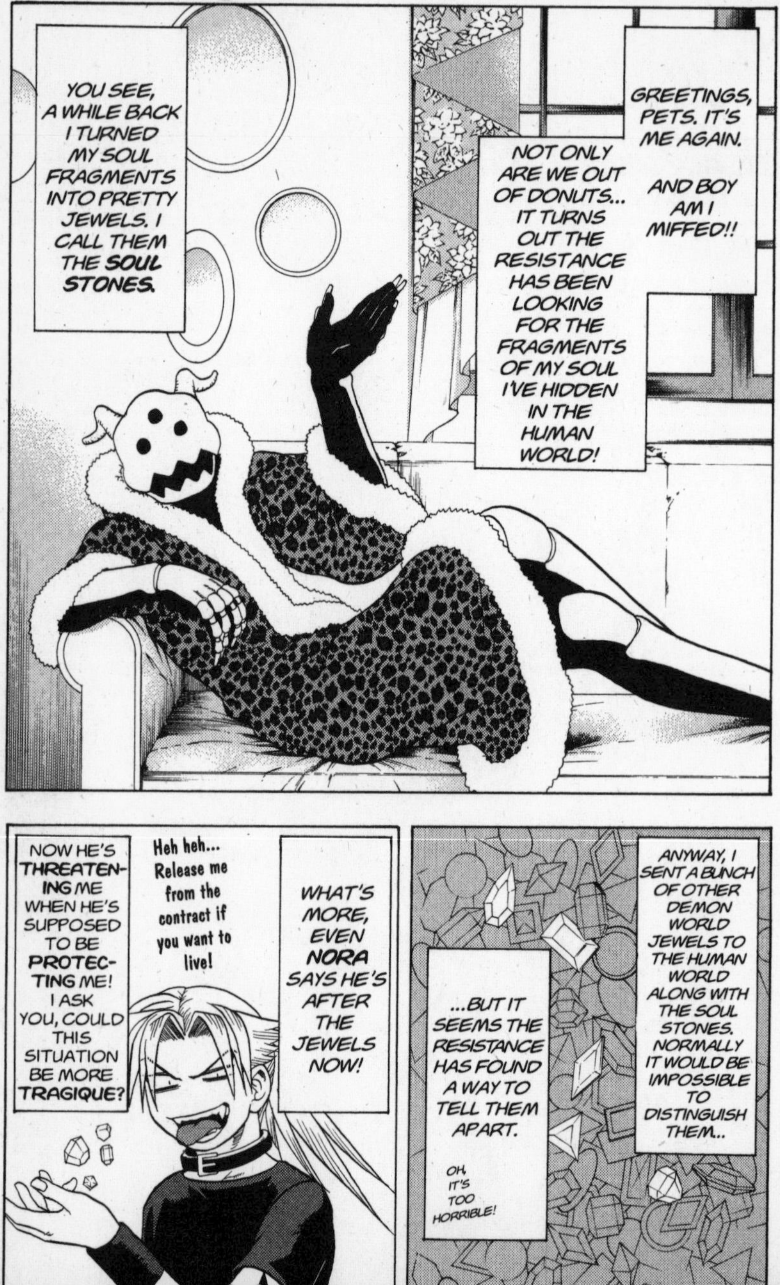
GREETINGS, PETS. IT'S ME AGAIN.
AND BOY AM I MIFFED!!
NOT ONLY ARE WE OUT OF DONUTS... IT TURNS OUT THE RESISTANCE HAS BEEN LOOKING FOR THE FRAGMENTS OF MY SOUL I'VE HIDDEN IN THE HUMAN WORLD!
YOU SEE, A WHILE BACK I TURNED MY SOUL FRAGMENTS INTO PRETTY JEWELS. I CALL THEM THE SOUL STONES.
ANYWAY, I SENT A BUNCH OF OTHER DEMON WORLD JEWELS TO THE HUMAN WORLD ALONG WITH THE SOUL STONES. NORMALLY IT WOULD BE IMPOSSIBLE TO DISTINGUISH THEM...
...BUT IT SEEMS THE RESISTANCE HAS FOUND A WAY TO TELL THEM APART.
OH, IT'S TOO HORRIBLE!
WHAT'S MORE, EVEN NORA SAYS HE'S AFTER THE JEWELS NOW!
Heh heh... Release me from the contract if you want to live!
NOW HE'S THREATENING ME WHEN HE'S SUPPOSED TO BE PROTECTING ME! I ASK YOU, COULD THIS SITUATION BE MORE TRAGIQUE?

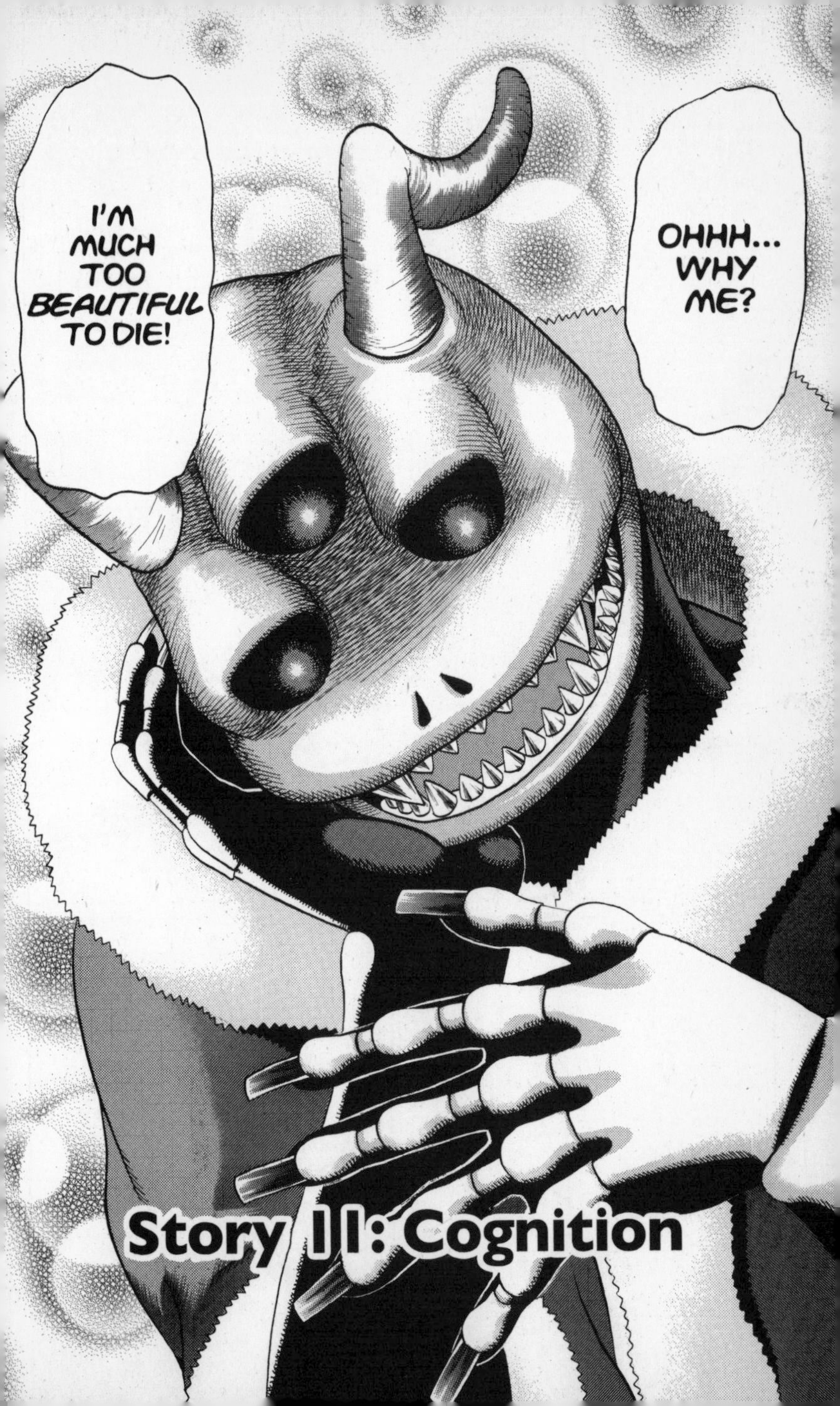
OHHH... WHY ME?
I'M MUCH TOO BEAUTIFUL TO DIE!

Story 11: Cognition

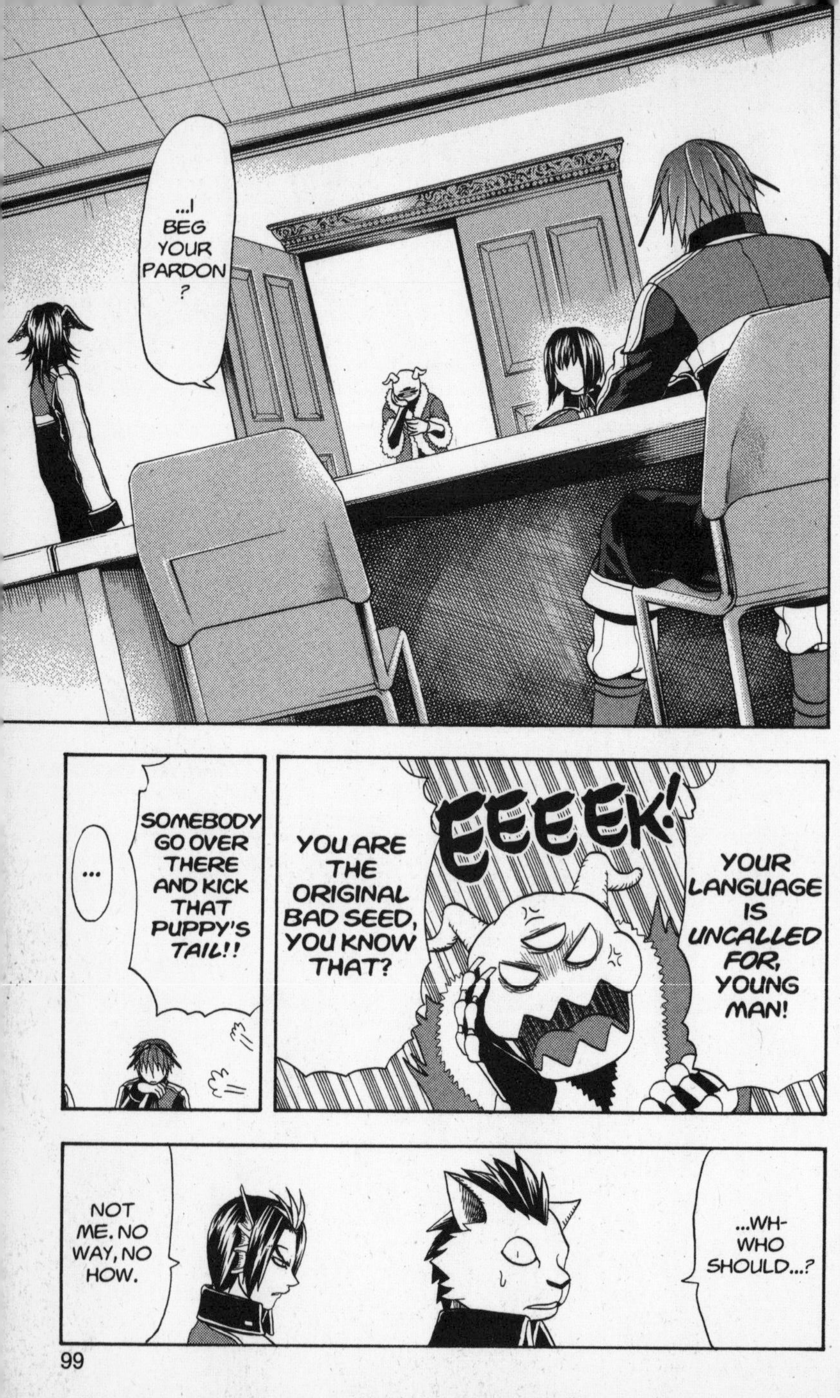
...I BEG YOUR PARDON?
YOUR LANGUAGE IS UNCALLED FOR, YOUNG MAN!
EEEEK!
YOU ARE THE ORIGINAL BAD SEED, YOU KNOW THAT?
SOMEBODY GO OVER THERE AND KICK THAT PUPPY'S TAIL!!
...
...WH-WHO SHOULD...?
NOT ME. NO WAY, NO HOW.

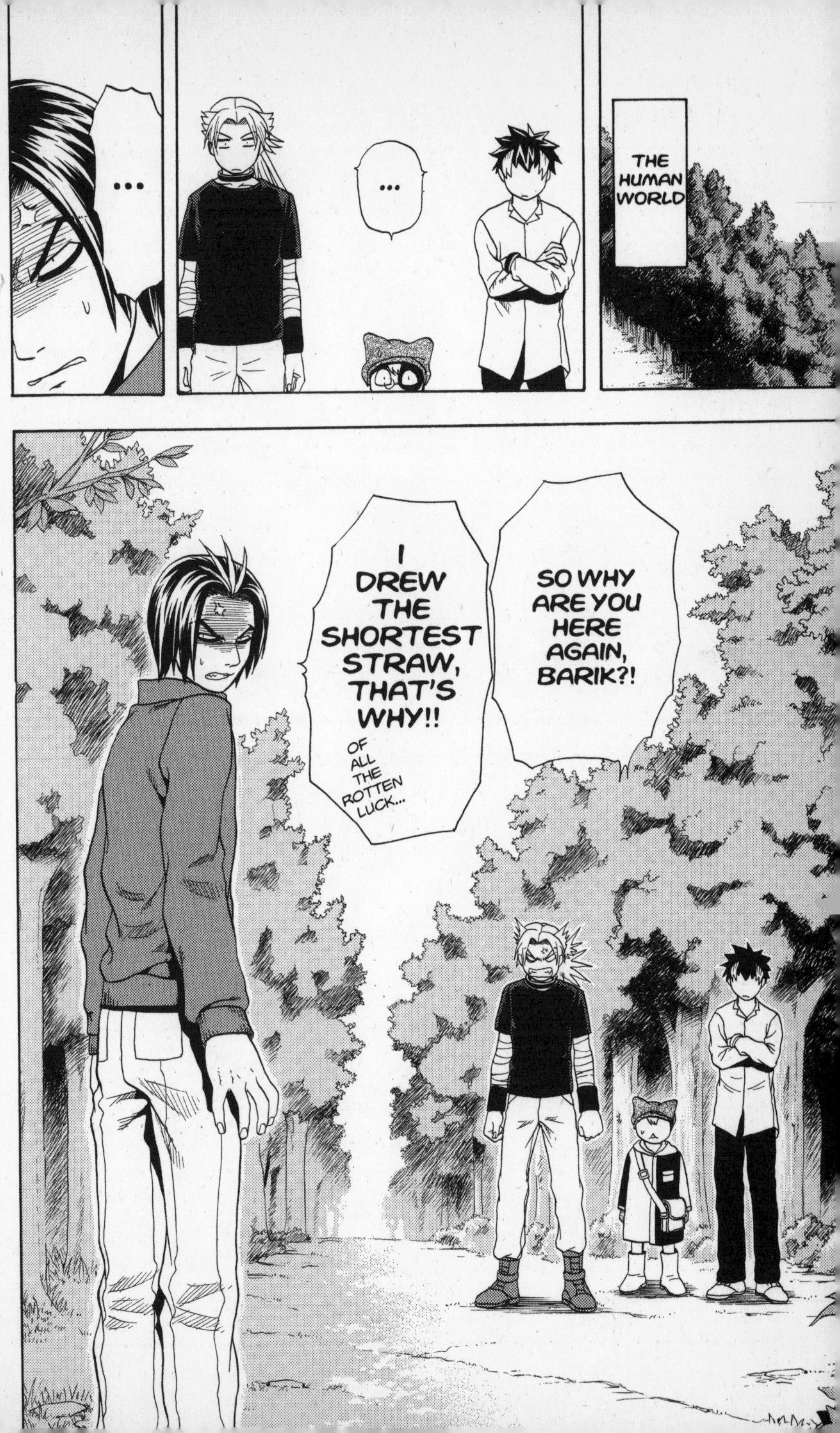
THE HUMAN WORLD
...
...
SO WHY ARE YOU HERE AGAIN, BARIK?!
I DREW THE SHORTEST STRAW, THAT'S WHY!!
OF ALL THE ROTTEN LUCK...

READ THIS WAY

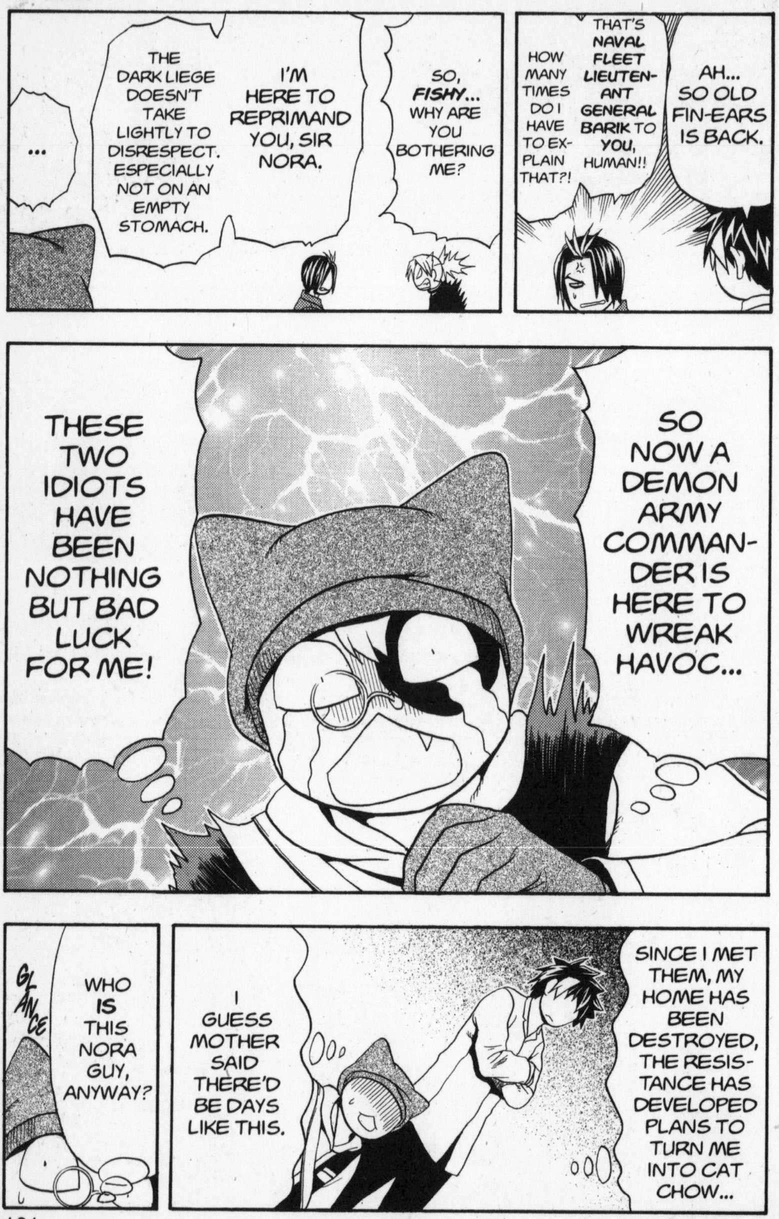

AH... SO OLD FIN-EARS IS BACK.
THAT'S **NAVAL FLEET LIEUTENANT GENERAL BARIK** TO **YOU**, HUMAN!!
HOW MANY TIMES DO I HAVE TO EXPLAIN THAT?!
SO, ***FISHY...*** WHY ARE YOU BOTHERING ME?
I'M HERE TO REPRIMAND YOU, SIR NORA.
THE DARK LIEGE DOESN'T TAKE LIGHTLY TO DISRESPECT. ESPECIALLY NOT ON AN EMPTY STOMACH.
...
SO NOW A DEMON ARMY COMMANDER IS HERE TO WREAK HAVOC...
THESE TWO IDIOTS HAVE BEEN NOTHING BUT BAD LUCK FOR ME!
SINCE I MET THEM, MY HOME HAS BEEN DESTROYED, THE RESISTANCE HAS DEVELOPED PLANS TO TURN ME INTO CAT CHOW...
I GUESS MOTHER SAID THERE'D BE DAYS LIKE THIS.
GLANCE
WHO **IS** THIS NORA GUY, ANYWAY?

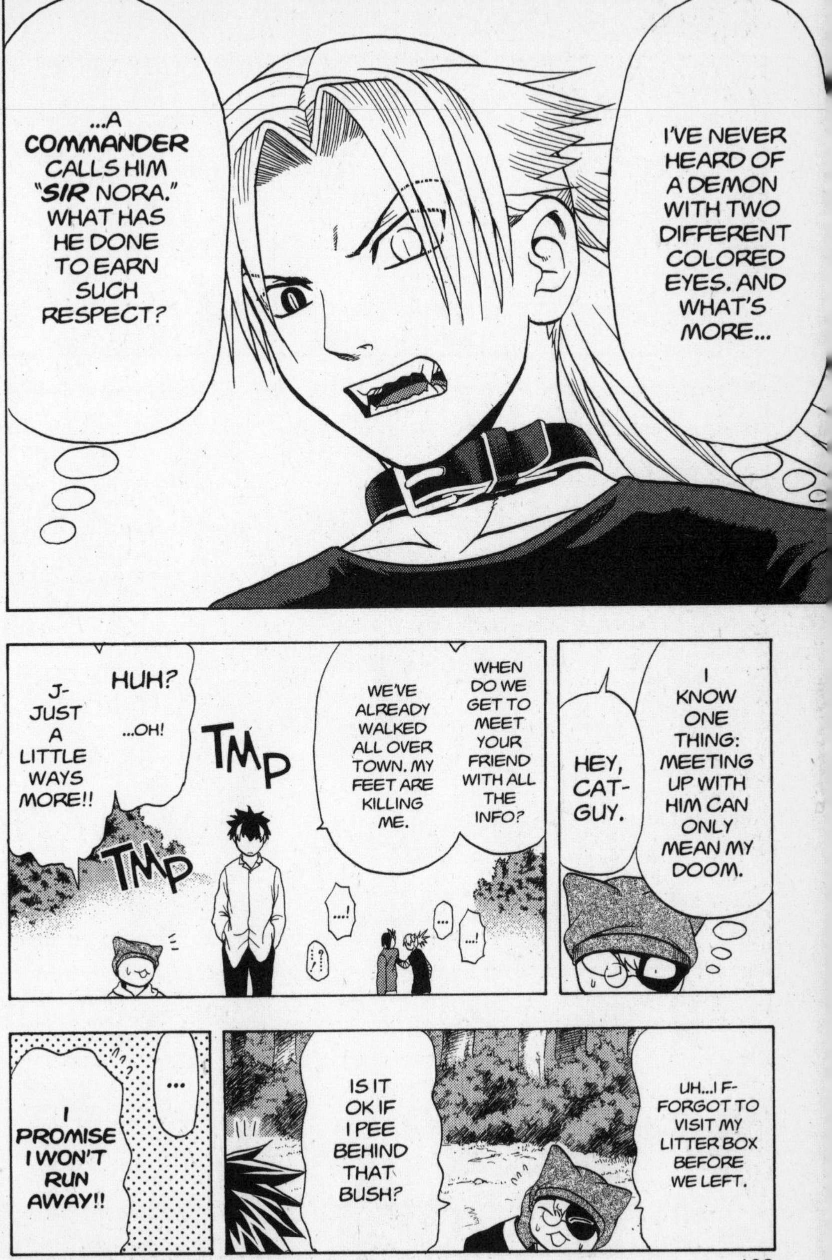
I'VE NEVER HEARD OF A DEMON WITH TWO DIFFERENT COLORED EYES. AND WHAT'S MORE...
...A COMMANDER CALLS HIM "SIR NORA." WHAT HAS HE DONE TO EARN SUCH RESPECT?
I KNOW ONE THING: MEETING UP WITH HIM CAN ONLY MEAN MY DOOM.
HEY, CAT-GUY.
WHEN DO WE GET TO MEET YOUR FRIEND WITH ALL THE INFO?
WE'VE ALREADY WALKED ALL OVER TOWN. MY FEET ARE KILLING ME.
...!
...
...!
!?
TMP
HUH?
...OH!
J-JUST A LITTLE WAYS MORE!!
TMP
UH...I F-FORGOT TO VISIT MY LITTER BOX BEFORE WE LEFT.
IS IT OK IF I PEE BEHIND THAT BUSH?
...
I PROMISE I WON'T RUN AWAY!!

READ THIS WAY

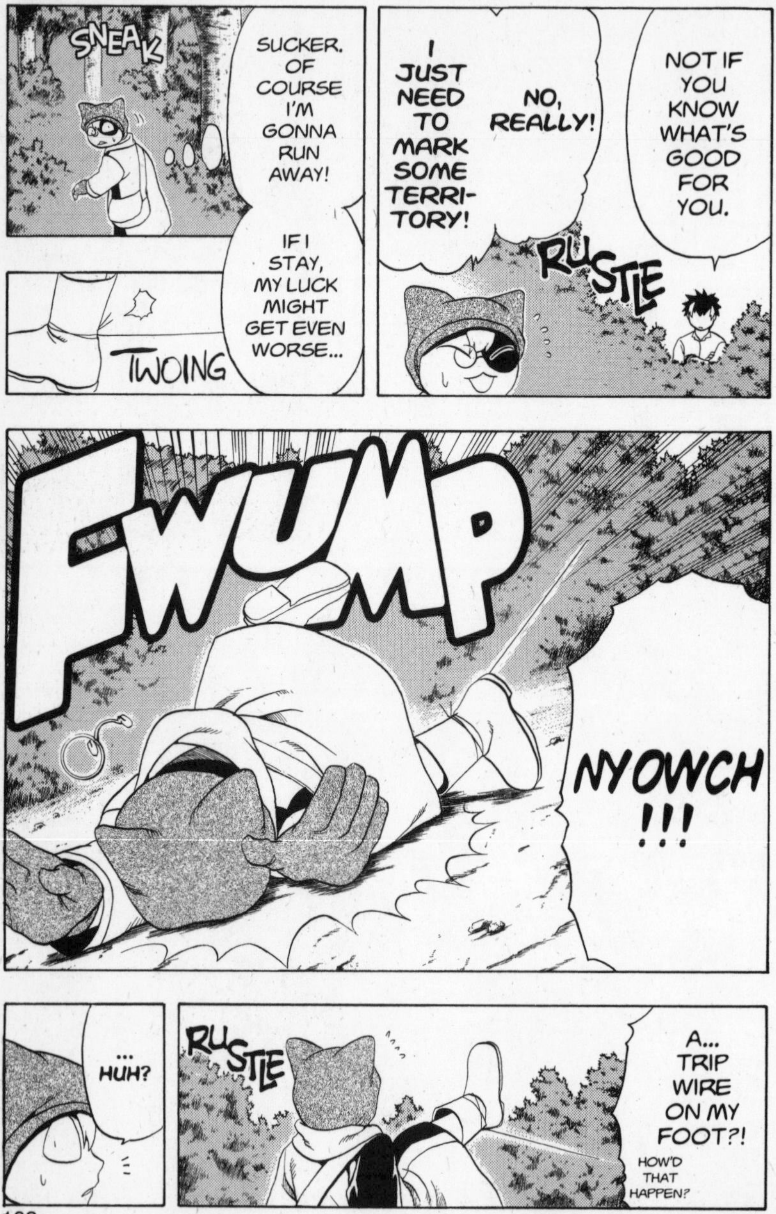
NOT IF YOU KNOW WHAT'S GOOD FOR YOU.
NO, REALLY!
I JUST NEED TO MARK SOME TERRITORY!
RUSTLE
SNEAK
SUCKER. OF COURSE I'M GONNA RUN AWAY!
IF I STAY, MY LUCK MIGHT GET EVEN WORSE...
TWOING
FWUMP
NYOWCH !!!
A... TRIP WIRE ON MY FOOT?!
HOW'D THAT HAPPEN?
RUSTLE
... HUH?

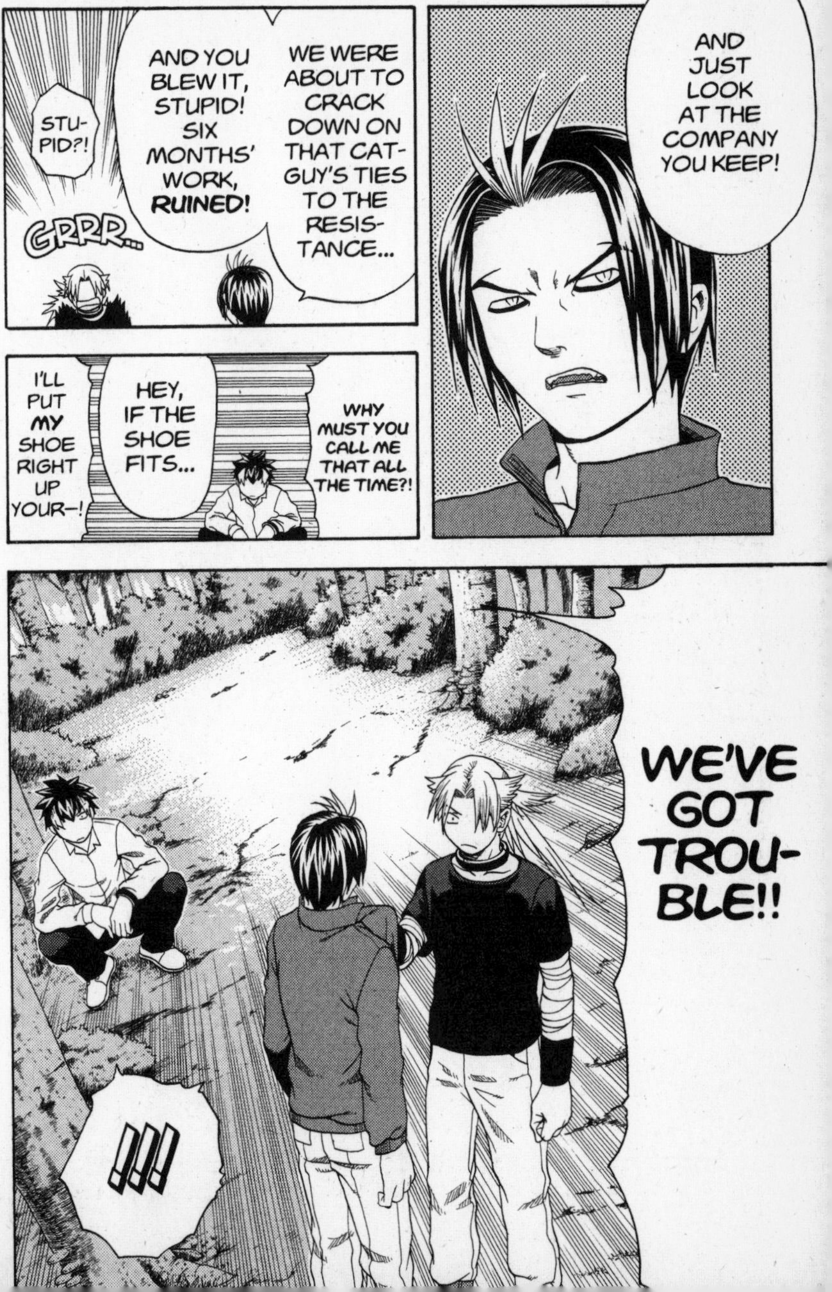
AND JUST LOOK AT THE COMPANY YOU KEEP!
WE WERE ABOUT TO CRACK DOWN ON THAT CAT-GUY'S TIES TO THE RESIS-TANCE...
AND YOU BLEW IT, STUPID! SIX MONTHS' WORK, RUINED!
STU-PID?!
GRRR...
WHY MUST YOU CALL ME THAT ALL THE TIME?!
HEY, IF THE SHOE FITS...
I'LL PUT MY SHOE RIGHT UP YOUR—!
WE'VE GOT TROU-BLE!!
!!!

READ THIS WAY

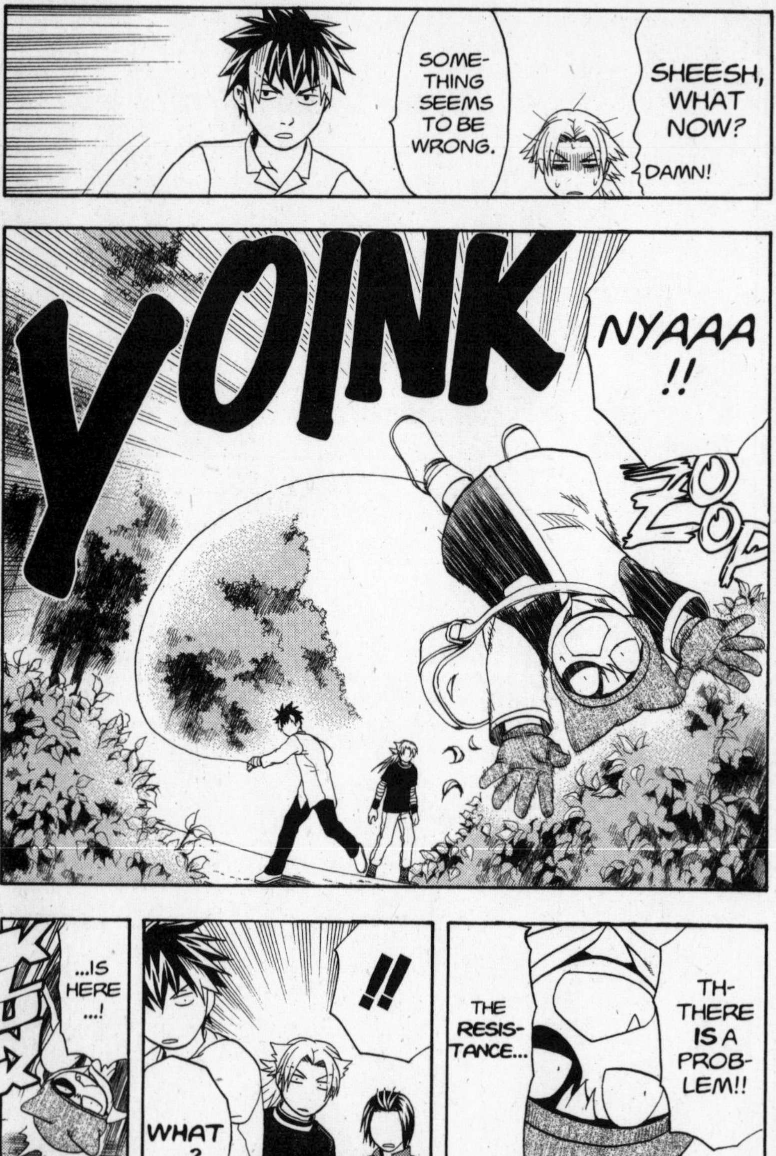

SHEESH, WHAT NOW?
DAMN!
SOME-THING SEEMS TO BE WRONG.
YOINK
NYAAA!!
ZOOP
TH-THERE IS A PROB-LEM!!
THE RESIS-TANCE...
!!
WHAT...?
...IS HERE...!

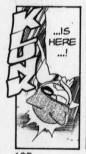

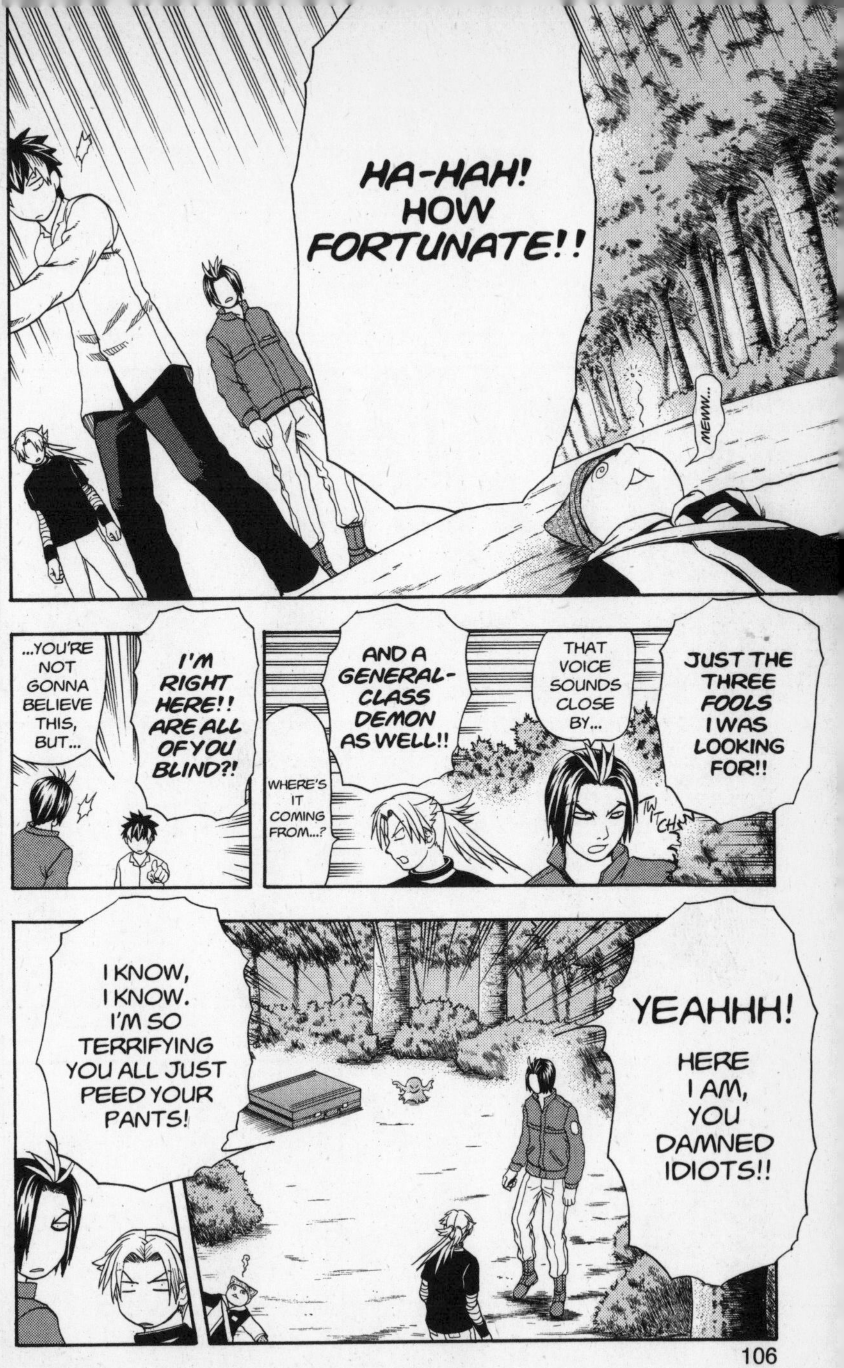
HA-HAH! HOW FORTUNATE!!
MEWW...
JUST THE THREE FOOLS I WAS LOOKING FOR!!
THAT VOICE SOUNDS CLOSE BY...
TWITCH
AND A GENERAL-CLASS DEMON AS WELL!!
WHERE'S IT COMING FROM...?
I'M RIGHT HERE!! ARE ALL OF YOU BLIND?!
...YOU'RE NOT GONNA BELIEVE THIS, BUT...
YEAHHH!
HERE I AM, YOU DAMNED IDIOTS!!
I KNOW, I KNOW. I'M SO TERRIFYING YOU ALL JUST PEED YOUR PANTS!

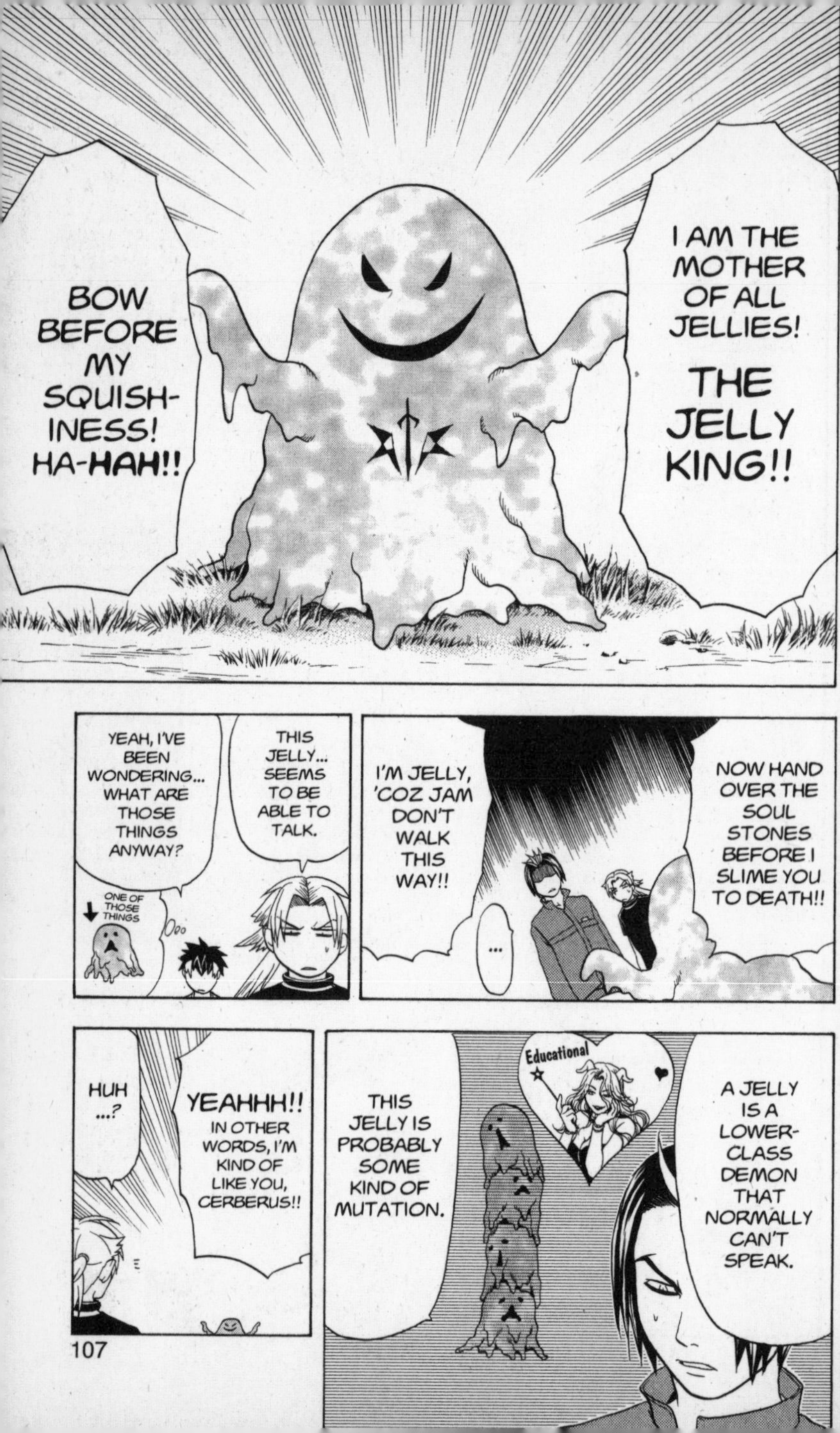
I AM THE MOTHER OF ALL JELLIES! THE JELLY KING!!
BOW BEFORE MY SQUISHINESS! HA-HAH!!
NOW HAND OVER THE SOUL STONES BEFORE I SLIME YOU TO DEATH!!
I'M JELLY, 'COZ JAM DON'T WALK THIS WAY!!
...
THIS JELLY... SEEMS TO BE ABLE TO TALK.
YEAH, I'VE BEEN WONDERING... WHAT ARE THOSE THINGS ANYWAY?
ONE OF THOSE THINGS
A JELLY IS A LOWER-CLASS DEMON THAT NORMALLY CAN'T SPEAK.
Educational
THIS JELLY IS PROBABLY SOME KIND OF MUTATION.
YEAHHH!! IN OTHER WORDS, I'M KIND OF LIKE YOU, CERBERUS!!
HUH ...?

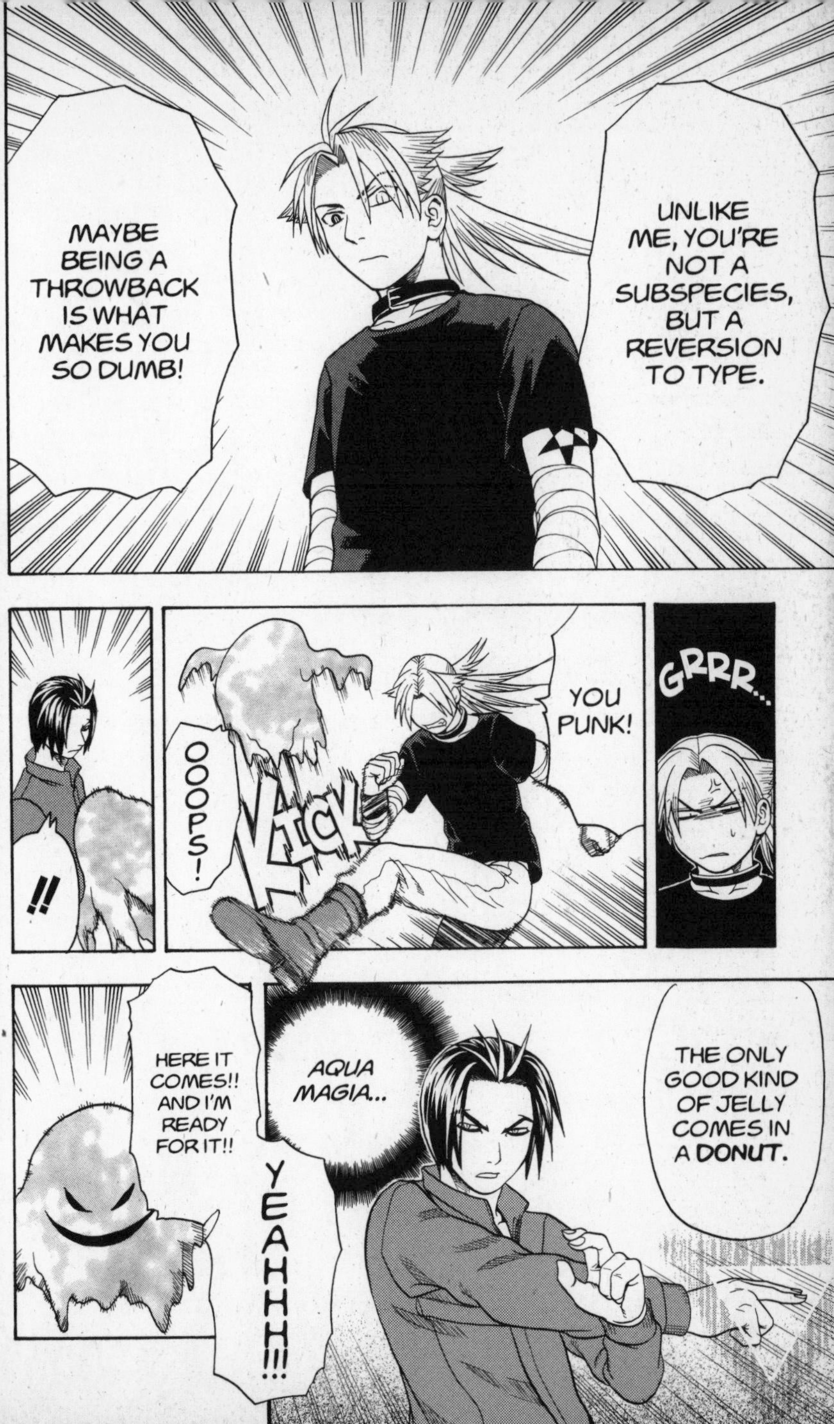
UNLIKE ME, YOU'RE NOT A SUBSPECIES, BUT A REVERSION TO TYPE.
MAYBE BEING A THROWBACK IS WHAT MAKES YOU SO DUMB!
GRRR...
YOU PUNK!
OOOPS!
KICK
!!
THE ONLY GOOD KIND OF JELLY COMES IN A **DONUT**.
AQUA MAGIA...
YEAHHH!!!
HERE IT COMES!! AND I'M READY FOR IT!!

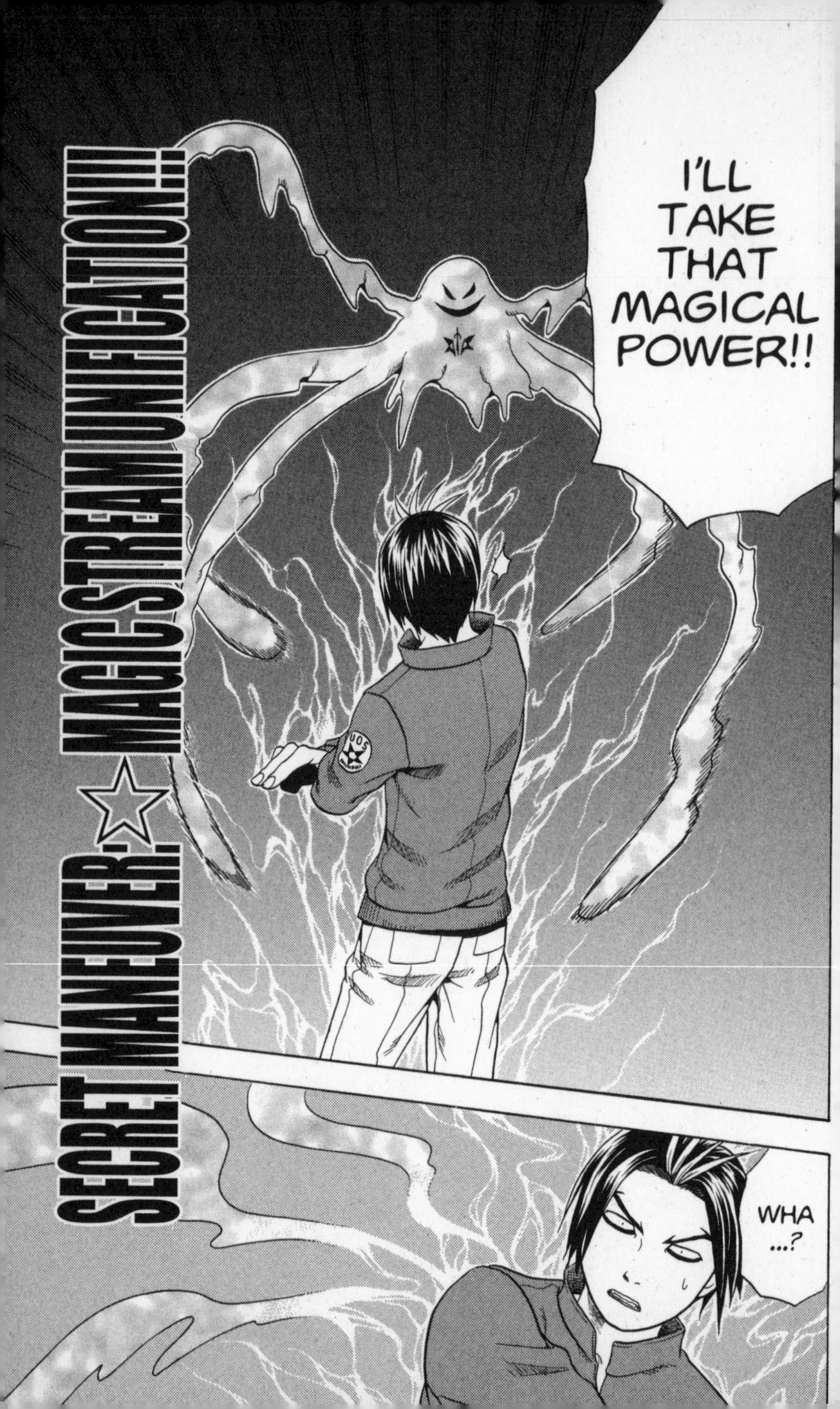
I'LL TAKE THAT MAGICAL POWER!!
SECRET MANEUVER: ☆ MAGIC STREAM UNIFICATION!!!
WHA ...?

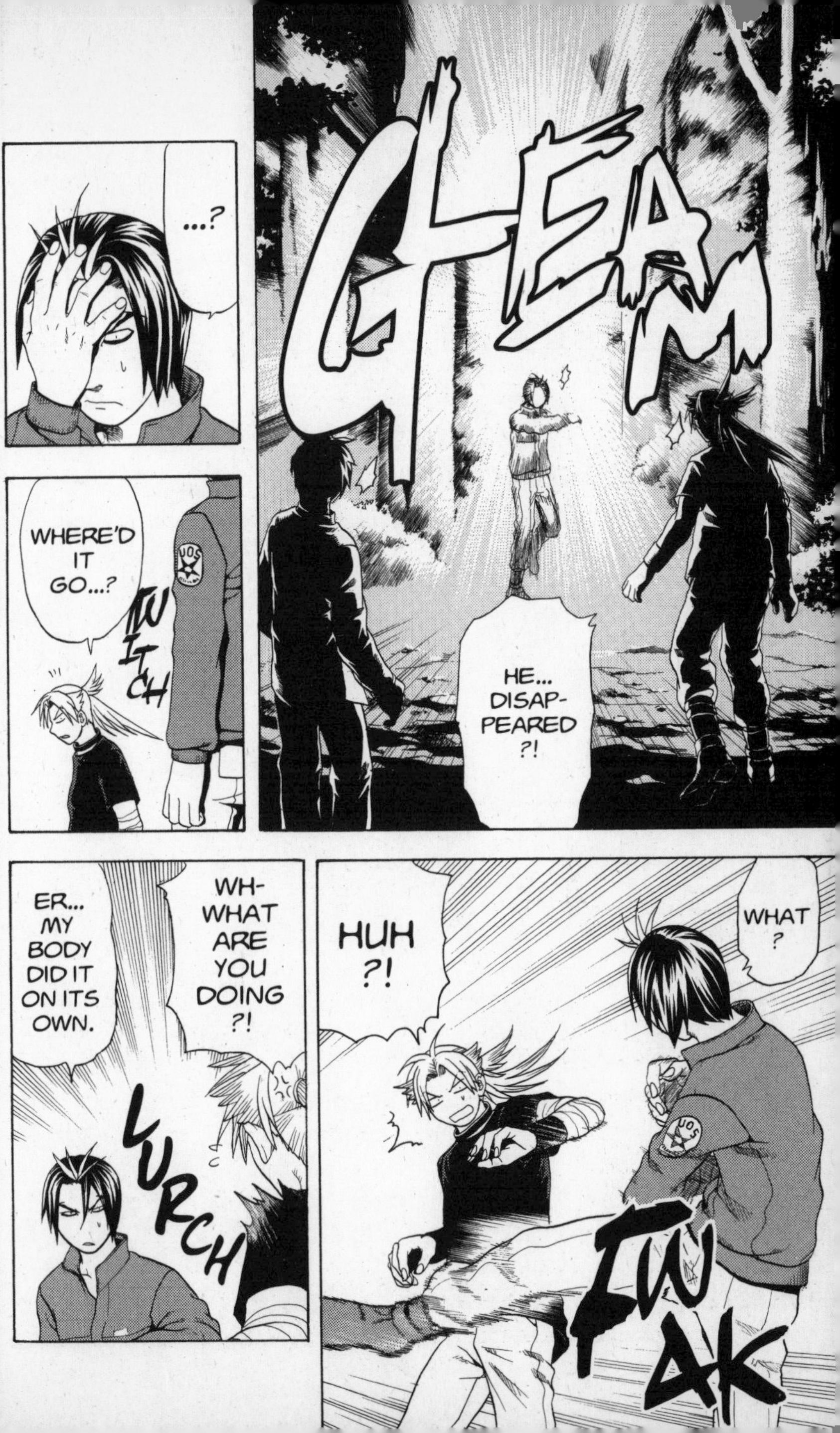
GLEAM
HE... DISAPPEARED?!
...?
WHERE'D IT GO...?
TWITCH
WHAT?
HUH?!
THWAK
WH-WHAT ARE YOU DOING?!
ER... MY BODY DID IT ON ITS OWN.
LURCH

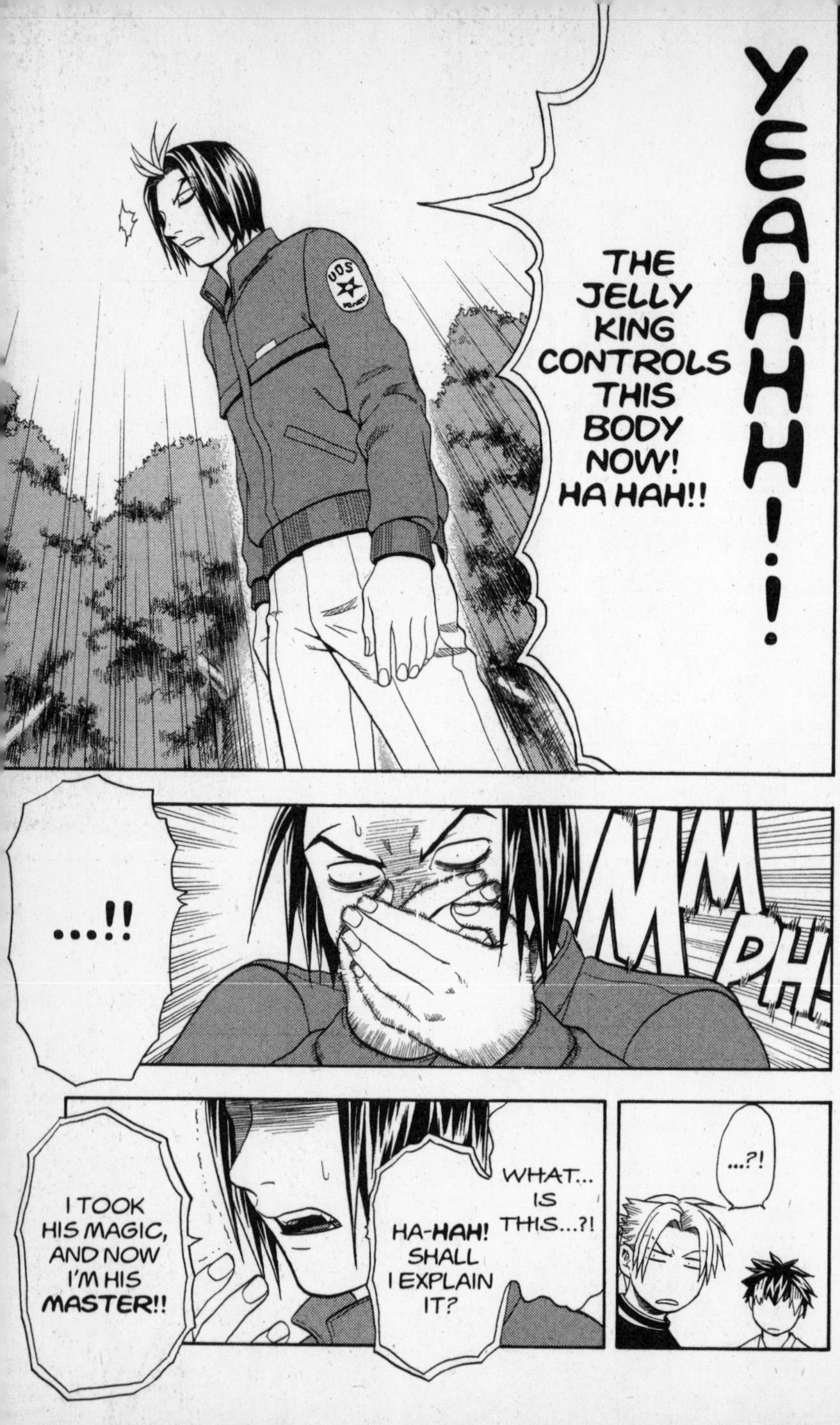

YEAHHH!!
THE JELLY KING CONTROLS THIS BODY NOW! HA HAH!!
MMMPH
...!!
...?!
WHAT... IS THIS...?!
HA-HAH! SHALL I EXPLAIN IT?
I TOOK HIS MAGIC, AND NOW I'M HIS MASTER!!

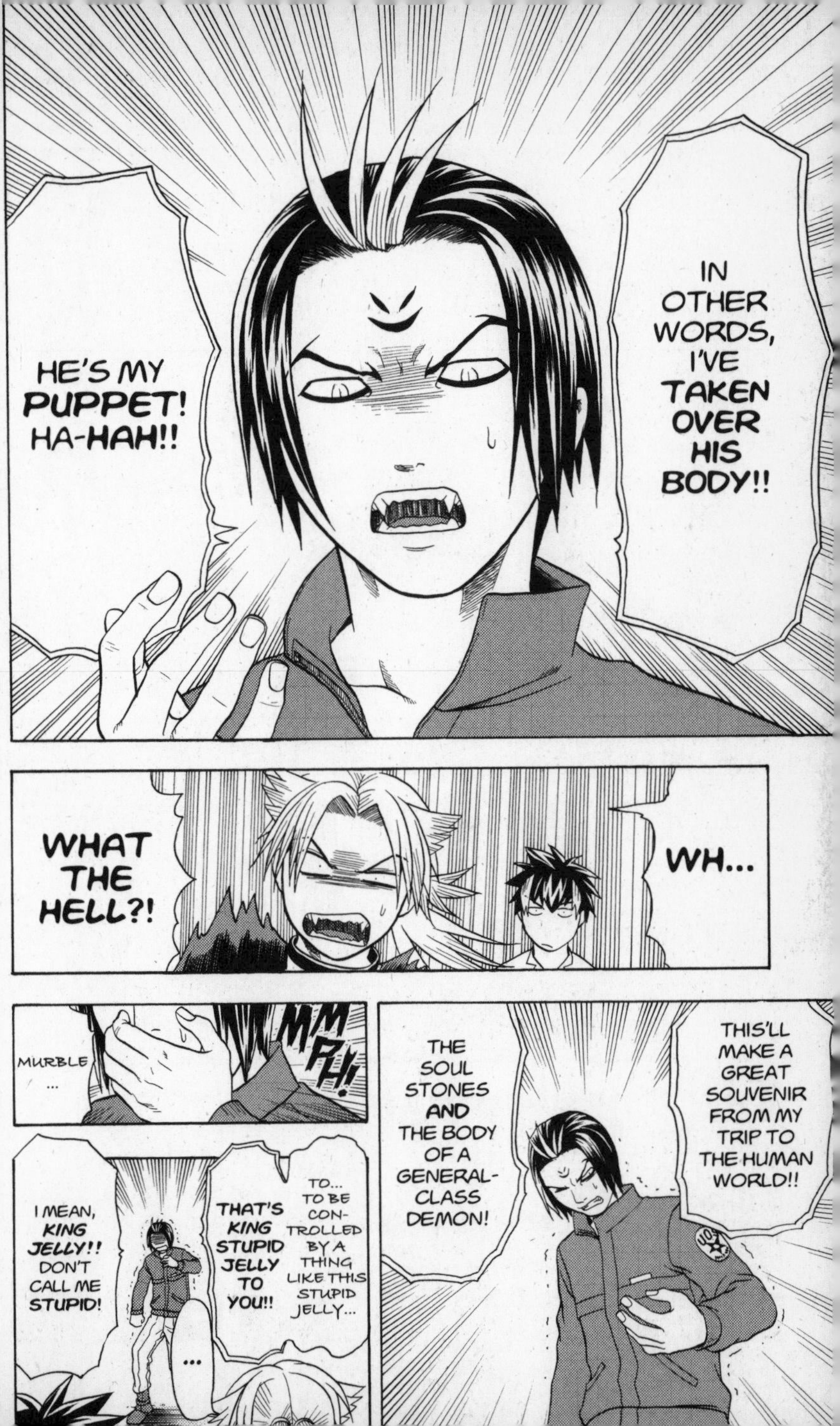
IN OTHER WORDS, I'VE TAKEN OVER HIS BODY!!
HE'S MY PUPPET! HA-HAH!!
WH...
WHAT THE HELL?!
THIS'LL MAKE A GREAT SOUVENIR FROM MY TRIP TO THE HUMAN WORLD!!
THE SOUL STONES AND THE BODY OF A GENERAL-CLASS DEMON!
MMPH!
MURBLE ...
TO... TO BE CON-TROLLED BY A THING LIKE THIS STUPID JELLY...
THAT'S KING STUPID JELLY TO YOU!!
I MEAN, KING JELLY!! DON'T CALL ME STUPID!
...

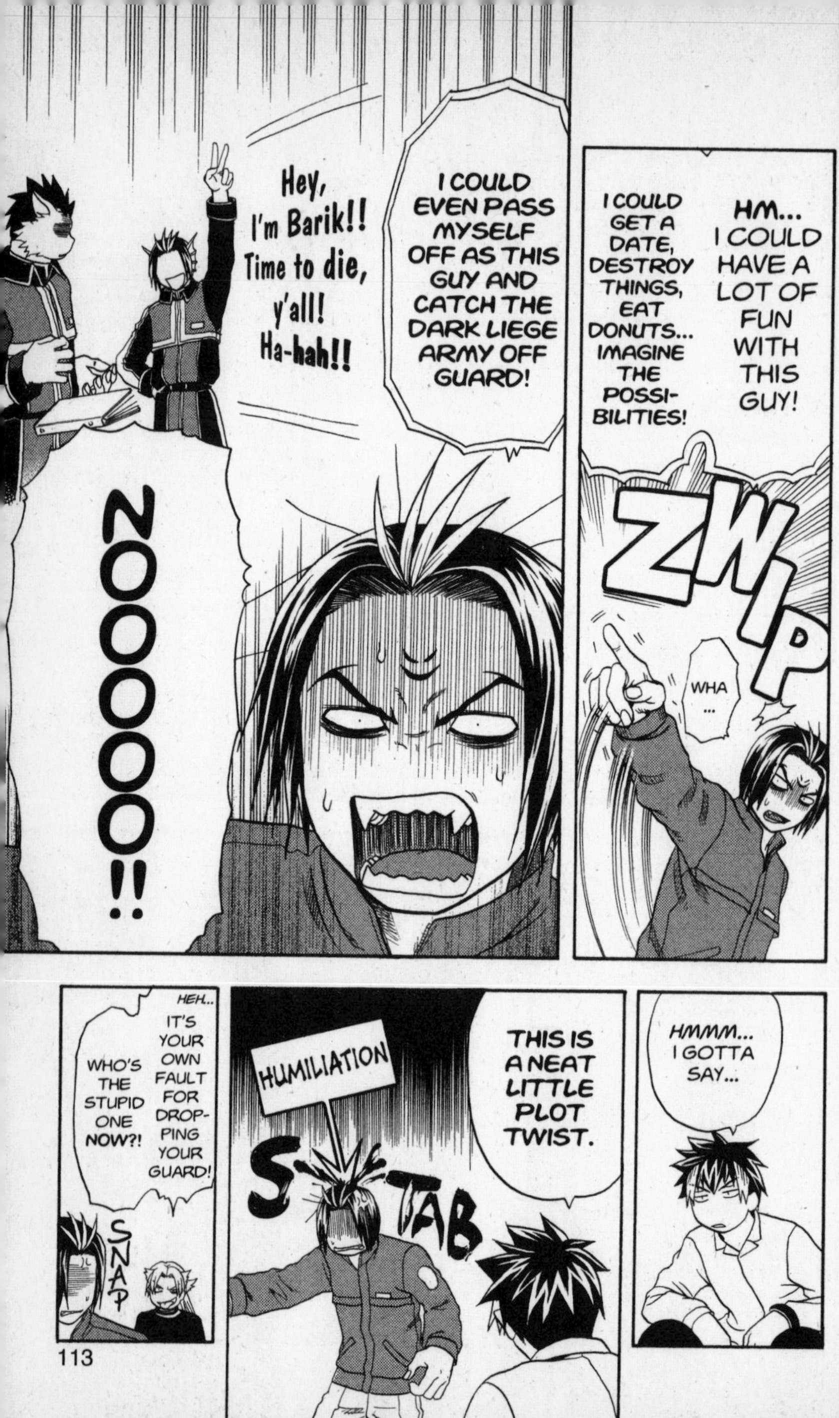
HM... I COULD HAVE A LOT OF FUN WITH THIS GUY!
I COULD GET A DATE, DESTROY THINGS, EAT DONUTS... IMAGINE THE POSSIBILITIES!
ZWIP
WHA...
I COULD EVEN PASS MYSELF OFF AS THIS GUY AND CATCH THE DARK LIEGE ARMY OFF GUARD!
Hey, I'm Barik!! Time to die, y'all! Ha-hah!!
NOOOOO!!
HMMM... I GOTTA SAY...
THIS IS A NEAT LITTLE PLOT TWIST.
HUMILIATION
STAB
HEH... IT'S YOUR OWN FAULT FOR DROPPING YOUR GUARD!
WHO'S THE STUPID ONE NOW?!
SNAP

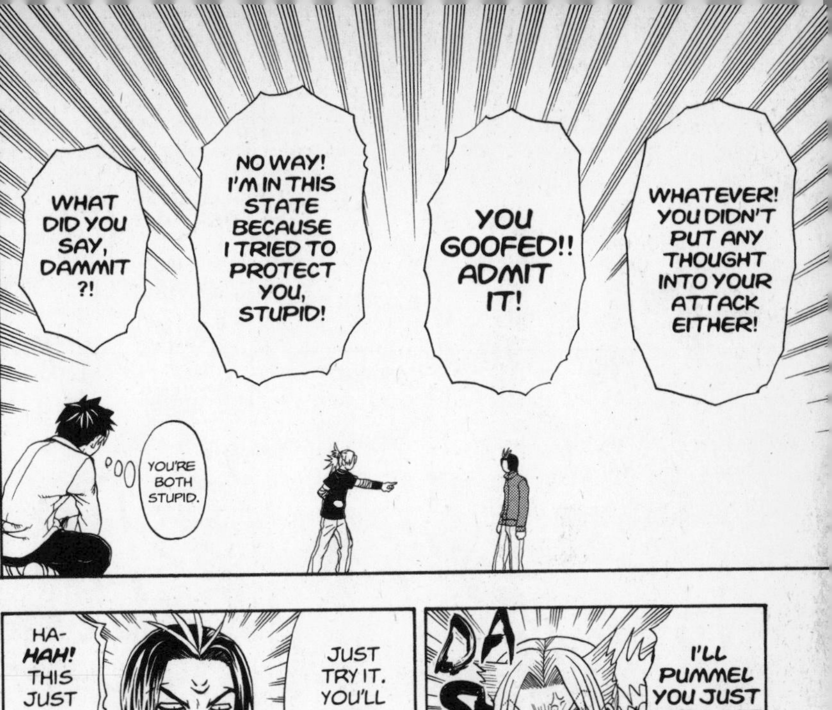

WHATEVER! YOU DIDN'T PUT ANY THOUGHT INTO YOUR ATTACK EITHER!
YOU GOOFED!! ADMIT IT!
NO WAY! I'M IN THIS STATE BECAUSE I TRIED TO PROTECT YOU, STUPID!
WHAT DID YOU SAY, DAMMIT?!
YOU'RE BOTH STUPID.
DASH
I'LL PUMMEL YOU JUST LIKE LAST TIME!!
JUST TRY IT. YOU'LL NEVER BEAT ME.
HA-HAH! THIS JUST GOT INTERESTING!!
ALL RIGHT, JELLY! PREPARE TO BE SQUISHED!!
POW
TOLD YOU YOU COULDN'T BEAT ME—
AQUA MAGIA: SNAKE MINIONS' CONSECUTIVE FANGS!!
HUH?

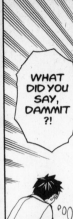

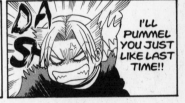

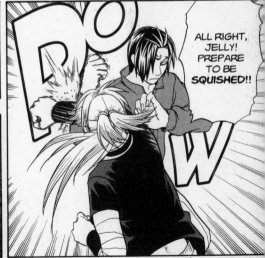

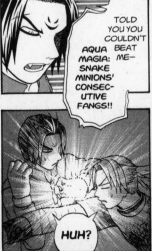

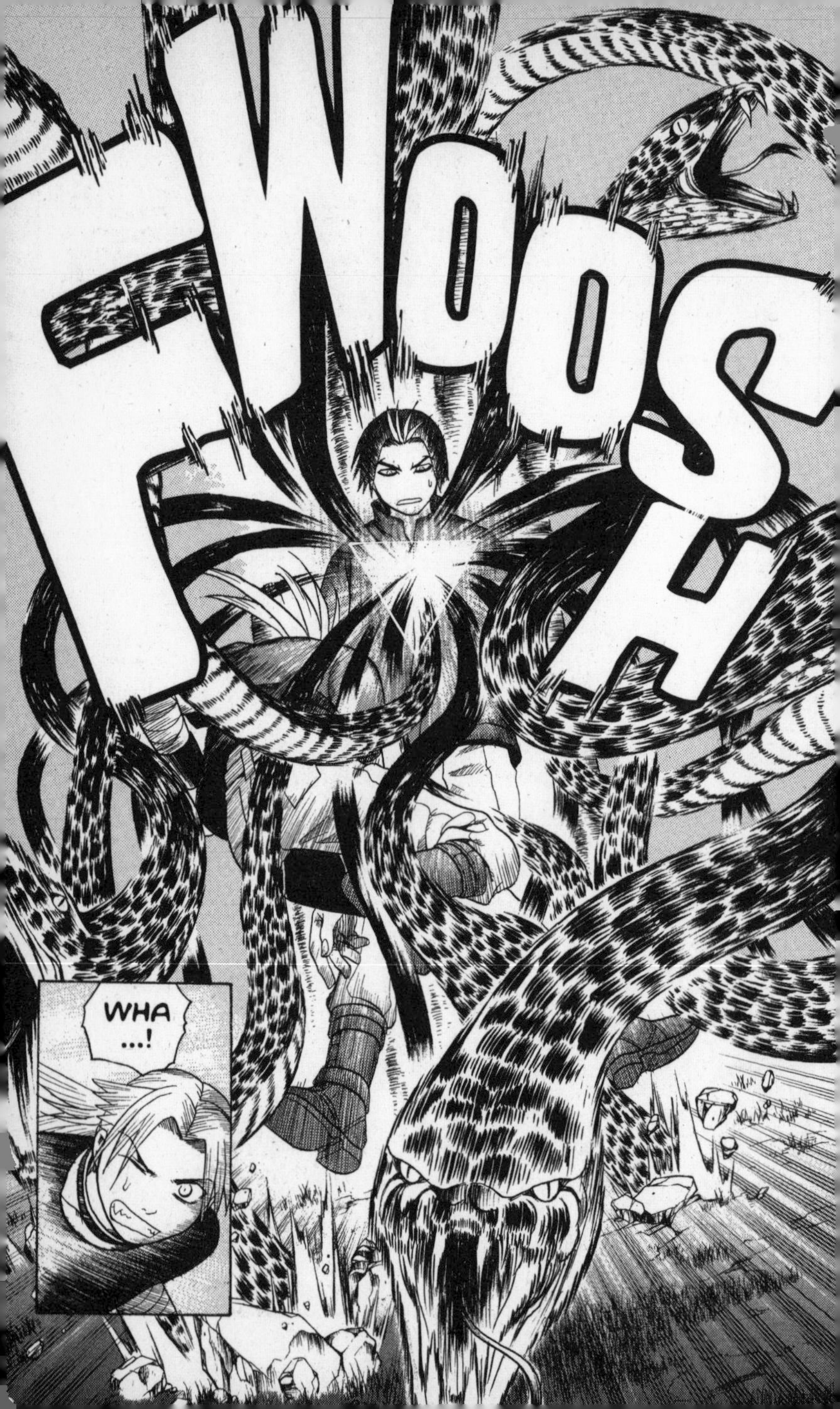
WHOOSH
WHA ...!

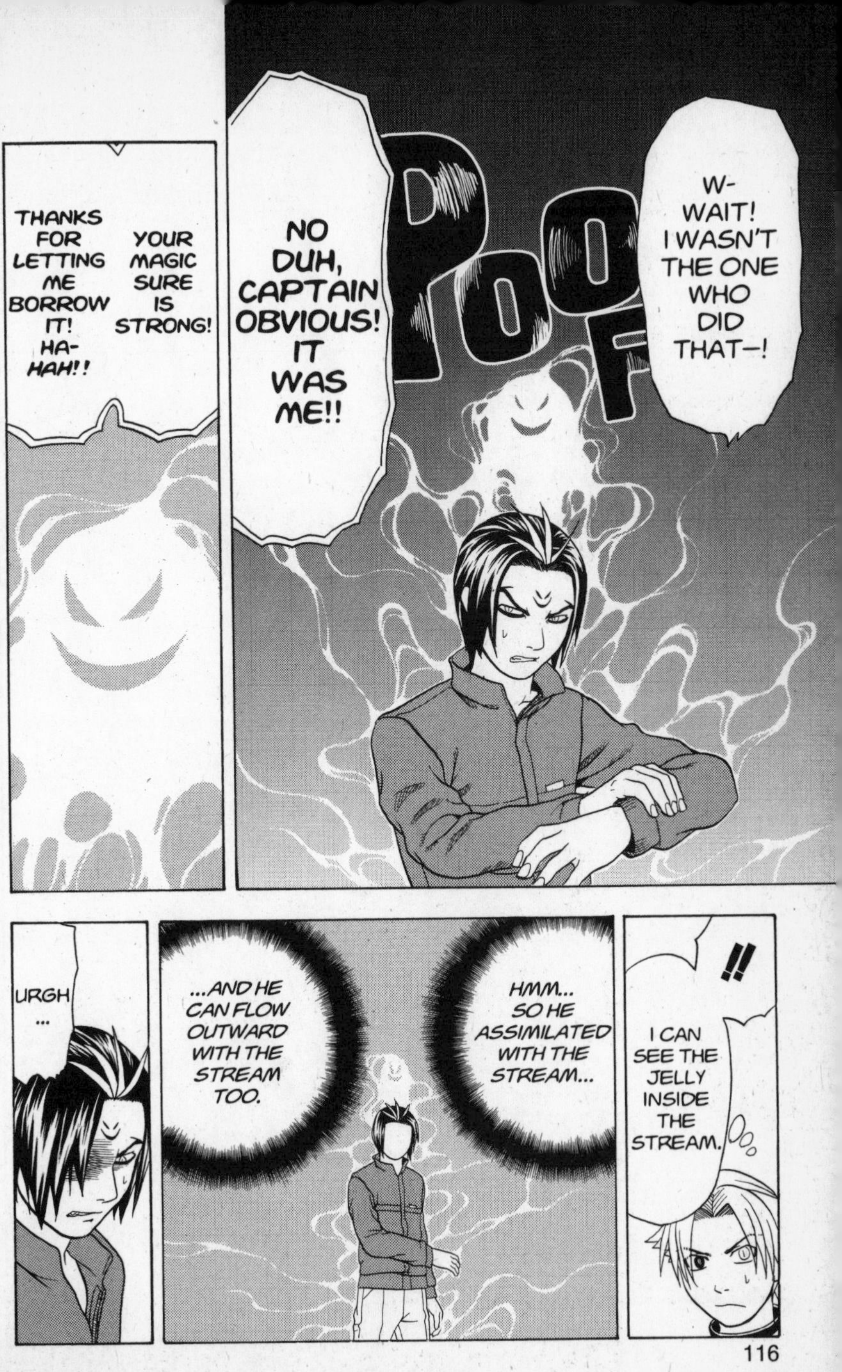

W- WAIT! I WASN'T THE ONE WHO DID THAT—!
POOF
NO DUH, CAPTAIN OBVIOUS! IT WAS ME!!
YOUR MAGIC SURE IS STRONG!
THANKS FOR LETTING ME BORROW IT! HA-HAH!!
!!
I CAN SEE THE JELLY INSIDE THE STREAM.
HMM... SO HE ASSIMILATED WITH THE STREAM...
...AND HE CAN FLOW OUTWARD WITH THE STREAM TOO.
URGH ...

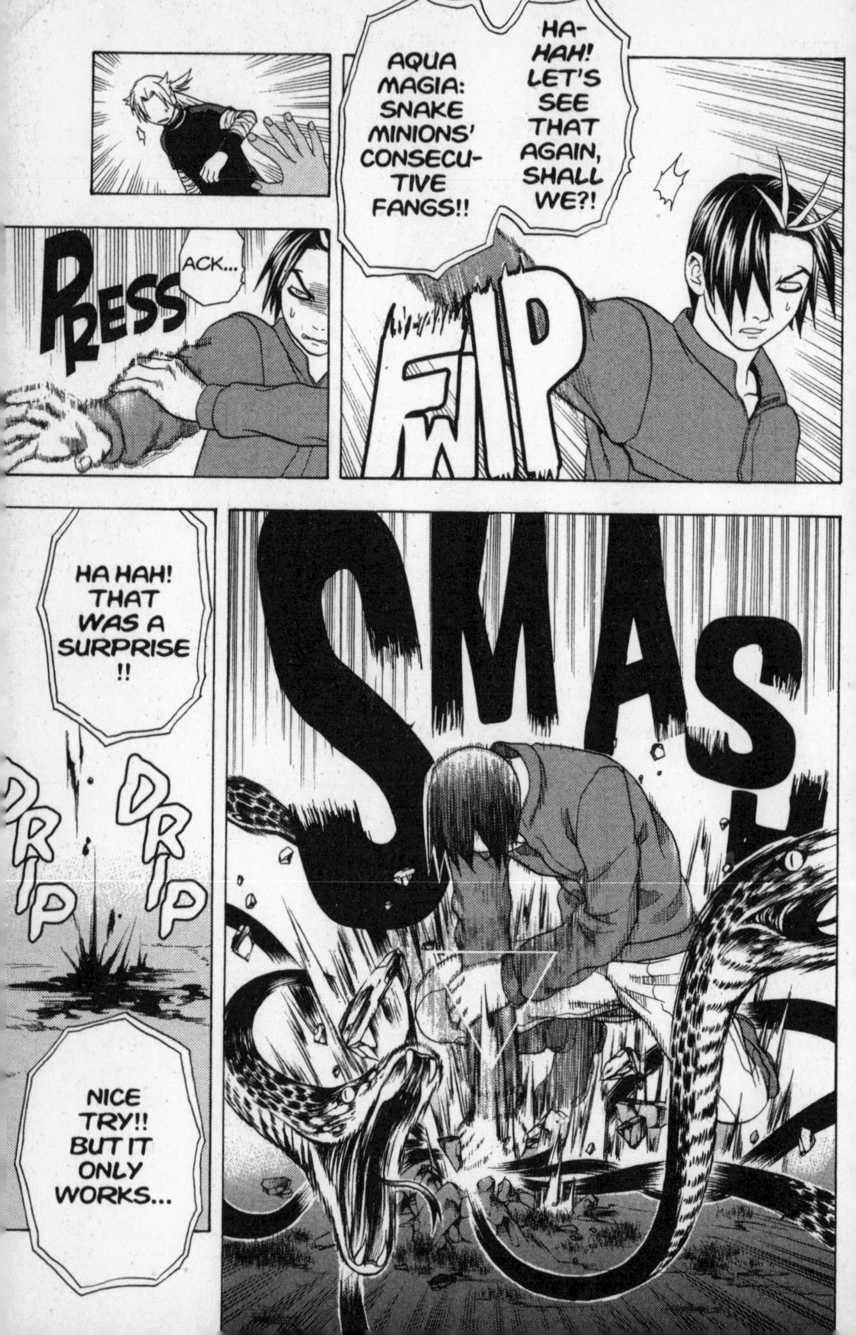
HA-HAH! LET'S SEE THAT AGAIN, SHALL WE?!
AQUA MAGIA: SNAKE MINIONS' CONSECU-TIVE FANGS!!
FWIP
PRESS
ACK...
SMASH
HA HAH! THAT WAS A SURPRISE!!
DRIP
DRIP
NICE TRY!! BUT IT ONLY WORKS...

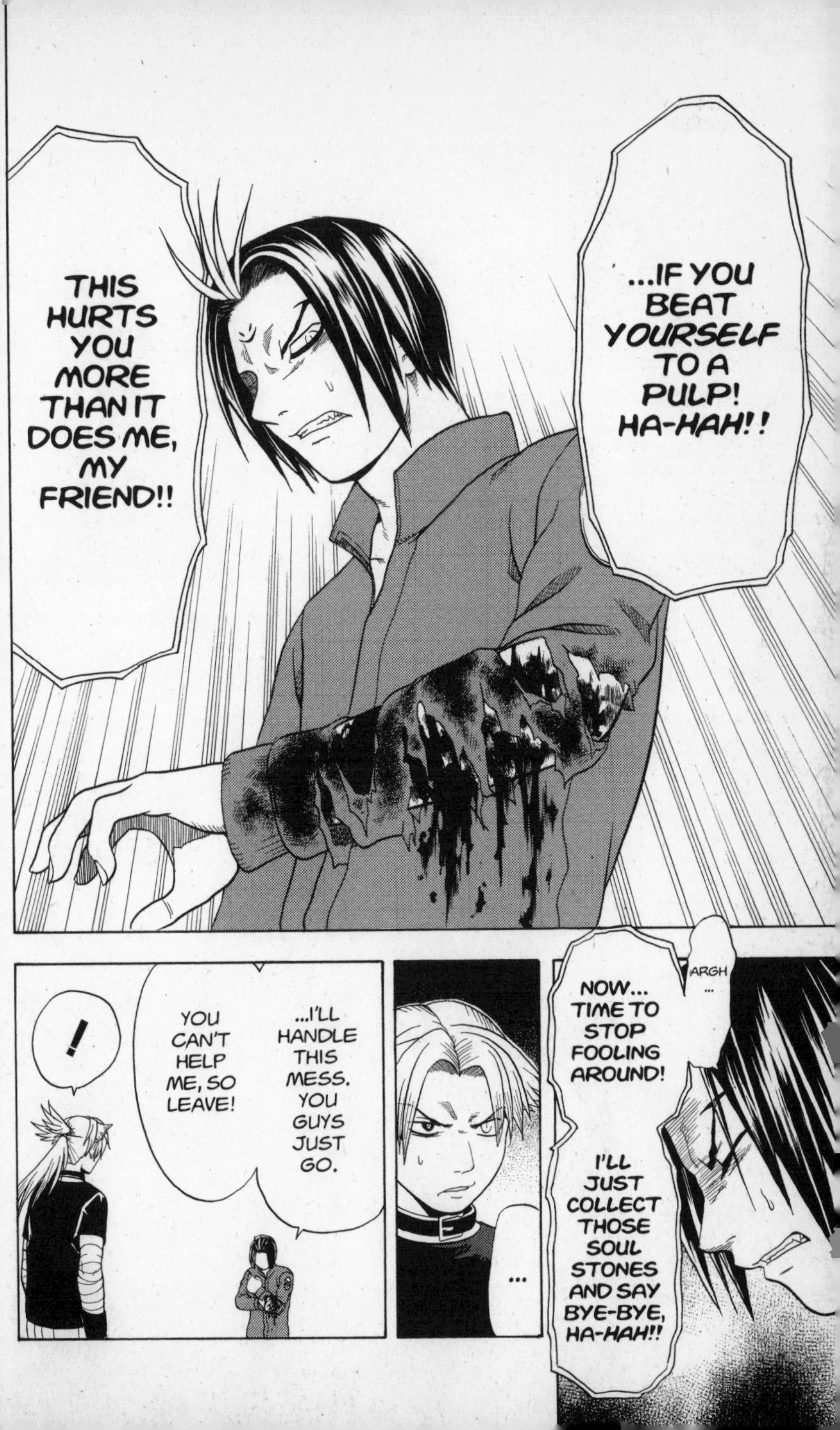
THIS HURTS YOU MORE THAN IT DOES ME, MY FRIEND!!
...IF YOU BEAT YOURSELF TO A PULP! HA-HAH!!
ARGH ...
NOW... TIME TO STOP FOOLING AROUND!
I'LL JUST COLLECT THOSE SOUL STONES AND SAY BYE-BYE, HA-HAH!!
...
...I'LL HANDLE THIS MESS. YOU GUYS JUST GO.
YOU CAN'T HELP ME, SO LEAVE!
!

READ THIS WAY

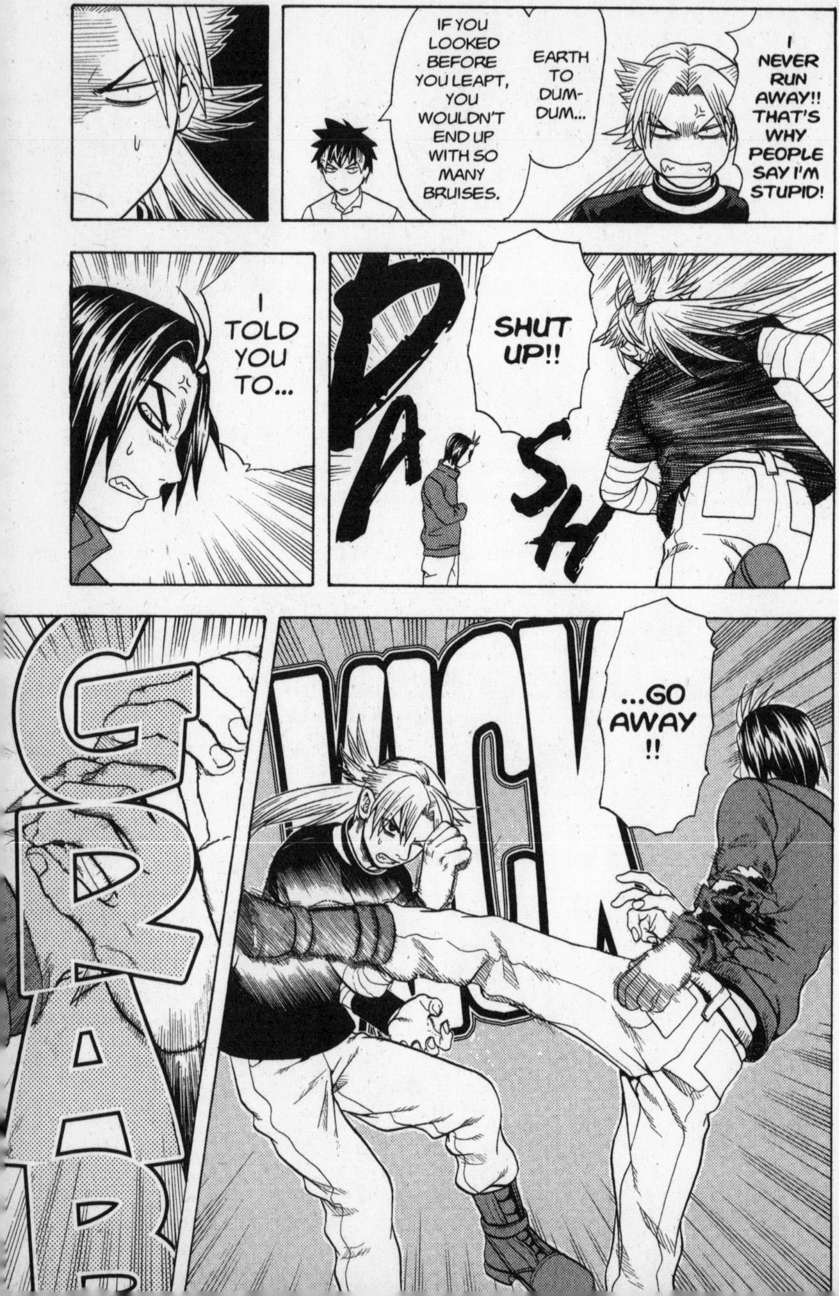
I NEVER RUN AWAY!! THAT'S WHY PEOPLE SAY I'M STUPID!
EARTH TO DUM-DUM...
IF YOU LOOKED BEFORE YOU LEAPT, YOU WOULDN'T END UP WITH SO MANY BRUISES.
SHUT UP!!
DASH
I TOLD YOU TO...
...GO AWAY!!

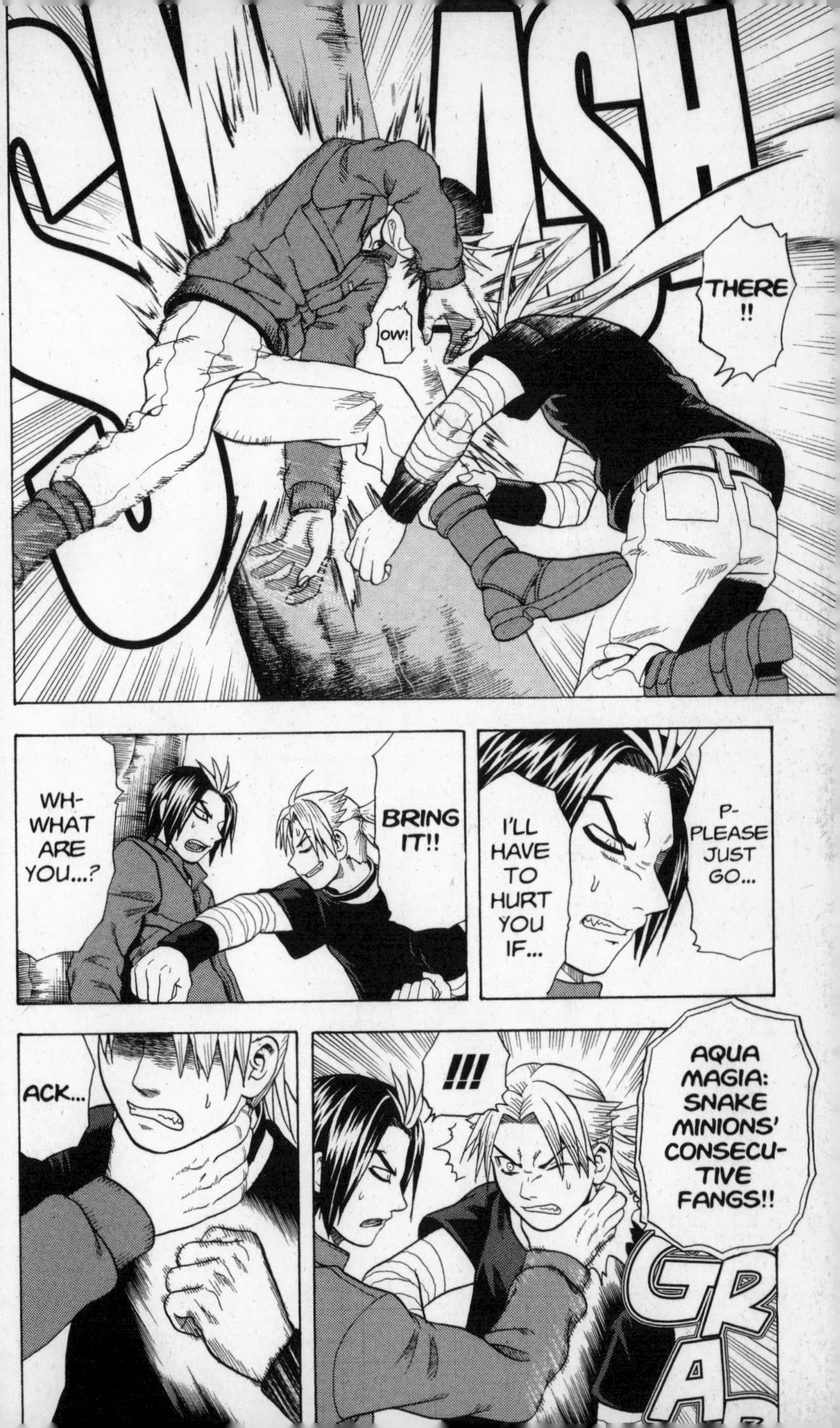
SMASH
THERE!!
OW!
P-PLEASE JUST GO...
I'LL HAVE TO HURT YOU IF...
BRING IT!!
WH-WHAT ARE YOU...?
AQUA MAGIA: SNAKE MINIONS' CONSECU-TIVE FANGS!!
!!!
GRA
ACK...

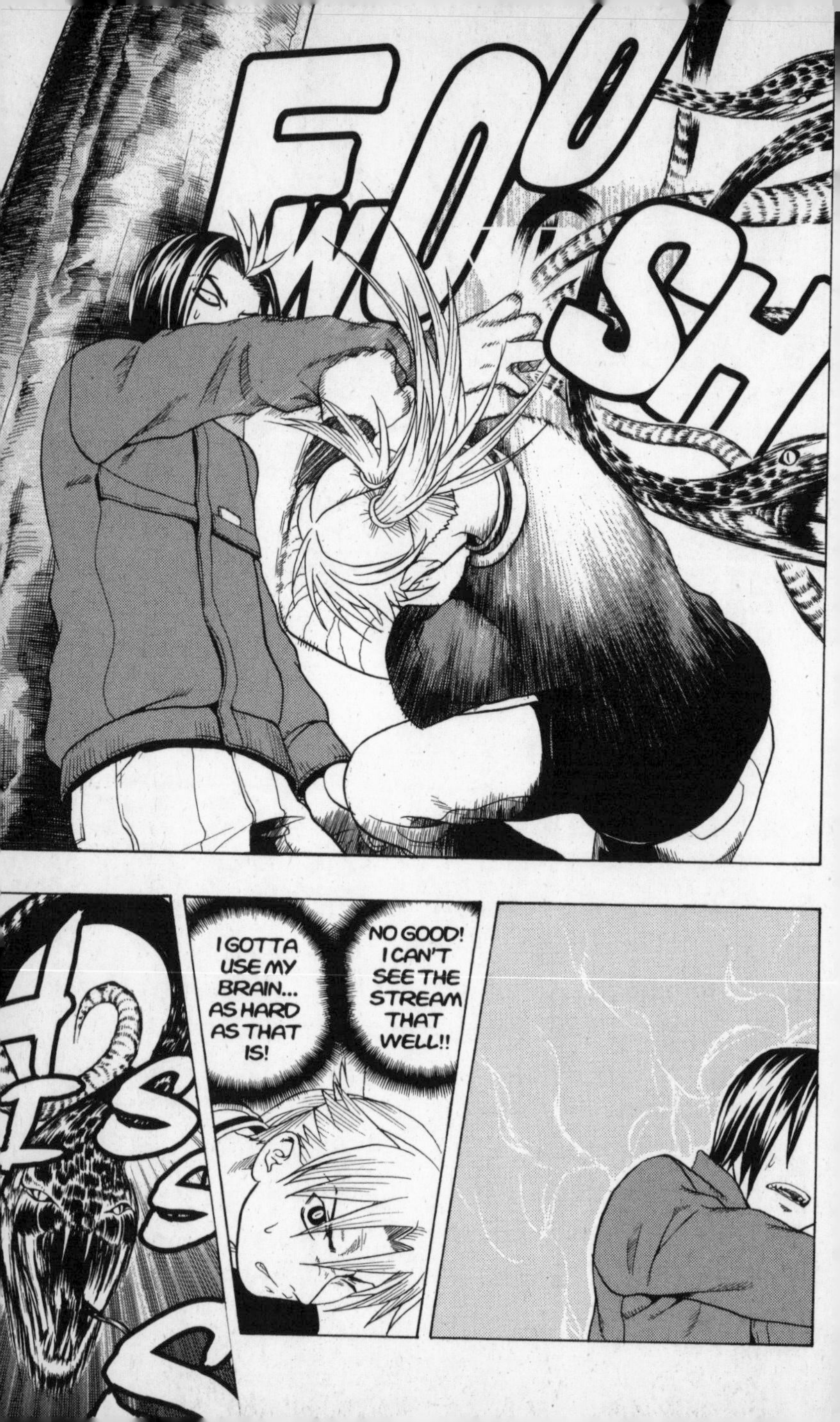
NO GOOD! I CAN'T SEE THE STREAM THAT WELL!!
I GOTTA USE MY BRAIN... AS HARD AS THAT IS!

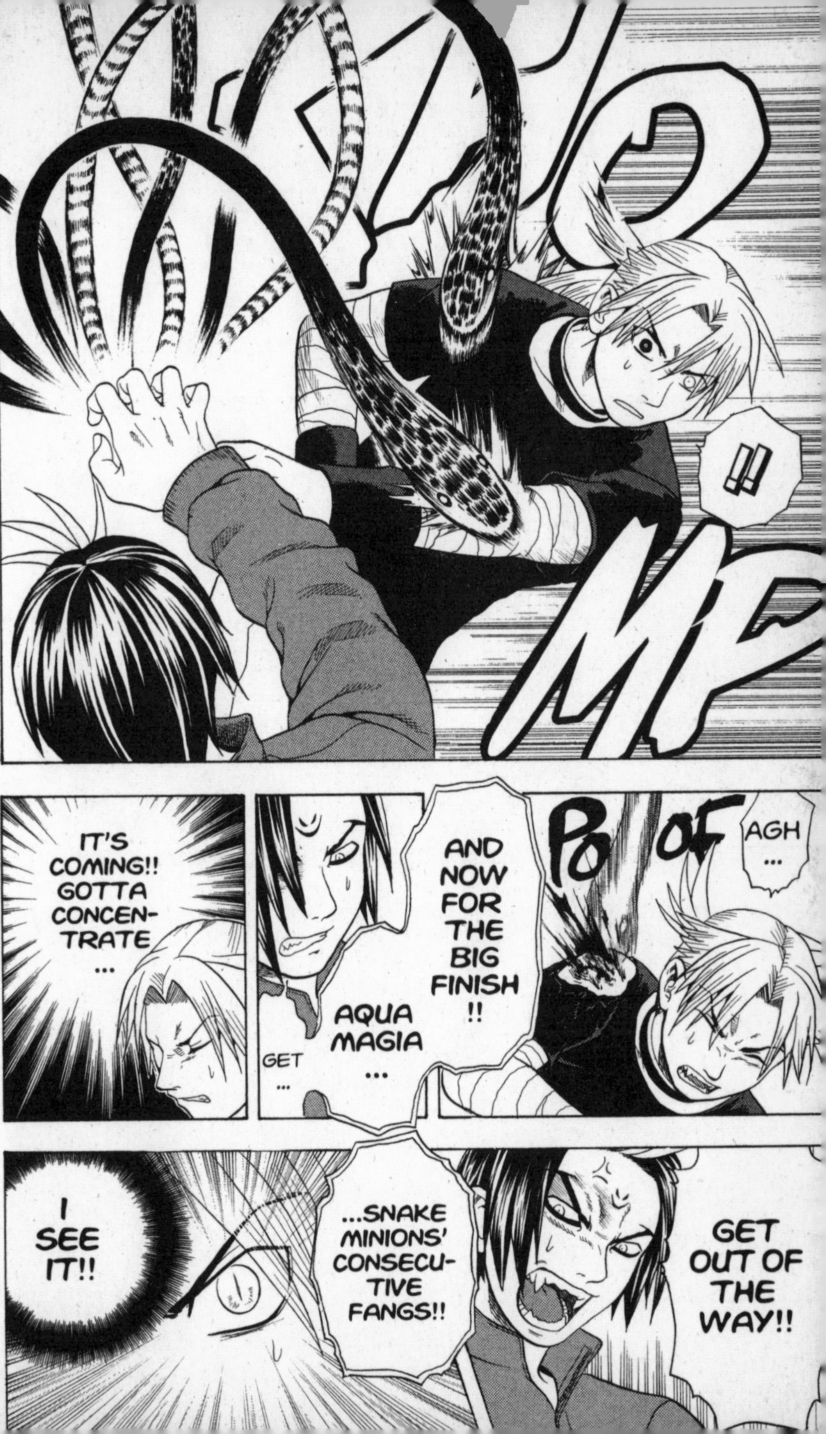
!!
POOF
AGH ...
AND NOW FOR THE BIG FINISH !!
AQUA MAGIA ...
GET ...
IT'S COMING!! GOTTA CONCENTRATE ...
GET OUT OF THE WAY!!
...SNAKE MINIONS' CONSECUTIVE FANGS!!
I SEE IT!!

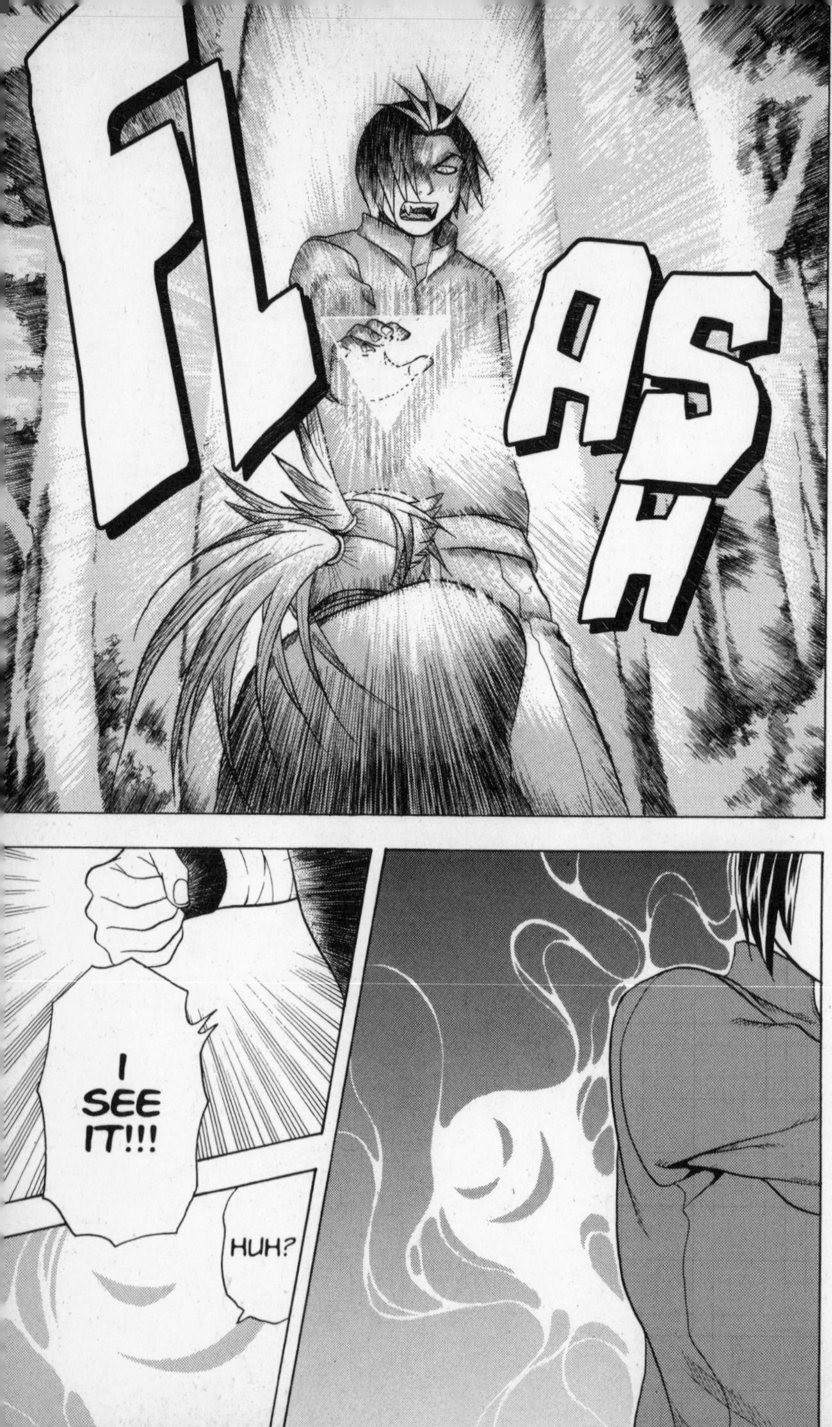
FLASH
I SEE IT!!!
HUH?

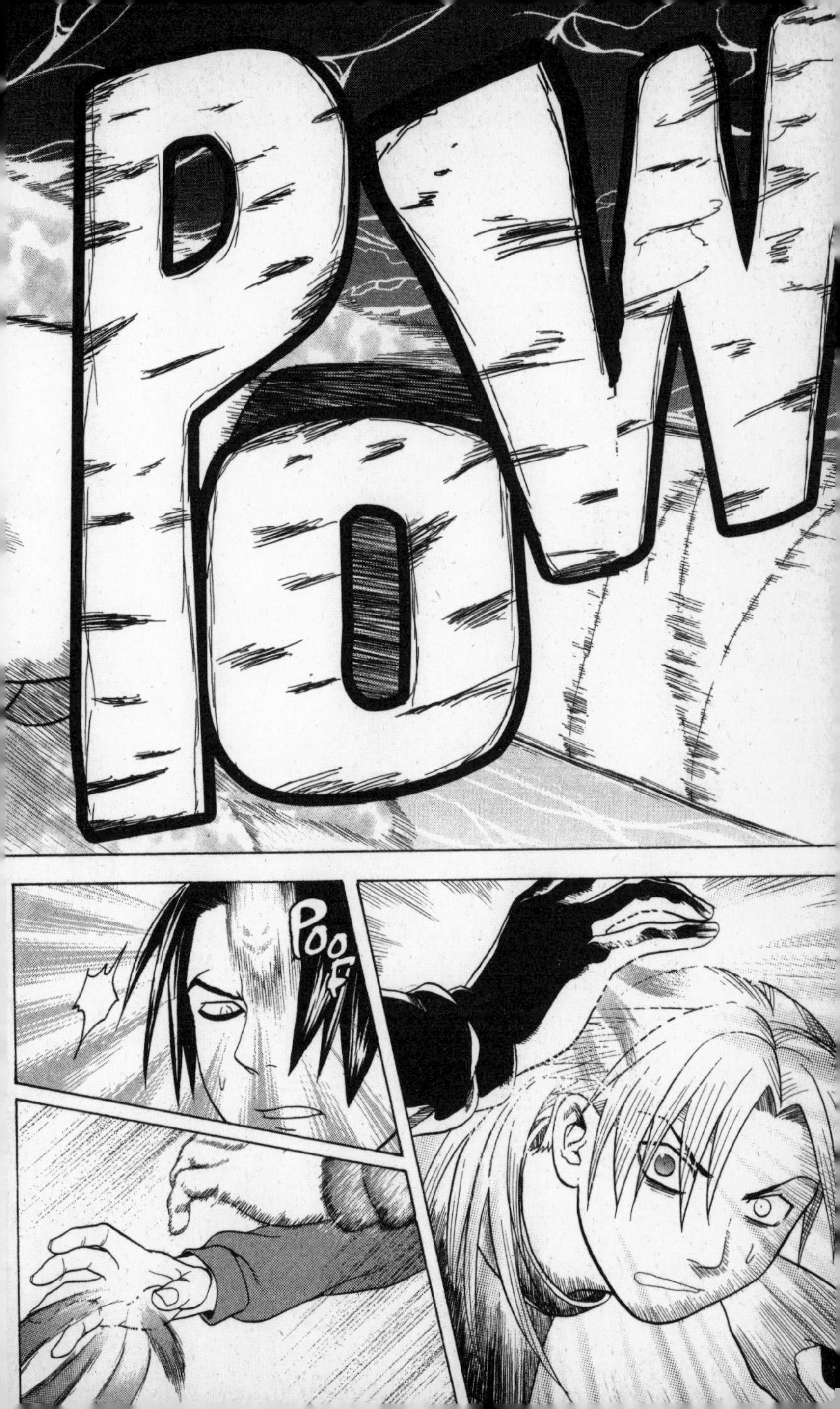
POW
POOF

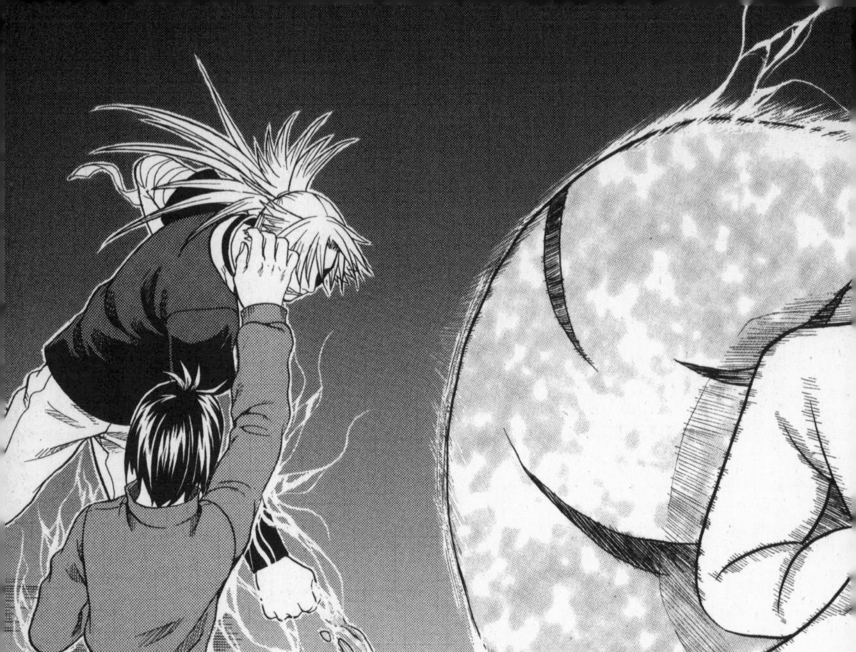

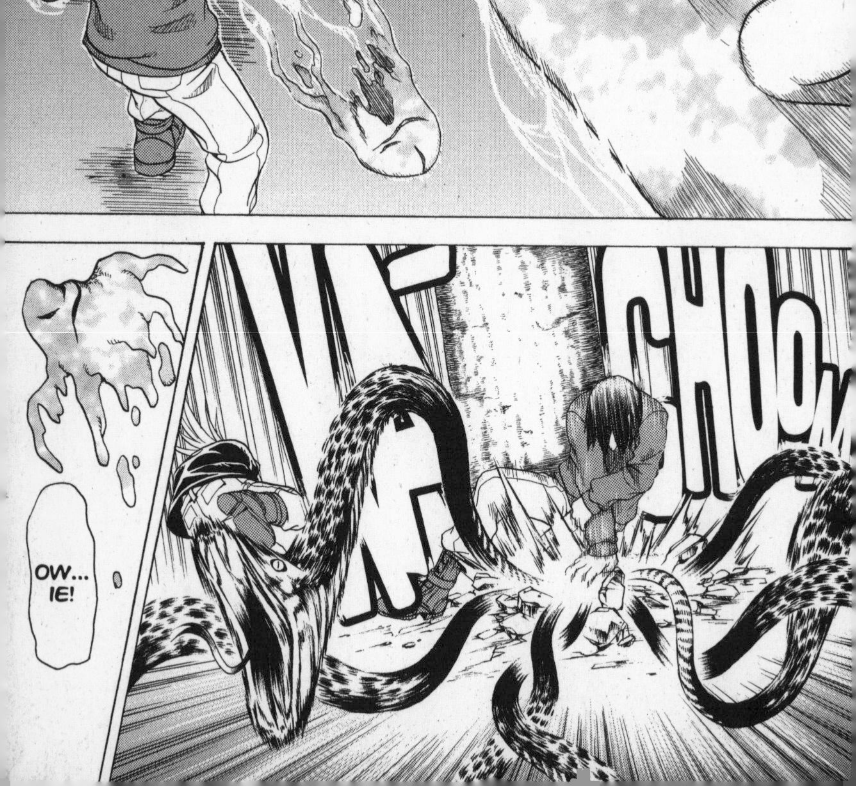
CHOM
OW... IE!

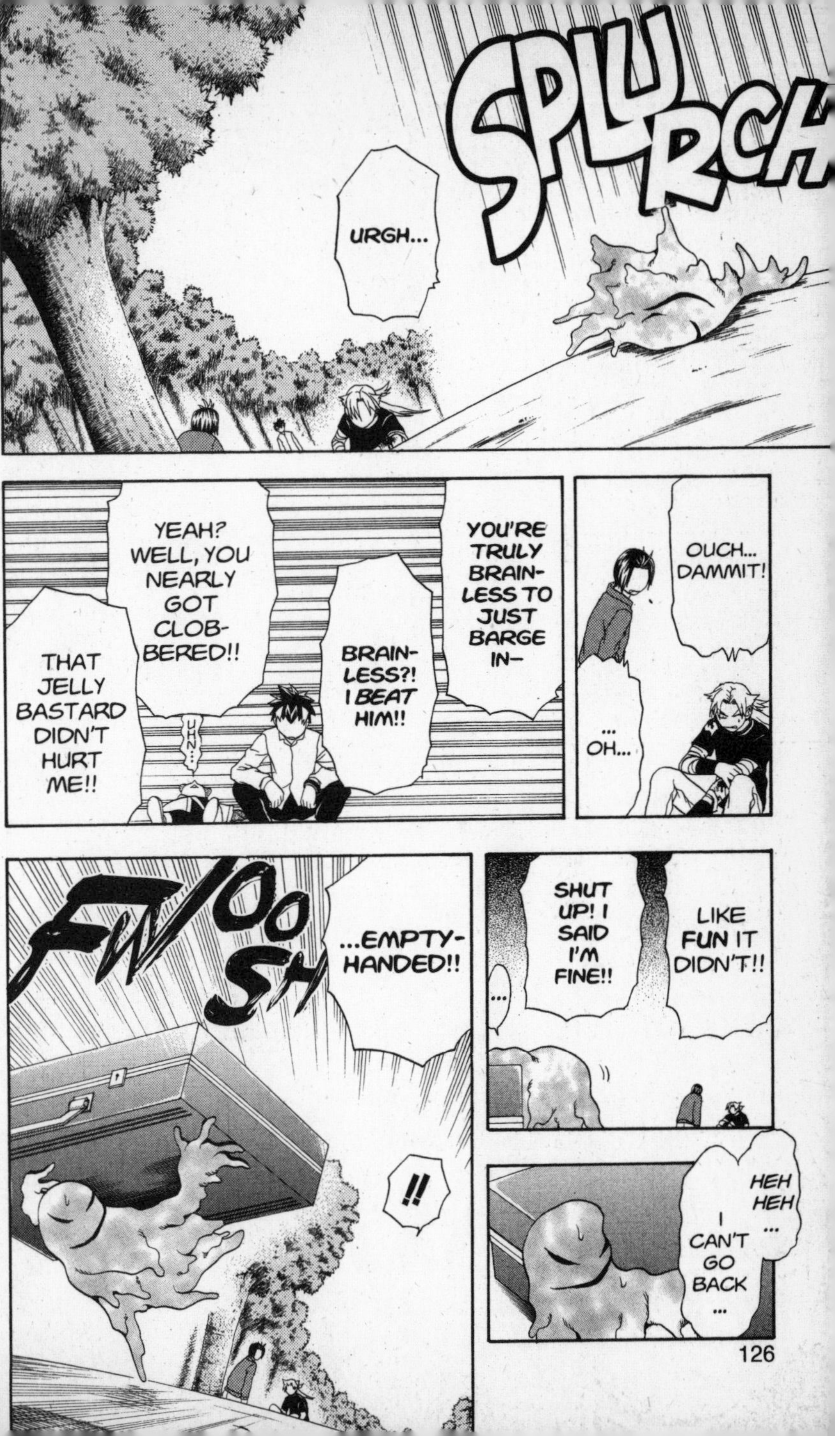
SPLURCH
URGH...
OUCH... DAMMIT!
... OH...
YOU'RE TRULY BRAIN-LESS TO JUST BARGE IN–
BRAIN-LESS?! I BEAT HIM!!
YEAH? WELL, YOU NEARLY GOT CLOB-BERED!!
UHN...
THAT JELLY BASTARD DIDN'T HURT ME!!
LIKE FUN IT DIDN'T!!
SHUT UP! I SAID I'M FINE!!
...
HEH HEH...
I CAN'T GO BACK...
...EMPTY-HANDED!!
!!
FWOOSH

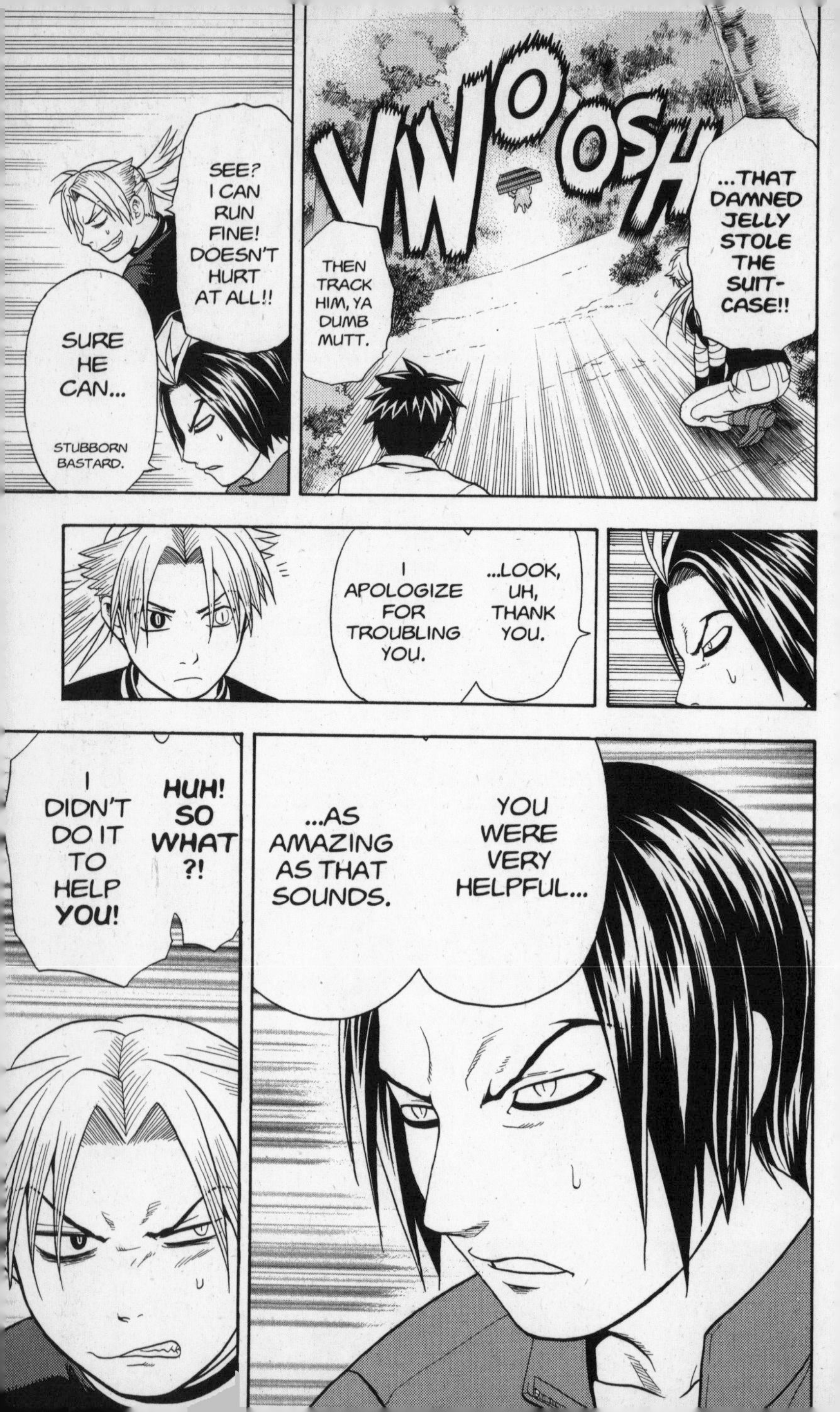
...THAT DAMNED JELLY STOLE THE SUIT-CASE!!
VWOOSH
THEN TRACK HIM, YA DUMB MUTT.
SEE? I CAN RUN FINE! DOESN'T HURT AT ALL!!
SURE HE CAN...
STUBBORN BASTARD.
...LOOK, UH, THANK YOU.
I APOLOGIZE FOR TROUBLING YOU.
YOU WERE VERY HELPFUL...
...AS AMAZING AS THAT SOUNDS.
HUH! SO WHAT?!
I DIDN'T DO IT TO HELP YOU!

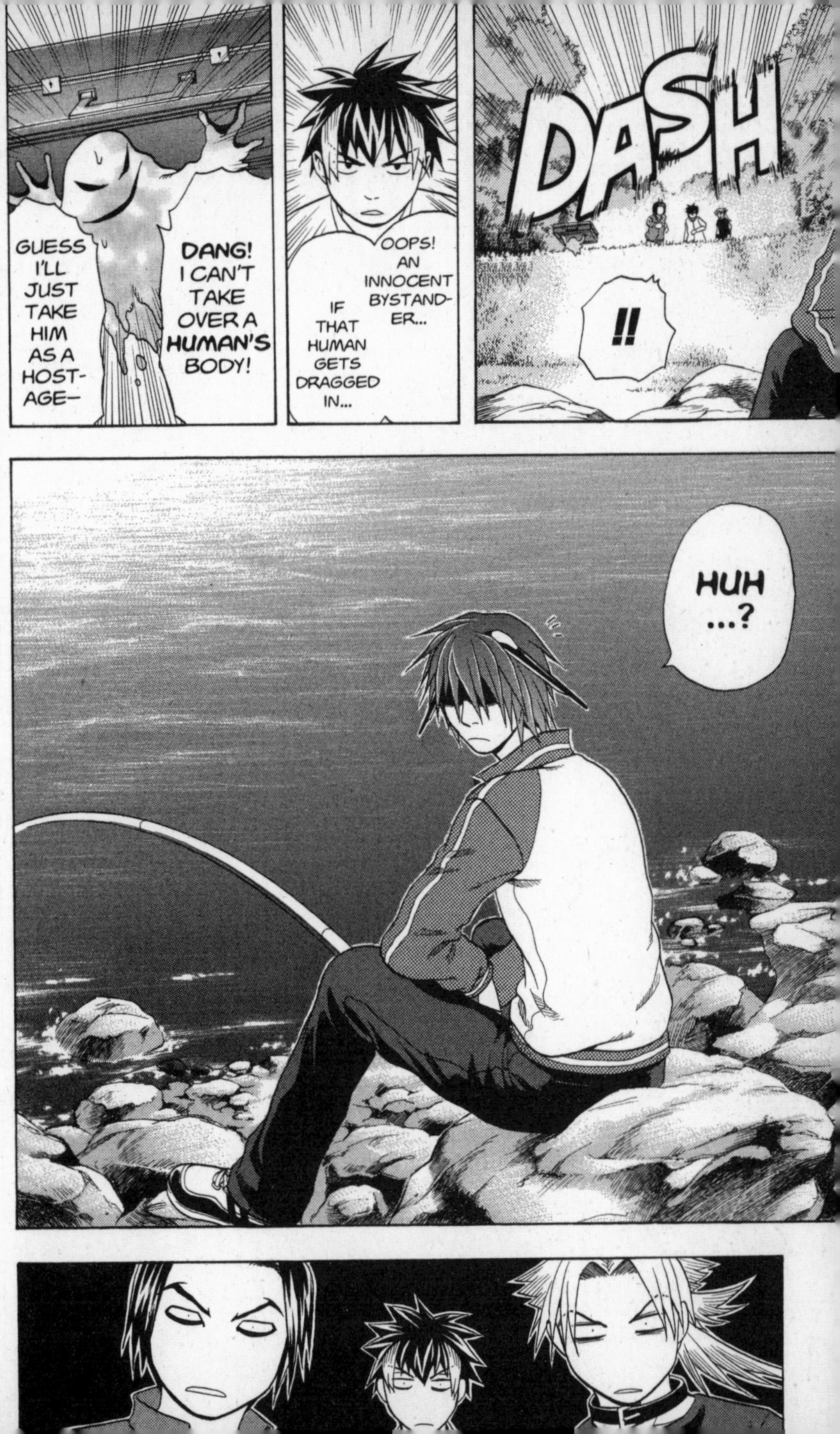
DASH
!!
OOPS! AN INNOCENT BYSTANDER...
IF THAT HUMAN GETS DRAGGED IN...
DANG! I CAN'T TAKE OVER A HUMAN'S BODY!
GUESS I'LL JUST TAKE HIM AS A HOSTAGE—
HUH ...?

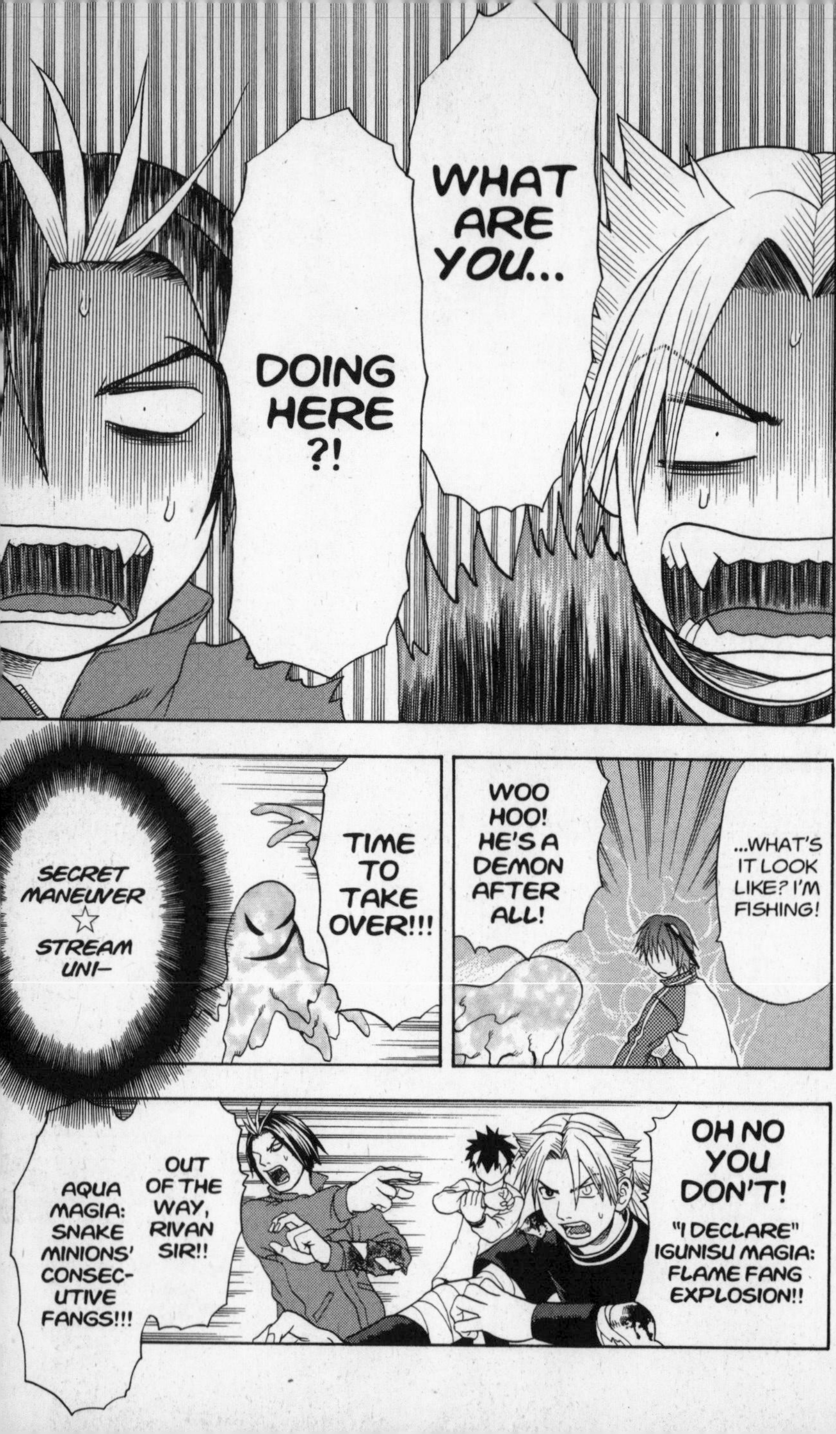
WHAT ARE YOU...
DOING HERE ?!
...WHAT'S IT LOOK LIKE? I'M FISHING!
WOO HOO! HE'S A DEMON AFTER ALL!
TIME TO TAKE OVER!!!
SECRET MANEUVER ☆ STREAM UNI–
OH NO YOU DON'T!
"I DECLARE" IGUNISU MAGIA: FLAME FANG EXPLOSION!!
OUT OF THE WAY, RIVAN SIR!!
AQUA MAGIA: SNAKE MINIONS' CONSEC-UTIVE FANGS!!!

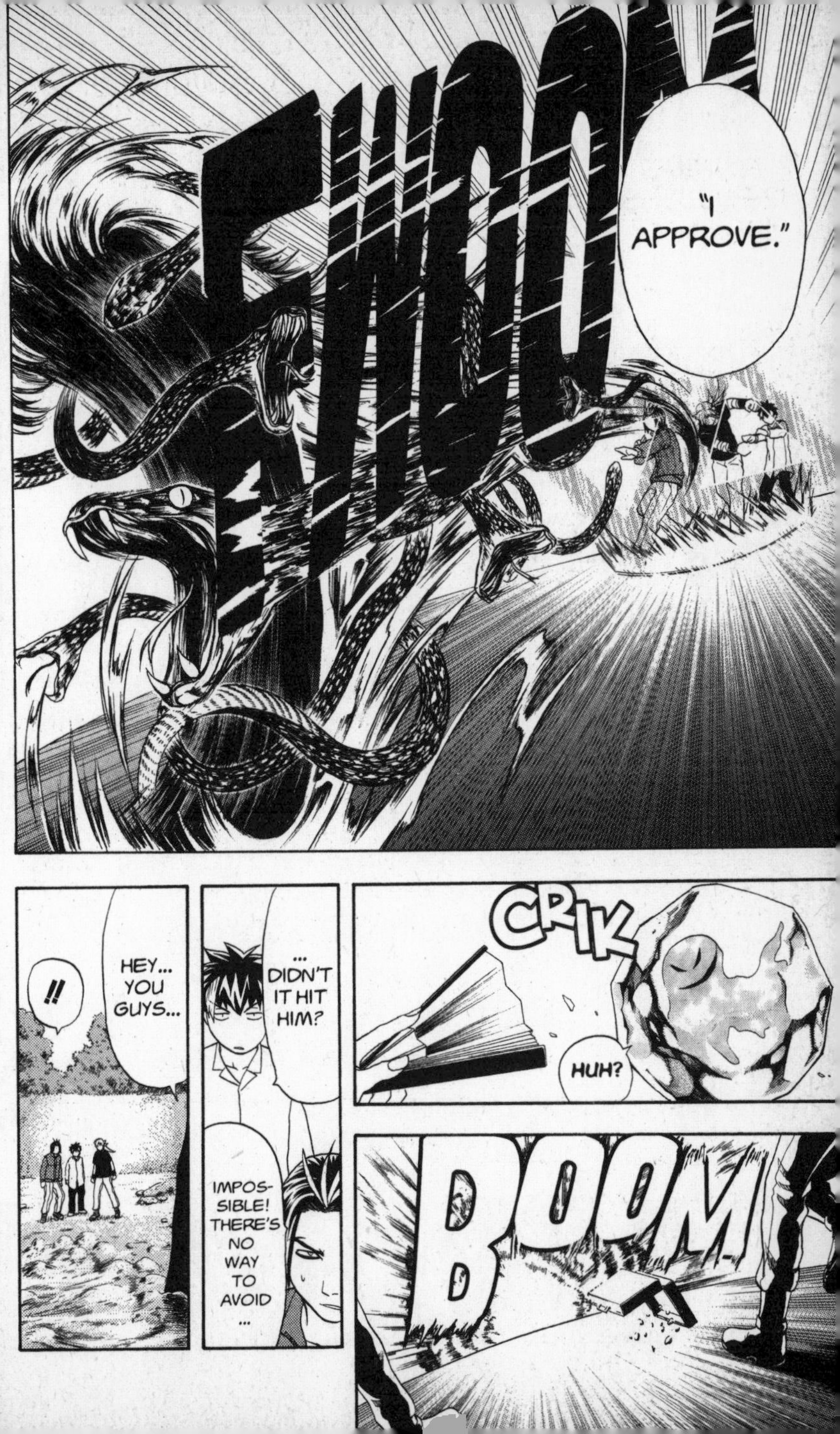
"I APPROVE."
CRIK
HUH?
BOOM
... DIDN'T IT HIT HIM?
IMPOS-SIBLE! THERE'S NO WAY TO AVOID ...
HEY... YOU GUYS...
!!

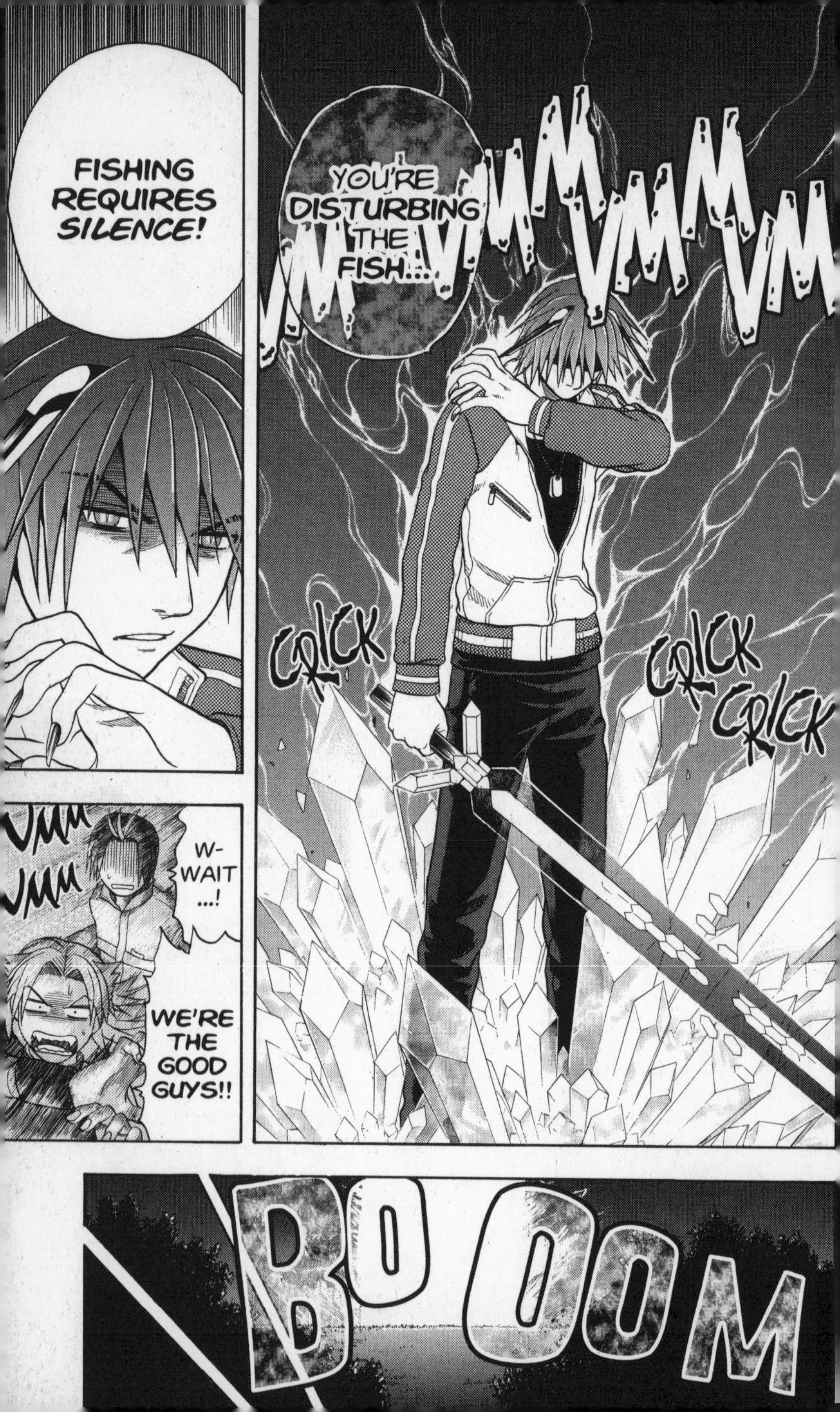
YOU'RE DISTURBING THE FISH...
CRICK
CRICK CRICK
FISHING REQUIRES SILENCE!
VMM VMM
W-WAIT ...!
WE'RE THE GOOD GUYS!!
BOOOM

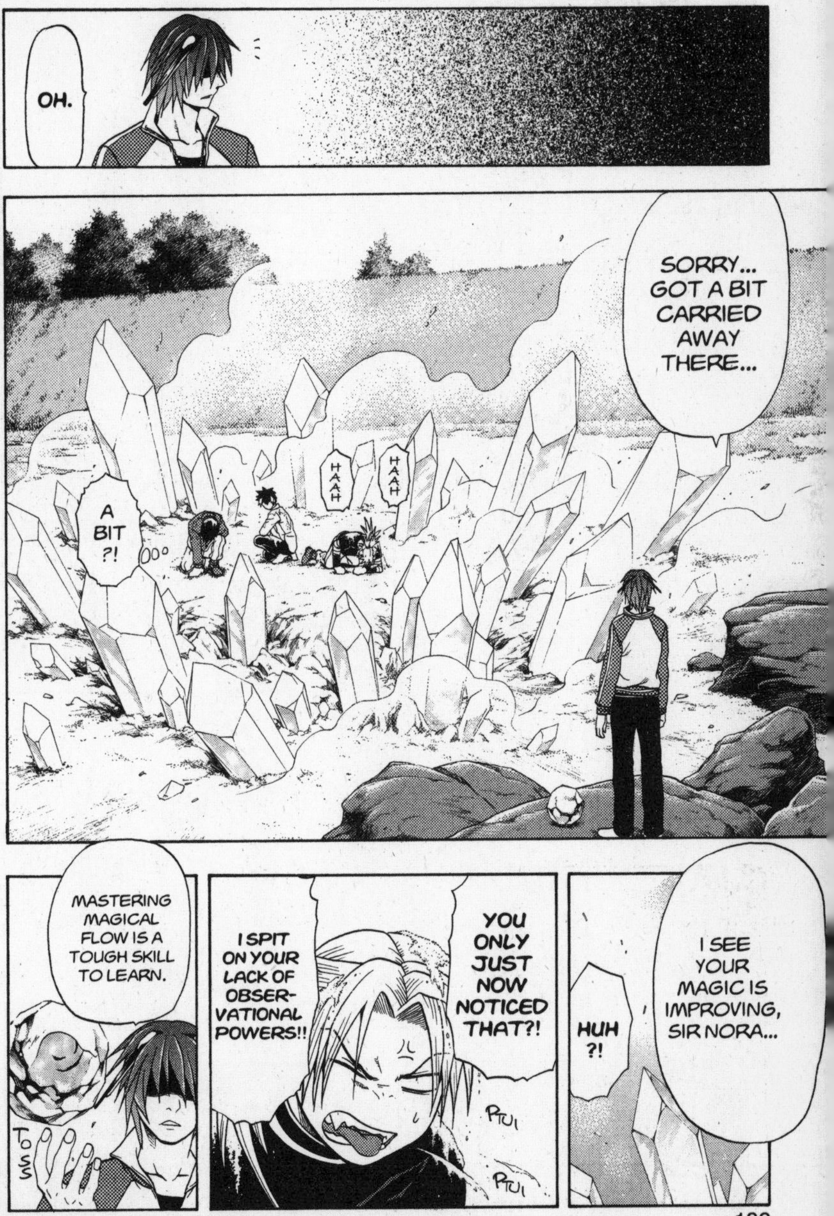
OH.
SORRY... GOT A BIT CARRIED AWAY THERE...
HAAH
HAAH
A BIT ?!
I SEE YOUR MAGIC IS IMPROVING, SIR NORA...
HUH ?!
YOU ONLY JUST NOW NOTICED THAT?!
I SPIT ON YOUR LACK OF OBSER-VATIONAL POWERS!!
PTUI
PTUI
MASTERING MAGICAL FLOW IS A TOUGH SKILL TO LEARN.
TOSS

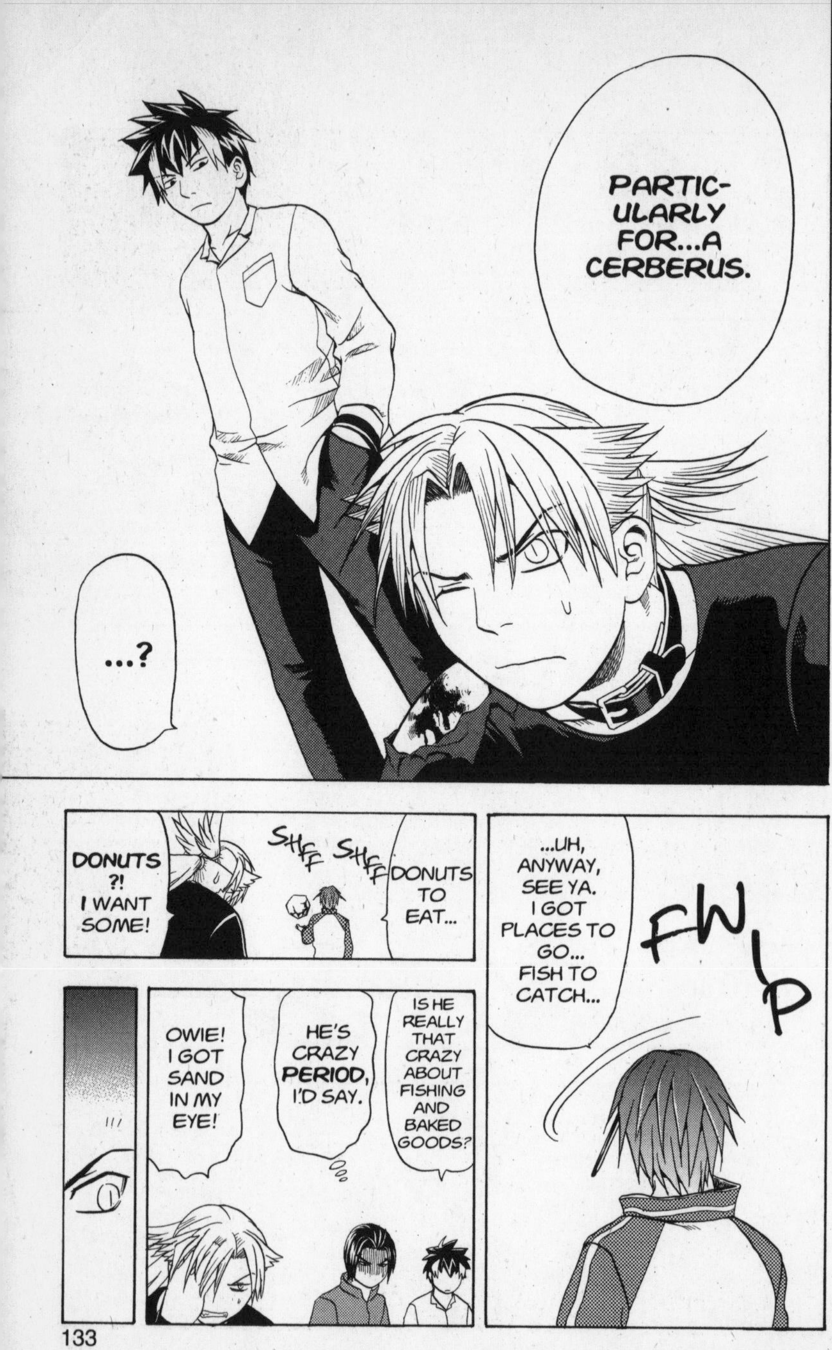
PARTICULARLY FOR...A CERBERUS.
...?
...UH, ANYWAY, SEE YA. I GOT PLACES TO GO... FISH TO CATCH...
FWIP
SHFF SHFF
DONUTS TO EAT...
DONUTS?! I WANT SOME!
IS HE REALLY THAT CRAZY ABOUT FISHING AND BAKED GOODS?
HE'S CRAZY **PERIOD**, I'D SAY.
OWIE! I GOT SAND IN MY EYE!

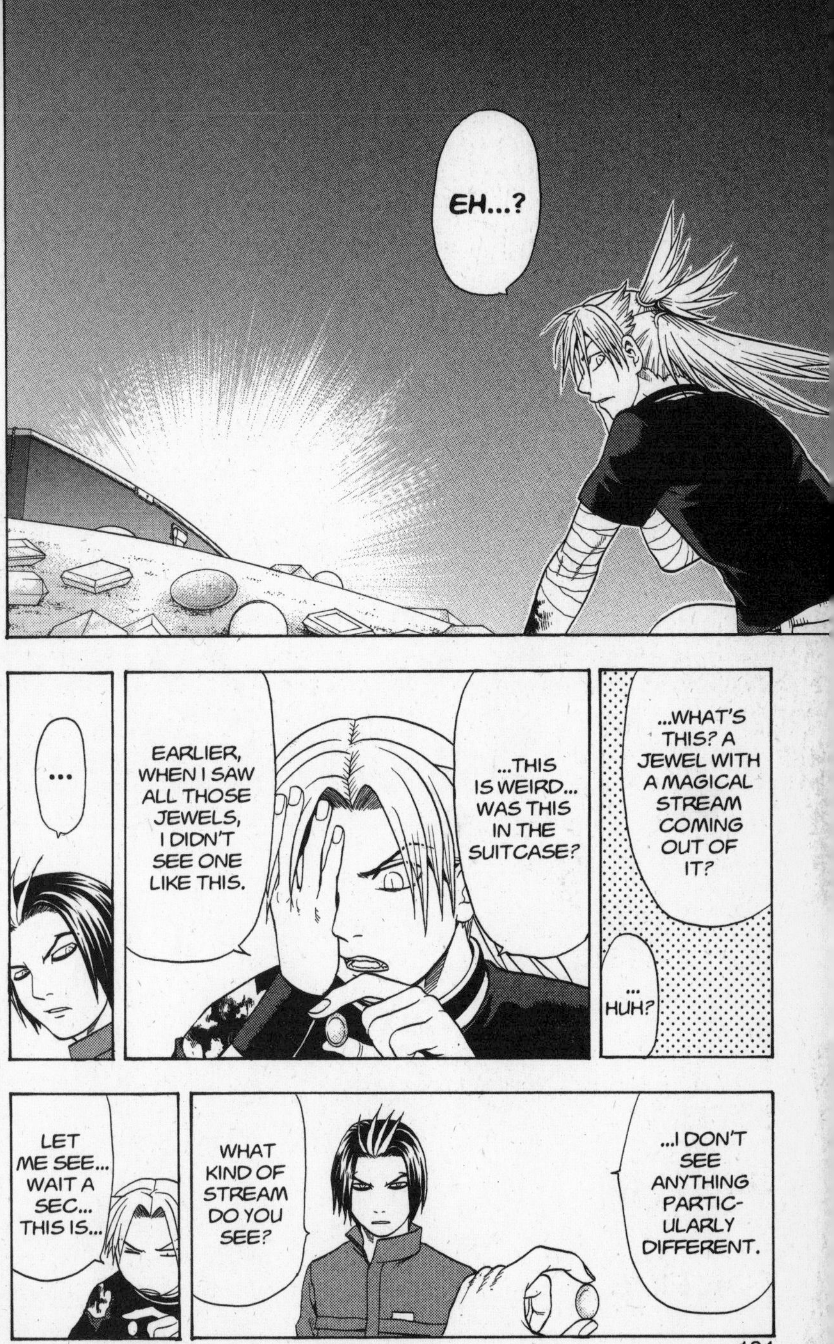
EH...?
...WHAT'S THIS? A JEWEL WITH A MAGICAL STREAM COMING OUT OF IT?
... HUH?
...THIS IS WEIRD... WAS THIS IN THE SUITCASE?
EARLIER, WHEN I SAW ALL THOSE JEWELS, I DIDN'T SEE ONE LIKE THIS.
...
...I DON'T SEE ANYTHING PARTIC-ULARLY DIFFERENT.
WHAT KIND OF STREAM DO YOU SEE?
LET ME SEE... WAIT A SEC... THIS IS...

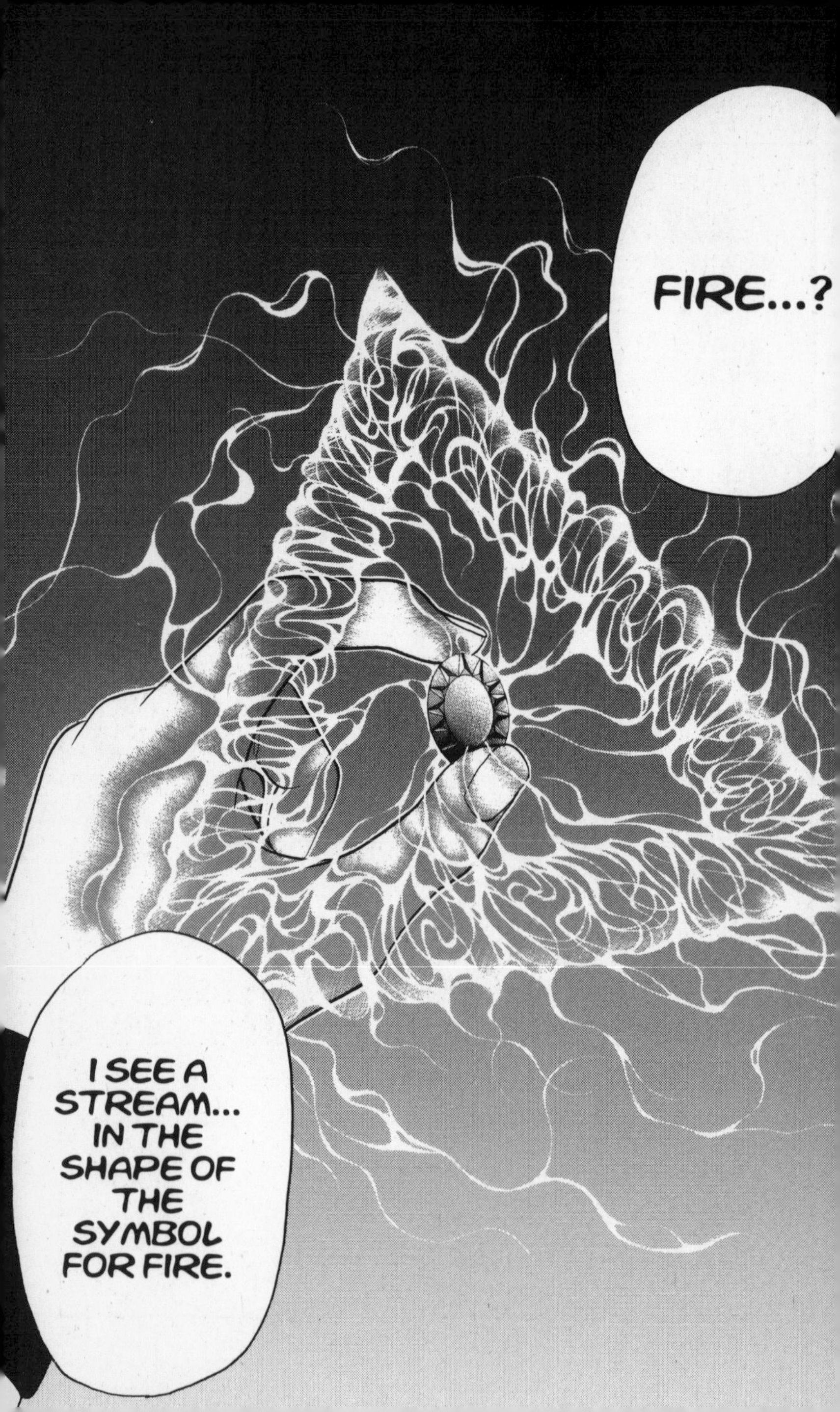
FIRE...?
I SEE A STREAM... IN THE SHAPE OF THE SYMBOL FOR FIRE.

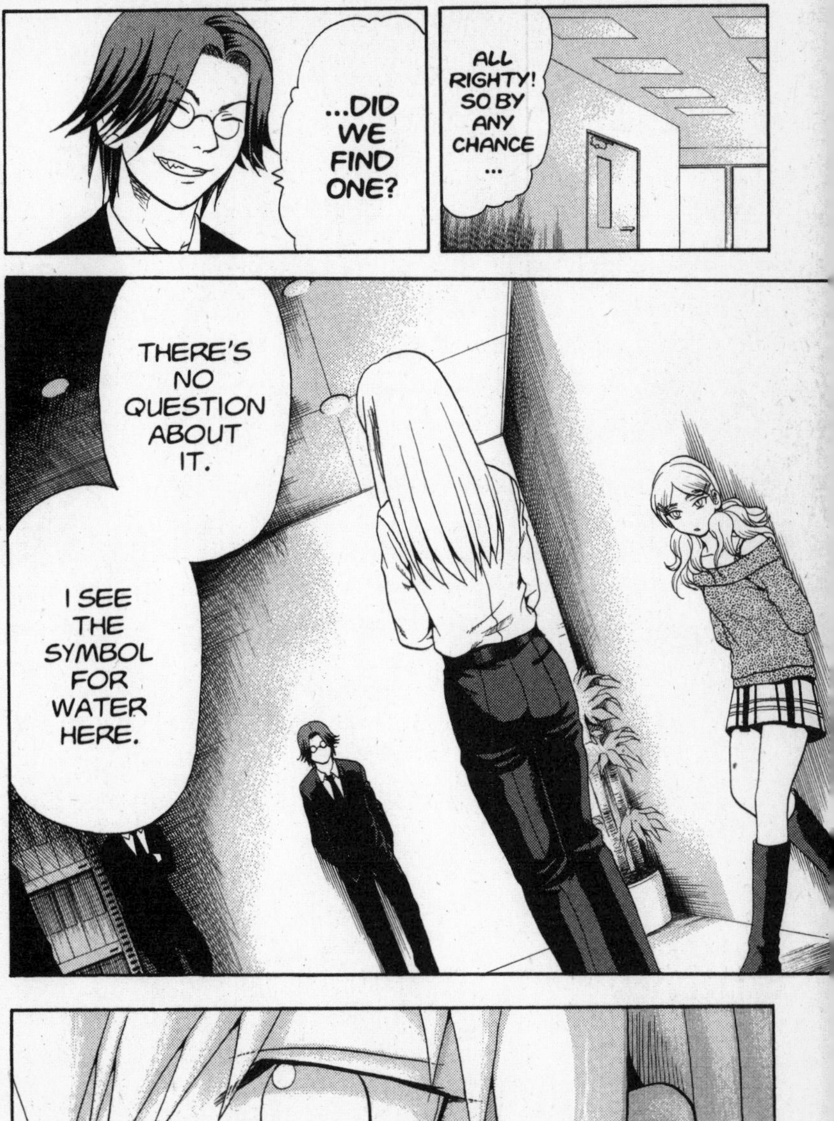
ALL RIGHTY! SO BY ANY CHANCE ...
...DID WE FIND ONE?
THERE'S NO QUESTION ABOUT IT.
I SEE THE SYMBOL FOR WATER HERE.

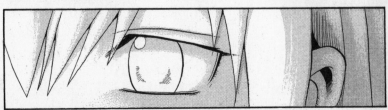

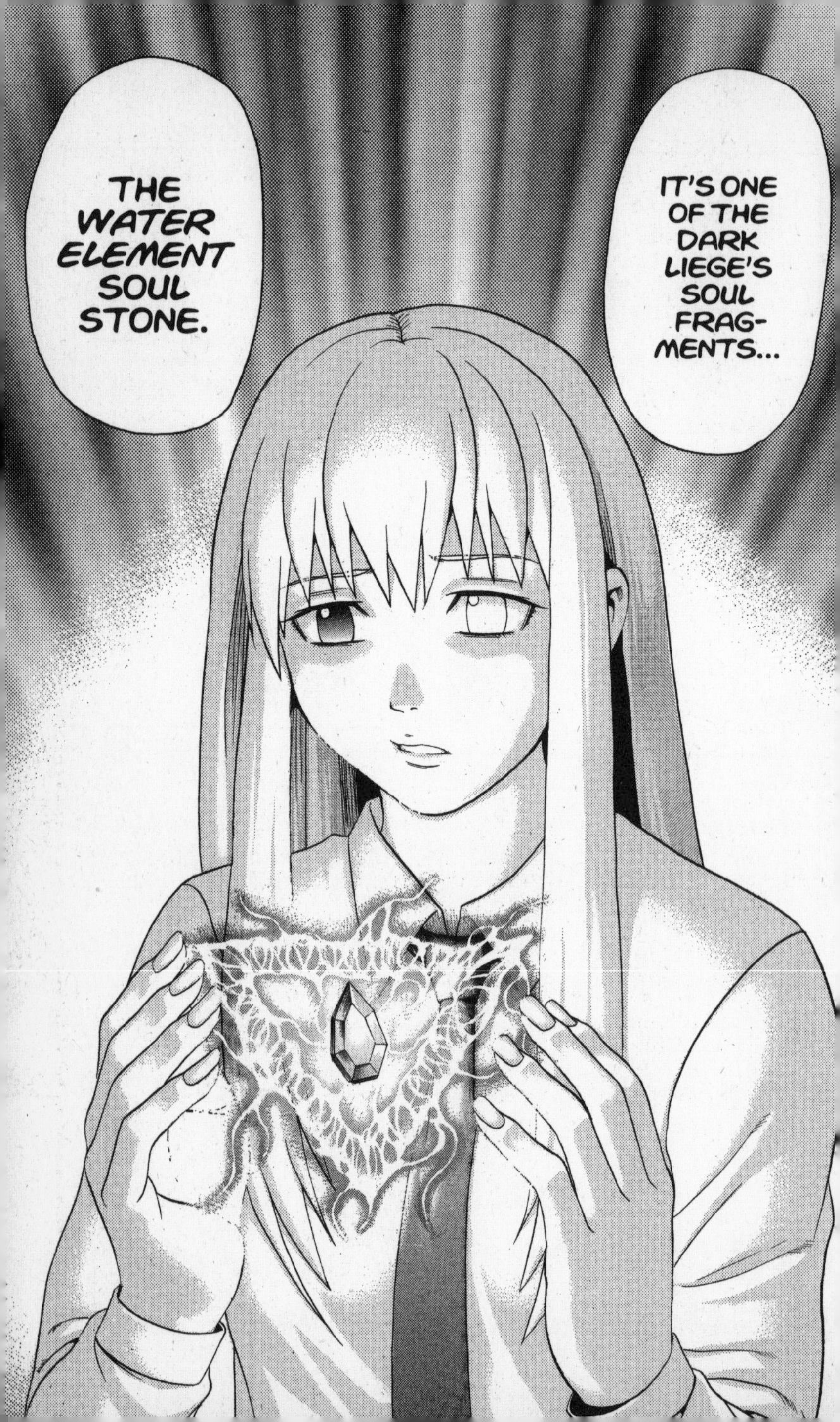
IT'S ONE OF THE DARK LIEGE'S SOUL FRAG-MENTS...
THE WATER ELEMENT SOUL STONE.

HUNGRY HUNGRY RIVAN

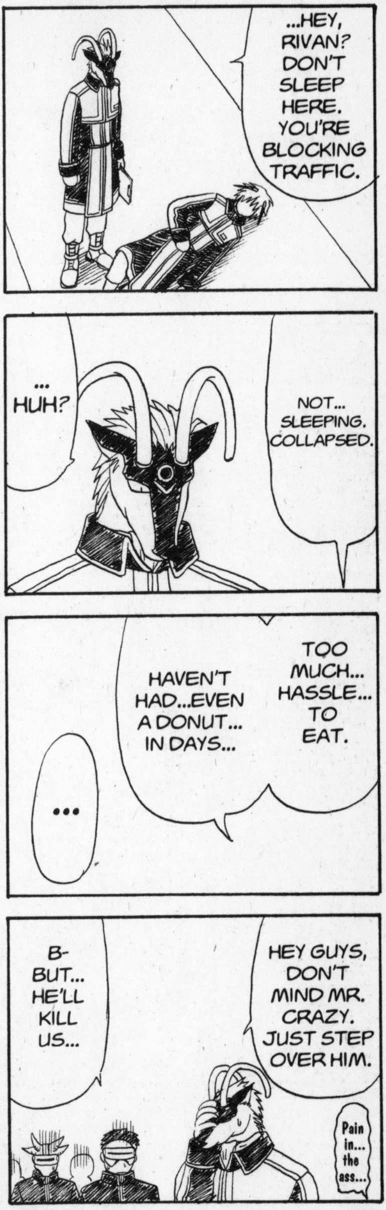
...HEY, RIVAN? DON'T SLEEP HERE. YOU'RE BLOCKING TRAFFIC.
NOT... SLEEPING. COLLAPSED.
... HUH?
TOO MUCH... HASSLE... TO EAT.
HAVEN'T HAD...EVEN A DONUT... IN DAYS...
...
HEY GUYS, DON'T MIND MR. CRAZY. JUST STEP OVER HIM.
B-BUT... HE'LL KILL US...
Pain in... the ass...

OL' JELLY BELLY

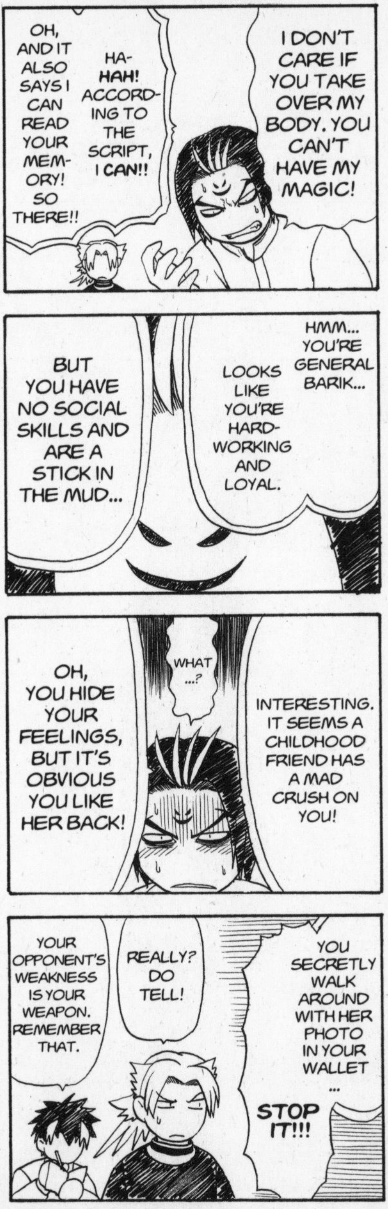
I DON'T CARE IF YOU TAKE OVER MY BODY. YOU CAN'T HAVE MY MAGIC!
HA-HAH! ACCORDING TO THE SCRIPT, I CAN!!
OH, AND IT ALSO SAYS I CAN READ YOUR MEMORY! SO THERE!!
HMM... YOU'RE GENERAL BARIK...
LOOKS LIKE YOU'RE HARD-WORKING AND LOYAL.
BUT YOU HAVE NO SOCIAL SKILLS AND ARE A STICK IN THE MUD...
INTERESTING. IT SEEMS A CHILDHOOD FRIEND HAS A MAD CRUSH ON YOU!
WHAT ...?
OH, YOU HIDE YOUR FEELINGS, BUT IT'S OBVIOUS YOU LIKE HER BACK!
YOU SECRETLY WALK AROUND WITH HER PHOTO IN YOUR WALLET ...
REALLY? DO TELL!
YOUR OPPONENT'S WEAKNESS IS YOUR WEAPON. REMEMBER THAT.
STOP IT!!!

Story 12: Do Your Business

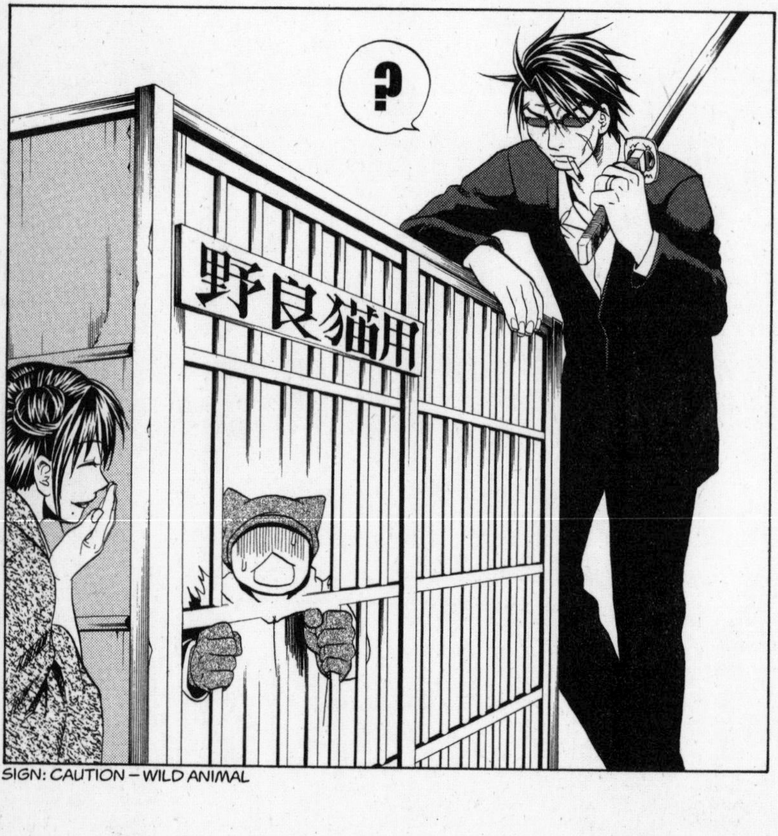
?
野良猫用

SIGN: CAUTION – WILD ANIMAL

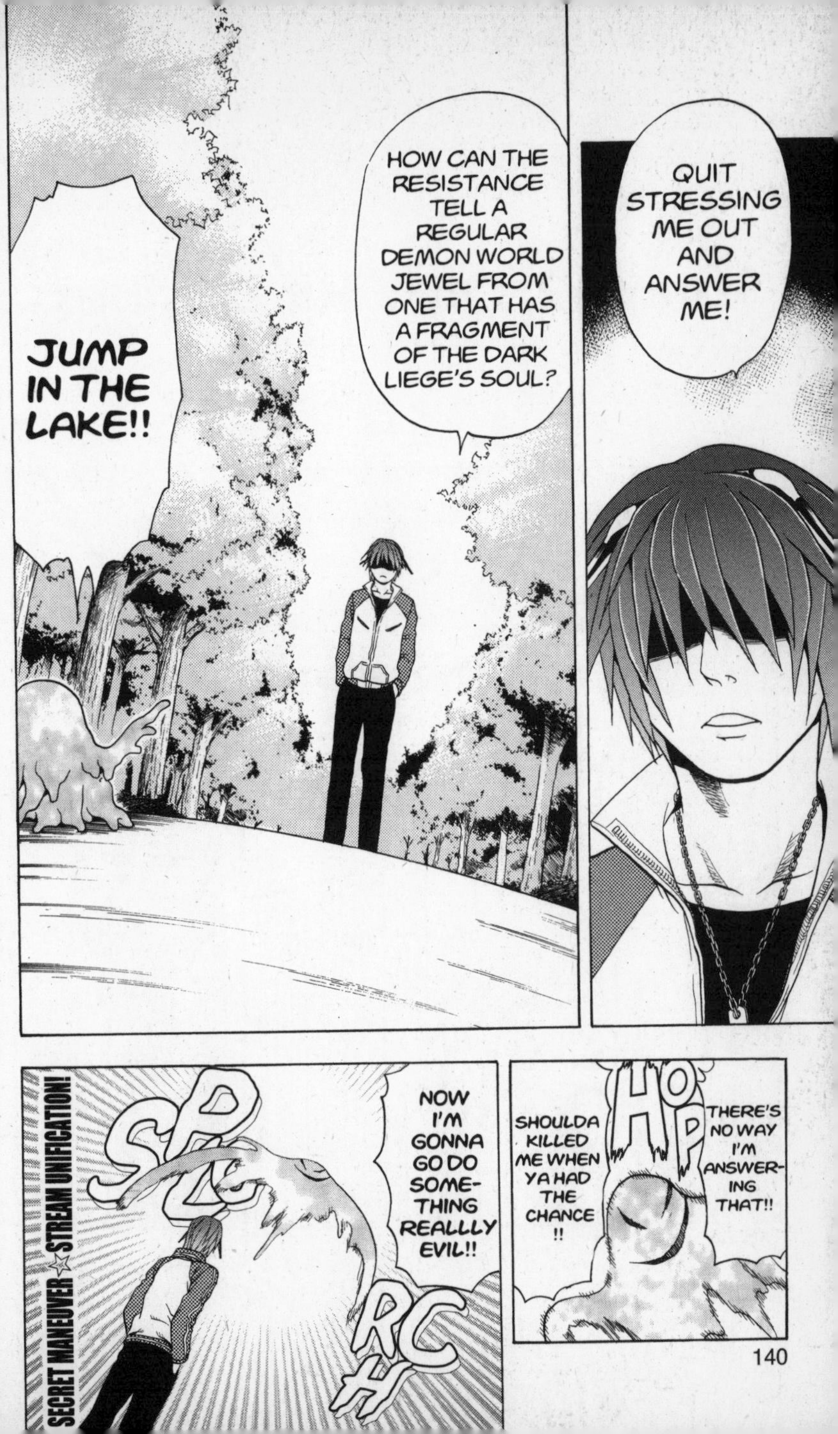
QUIT STRESSING ME OUT AND ANSWER ME!
HOW CAN THE RESISTANCE TELL A REGULAR DEMON WORLD JEWEL FROM ONE THAT HAS A FRAGMENT OF THE DARK LIEGE'S SOUL?
JUMP IN THE LAKE!!
HOP
THERE'S NO WAY I'M ANSWER-ING THAT!!
SHOULDA KILLED ME WHEN YA HAD THE CHANCE!!
NOW I'M GONNA GO DO SOME-THING REALLLY EVIL!!
SPLORCH
SECRET MANEUVER☆STREAM UNIFICATION!

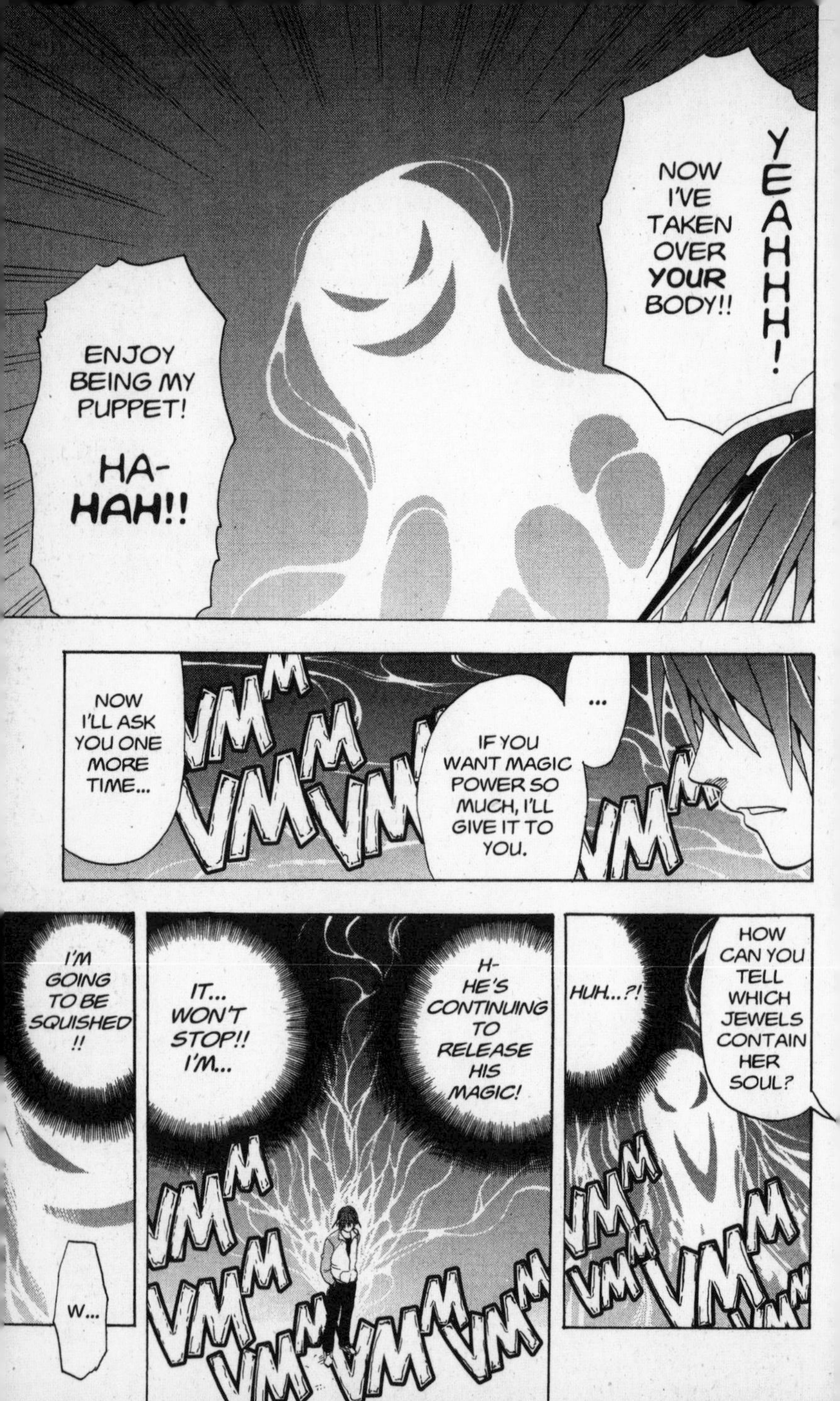
YEAHHH!
NOW I'VE TAKEN OVER YOUR BODY!!
ENJOY BEING MY PUPPET!
HA-HAH!!
...
IF YOU WANT MAGIC POWER SO MUCH, I'LL GIVE IT TO YOU.
NOW I'LL ASK YOU ONE MORE TIME...
VMMM
HOW CAN YOU TELL WHICH JEWELS CONTAIN HER SOUL?
HUH...?!
H-HE'S CONTINUING TO RELEASE HIS MAGIC!
IT... WON'T STOP!! I'M...
VMMM
I'M GOING TO BE SQUISHED!!
W...

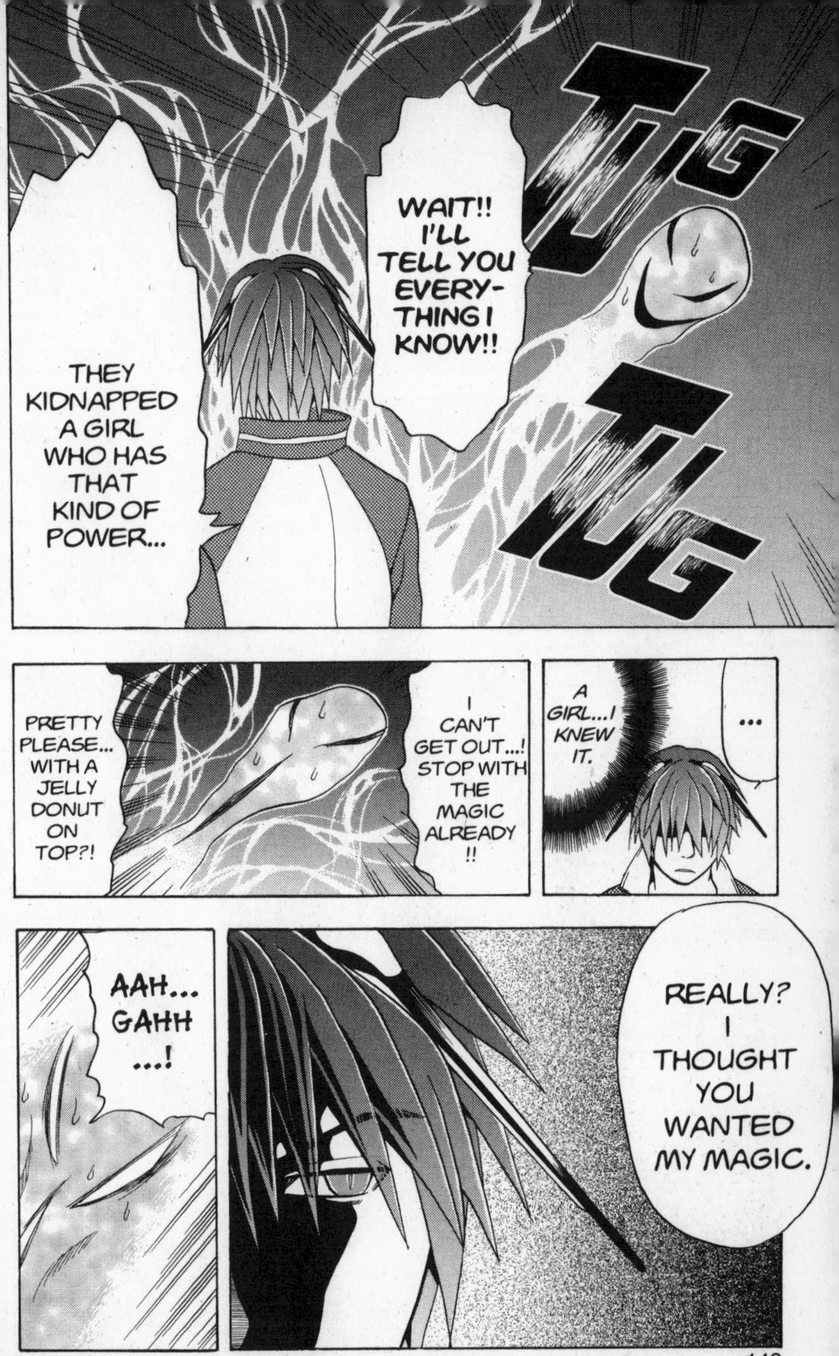
TUG TUG
WAIT!! I'LL TELL YOU EVERY-THING I KNOW!!
THEY KIDNAPPED A GIRL WHO HAS THAT KIND OF POWER...
...
A GIRL...I KNEW IT.
I CAN'T GET OUT...! STOP WITH THE MAGIC ALREADY !!
PRETTY PLEASE... WITH A JELLY DONUT ON TOP?!
REALLY? I THOUGHT YOU WANTED MY MAGIC.
AAH... GAHH ...!

READ THIS WAY

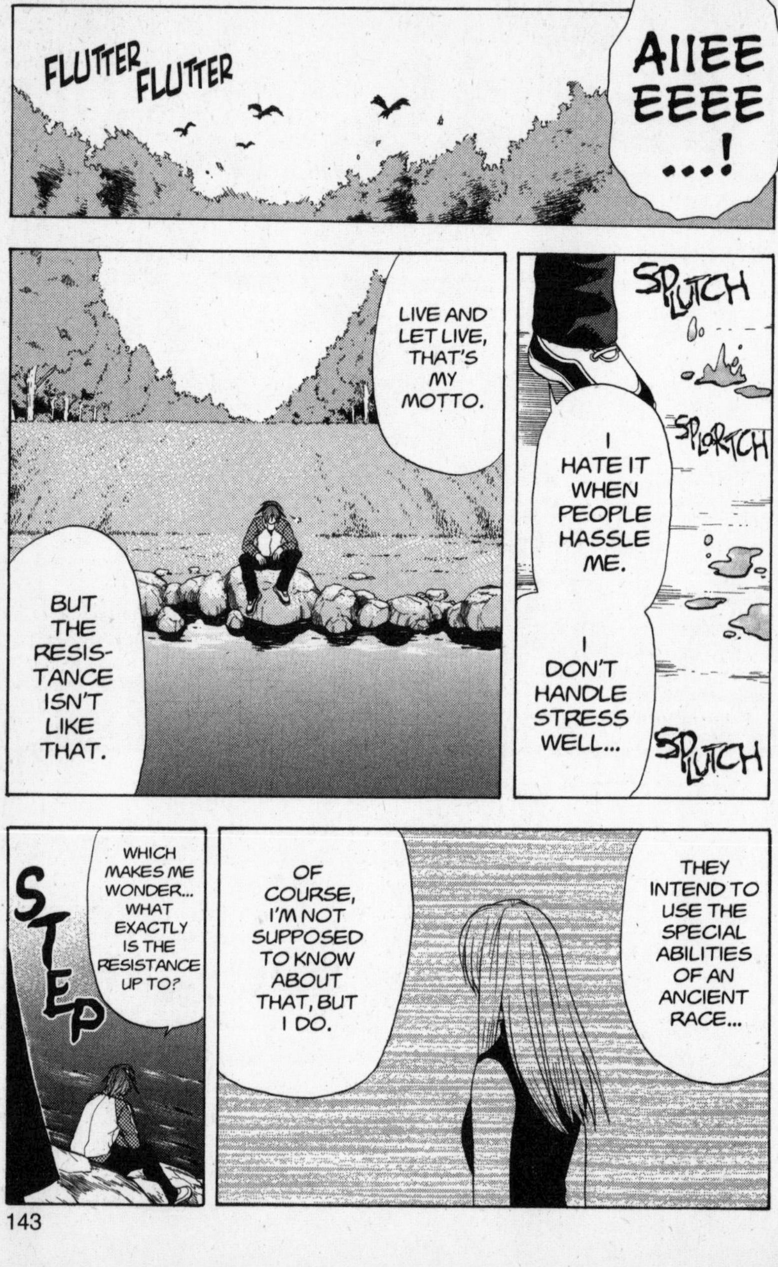
AIIEEEEEE...!
FLUTTER FLUTTER
SPLUTCH
I HATE IT WHEN PEOPLE HASSLE ME.
SPLORTCH
I DON'T HANDLE STRESS WELL...
SPLUTCH
LIVE AND LET LIVE, THAT'S MY MOTTO.
BUT THE RESIS-TANCE ISN'T LIKE THAT.
THEY INTEND TO USE THE SPECIAL ABILITIES OF AN ANCIENT RACE...
OF COURSE, I'M NOT SUPPOSED TO KNOW ABOUT THAT, BUT I DO.
WHICH MAKES ME WONDER... WHAT EXACTLY IS THE RESISTANCE UP TO?
STEP

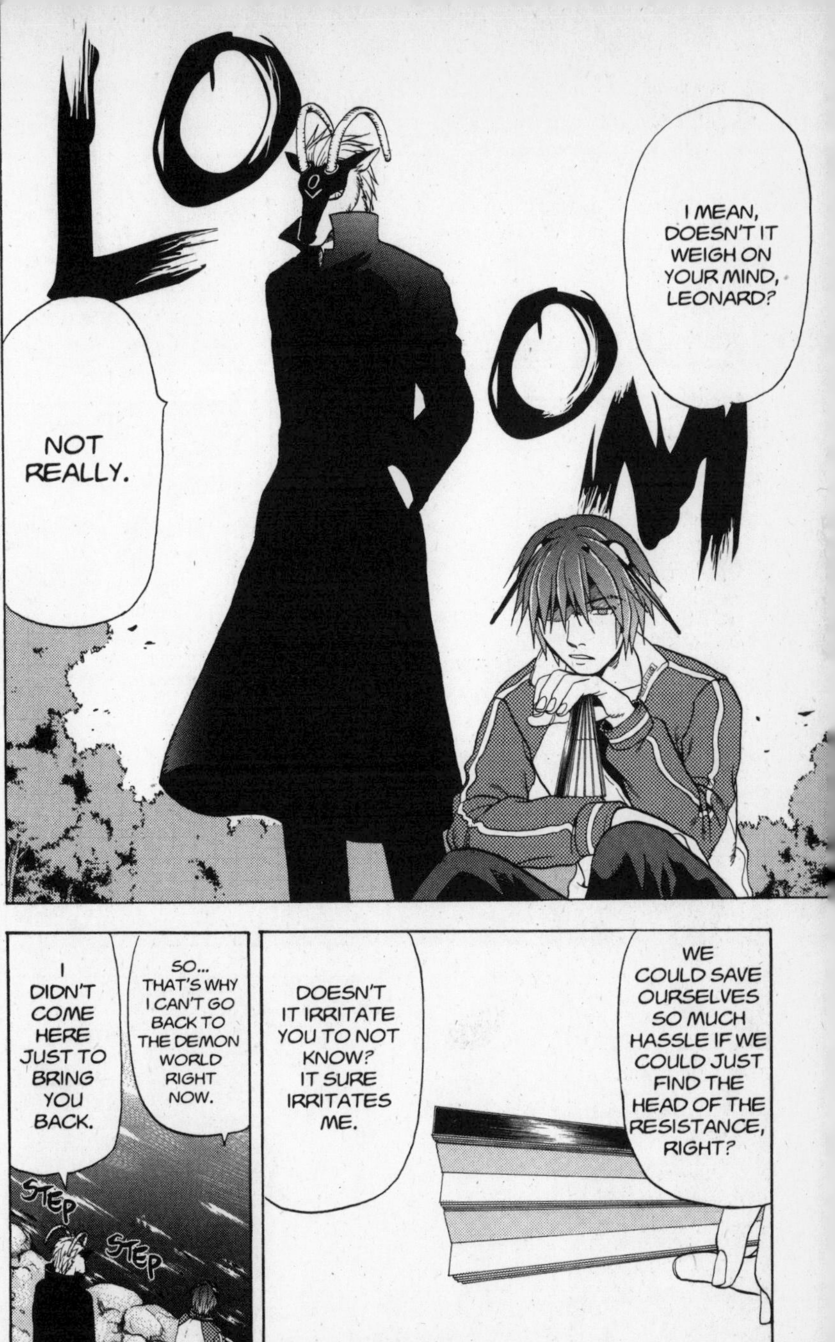
I MEAN, DOESN'T IT WEIGH ON YOUR MIND, LEONARD?
LOOM
NOT REALLY.
WE COULD SAVE OURSELVES SO MUCH HASSLE IF WE COULD JUST FIND THE HEAD OF THE RESISTANCE, RIGHT?
DOESN'T IT IRRITATE YOU TO NOT KNOW? IT SURE IRRITATES ME.
SO... THAT'S WHY I CAN'T GO BACK TO THE DEMON WORLD RIGHT NOW.
I DIDN'T COME HERE JUST TO BRING YOU BACK.
STEP
STEP

READ THIS WAY

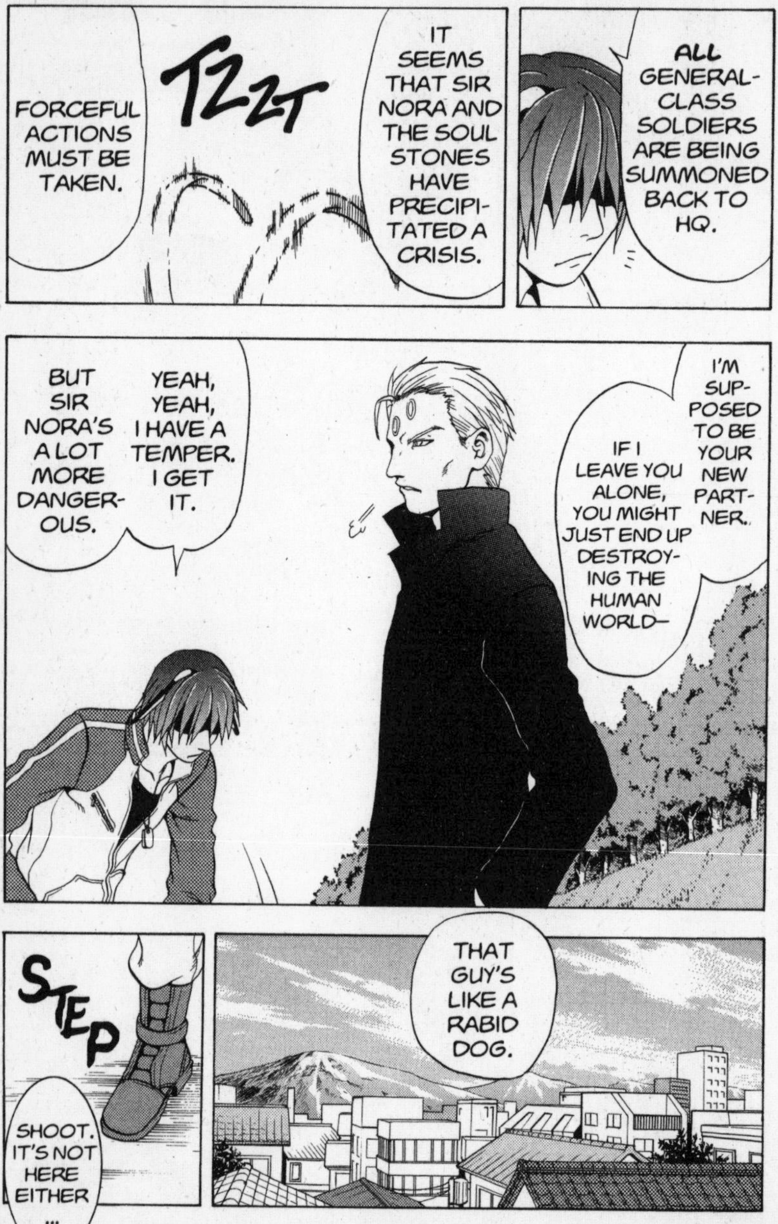
ALL GENERAL-CLASS SOLDIERS ARE BEING SUMMONED BACK TO HQ.
IT SEEMS THAT SIR NORA AND THE SOUL STONES HAVE PRECIPITATED A CRISIS.
TZZT
FORCEFUL ACTIONS MUST BE TAKEN.
I'M SUPPOSED TO BE YOUR NEW PARTNER.
IF I LEAVE YOU ALONE, YOU MIGHT JUST END UP DESTROYING THE HUMAN WORLD—
YEAH, YEAH, I HAVE A TEMPER. I GET IT.
BUT SIR NORA'S A LOT MORE DANGEROUS.
THAT GUY'S LIKE A RABID DOG.
STEP
SHOOT. IT'S NOT HERE EITHER ...

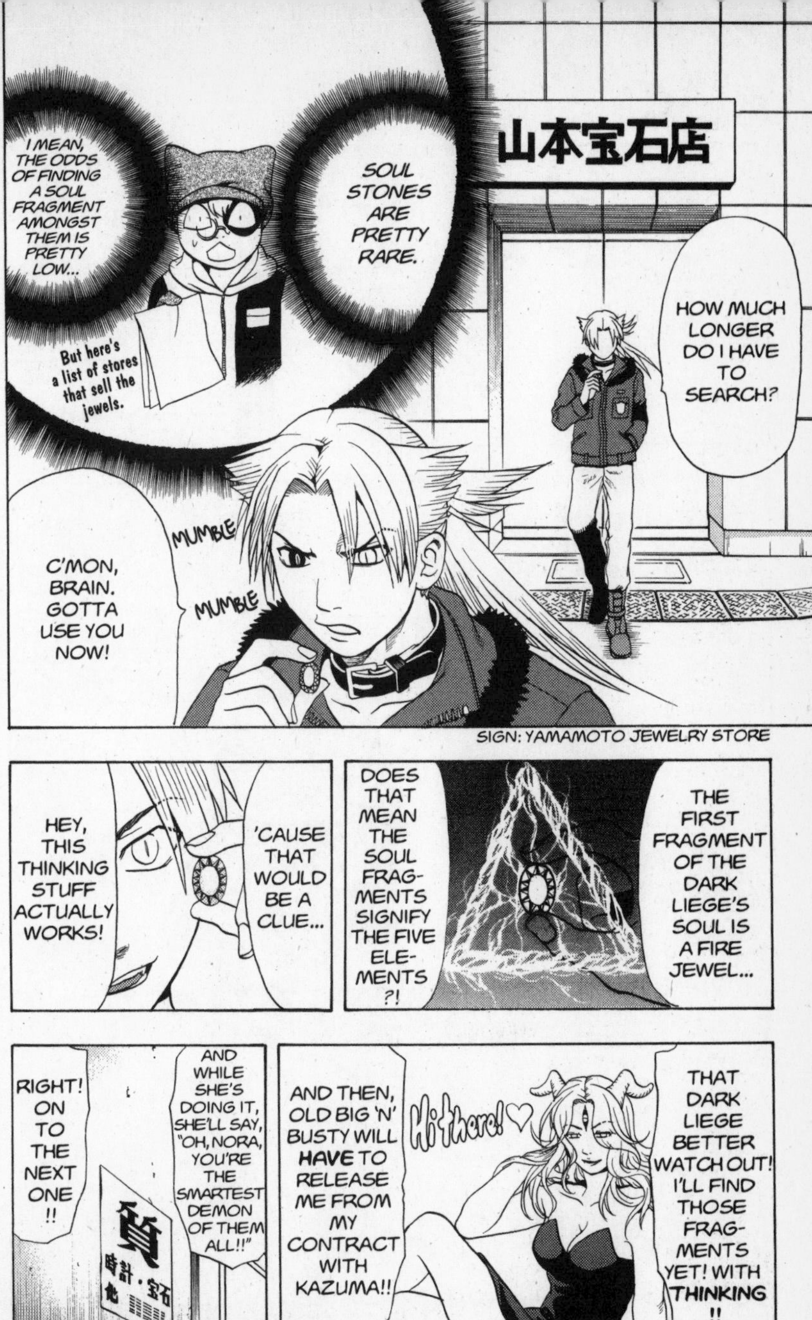
山本宝石店
HOW MUCH LONGER DO I HAVE TO SEARCH?
SOUL STONES ARE PRETTY RARE.
I MEAN, THE ODDS OF FINDING A SOUL FRAGMENT AMONGST THEM IS PRETTY LOW...
But here's a list of stores that sell the jewels.
MUMBLE
MUMBLE
C'MON, BRAIN. GOTTA USE YOU NOW!
SIGN: YAMAMOTO JEWELRY STORE
THE FIRST FRAGMENT OF THE DARK LIEGE'S SOUL IS A FIRE JEWEL...
DOES THAT MEAN THE SOUL FRAGMENTS SIGNIFY THE FIVE ELEMENTS?!
'CAUSE THAT WOULD BE A CLUE...
HEY, THIS THINKING STUFF ACTUALLY WORKS!
THAT DARK LIEGE BETTER WATCH OUT! I'LL FIND THOSE FRAGMENTS YET! WITH **THINKING**!!
Hi there! ♥
AND THEN, OLD BIG 'N' BUSTY WILL **HAVE** TO RELEASE ME FROM MY CONTRACT WITH KAZUMA!!
AND WHILE SHE'S DOING IT, SHE'LL SAY, "OH, NORA, YOU'RE THE SMARTEST DEMON OF THEM ALL!!"
RIGHT! ON TO THE NEXT ONE!!
質
時計・宝石
他
SIGN: PAWNSHOP

READ THIS WAY

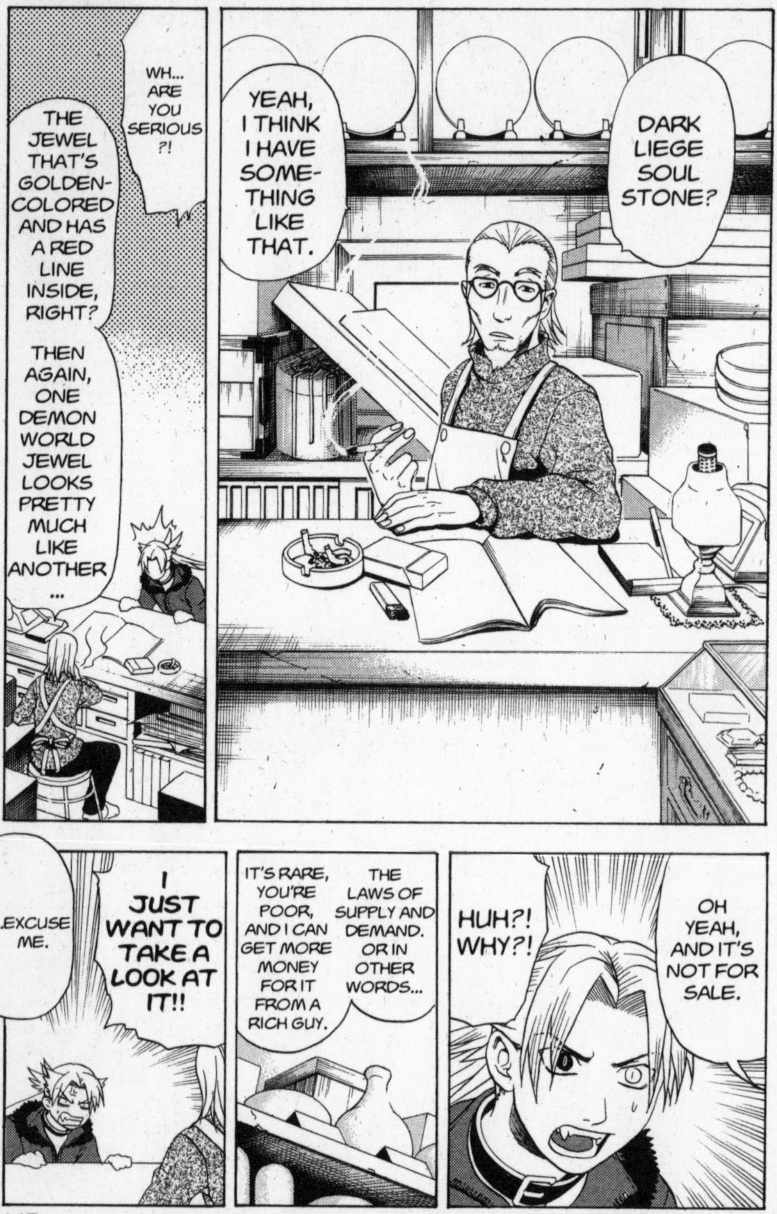

DARK LIEGE SOUL STONE?
YEAH, I THINK I HAVE SOME-THING LIKE THAT.
WH... ARE YOU SERIOUS?!
THE JEWEL THAT'S GOLDEN-COLORED AND HAS A RED LINE INSIDE, RIGHT?
THEN AGAIN, ONE DEMON WORLD JEWEL LOOKS PRETTY MUCH LIKE ANOTHER...
OH YEAH, AND IT'S NOT FOR SALE.
HUH?! WHY?!
THE LAWS OF SUPPLY AND DEMAND. OR IN OTHER WORDS...
IT'S RARE, YOU'RE POOR, AND I CAN GET MORE MONEY FOR IT FROM A RICH GUY.
I JUST WANT TO TAKE A LOOK AT IT!!
...EXCUSE ME.

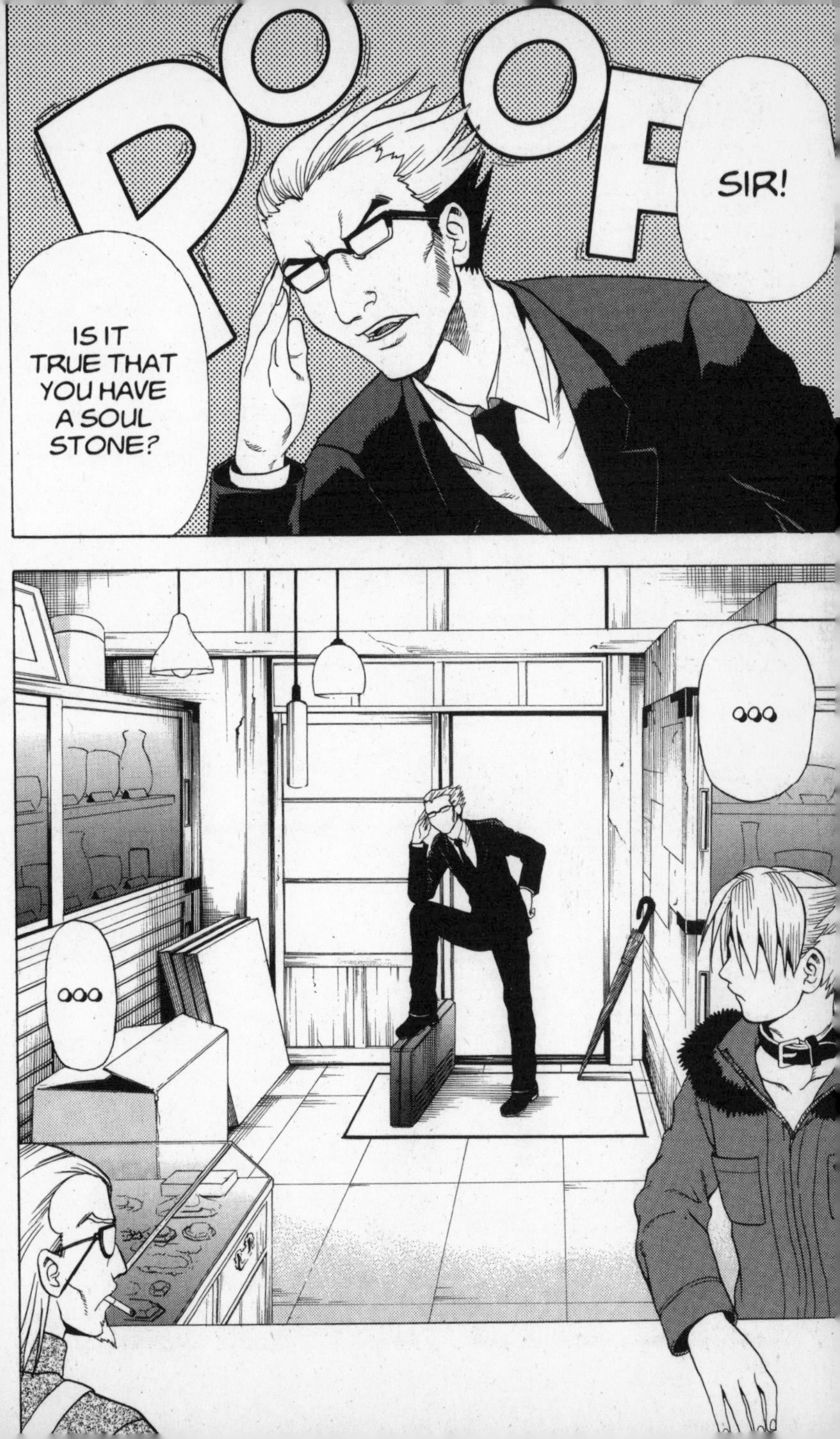
POOF
SIR!
IS IT TRUE THAT YOU HAVE A SOUL STONE?
...
...

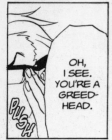

OH, I SEE. YOU'RE A GREED-HEAD.

PUSH

WHO IS THIS...?

STEP

STEP

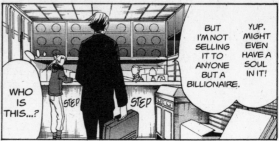

BUT I'M NOT SELLING IT TO ANYONE BUT A BILLIONAIRE.

YUP. MIGHT EVEN HAVE A SOUL IN IT!

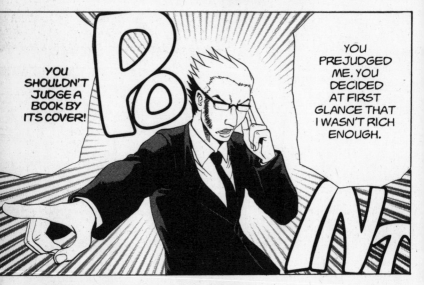

YOU SHOULDN'T JUDGE A BOOK BY ITS COVER!

YOU PREJUDGED ME. YOU DECIDED AT FIRST GLANCE THAT I WASN'T RICH ENOUGH.

Po INT

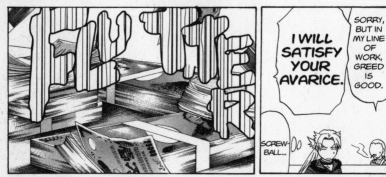

FLUTTER

I WILL SATISFY YOUR AVARICE.

SORRY, BUT IN MY LINE OF WORK, GREED IS GOOD.

SCREW-BALL...

149

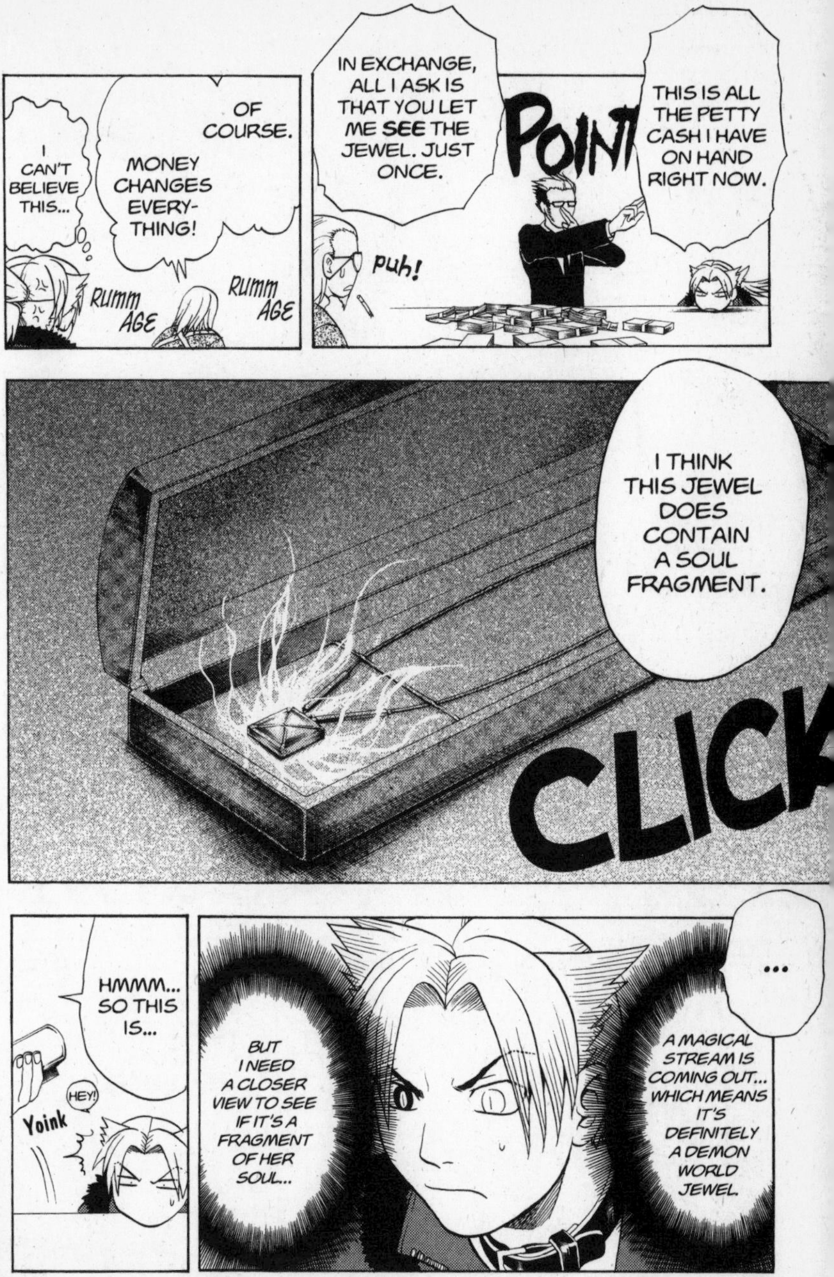
THIS IS ALL THE PETTY CASH I HAVE ON HAND RIGHT NOW.
POINT
IN EXCHANGE, ALL I ASK IS THAT YOU LET ME **SEE** THE JEWEL. JUST ONCE.
puh!
OF COURSE.
MONEY CHANGES EVERY-THING!
RUMMAGE
RUMMAGE
I CAN'T BELIEVE THIS...
I THINK THIS JEWEL DOES CONTAIN A SOUL FRAGMENT.
CLICK
...
A MAGICAL STREAM IS COMING OUT... WHICH MEANS IT'S DEFINITELY A DEMON WORLD JEWEL.
BUT I NEED A CLOSER VIEW TO SEE IF IT'S A FRAGMENT OF HER SOUL...
HMMM... SO THIS IS...
HEY!
Yoink

POSE
...THE MOST BEAUTIFUL, MYSTERIOUS JEWEL EVER!
SURELY THIS IS WHAT I SEEK!!
...
IT'S AN EXCELLENT ARTICLE, TRULY WORTHY OF MY COLLECTION!!
WILL YOU SELL THIS TO ME? MONEY IS NO OBJECT.
...
OF COURSE!
KLUNK
IN THAT CASE, I'LL COME AGAIN... AND BRING MY MONEY BELT.
HUH?
I CAN'T SEE THE STREAM AT ALL NOW!
THIS ISN'T... LIKE BEFORE...
IT'S **NOT** A SOUL STONE?!
Wait a sec.
WHERE DID THAT GUY GO?
WHAT? HE JUST LEFT.
THAT GUY...
DASH

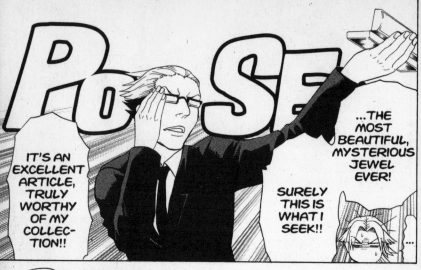

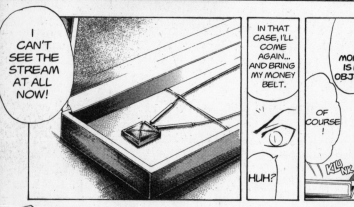

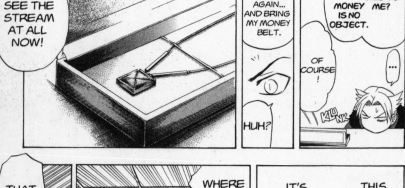

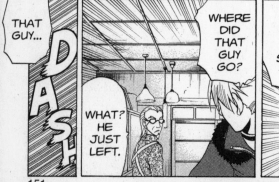

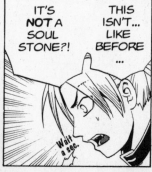

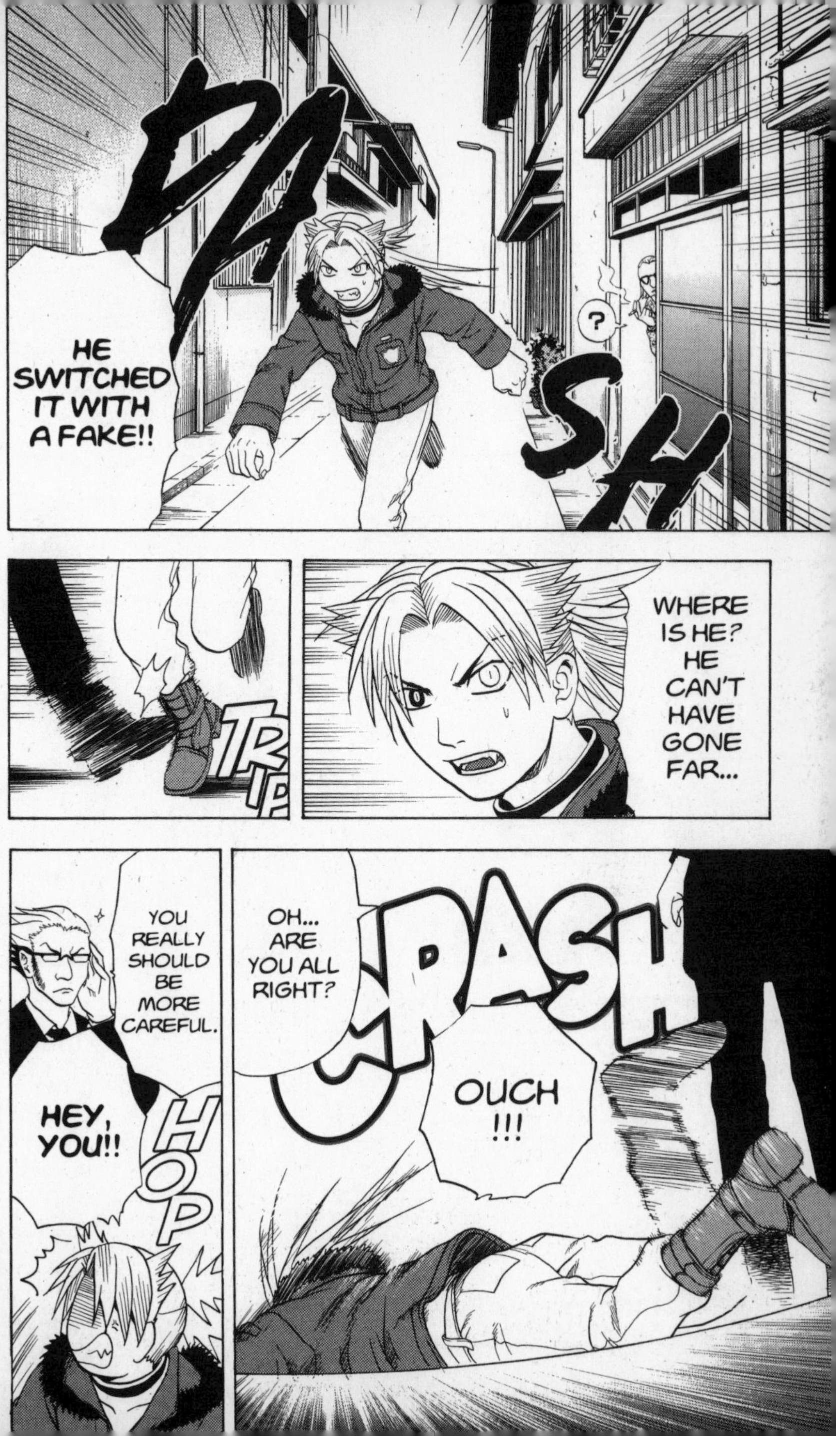
?
DA
SH
HE SWITCHED IT WITH A FAKE!!
WHERE IS HE? HE CAN'T HAVE GONE FAR...
TRIP
CRASH
OH... ARE YOU ALL RIGHT?
OUCH !!!
YOU REALLY SHOULD BE MORE CAREFUL.
HEY, YOU!!
HOP

READ THIS WAY

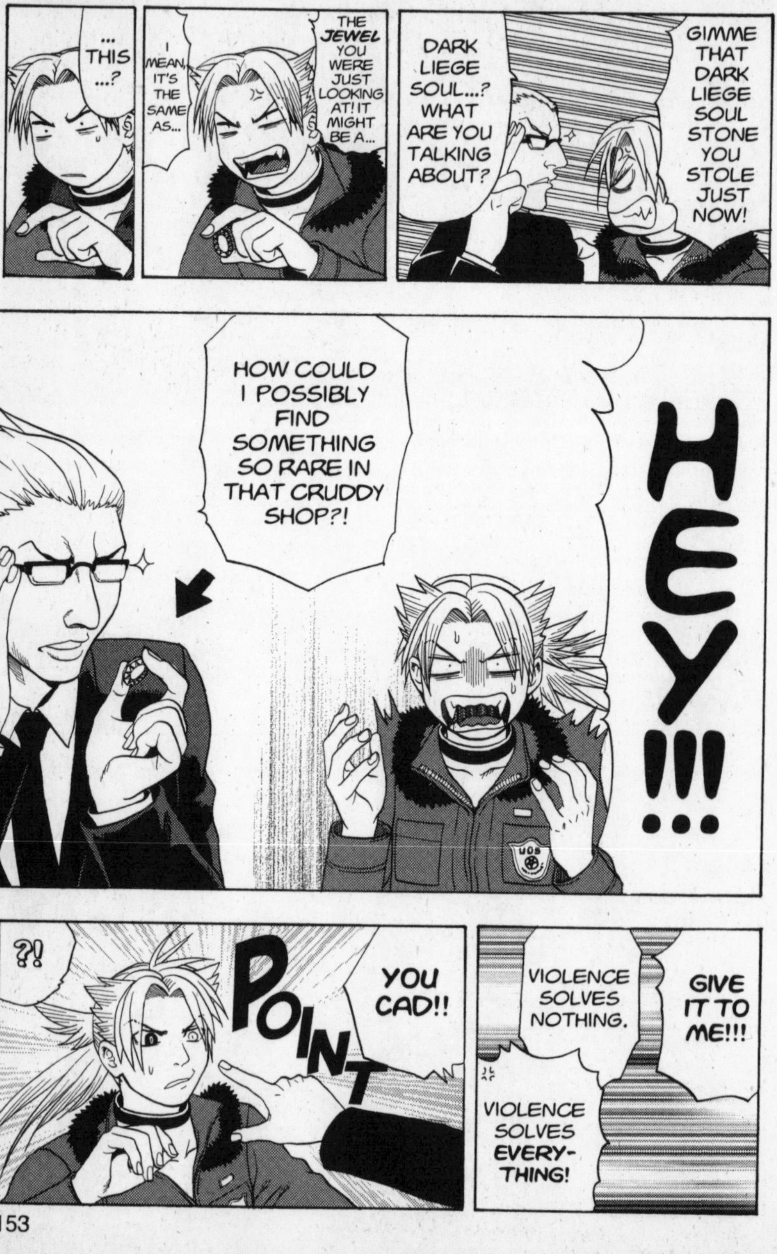

GIMME THAT DARK LIEGE SOUL STONE YOU STOLE JUST NOW!
DARK LIEGE SOUL...? WHAT ARE YOU TALKING ABOUT?
THE JEWEL YOU WERE JUST LOOKING AT! IT MIGHT BE A...
I MEAN, IT'S THE SAME AS...
... THIS ...?
HEY!!!
HOW COULD I POSSIBLY FIND SOMETHING SO RARE IN THAT CRUDDY SHOP?!
GIVE IT TO ME!!!
VIOLENCE SOLVES NOTHING.
VIOLENCE SOLVES EVERY-THING!
YOU CAD!!
POINT
?!

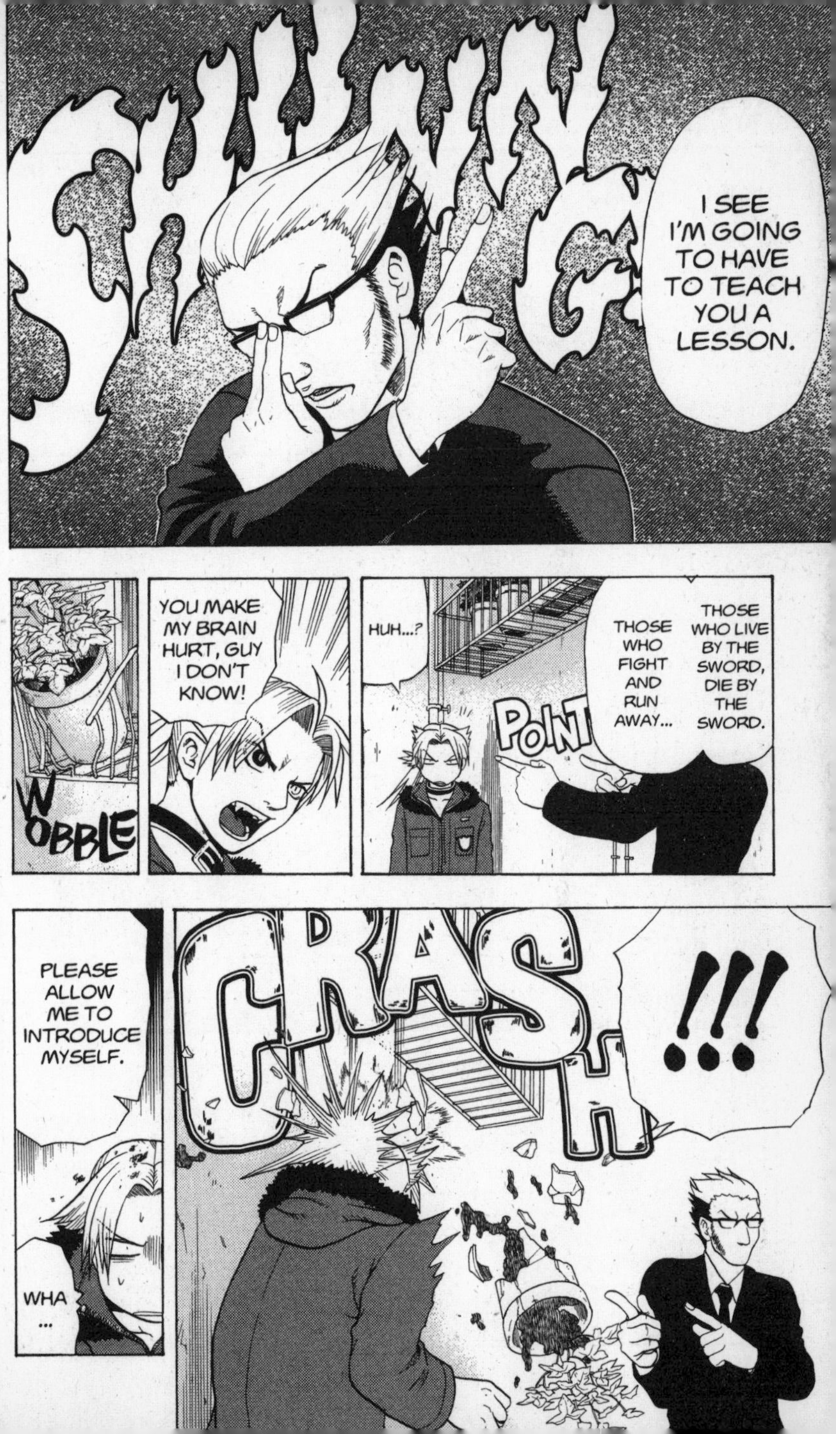
I SEE I'M GOING TO HAVE TO TEACH YOU A LESSON.
THOSE WHO LIVE BY THE SWORD, DIE BY THE SWORD.
THOSE WHO FIGHT AND RUN AWAY...
POINT
HUH...?
YOU MAKE MY BRAIN HURT, GUY I DON'T KNOW!
WOBBLE
CRASH
!!!
PLEASE ALLOW ME TO INTRODUCE MYSELF.
WHA ...

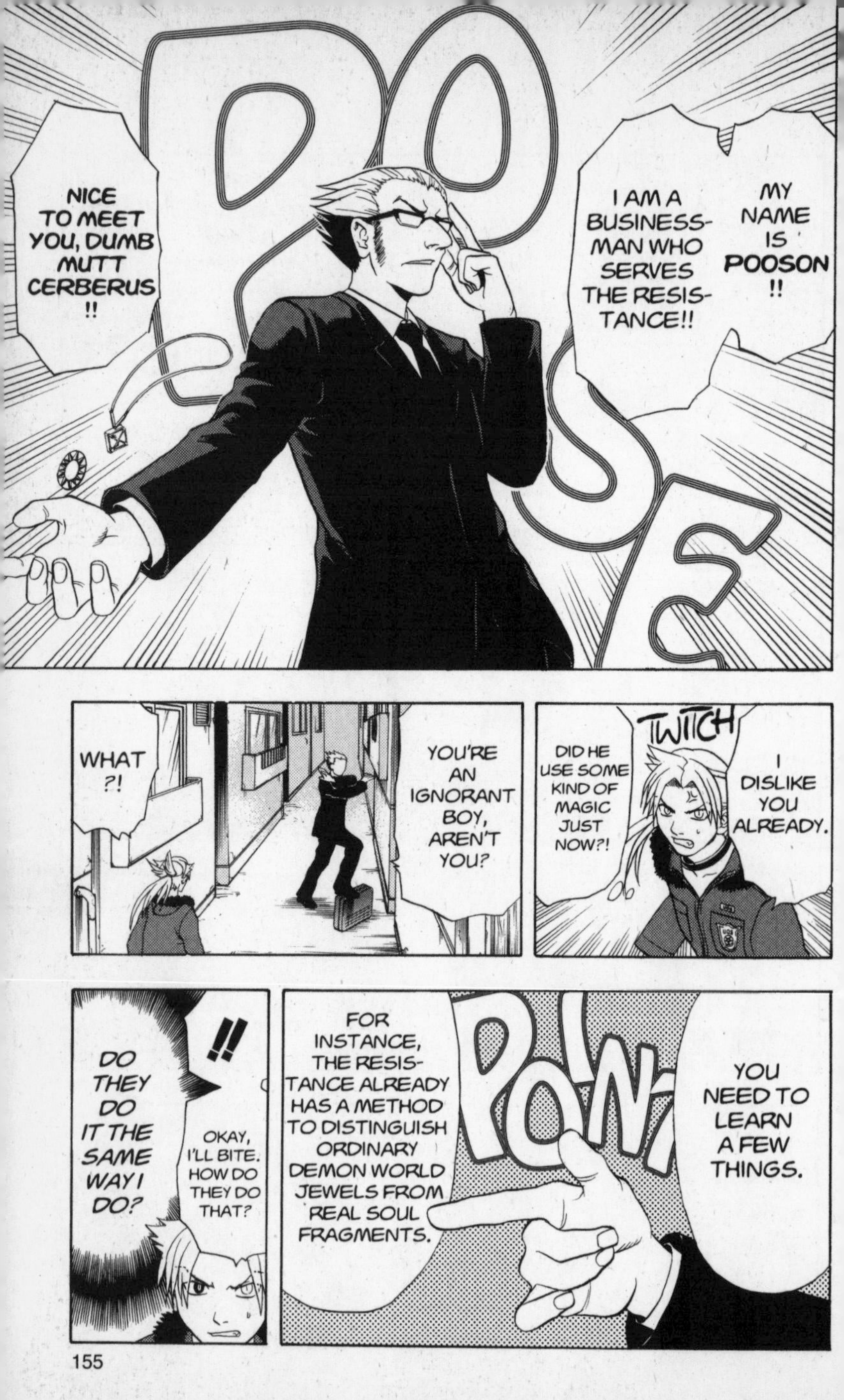
MY NAME IS POOSON!!
I AM A BUSINESSMAN WHO SERVES THE RESISTANCE!!
NICE TO MEET YOU, DUMB MUTT CERBERUS!!
I DISLIKE YOU ALREADY.
TWITCH
DID HE USE SOME KIND OF MAGIC JUST NOW?!
YOU'RE AN IGNORANT BOY, AREN'T YOU?
WHAT?!
YOU NEED TO LEARN A FEW THINGS.
FOR INSTANCE, THE RESISTANCE ALREADY HAS A METHOD TO DISTINGUISH ORDINARY DEMON WORLD JEWELS FROM REAL SOUL FRAGMENTS.
!!
OKAY, I'LL BITE. HOW DO THEY DO THAT?
DO THEY DO IT THE SAME WAY I DO?

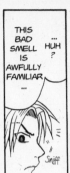

SIMPLE. I'LL SHOW YOU.
FIRST, I PREPARE A FIRE WITH THIS LIGHTER.
TOSS
...
CLICK CLICK CLICK CLICK CLICK CLICK
OW, MY FINGER!
fwoosh
FIRE PLUS GAS MAKES FOR A STRONG CHEMICAL REACTION.
SPLORP
SPLORP
... HUH?
THIS BAD SMELL IS AWFULLY FAMILIAR...
Sniff
... HEY !!
SPLASH
THIS IS THE FLAME-STARTING STUFF FROM THAT TIME WITH THE SHARK-GUY !!
THAT STUFF MAKES FIRE GO BOOM!!
OH? YOU KNOW ABOUT IT ALREADY? HOW SAD!!
SAD? THAT'S A TOTAL UNDER-STATEMENT!!
火気厳禁
灯油
HEY ...
GIMME THE JEWEL, YA JERK!!

SIGN: CAUTION — GASOLINE

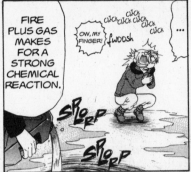

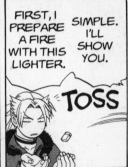

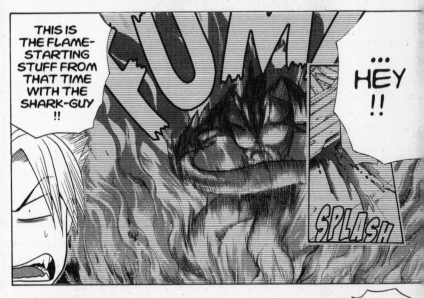

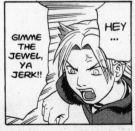

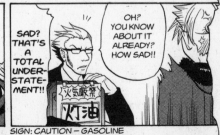

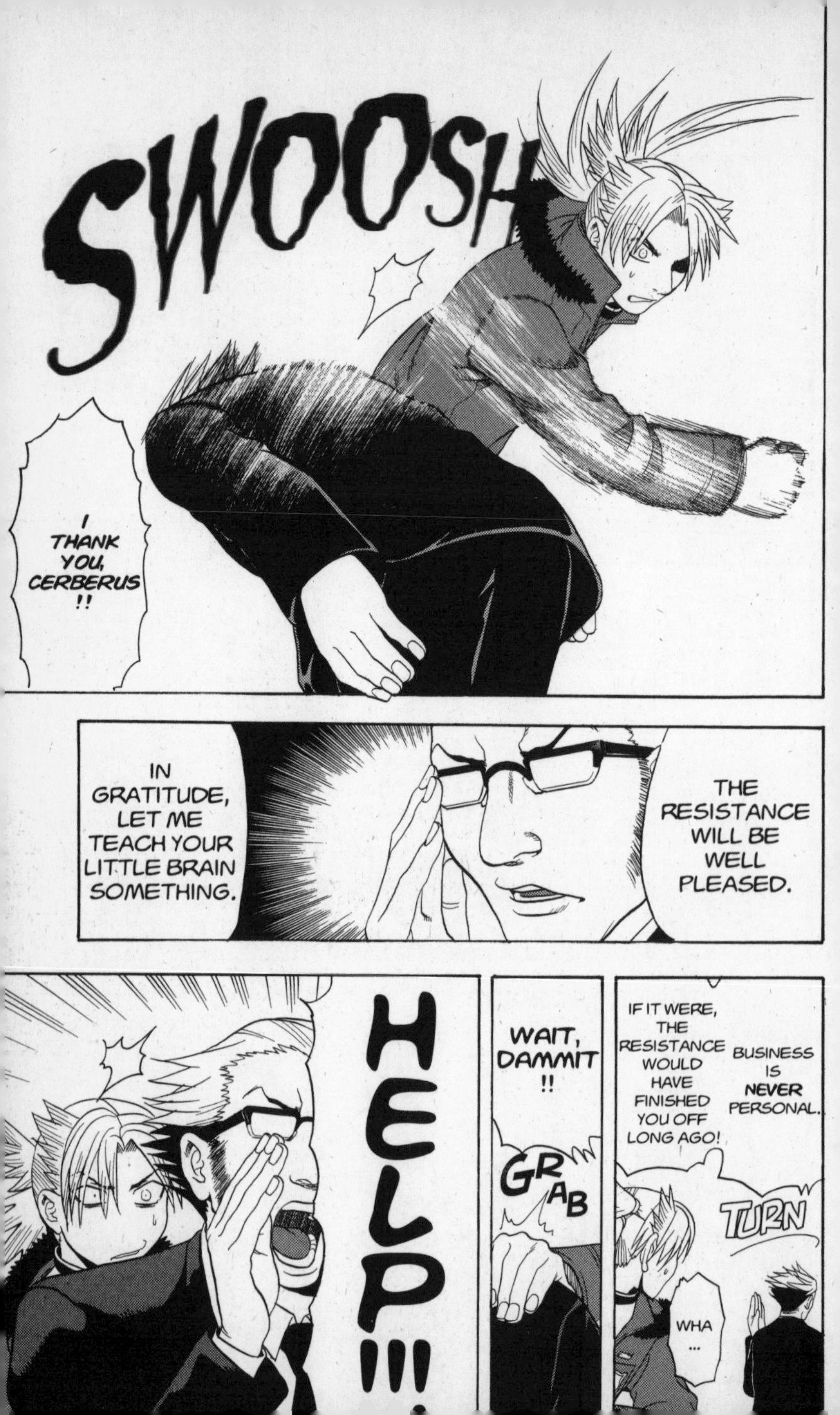
SWOOSH
I THANK YOU, CERBERUS!!
THE RESISTANCE WILL BE WELL PLEASED.
IN GRATITUDE, LET ME TEACH YOUR LITTLE BRAIN SOMETHING.
BUSINESS IS **NEVER** PERSONAL.
IF IT WERE, THE RESISTANCE WOULD HAVE FINISHED YOU OFF LONG AGO!
TURN
WHA...
WAIT, DAMMIT!!
GRAB
HELP!!!

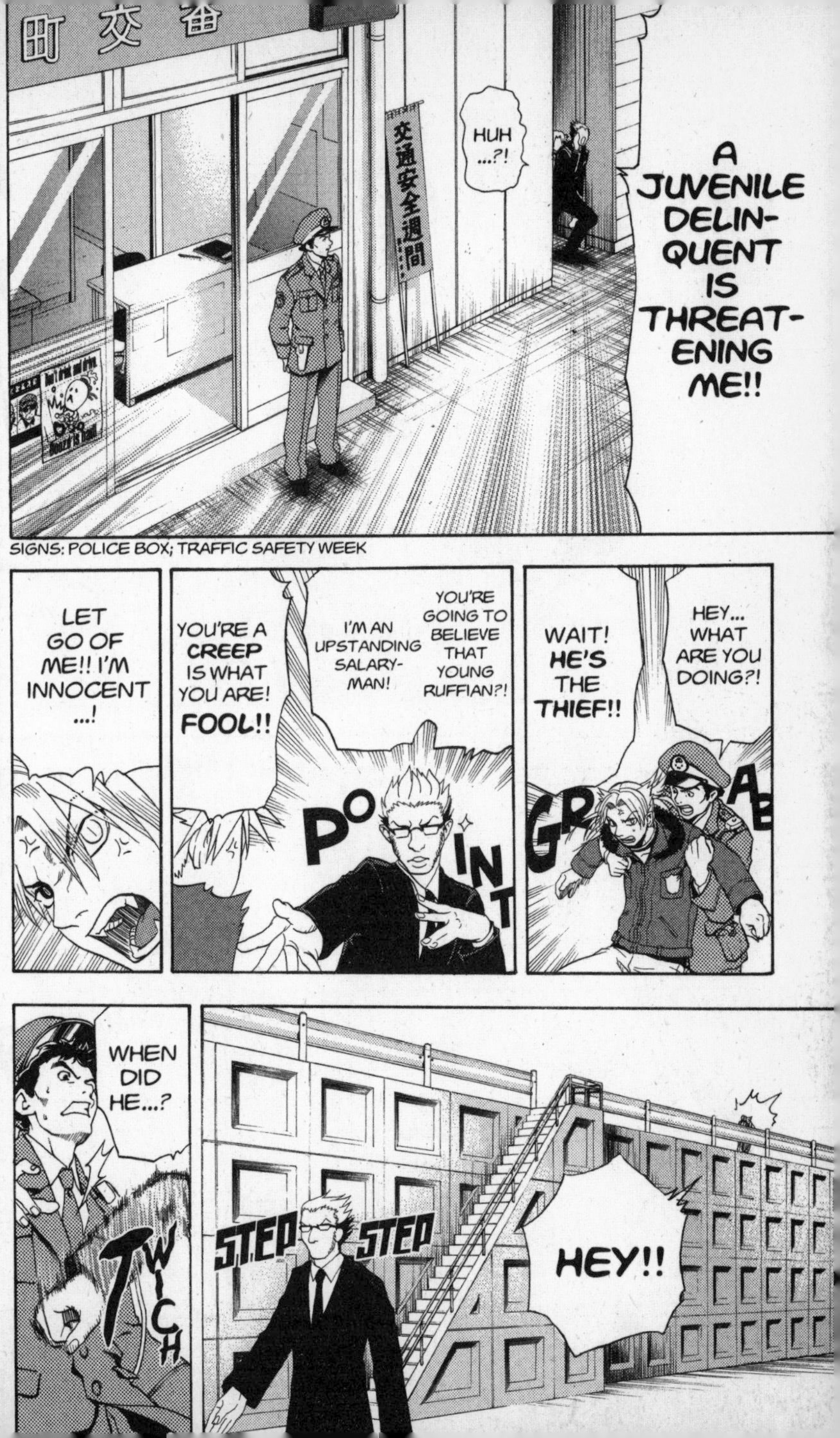
町交番
交通安全週間
A JUVENILE DELINQUENT IS THREATENING ME!!
HUH ...?!
SIGNS: POLICE BOX; TRAFFIC SAFETY WEEK
HEY... WHAT ARE YOU DOING?!
WAIT! HE'S THE THIEF!!
GRAB
YOU'RE GOING TO BELIEVE THAT YOUNG RUFFIAN?!
I'M AN UPSTANDING SALARYMAN!
YOU'RE A CREEP IS WHAT YOU ARE! FOOL!!
POINT
LET GO OF ME!! I'M INNOCENT ...!
HEY!!
STEP STEP
WHEN DID HE...?
TWITCH

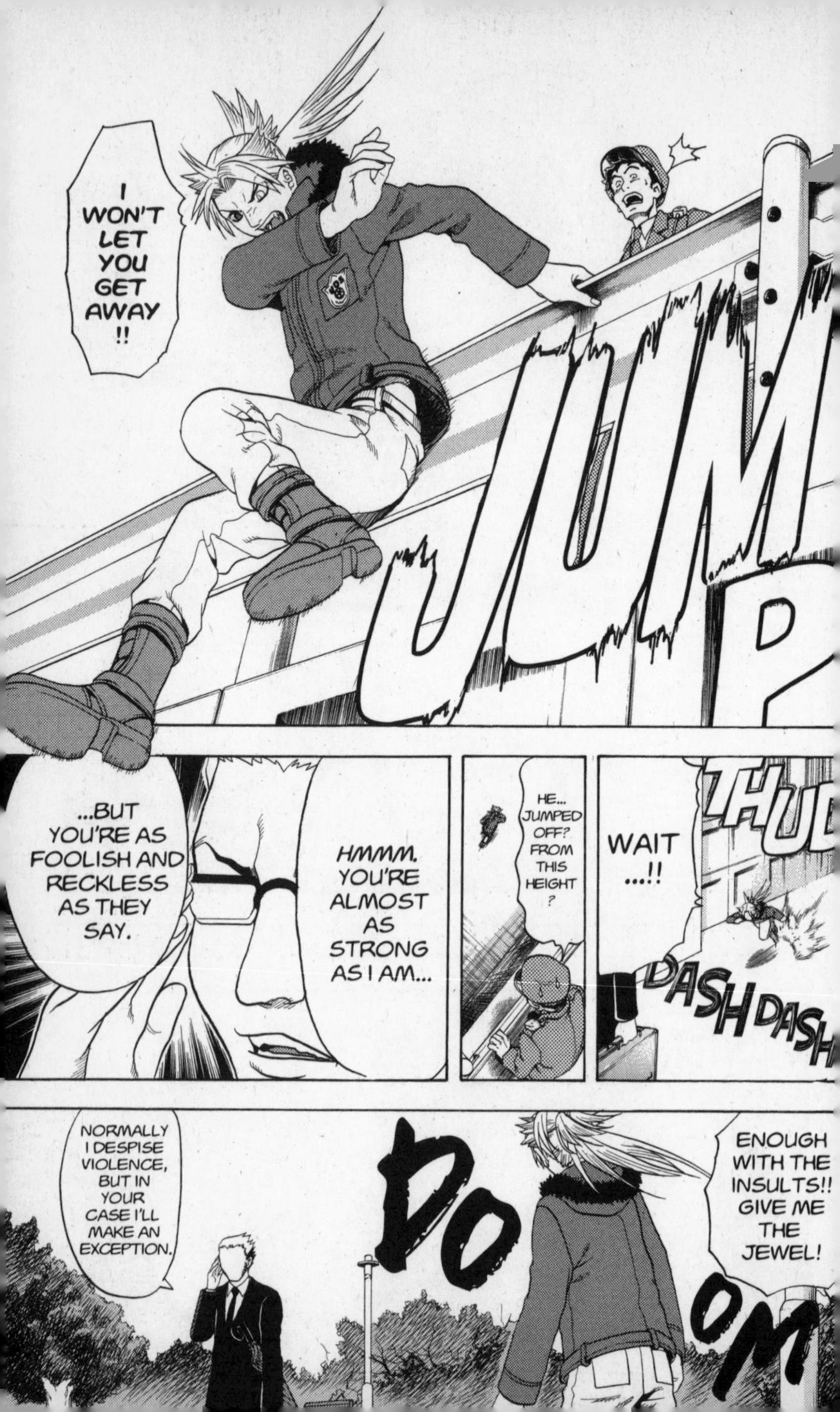
I WON'T LET YOU GET AWAY!!
JUMP
THUD
WAIT...!!
DASH DASH
HE... JUMPED OFF? FROM THIS HEIGHT?
HMMM. YOU'RE ALMOST AS STRONG AS I AM...
...BUT YOU'RE AS FOOLISH AND RECKLESS AS THEY SAY.
ENOUGH WITH THE INSULTS!! GIVE ME THE JEWEL!
DOOM
NORMALLY I DESPISE VIOLENCE, BUT IN YOUR CASE I'LL MAKE AN EXCEPTION.

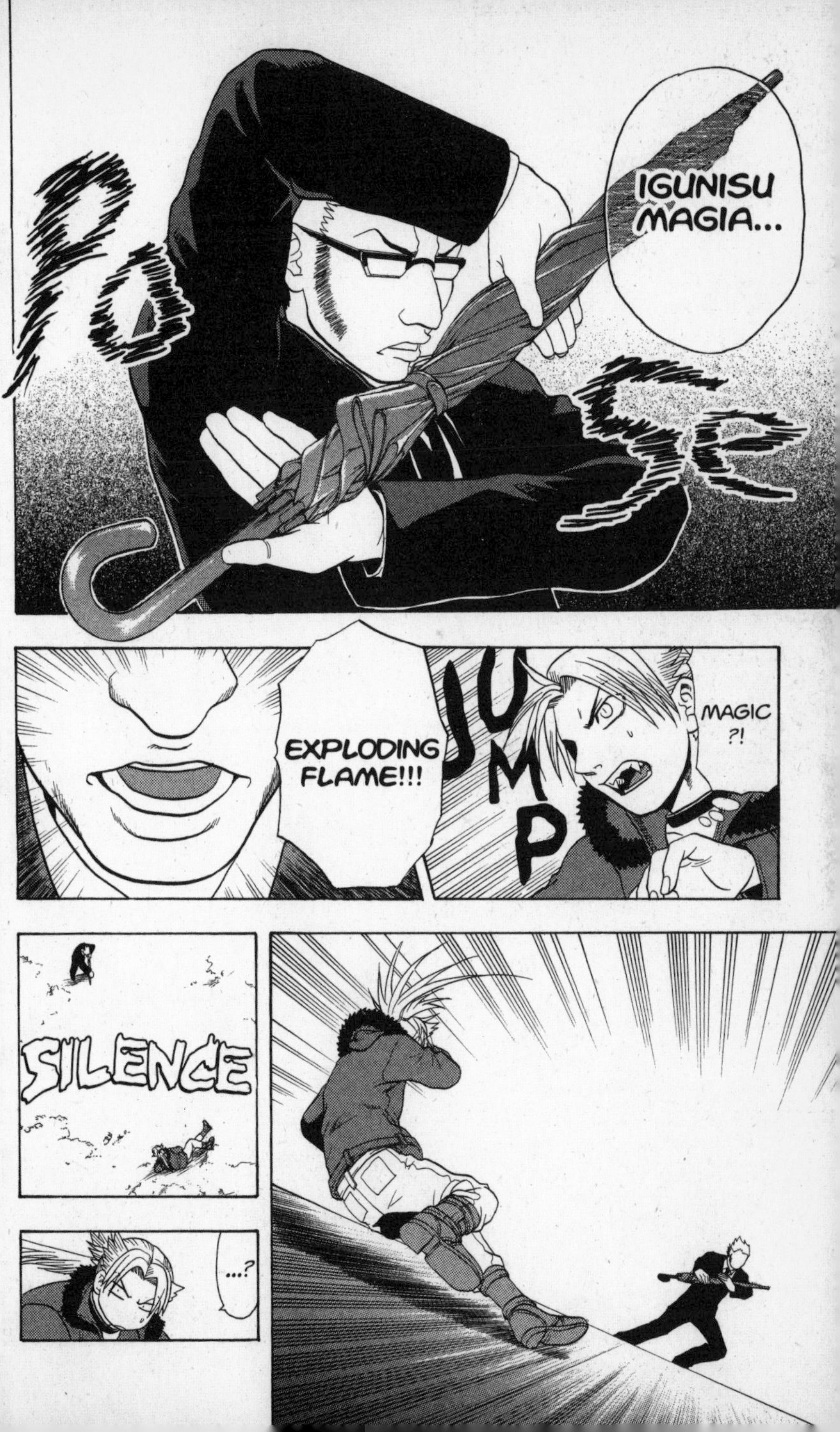
IGUNISU MAGIA...
MAGIC ?!
JUMP
EXPLODING FLAME!!!
SILENCE
...?

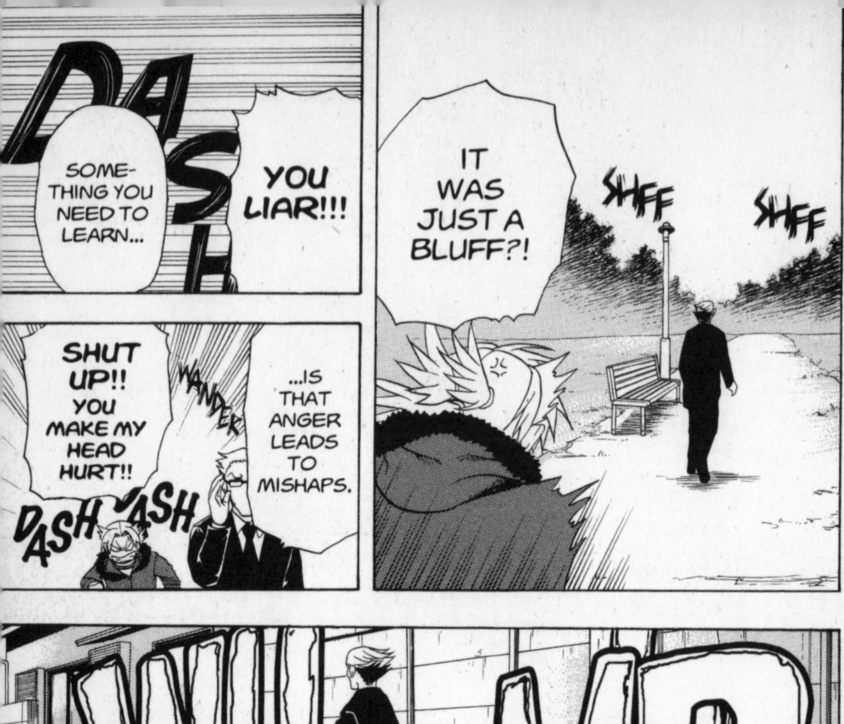
IT WAS JUST A BLUFF?!
SHFF
SHFF
YOU LIAR!!!
SOME-THING YOU NEED TO LEARN...
DASH
...IS THAT ANGER LEADS TO MISHAPS.
WANDER
SHUT UP!! YOU MAKE MY HEAD HURT!!
DASH DASH
WUMP

SIGNS: SAFETY FIRST

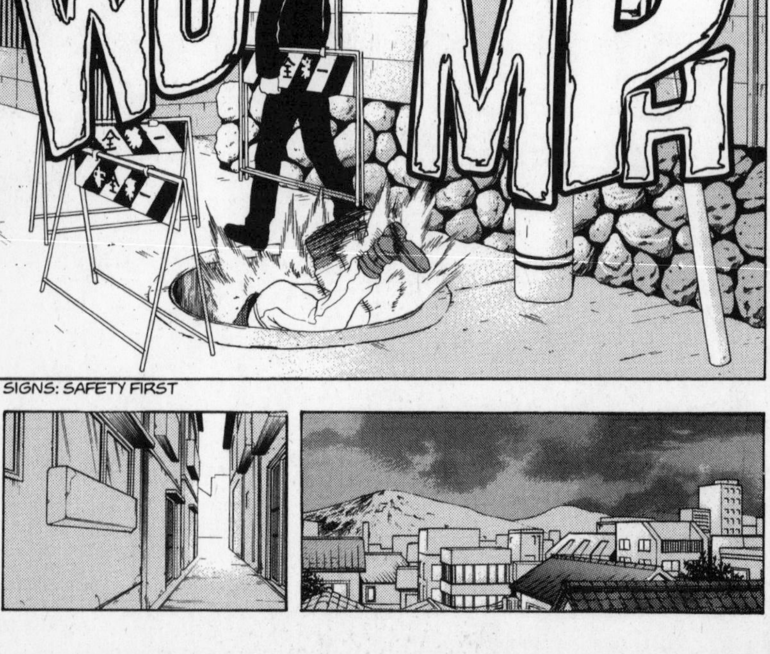

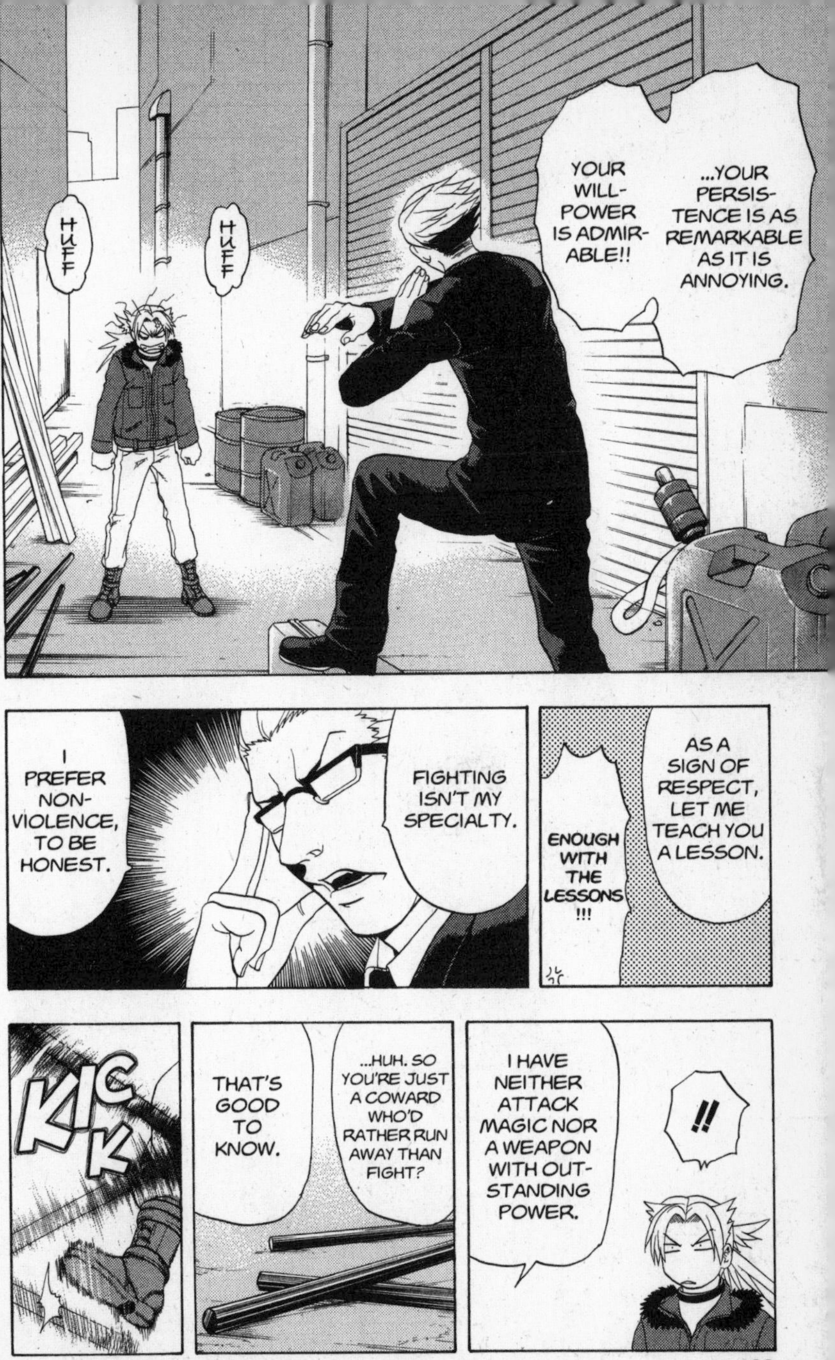
...YOUR PERSISTENCE IS AS REMARKABLE AS IT IS ANNOYING.
YOUR WILL-POWER IS ADMIRABLE!!
HUFF
HUFF
AS A SIGN OF RESPECT, LET ME TEACH YOU A LESSON.
ENOUGH WITH THE LESSONS!!!
FIGHTING ISN'T MY SPECIALTY.
I PREFER NON-VIOLENCE, TO BE HONEST.
I HAVE NEITHER ATTACK MAGIC NOR A WEAPON WITH OUT-STANDING POWER.
!!
...HUH. SO YOU'RE JUST A COWARD WHO'D RATHER RUN AWAY THAN FIGHT?
THAT'S GOOD TO KNOW.
KICK

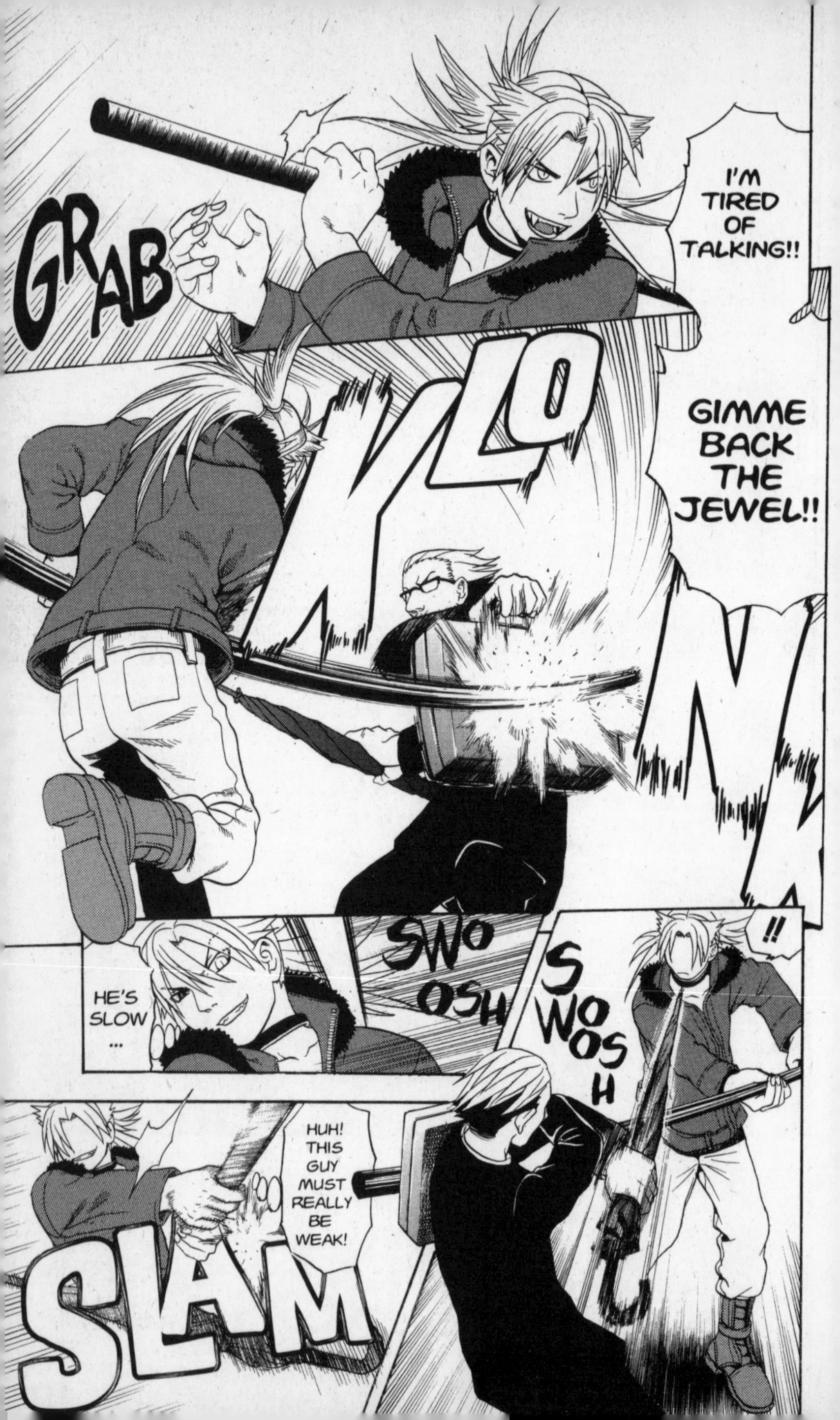
I'M TIRED OF TALKING!!
GRAB
GIMME BACK THE JEWEL!!
KLON
!!
SWOOSH
SWOOSH
HE'S SLOW ...
HUH! THIS GUY MUST REALLY BE WEAK!
SLAM

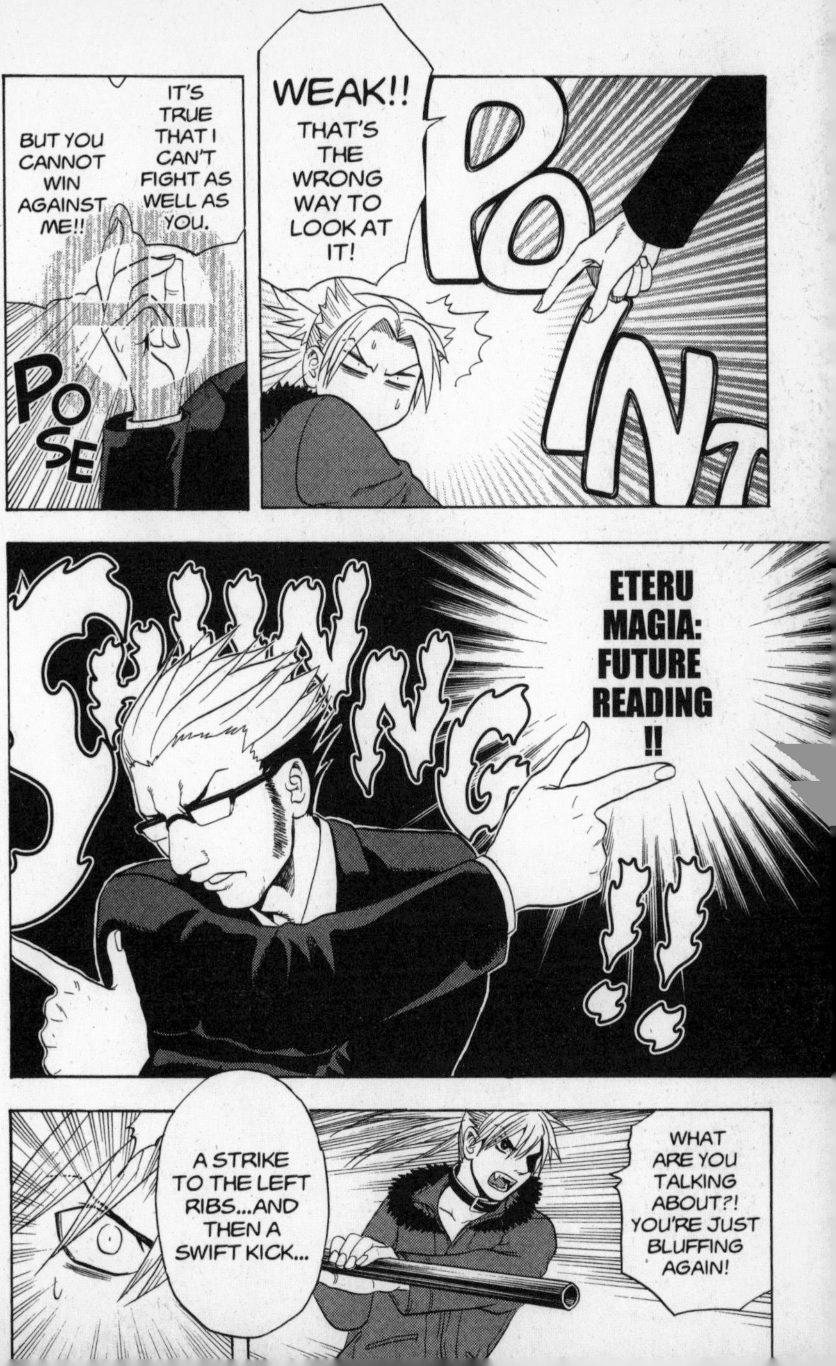
WEAK!!
THAT'S THE WRONG WAY TO LOOK AT IT!
POINT
IT'S TRUE THAT I CAN'T FIGHT AS WELL AS YOU.
BUT YOU CANNOT WIN AGAINST ME!!
POSE
ETERU MAGIA: FUTURE READING!!
WHAT ARE YOU TALKING ABOUT?! YOU'RE JUST BLUFFING AGAIN!
A STRIKE TO THE LEFT RIBS...AND THEN A SWIFT KICK...

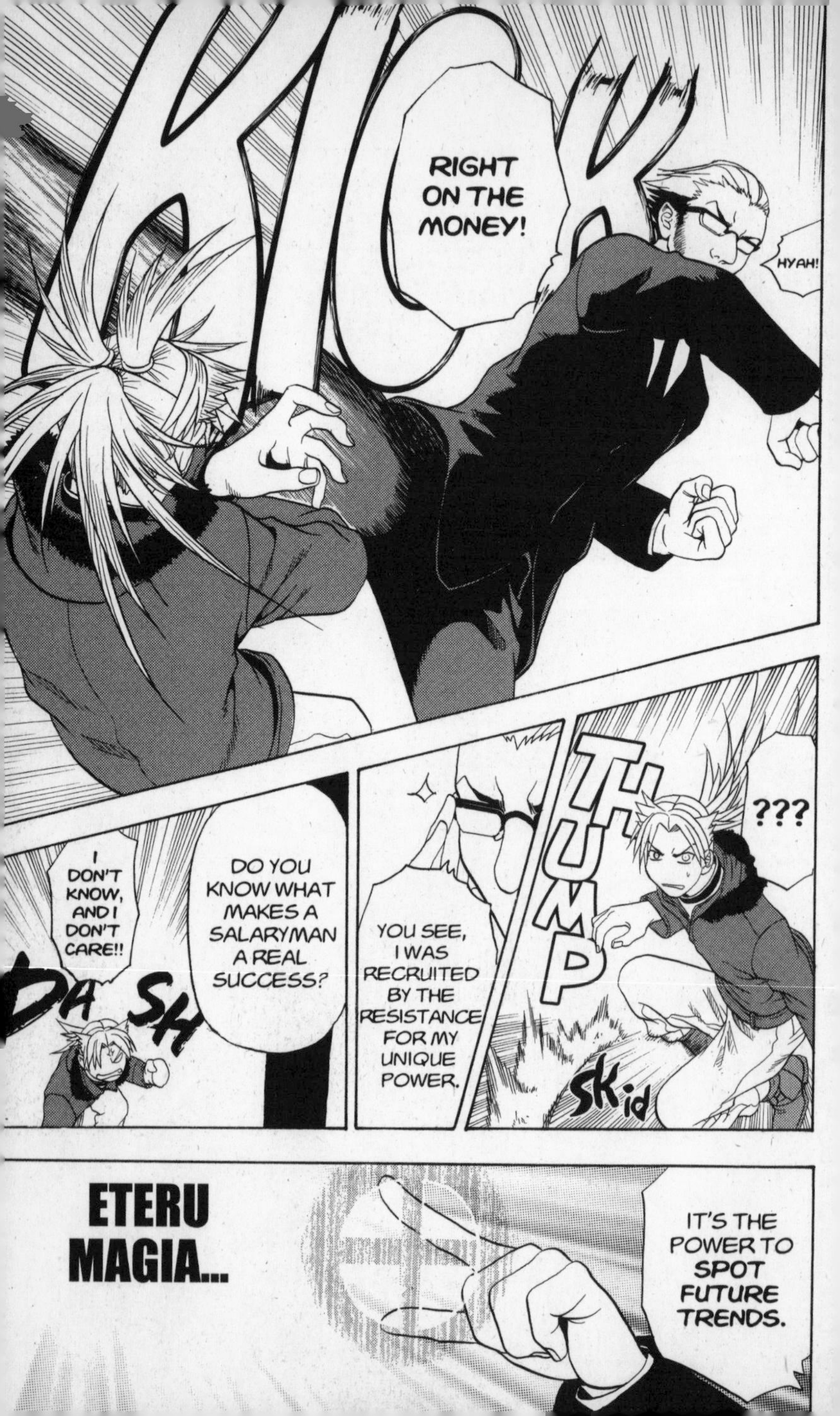
HYAH!
RIGHT ON THE MONEY!
???
THUMP
SKid
YOU SEE, I WAS RECRUITED BY THE RESISTANCE FOR MY UNIQUE POWER.
DO YOU KNOW WHAT MAKES A SALARYMAN A REAL SUCCESS?
I DON'T KNOW, AND I DON'T CARE!!
DASH
IT'S THE POWER TO SPOT FUTURE TRENDS.
ETERU MAGIA...

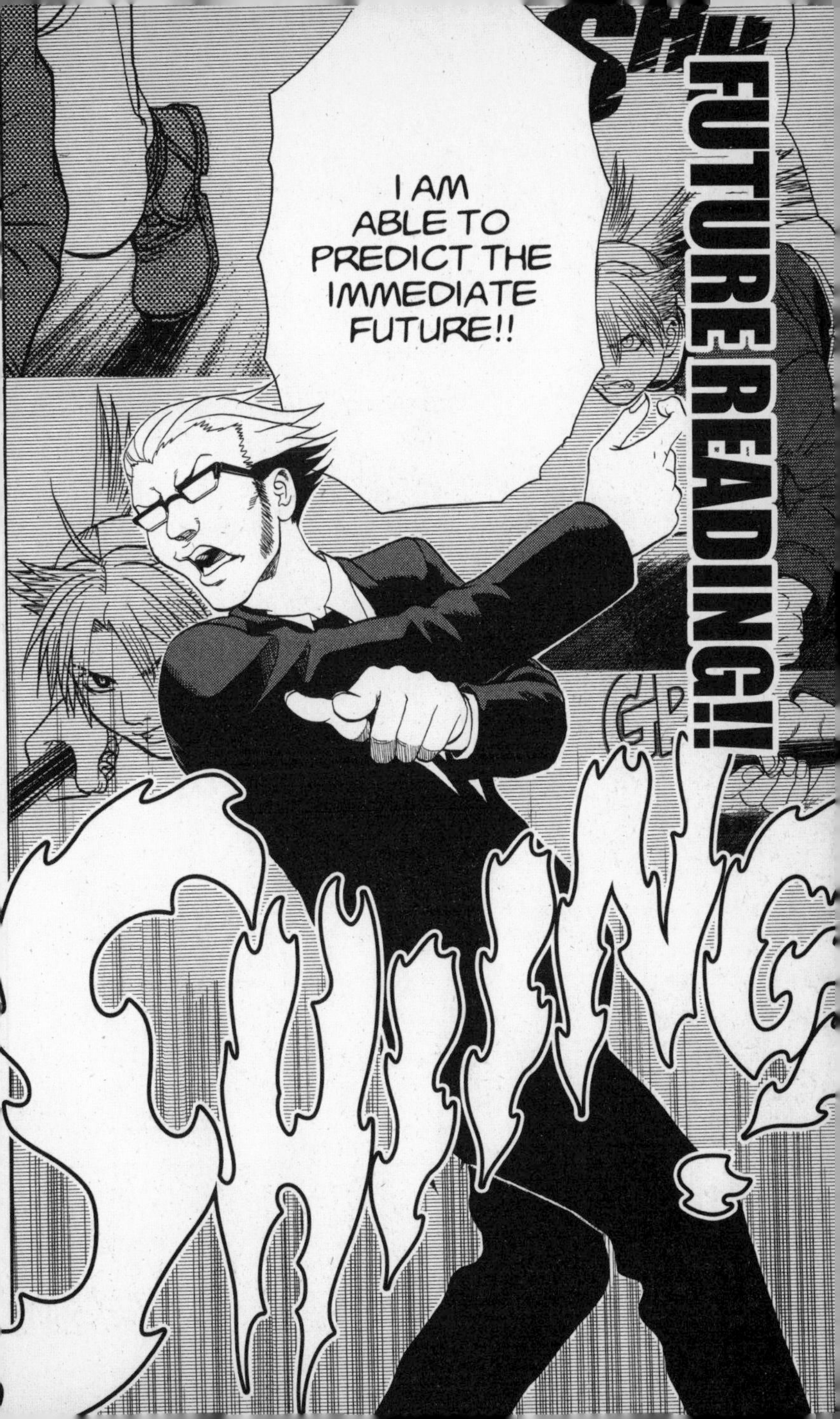
I AM ABLE TO PREDICT THE IMMEDIATE FUTURE!!
FUTURE READING!!

READ THIS WAY

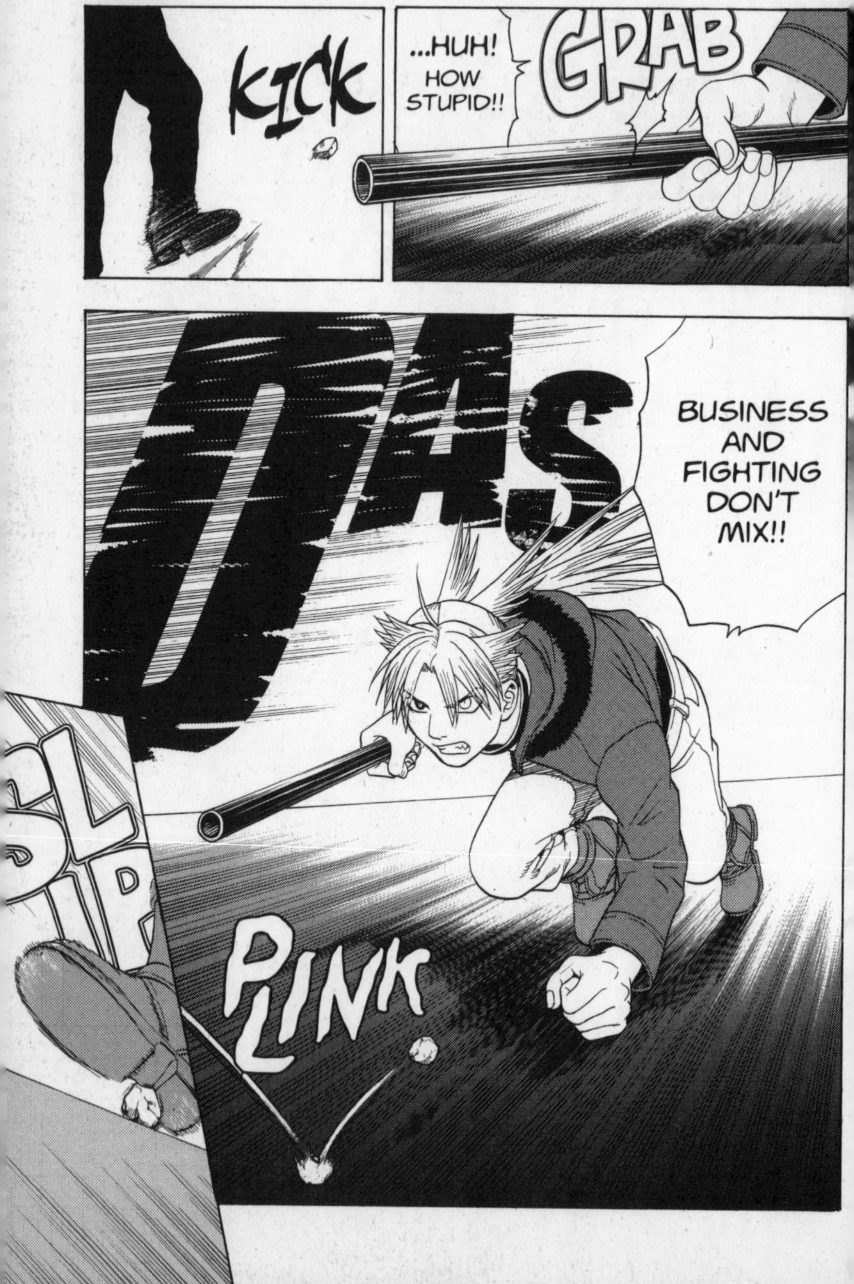
GRAB
...HUH! HOW STUPID!!
KICK
DAS
BUSINESS AND FIGHTING DON'T MIX!!
PLINK

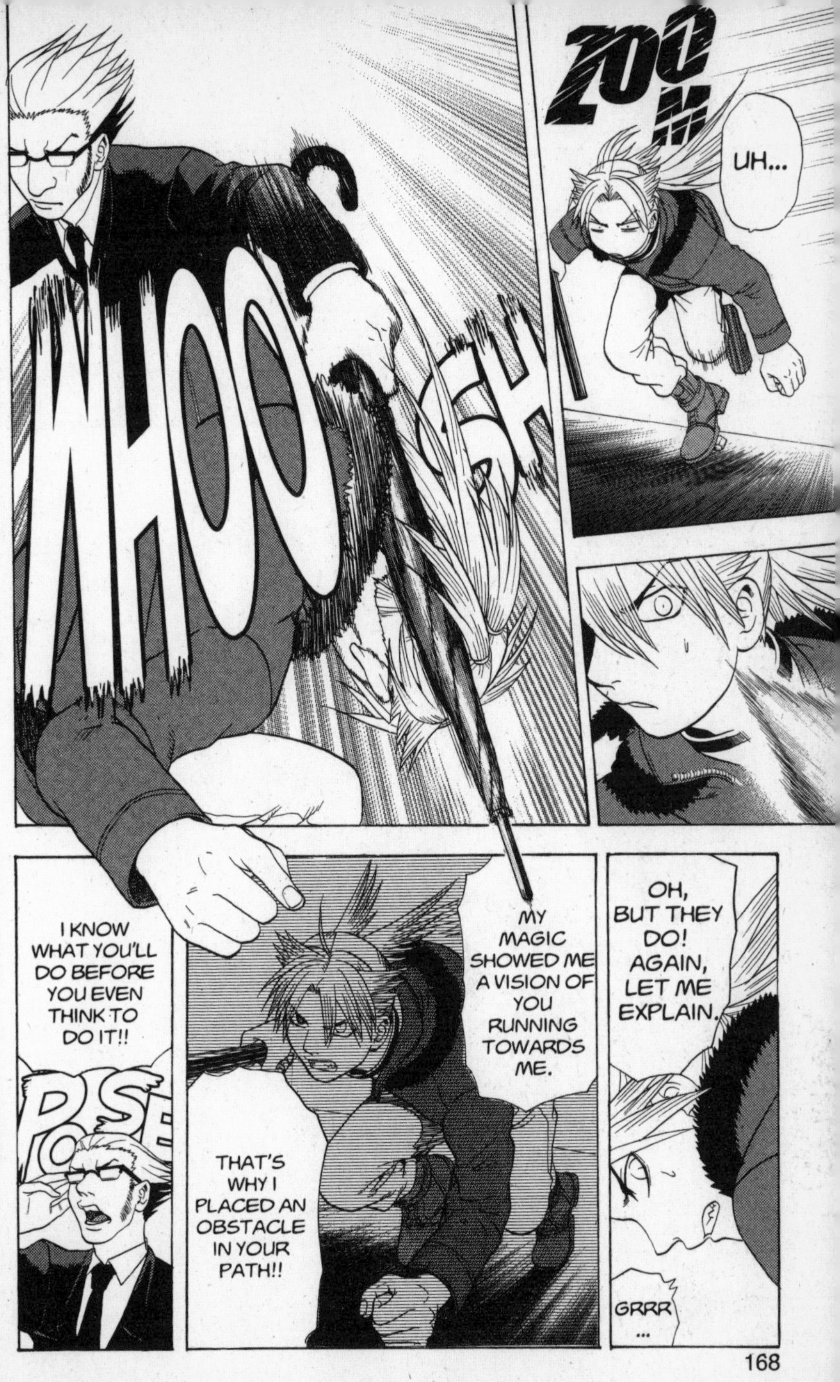
ZOOM
UH...
WHOOSH
OH, BUT THEY DO! AGAIN, LET ME EXPLAIN.
GRRR ...
MY MAGIC SHOWED ME A VISION OF YOU RUNNING TOWARDS ME.
THAT'S WHY I PLACED AN OBSTACLE IN YOUR PATH!!
I KNOW WHAT YOU'LL DO BEFORE YOU EVEN THINK TO DO IT!!

READ THIS WAY

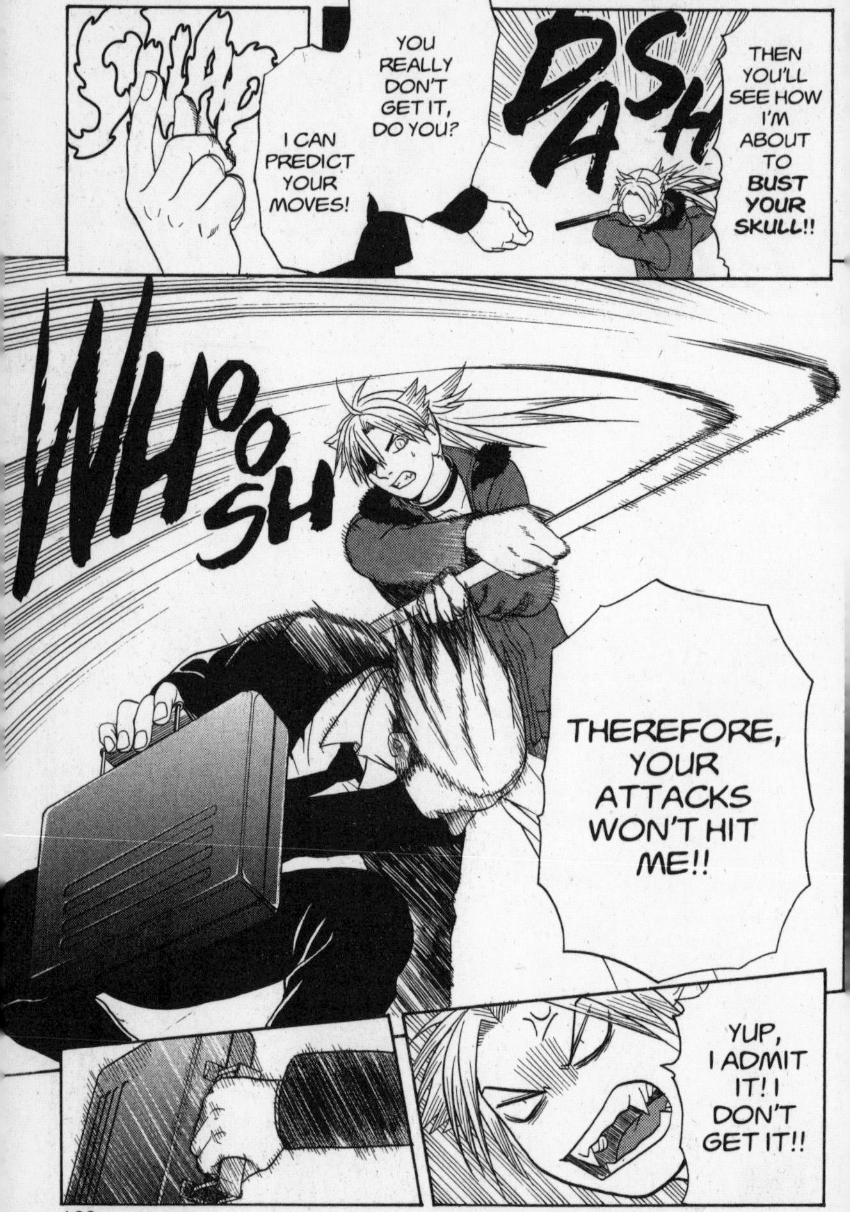

DASH
THEN YOU'LL SEE HOW I'M ABOUT TO **BUST YOUR SKULL!!**
YOU REALLY DON'T GET IT, DO YOU?
I CAN PREDICT YOUR MOVES!
WHOOSH
THEREFORE, YOUR ATTACKS WON'T HIT ME!!
YUP, I ADMIT IT! I DON'T GET IT!!

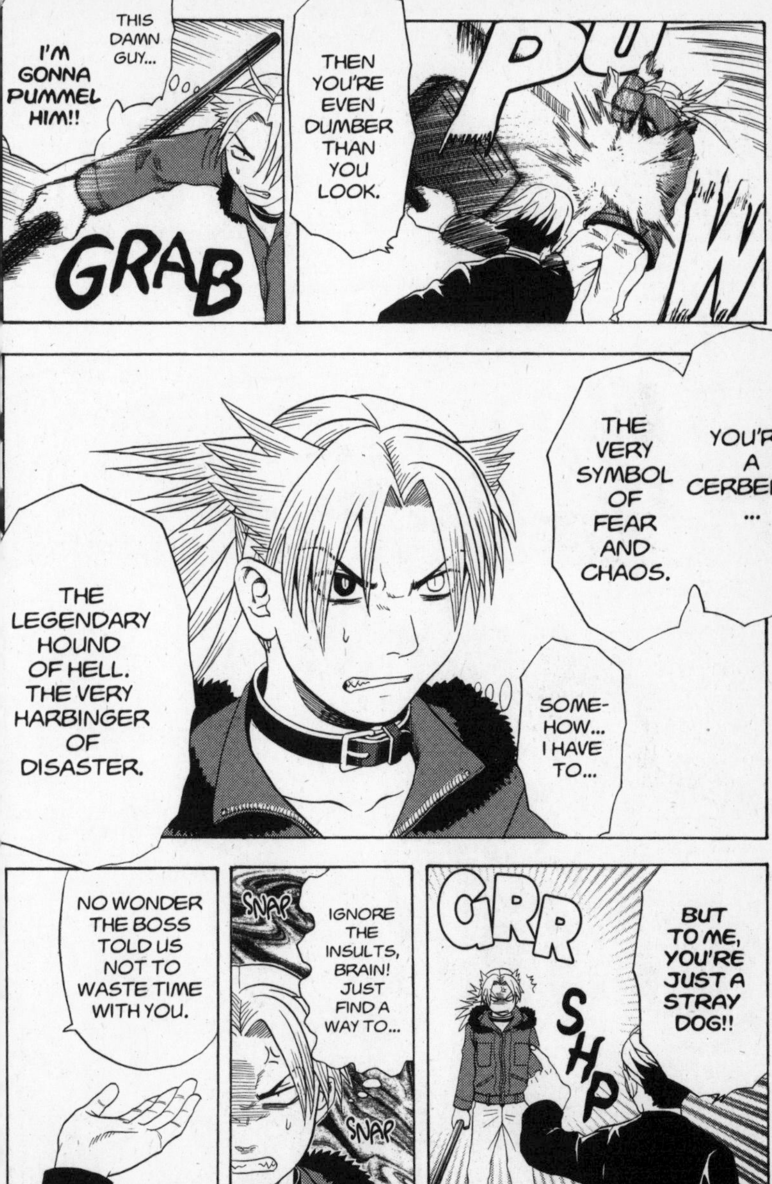
PUW
THEN YOU'RE EVEN DUMBER THAN YOU LOOK.
THIS DAMN GUY...
I'M GONNA PUMMEL HIM!!
GRAB
YOU'RE A CERBERUS...
THE VERY SYMBOL OF FEAR AND CHAOS.
THE LEGENDARY HOUND OF HELL. THE VERY HARBINGER OF DISASTER.
SOME-HOW... I HAVE TO...
GRR
BUT TO ME, YOU'RE JUST A STRAY DOG!!
SHP
SNAP
IGNORE THE INSULTS, BRAIN! JUST FIND A WAY TO...
SNAP
NO WONDER THE BOSS TOLD US NOT TO WASTE TIME WITH YOU.

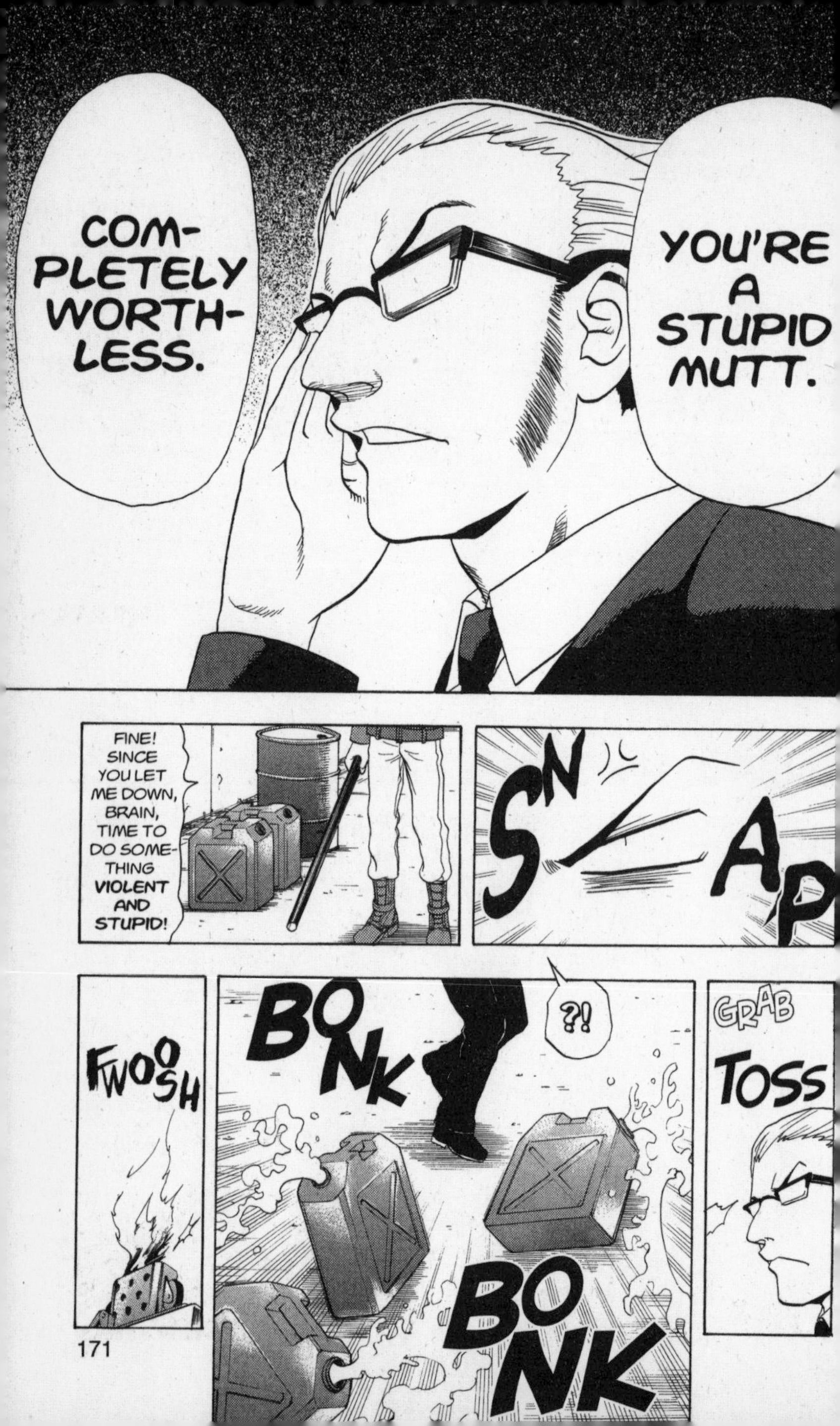
YOU'RE A STUPID MUTT.
COMPLETELY WORTHLESS.
SNAP
FINE! SINCE YOU LET ME DOWN, BRAIN, TIME TO DO SOMETHING VIOLENT AND STUPID!
GRAB
TOSS
BONK
?!
BONK
FWOOSH

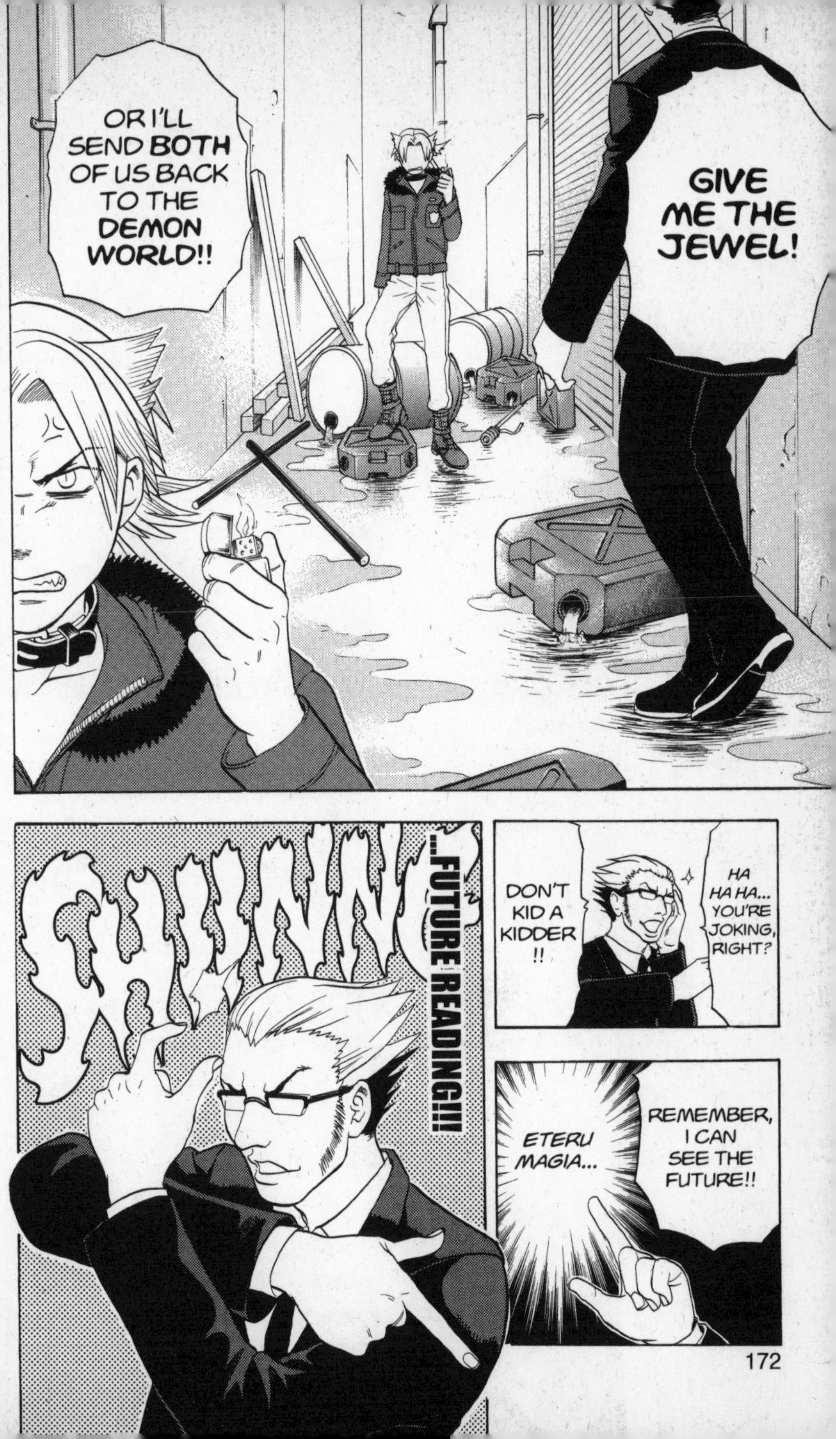
GIVE ME THE JEWEL!
OR I'LL SEND BOTH OF US BACK TO THE DEMON WORLD!!
HA HA HA... YOU'RE JOKING, RIGHT?
DON'T KID A KIDDER!!
REMEMBER, I CAN SEE THE FUTURE!!
ETERU MAGIA...
...FUTURE READING!!!
SHUNN

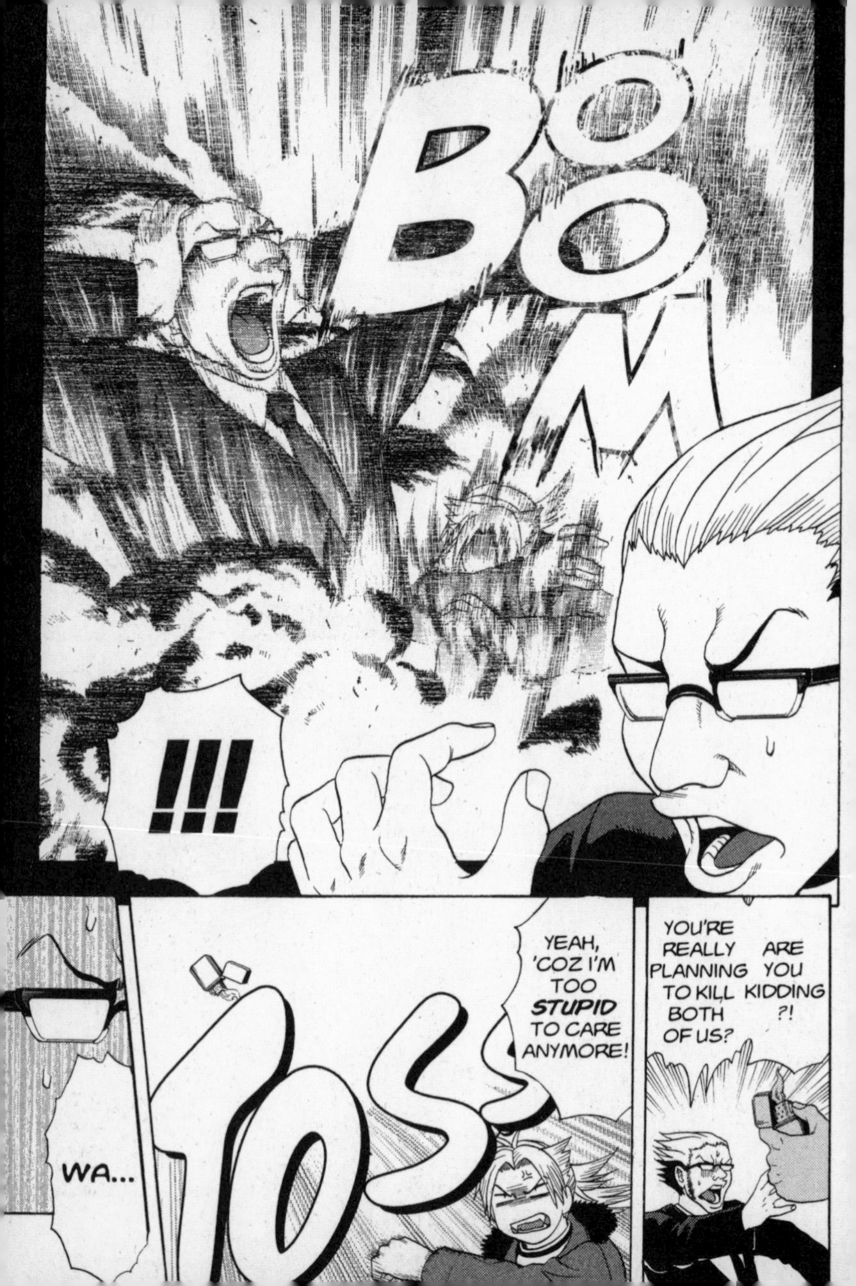
BOOM
!!!
ARE YOU KIDDING?!
YOU'RE REALLY PLANNING TO KILL BOTH OF US?
YEAH, 'COZ I'M TOO STUPID TO CARE ANYMORE!
TOSS
WA...

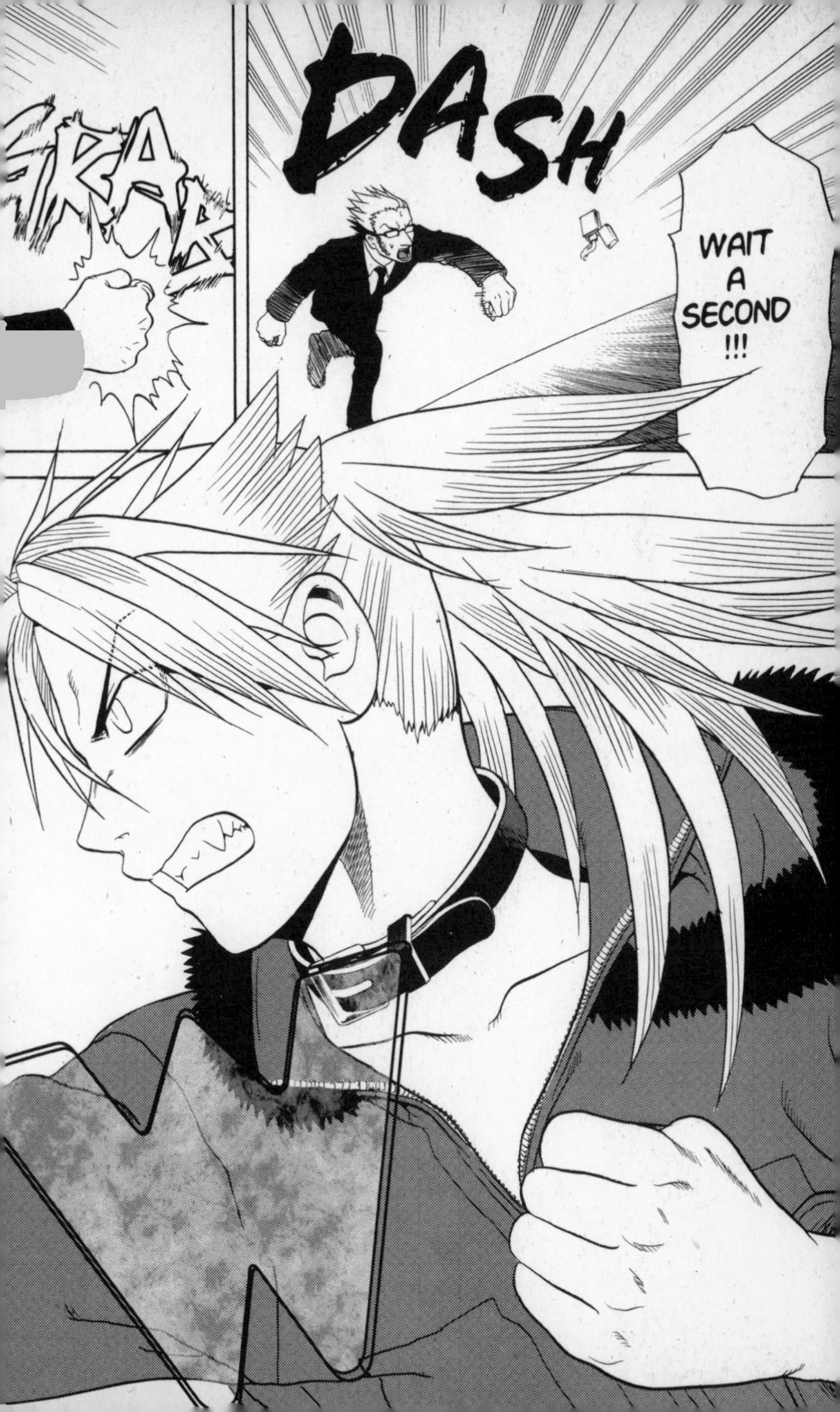
DASH
WAIT A SECOND !!!
GRAB

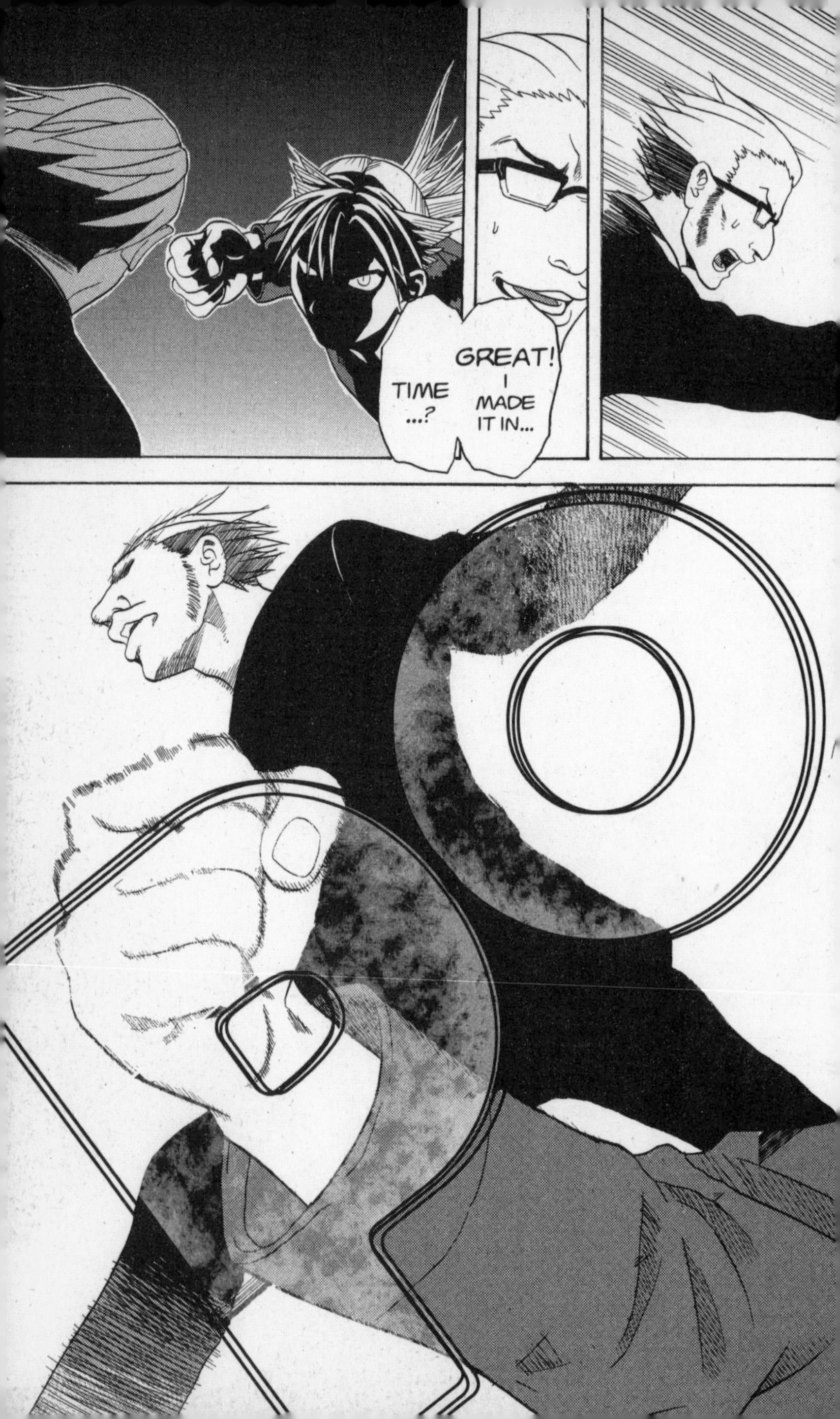
GREAT! I MADE IT IN... TIME ...?

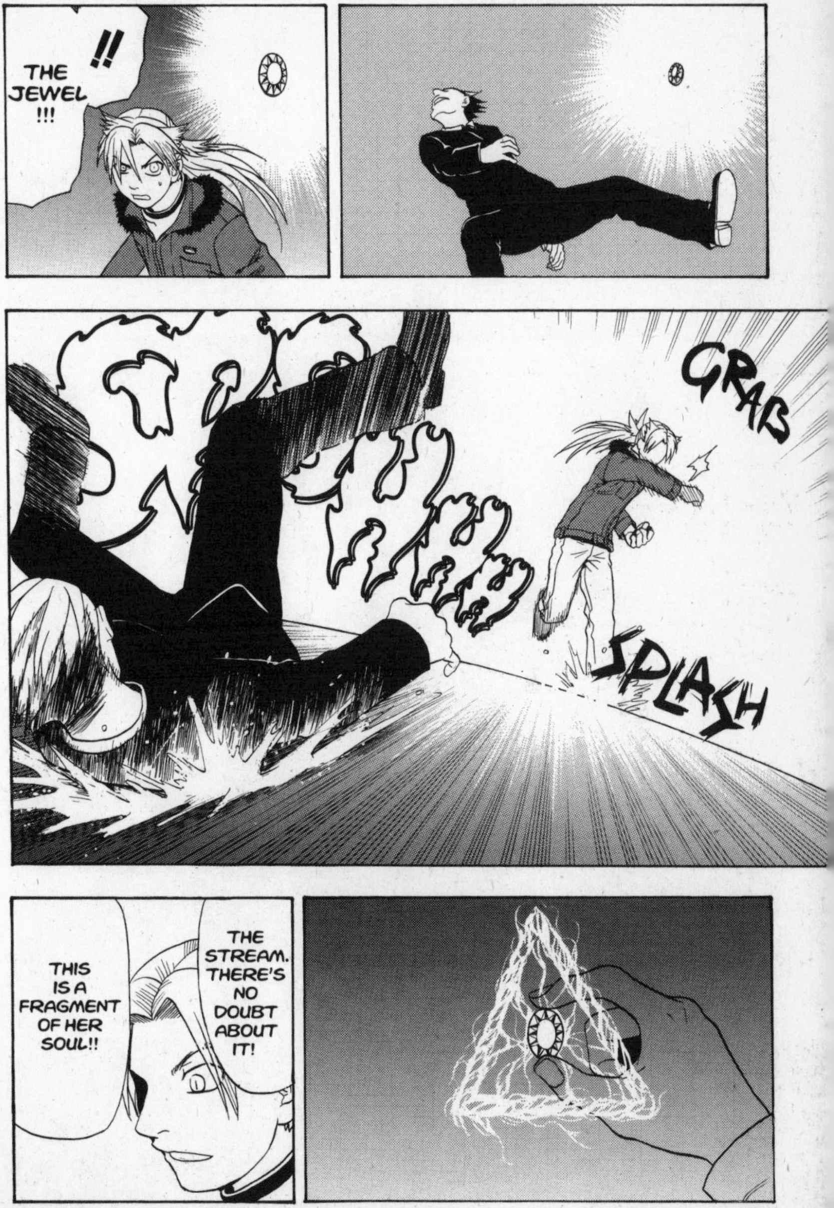
!!
THE JEWEL !!!
GRAB
SPLASH
THE STREAM. THERE'S NO DOUBT ABOUT IT!
THIS IS A FRAGMENT OF HER SOUL!!

READ THIS WAY

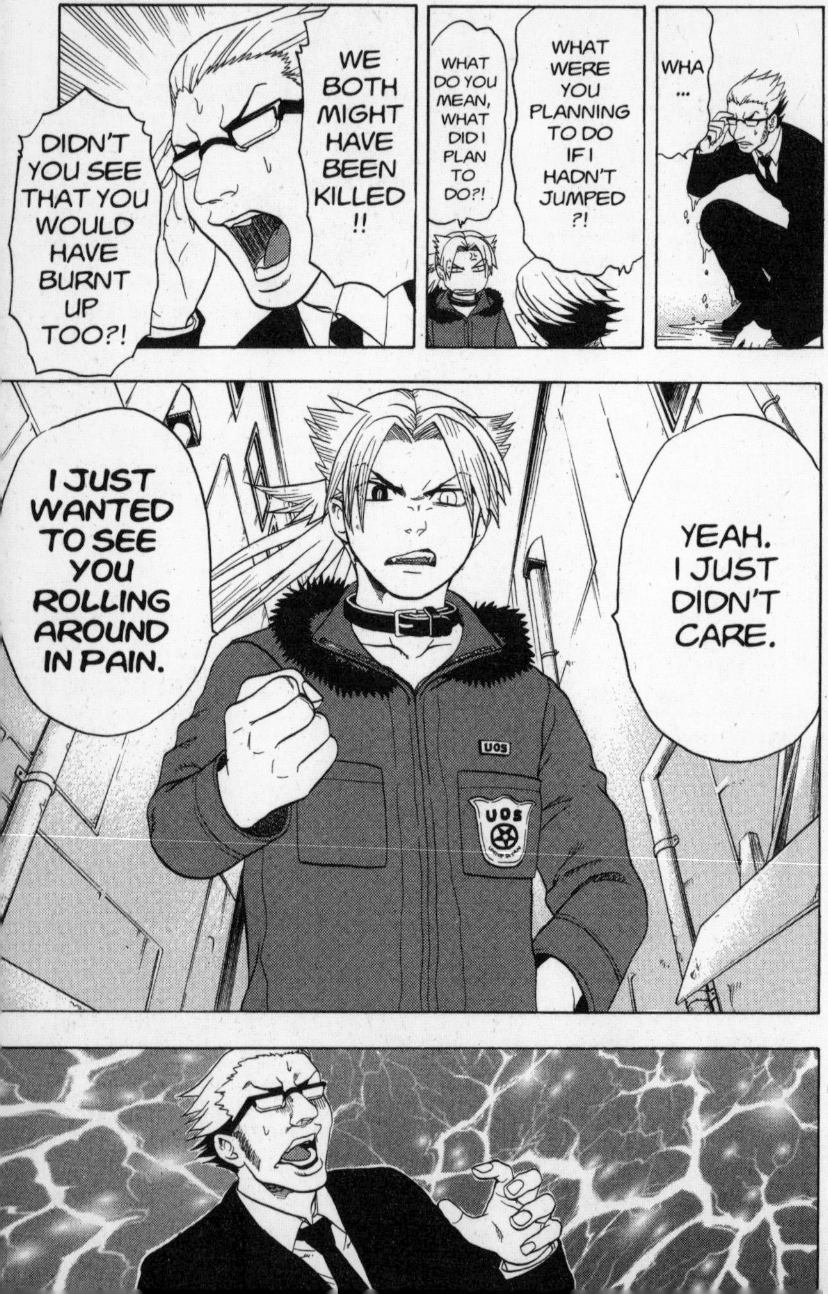
WHA ...
WHAT WERE YOU PLANNING TO DO IF I HADN'T JUMPED?!
WHAT DO YOU MEAN, WHAT DID I PLAN TO DO?!
WE BOTH MIGHT HAVE BEEN KILLED!!
DIDN'T YOU SEE THAT YOU WOULD HAVE BURNT UP TOO?!
YEAH. I JUST DIDN'T CARE.
I JUST WANTED TO SEE YOU ROLLING AROUND IN PAIN.
UOS
UOS

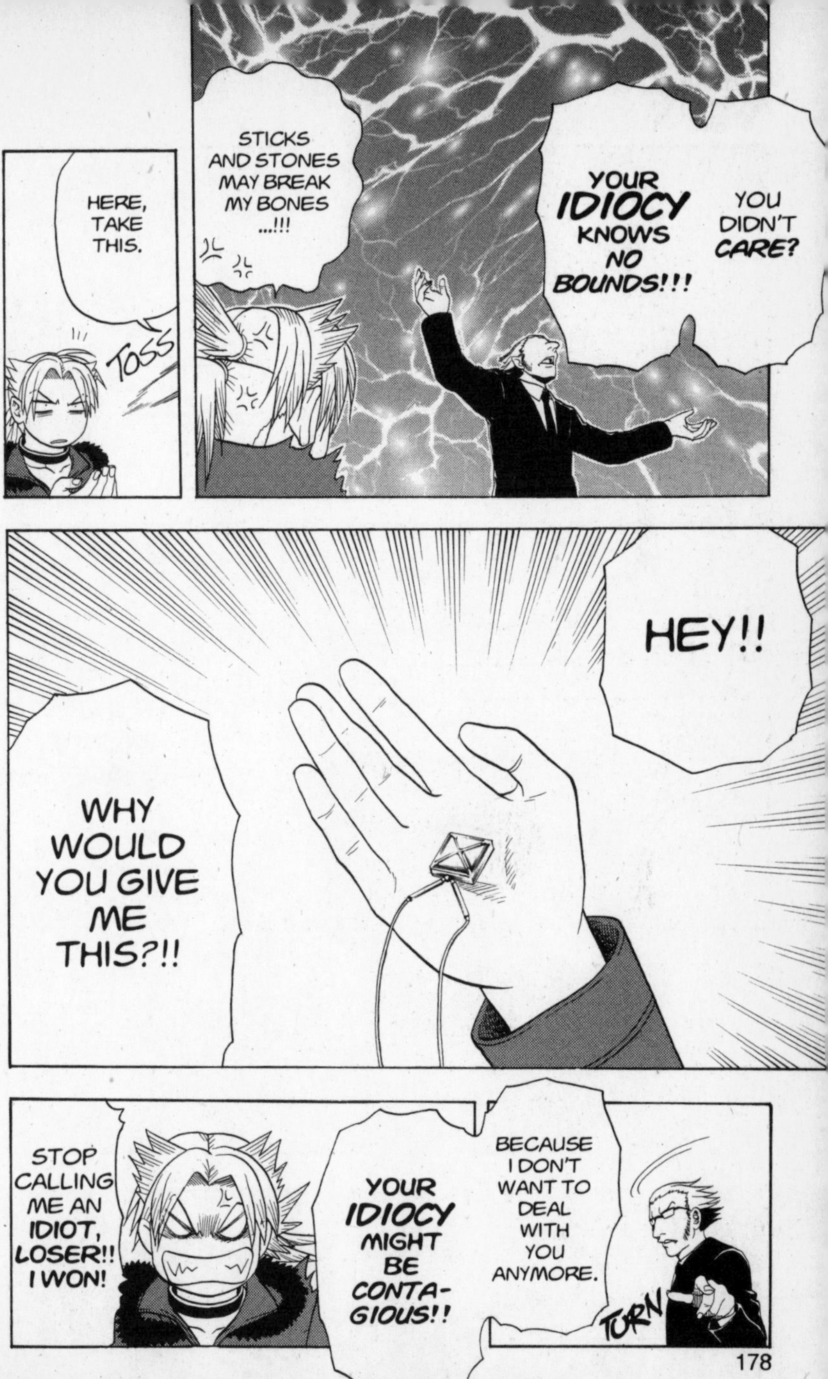
YOU DIDN'T CARE?
YOUR IDIOCY KNOWS NO BOUNDS!!!
STICKS AND STONES MAY BREAK MY BONES ...!!!
HERE, TAKE THIS.
TOSS
HEY!!
WHY WOULD YOU GIVE ME THIS?!!
BECAUSE I DON'T WANT TO DEAL WITH YOU ANYMORE.
TURN
YOUR IDIOCY MIGHT BE CONTA-GIOUS!!
STOP CALLING ME AN IDIOT, LOSER!! I WON!

READ THIS WAY

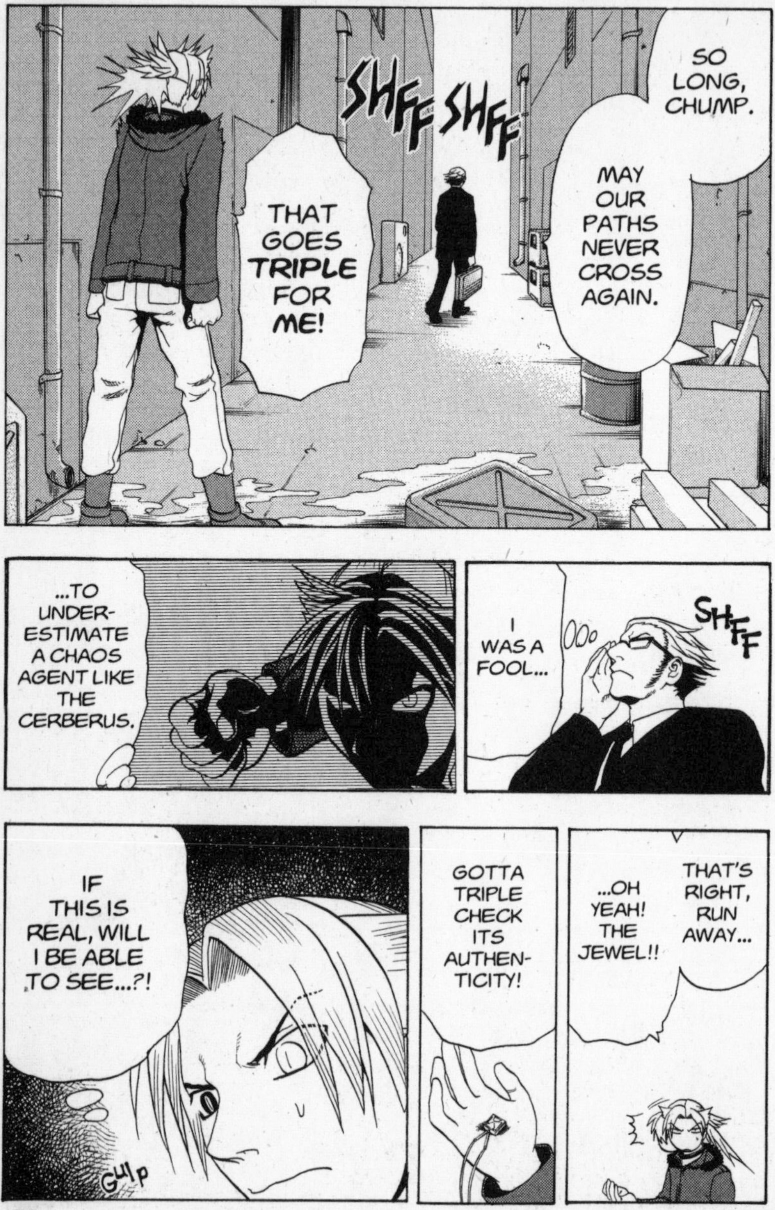
SO LONG, CHUMP.
MAY OUR PATHS NEVER CROSS AGAIN.
SHFF SHFF
THAT GOES TRIPLE FOR ME!
SHFF
I WAS A FOOL...
...TO UNDER-ESTIMATE A CHAOS AGENT LIKE THE CERBERUS.
THAT'S RIGHT, RUN AWAY...
...OH YEAH! THE JEWEL!!
GOTTA TRIPLE CHECK ITS AUTHEN-TICITY!
IF THIS IS REAL, WILL I BE ABLE TO SEE...?!
GULP

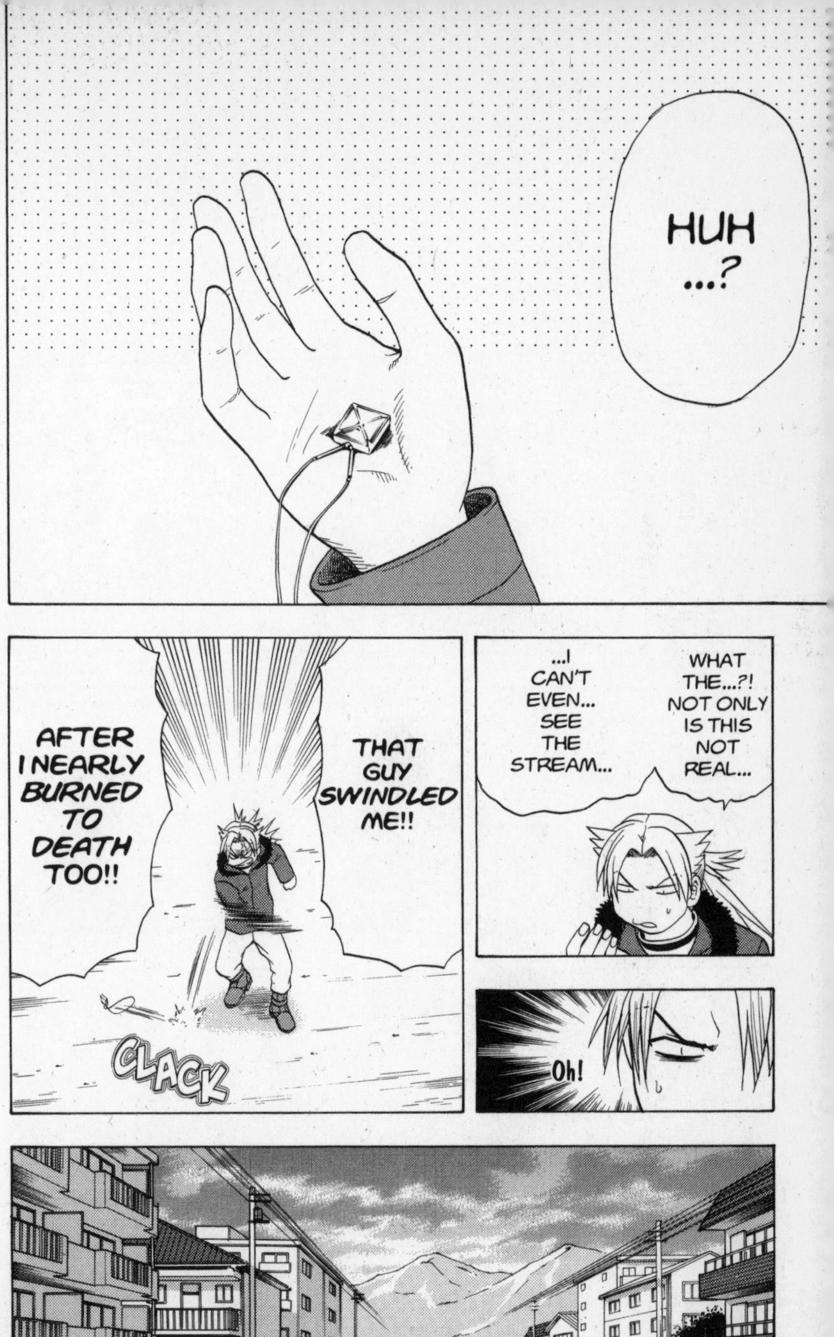
HUH ...?
WHAT THE...?! NOT ONLY IS THIS NOT REAL...
...I CAN'T EVEN... SEE THE STREAM...
Oh!
THAT GUY SWINDLED ME!!
AFTER I NEARLY BURNED TO DEATH TOO!!
CLACK

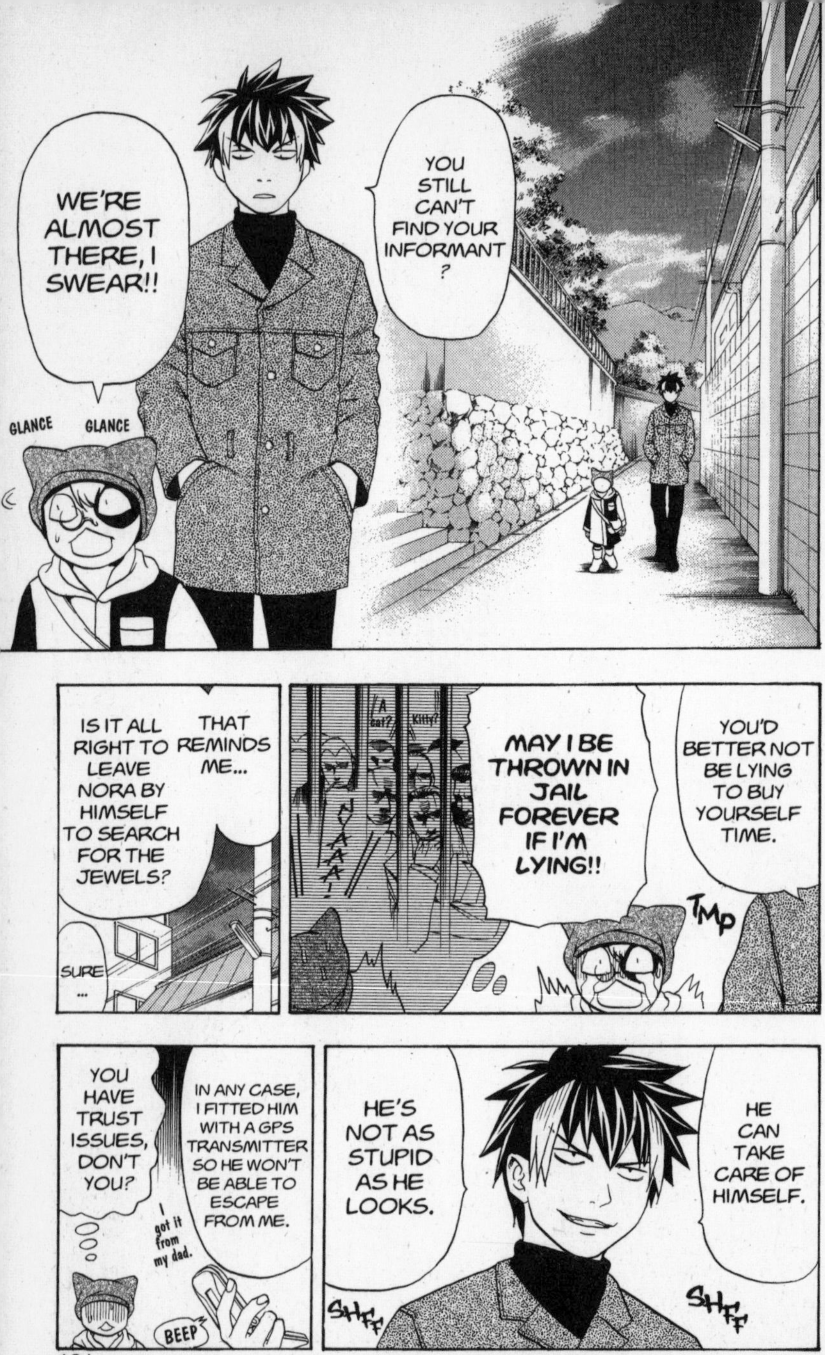
YOU STILL CAN'T FIND YOUR INFORMANT?
WE'RE ALMOST THERE, I SWEAR!!
GLANCE
GLANCE
YOU'D BETTER NOT BE LYING TO BUY YOURSELF TIME.
TMP
MAY I BE THROWN IN JAIL FOREVER IF I'M LYING!!
Kitty?
A cat?
NYAAAA!
THAT REMINDS ME...
IS IT ALL RIGHT TO LEAVE NORA BY HIMSELF TO SEARCH FOR THE JEWELS?
SURE...
HE CAN TAKE CARE OF HIMSELF.
HE'S NOT AS STUPID AS HE LOOKS.
SHFF
SHFF
IN ANY CASE, I FITTED HIM WITH A GPS TRANSMITTER SO HE WON'T BE ABLE TO ESCAPE FROM ME.
YOU HAVE TRUST ISSUES, DON'T YOU?
I got it from my dad.
BEEP

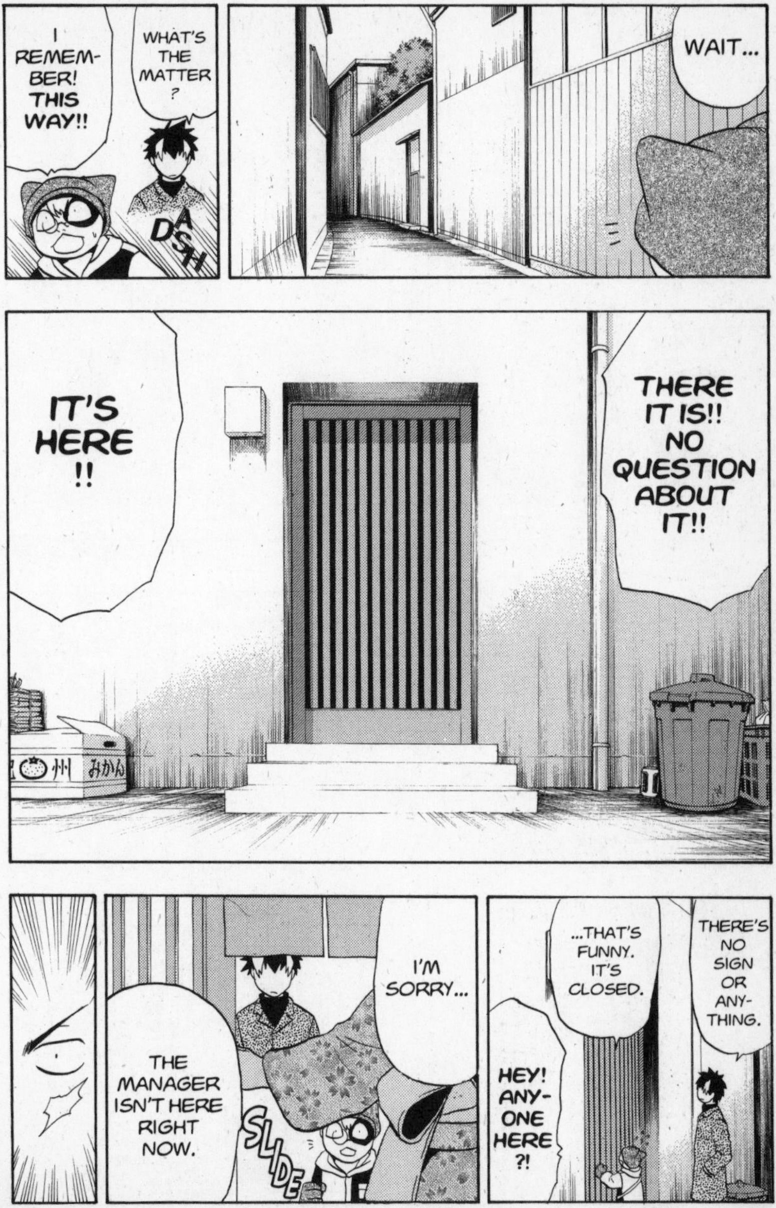
WAIT...
WHAT'S THE MATTER?
I REMEMBER! THIS WAY!!
DASH
THERE IT IS!! NO QUESTION ABOUT IT!!
IT'S HERE!!
みかん
THERE'S NO SIGN OR ANYTHING.
...THAT'S FUNNY. IT'S CLOSED.
HEY! ANYONE HERE?!
I'M SORRY...
THE MANAGER ISN'T HERE RIGHT NOW.
SLIDE

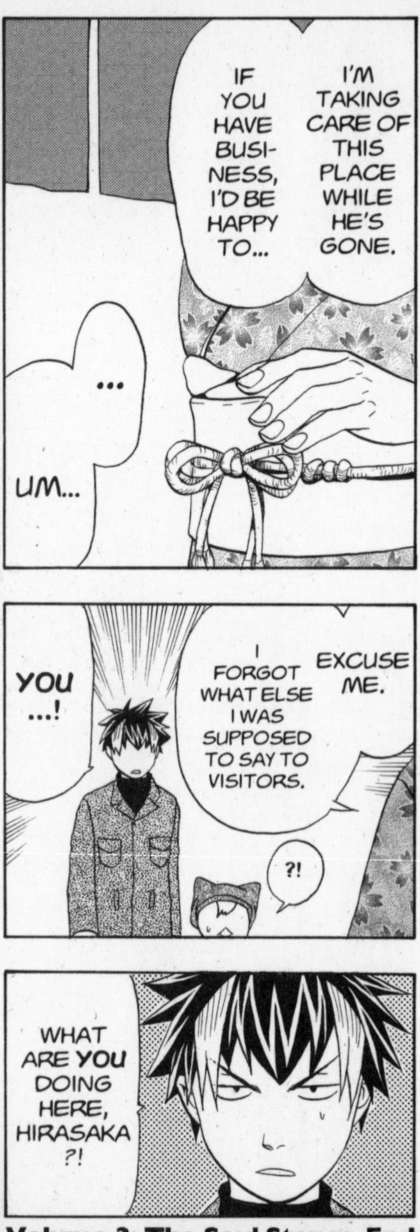
I'M TAKING CARE OF THIS PLACE WHILE HE'S GONE.
IF YOU HAVE BUSI-NESS, I'D BE HAPPY TO...
... UM...
EXCUSE ME.
I FORGOT WHAT ELSE I WAS SUPPOSED TO SAY TO VISITORS.
YOU ...!
?!
WHAT ARE YOU DOING HERE, HIRASAKA ?!

Volume 3: The Soul Stones–End

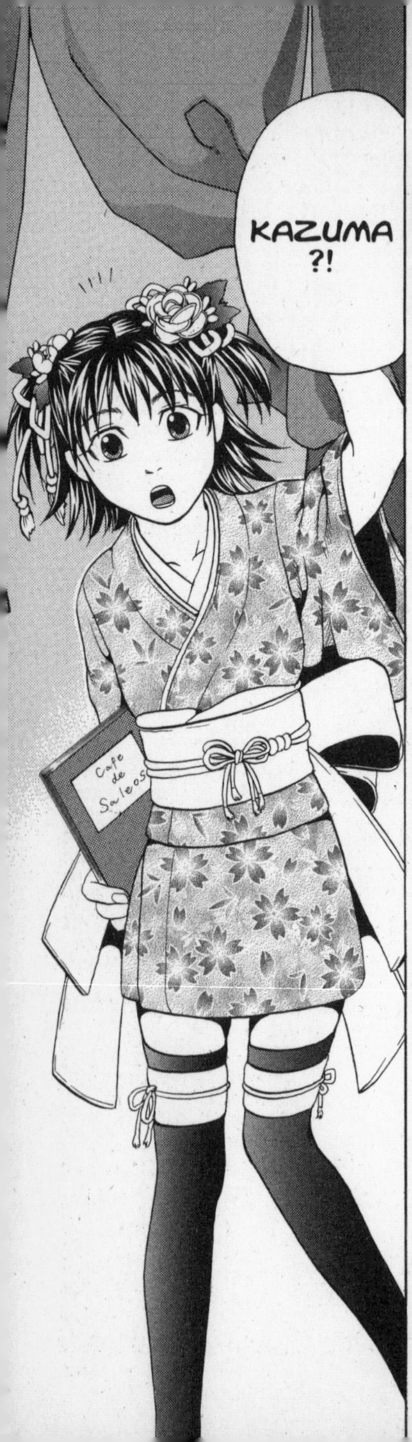
KAZUMA ?!
Cafe de Saleos

CHARACTER DATA

KAIN

HEIGHT: 183 CM
VORITE FOOD: ?
OD HE HATES: ?
RESTS AND
CIAL TALENTS: ?
NOTES: KAIN IS THE DARK LIEGE'S RIGHT
HAND BECAUSE OF HIS RESERVED
AND CIRCUMSPECT CHARACTER.
SHE TRUSTS HIM, WHICH MAKES KAIN THE
"POWER BEHIND THE THRONE." FROM ALL
INDICATIONS, THEY'RE OLD FRIENDS.

LEONARD

HEIGHT: 189 CM
FAVORITE FOOD: WINE... AND TIN CANS
FOOD HE HATES: JUNK FOOD
INTERESTS AND
SPECIAL TALENTS: TENDS TO HAVE A NERVOUS
DISPOSITION.
NOTES: THE DARK LIEGE ARMY LAND CORPS GENERAL
WHO WORRIES TOO MUCH. BECAUSE OF HIS
GREAT ABILITY AND NOBLE CHARACTER, HE
ENDS UP TAKING ON THE MOST CHALLENGING
TASKS. RIVAN, WHOM HE HAS KNOWN SINCE
CHILDHOOD, HAS GIVEN HIM ALL SORTS OF
TROUBLE.

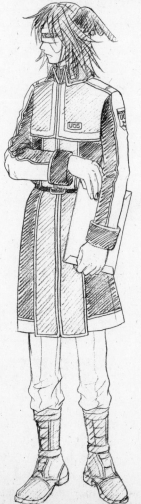
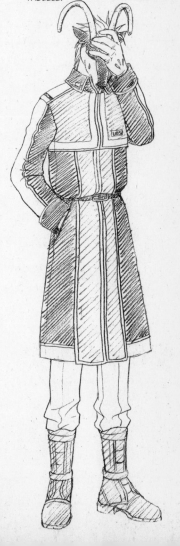

NORA LETTER CORNER

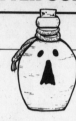

KAZUNARI KAKEI ANSWERS

YOUR QUESTIONS

Illustration by said friend →

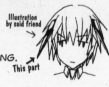

This part ↗

Q : PARDON ME IF I SEEM RUDE, BUT WHAT IS THAT THING ON GENERAL RIVAN'S HEAD? MY FRIEND SAYS IT'S A STORAGE CASE FOR THAT FAN HE'S ALWAYS HOLDING. WILL IT BECOME CLEAR WHEN HE RELEASES HIS SEAL SPELL? —DOIKO, IBARAKI PREFECTURE

A : A STORAGE CASE!! GREAT IDEA! LET'S GO WITH THAT!!

Q : WHAT EXACTLY IS "LAND-TYPE MAGIC"? —KAZUKI GAIKIN, KAGOSHIMA PREFECTURE

A : IT'S ACTUALLY KNOWN AS "TERRA MAGIA." THE LINE THAT EXPLAINS IT GOT LOST IN THE MAGAZINE EDITION, BUT WAS ADDED FOR THE BOOK. IT'S JUST A TYPE OF MAGIC. NO NEED TO STRESS ABOUT IT.

Q : CAN OTHER CHARACTERS BECOME BIG WHEN THEY TRANSFORM, LIKE NORA? —SHIGECO

A : THAT REMAINS TO BE SEEN.

Q : WHERE DO YOU GET YOUR FASCINATING IDEAS? —TAMAMI MIHIRA, CHIBA PREFECTURE

A : THANKS FOR THE COMPLIMENT. I LOVE FANS LIKE YOU.

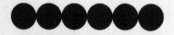

WE LOVE HEARING FROM YOU!

WRITE TO:
KAZUNARI KAKEI
C/O NORA EDITOR, VIZ MEDIA
P.O. BOX 77010
SAN FRANCISCO, CA
94107

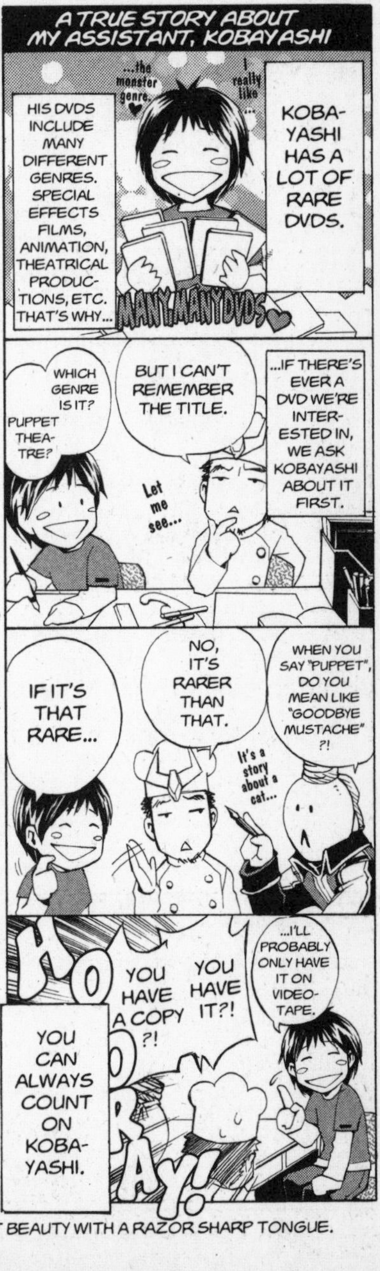
A TRUE STORY ABOUT MY ASSISTANT, KOBAYASHI
KOBA-YASHI HAS A LOT OF RARE DVDS.
I really like ...
...the monster genre.
HIS DVDS INCLUDE MANY DIFFERENT GENRES. SPECIAL EFFECTS FILMS, ANIMATION, THEATRICAL PRODUC-TIONS, ETC. THAT'S WHY...
MANY, MANY DVDS
...IF THERE'S EVER A DVD WE'RE INTER-ESTED IN, WE ASK KOBAYASHI ABOUT IT FIRST.
BUT I CAN'T REMEMBER THE TITLE.
Let me see...
WHICH GENRE IS IT?
PUPPET THEA-TRE?
WHEN YOU SAY "PUPPET", DO YOU MEAN LIKE "GOODBYE MUSTACHE" ?!
NO, IT'S RARER THAN THAT.
It's a story about a cat...
IF IT'S THAT RARE...
...I'LL PROBABLY ONLY HAVE IT ON VIDEO-TAPE.
YOU HAVE IT?!
YOU HAVE A COPY ?!
YOU CAN ALWAYS COUNT ON KOBA-YASHI.
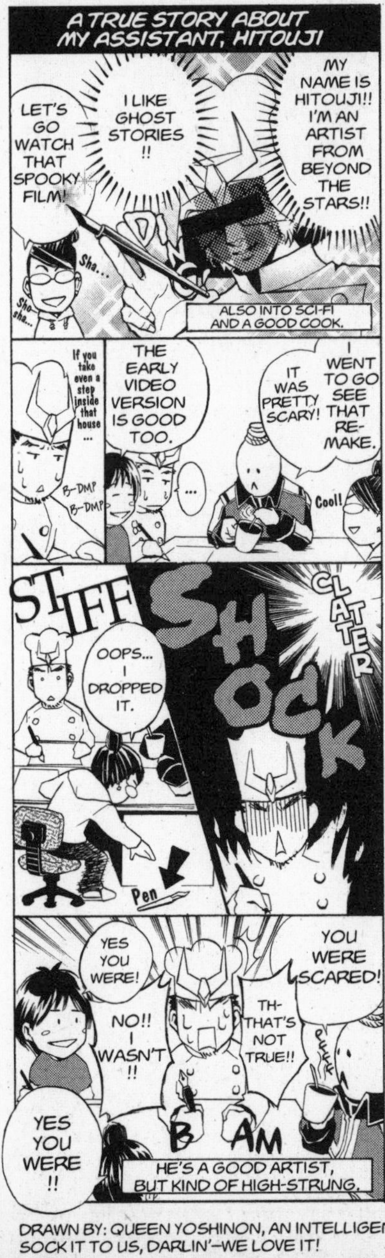
A TRUE STORY ABOUT MY ASSISTANT, HITOUJI
MY NAME IS HITOUJI!! I'M AN ARTIST FROM BEYOND THE STARS!!
I LIKE GHOST STORIES !!
LET'S GO WATCH THAT SPOOKY FILM!
Sha...
Sho-sha...
ALSO INTO SCI-FI AND A GOOD COOK.
I WENT TO GO SEE THAT RE-MAKE.
IT WAS PRETTY SCARY!
Cool!
THE EARLY VIDEO VERSION IS GOOD TOO.
...
If you take even a step inside that house ...
B-DMP B-DMP
CLATTER
SHOCK
STIFF
OOPS... I DROPPED IT.
Pen
YOU WERE SCARED!
TH-THAT'S NOT TRUE!!
YES YOU WERE!
NO!! I WASN'T !!
YES YOU WERE !!
BAM
HE'S A GOOD ARTIST, BUT KIND OF HIGH-STRUNG.

DRAWN BY: QUEEN YOSHINON, AN INTELLIGENT BEAUTY WITH A RAZOR SHARP TONGUE.
SOCK IT TO US, DARLIN'—WE LOVE IT!

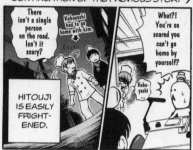

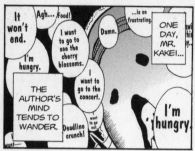

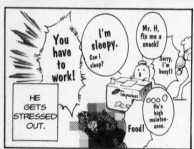

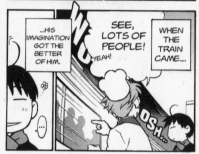

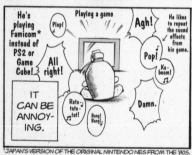

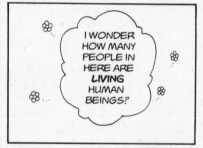

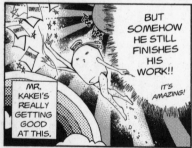

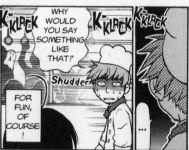

CONTINUATION OF THE PREVIOUS STORY→

What?! You're so scared you can't go home by yourself?
Koba-yashi...
There isn't a single person on the road. Isn't it scary?
Kobayashi had to go home with him.
glance
HITOUJI IS EASILY FRIGHTENED.
WHEN THE TRAIN CAME...
SEE, LOTS OF PEOPLE!
YEAH!
WOOSH...
...HIS IMAGINATION GOT THE BETTER OF HIM.
...
I WONDER HOW MANY PEOPLE IN HERE ARE **LIVING** HUMAN BEINGS?
K-KLACK
K-KLACK
WHY WOULD YOU SAY SOMETHING LIKE THAT?
K-KLACK
...
Shudder
FOR FUN, OF COURSE!

↑To combat his fear, he spent the whole time playing with his cell phone. -Kakei

DRAWN BY: KOBAYASHI, DVD MASTER AND ALL-AROUND TECHIE.

ONE DAY, MR. KAKEI...
...is so frustrating.
Damn.
Food!
Agh...
It won't end.
I want to go to see the cherry blossoms.
I'm hungry.
I want to go to the concert.
I'm hungry.
I want to go out.
Deadline crunch!
THE AUTHOR'S MIND TENDS TO WANDER.
Mr. H, fix me a snack!
Sorry, I'm busy!!
I'm sleepy.
Can I sleep?
You have to work!
Tangerines
He's high mainten-ance.
Food!
HE GETS STRESSED OUT.
He likes to repeat the sound effects from his game.
Agh!
Playing a game
Plop!
He's playing Famicom* instead of PS2 or Game Cube!
Pop!
Ka-boom!
All right!
Damn.
Rata-tata-tat!
Bang! Bang!
IT CAN BE ANNOYING.
*JAPAN'S VERSION OF THE ORIGINAL NINTENDO NES FROM THE '80S.
BUT SOMEHOW HE STILL FINISHES HIS WORK!!
IT'S AMAZING!
Tee hee
COMPLETE
COMPLETE
COMPLETE
MR. KAKEI'S REALLY GETTING GOOD AT THIS.

DRAWN BY: SHIBAYAN, THE ANGEL WHO BOUGHT ME A GAME WHEN I SAID I WANTED TO PLAY IT.

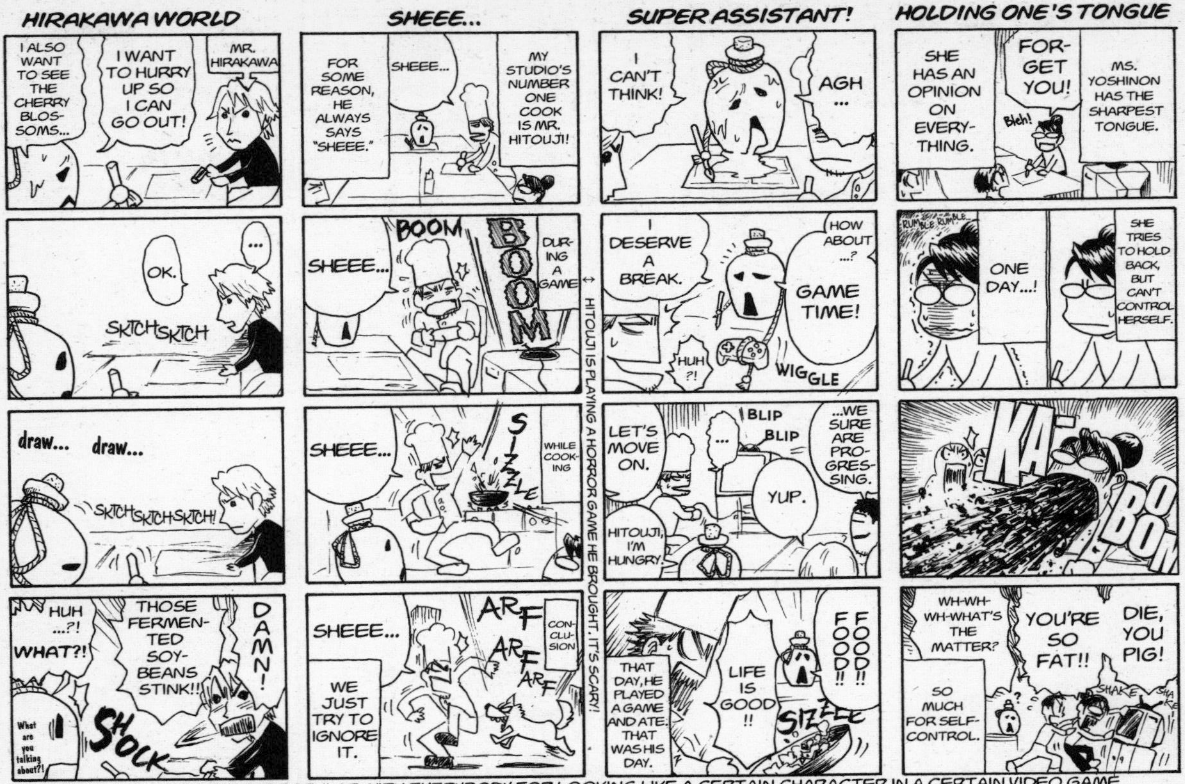
HOLDING ONE'S TONGUE
MS. YOSHINON HAS THE SHARPEST TONGUE.
FOR-GET YOU!
Bleh!
SHE HAS AN OPINION ON EVERY-THING.
SHE TRIES TO HOLD BACK, BUT CAN'T CONTROL HERSELF.
ONE DAY...!
RUMBLE RUMBLE
KA-
BOOM
DIE, YOU PIG!
YOU'RE SO FAT!!
SHAKE SHAKE
WH-WH-WH-WHAT'S THE MATTER?
SO MUCH FOR SELF-CONTROL.
SUPER ASSISTANT!
AGH ...
I CAN'T THINK!
HOW ABOUT ...?
GAME TIME!
WIGGLE
I DESERVE A BREAK.
HUH ?!
...WE SURE ARE PRO-GRES-SING.
BLIP BLIP
YUP.
...
LET'S MOVE ON.
HITOUJI, I'M HUNGRY.
FOOD!! FOOD!!
LIFE IS GOOD !!
SIZZLE
THAT DAY, HE PLAYED A GAME AND ATE. THAT WAS HIS DAY.
↔ HITOUJI IS PLAYING A HORROR GAME HE BROUGHT. IT'S SCARY!
SHEEE...
MY STUDIO'S NUMBER ONE COOK IS MR. HITOUJI!
SHEEE...
FOR SOME REASON, HE ALWAYS SAYS "SHEEE."
DUR-ING A GAME
BOOM
BOOM
SHEEE...
WHILE COOK-ING
SIZZLE
SHEEE...
CON-CLU-SION
ARF ARF ARF
SHEEE...
WE JUST TRY TO IGNORE IT.
HIRAKAWA WORLD
MR. HIRAKAWA
I WANT TO HURRY UP SO I CAN GO OUT!
I ALSO WANT TO SEE THE CHERRY BLOS-SOMS...
...
OK.
SKTCH SKTCH
SKTCH SKTCH SKTCH!
draw... draw...
DAMN!
THOSE FERMEN-TED SOY-BEANS STINK!!
HUH ...?! WHAT?!
SHOCK
What are you talking about?!

DRAWN BY: OHGA KING, WHO IS POPULAR WITH EVERYBODY FOR LOOKING LIKE A CERTAIN CHARACTER IN A CERTAIN VIDEO GAME (GUESS WHICH ONE!). HIS SPECIALTIES ARE VIDEO, MD EDITING, AND PLAYING THE GUITAR!

SEND YOUR FAN MAIL TO GENIUS COOK HITOUJI!!

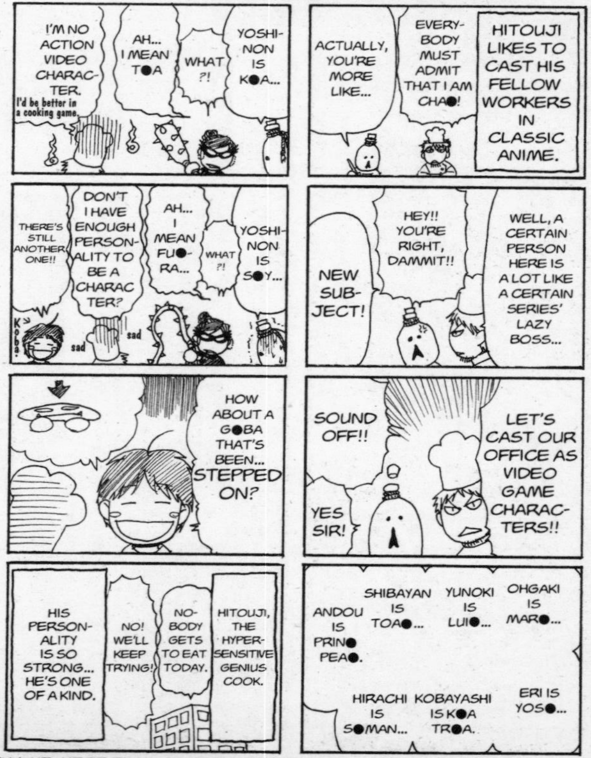
HITOUJI LIKES TO CAST HIS FELLOW WORKERS IN CLASSIC ANIME.
EVERYBODY MUST ADMIT THAT I AM CHA●!
ACTUALLY, YOU'RE MORE LIKE...
WELL, A CERTAIN PERSON HERE IS A LOT LIKE A CERTAIN SERIES' LAZY BOSS...
HEY!! YOU'RE RIGHT, DAMMIT!!
NEW SUBJECT!
LET'S CAST OUR OFFICE AS VIDEO GAME CHARACTERS!!
SOUND OFF!!
YES SIR!
OHGAKI IS MAR●...
YUNOKI IS LUI●...
SHIBAYAN IS TOA●...
ANDOU IS PRIN● PEA●.
ERI IS YOS●...
KOBAYASHI IS K●A TR●A.
HIRACHI IS S●MAN...
YOSHINON IS K●A...
WHAT ?!
AH... I MEAN T●A
I'M NO ACTION VIDEO CHARACTER.
I'd be better in a cooking game.
YOSHINON IS S●Y...
WHAT ?!
AH... I MEAN FU●RA...
DON'T I HAVE ENOUGH PERSONALITY TO BE A CHARACTER?
THERE'S STILL ANOTHER ONE!!
Koba
sad
sad
HOW ABOUT A G●BA THAT'S BEEN... STEPPED ON?
HITOUJI, THE HYPERSENSITIVE GENIUS COOK.
NOBODY GETS TO EAT TODAY.
NO! WE'LL KEEP TRYING!
HIS PERSONALITY IS SO STRONG... HE'S ONE OF A KIND.

HIRAKAWA WORLD, PART TWO

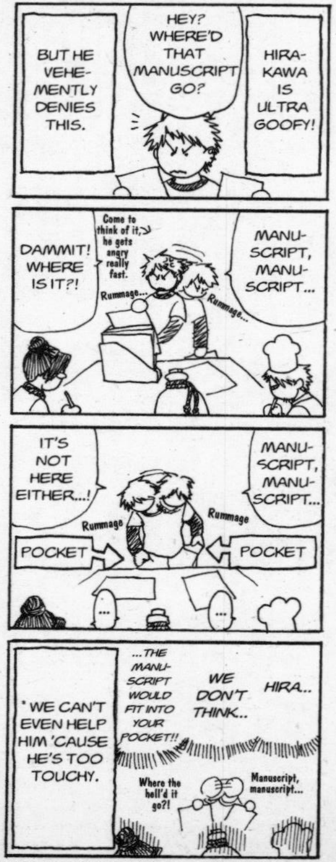
HIRAKAWA IS ULTRA GOOFY!
HEY? WHERE'D THAT MANUSCRIPT GO?
BUT HE VEHEMENTLY DENIES THIS.
MANUSCRIPT, MANUSCRIPT...
Rummage...
Come to think of it, he gets angry really fast.
Rummage...
DAMMIT! WHERE IS IT?!
MANUSCRIPT, MANUSCRIPT...
Rummage
POCKET
Rummage
POCKET
IT'S NOT HERE EITHER...!
...
...
HIRA...
WE DON'T THINK...
...THE MANUSCRIPT WOULD FIT INTO YOUR POCKET!!
Manuscript, manuscript...
Where the hell'd it go?!
"WE CAN'T EVEN HELP HIM 'CAUSE HE'S TOO TOUCHY.

THE COOKING MANGAKA

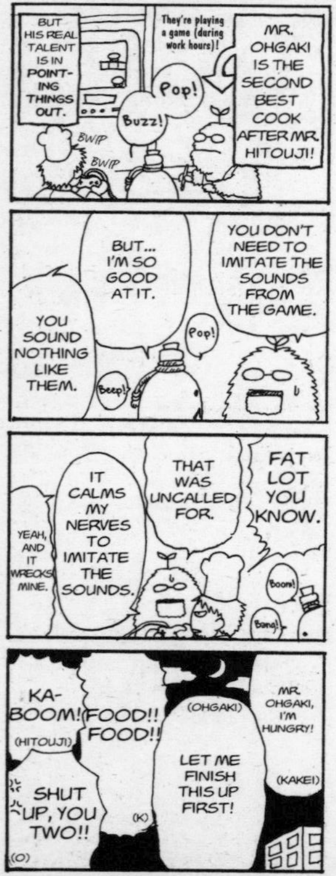
MR. OHGAKI IS THE SECOND BEST COOK AFTER MR. HITOUJI!
They're playing a game (during work hours)!
Pop!
Buzz!
BUT HIS REAL TALENT IS IN POINTING THINGS OUT.
BWIP
BWIP
YOU DON'T NEED TO IMITATE THE SOUNDS FROM THE GAME.
BUT... I'M SO GOOD AT IT.
Pop!
YOU SOUND NOTHING LIKE THEM.
Beep!
FAT LOT YOU KNOW.
THAT WAS UNCALLED FOR.
IT CALMS MY NERVES TO IMITATE THE SOUNDS.
YEAH, AND IT WRECKS MINE.
Boom!
Bang!
MR. OHGAKI, I'M HUNGRY!
(KAKEI)
(OHGAKI)
LET ME FINISH THIS UP FIRST!
FOOD!! FOOD!!
(K)
KA-BOOM!
(HITOUJI)
SHUT UP, YOU TWO!!
(O)

DRAWN BY KAZUNARI KAKEI, WHO HAD TO EXPLAIN TO OUR EDITOR WHY WE WERE PLAYING VIDEO GAMES INSTEAD OF WORKING.

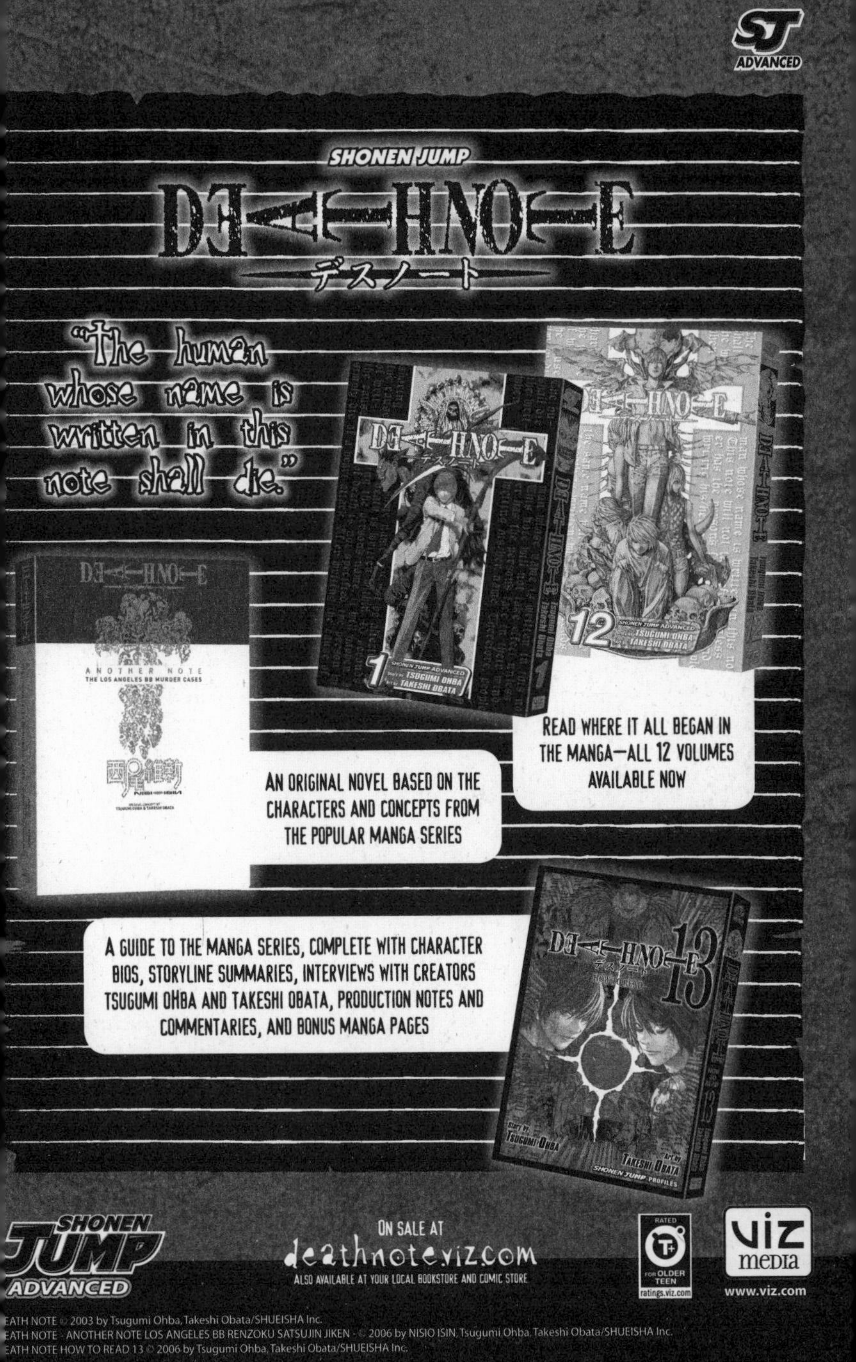
SJ ADVANCED
SHONEN JUMP
DEATH NOTE
デスノート
"The human whose name is written in this note shall die."
AN ORIGINAL NOVEL BASED ON THE CHARACTERS AND CONCEPTS FROM THE POPULAR MANGA SERIES
READ WHERE IT ALL BEGAN IN THE MANGA—ALL 12 VOLUMES AVAILABLE NOW
A GUIDE TO THE MANGA SERIES, COMPLETE WITH CHARACTER BIOS, STORYLINE SUMMARIES, INTERVIEWS WITH CREATORS TSUGUMI OHBA AND TAKESHI OBATA, PRODUCTION NOTES AND COMMENTARIES, AND BONUS MANGA PAGES
ANOTHER NOTE
THE LOS ANGELES BB MURDER CASES
SHONEN JUMP ADVANCED
TSUGUMI OHBA
TAKESHI OBATA
Story by TSUGUMI OHBA
Art by TAKESHI OBATA
SHONEN JUMP PROFILES
SHONEN JUMP ADVANCED
ON SALE AT
deathnote.viz.com
ALSO AVAILABLE AT YOUR LOCAL BOOKSTORE AND COMIC STORE
RATED T+ FOR OLDER TEEN
ratings.viz.com
viz media
www.viz.com

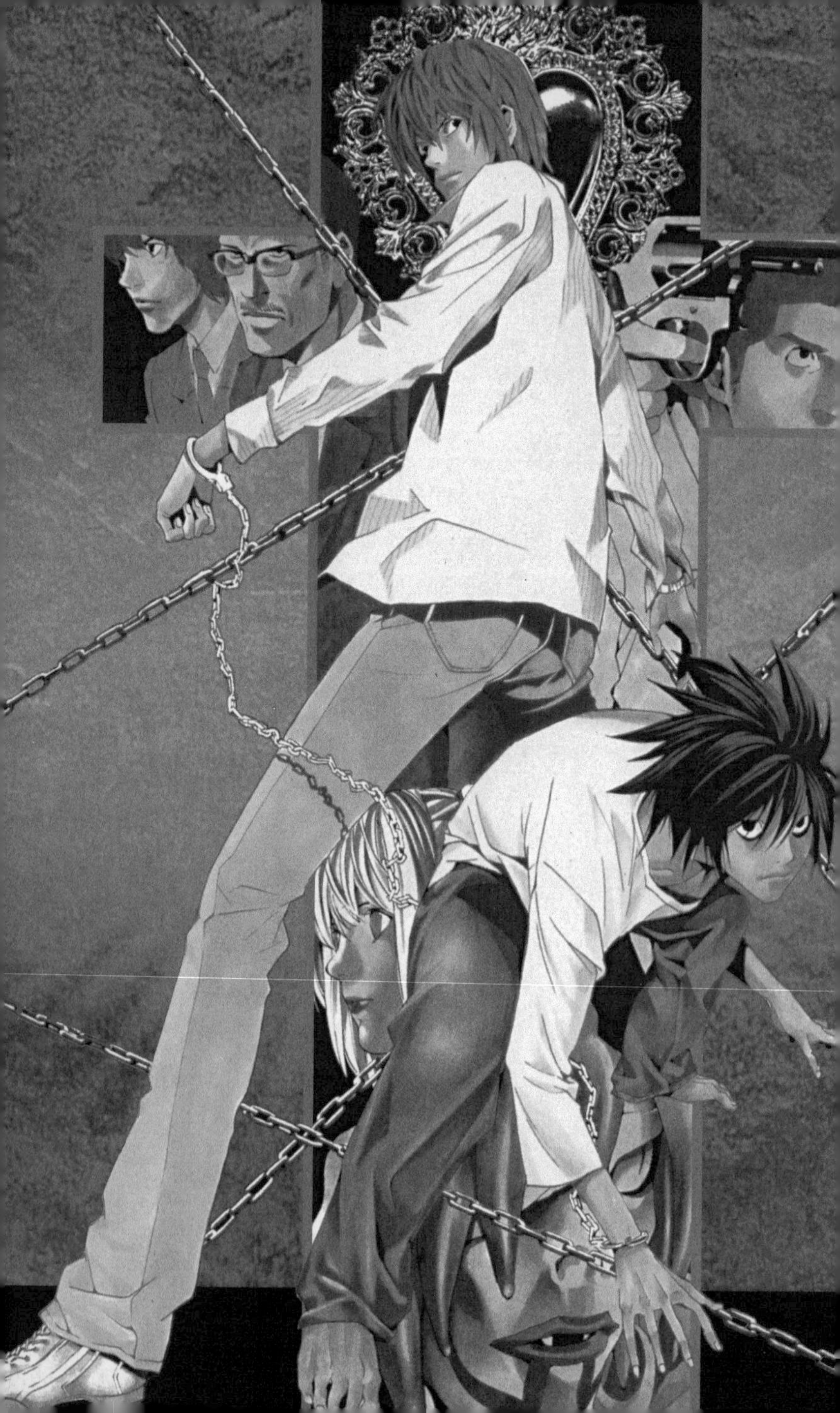

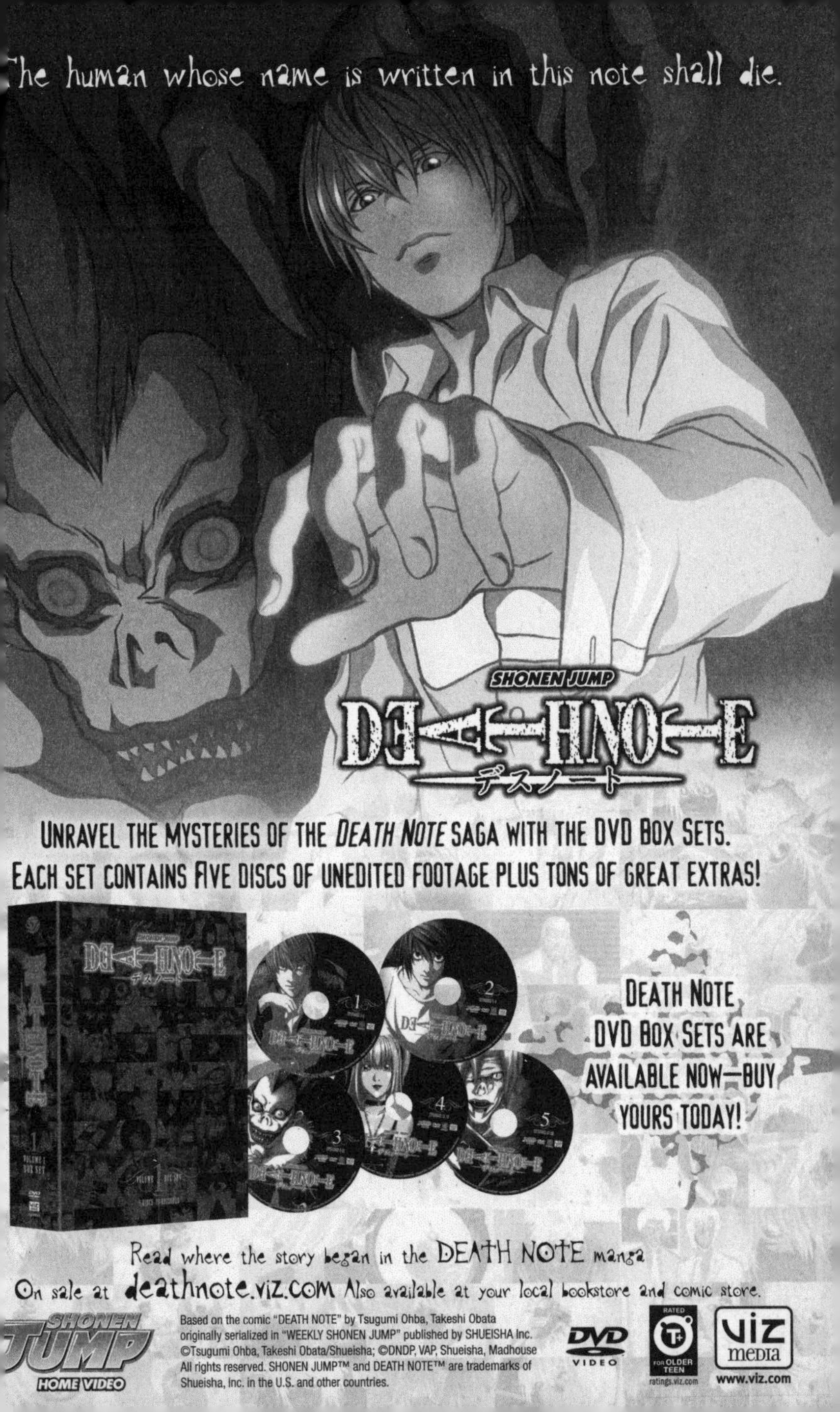

The human whose name is written in this note shall die.
SHONEN JUMP
DEATH NOTE
デスノート
UNRAVEL THE MYSTERIES OF THE DEATH NOTE SAGA WITH THE DVD BOX SETS.
EACH SET CONTAINS FIVE DISCS OF UNEDITED FOOTAGE PLUS TONS OF GREAT EXTRAS!
DEATH NOTE DVD BOX SETS ARE AVAILABLE NOW—BUY YOURS TODAY!
Read where the story began in the DEATH NOTE manga
On sale at deathnote.viz.com Also available at your local bookstore and comic store.
SHONEN JUMP HOME VIDEO
Based on the comic "DEATH NOTE" by Tsugumi Ohba, Takeshi Obata originally serialized in "WEEKLY SHONEN JUMP" published by SHUEISHA Inc. ©Tsugumi Ohba, Takeshi Obata/Shueisha; ©DNDP, VAP, Shueisha, Madhouse All rights reserved. SHONEN JUMP™ and DEATH NOTE™ are trademarks of Shueisha, Inc. in the U.S. and other countries.
DVD VIDEO
RATED T+ FOR OLDER TEEN
ratings.viz.com
viz media
www.viz.com

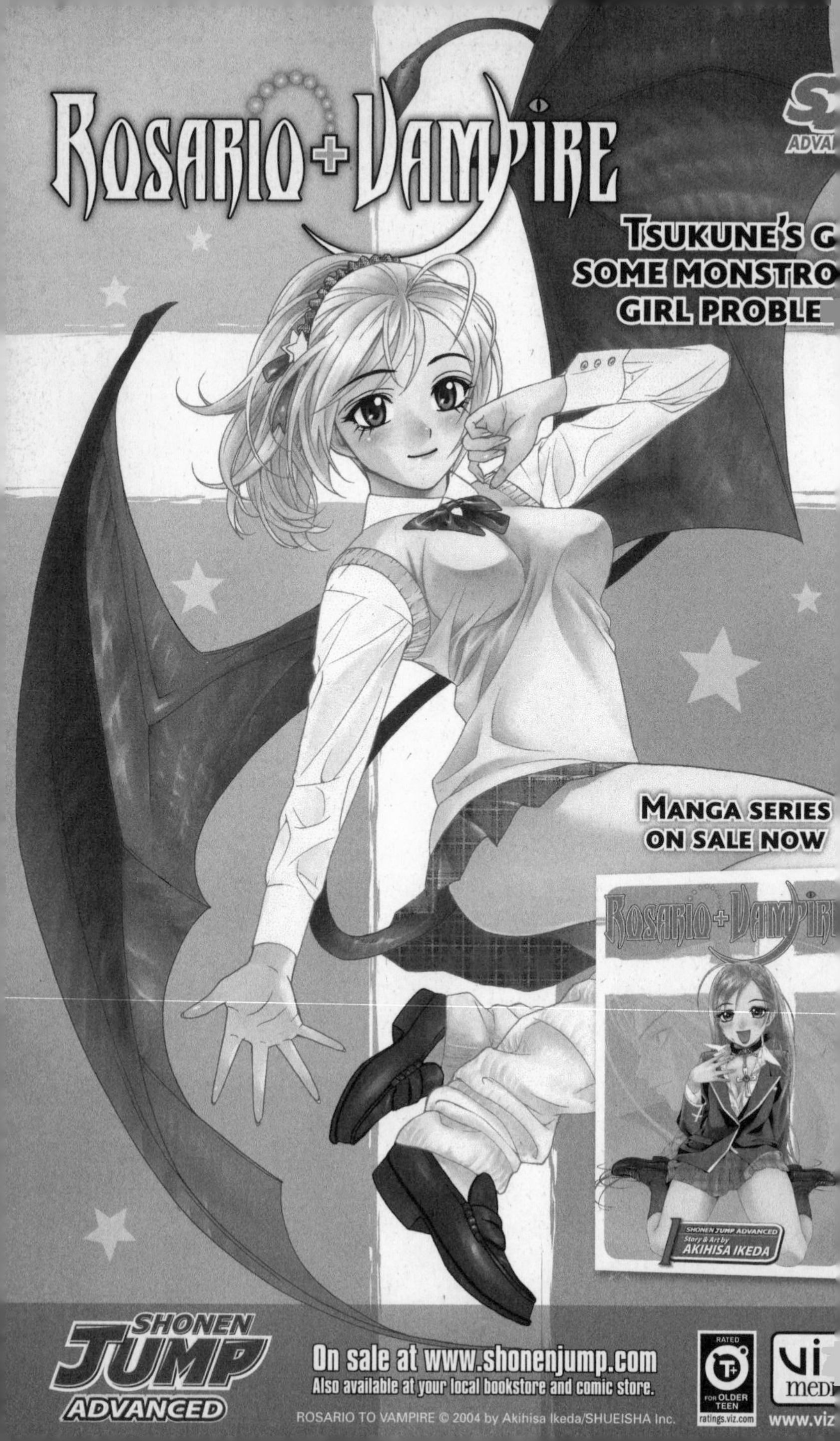
ROSARIO+VAMPIRE
TSUKUNE'S G
SOME MONSTRO
GIRL PROBLE
MANGA SERIES
ON SALE NOW
ROSARIO+VAMPIRE
SHONEN JUMP ADVANCED
Story & Art by
AKIHISA IKEDA
SHONEN JUMP ADVANCED
On sale at www.shonenjump.com
Also available at your local bookstore and comic store.
ROSARIO TO VAMPIRE © 2004 by Akihisa Ikeda/SHUEISHA Inc.
RATED T+ FOR OLDER TEEN
ratings.viz.com
www.viz

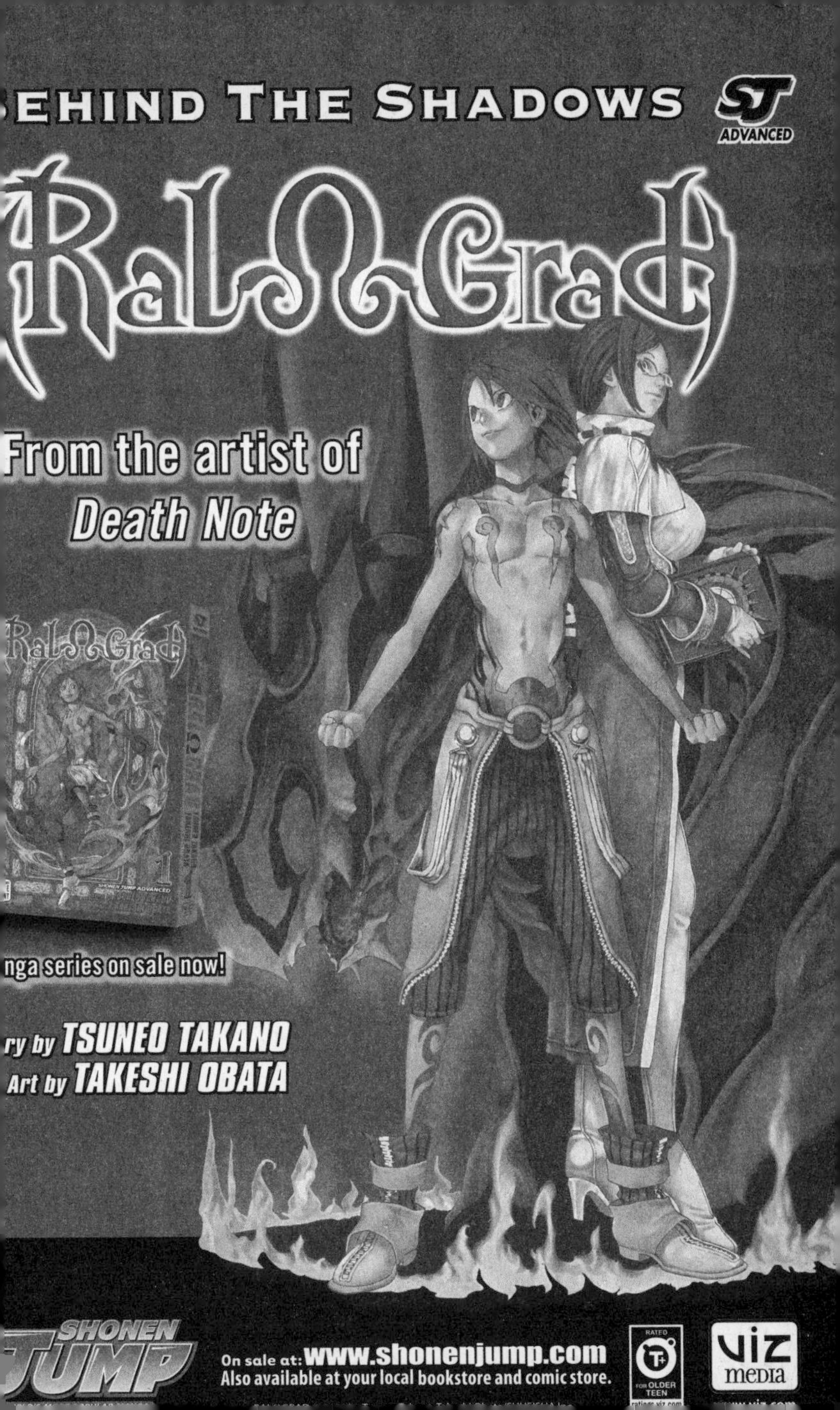

EHIND THE SHADOWS
SJ ADVANCED
RalΩGrad
From the artist of
Death Note
RalΩGrad
SHONEN JUMP ADVANCED
1
nga series on sale now!
ry by TSUNEO TAKANO
Art by TAKESHI OBATA
SHONEN JUMP
On sale at: www.shonenjump.com
Also available at your local bookstore and comic store.
RATED T+ FOR OLDER TEEN
viz media

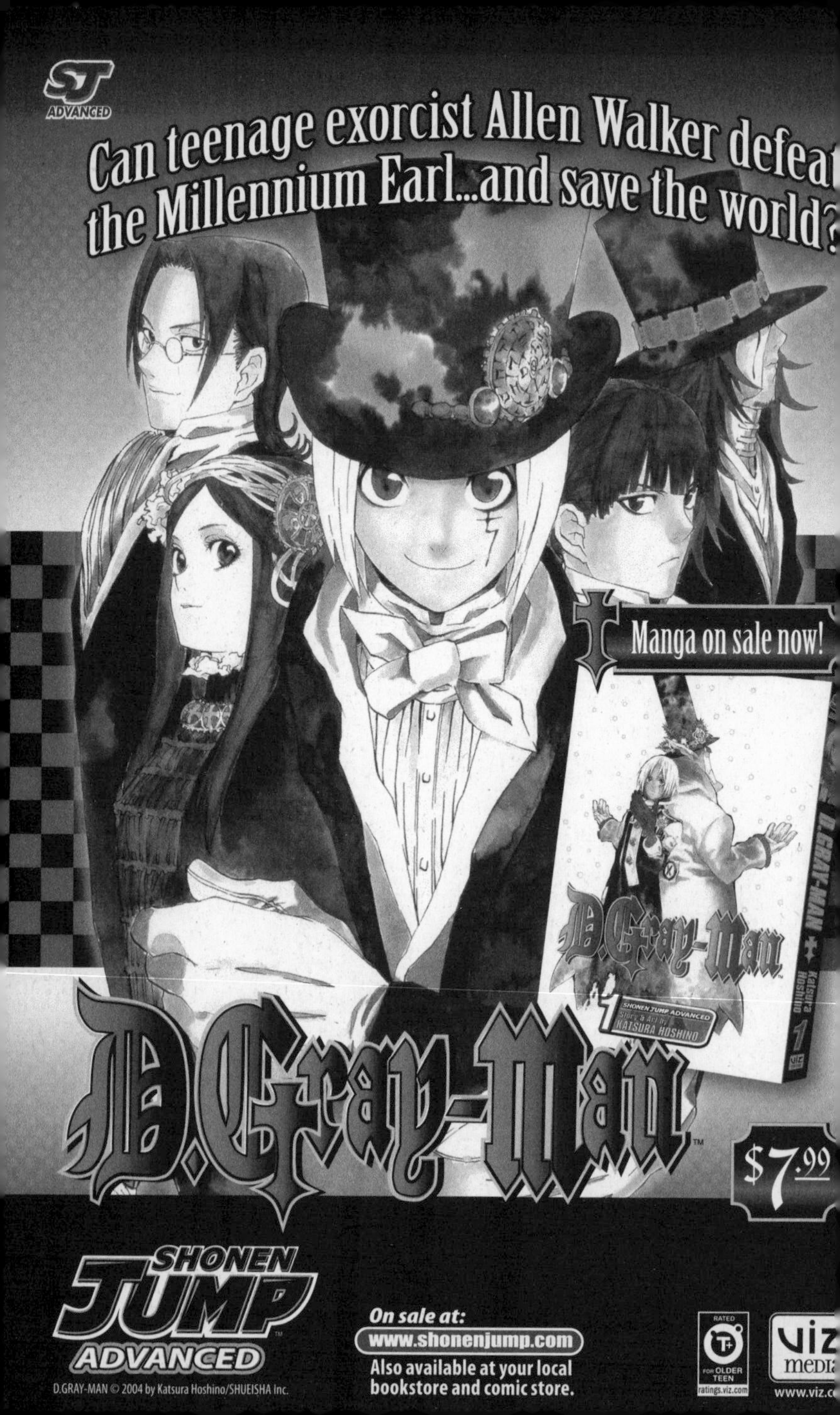
SJ ADVANCED
Can teenage exorcist Allen Walker defeat the Millennium Earl...and save the world?
Manga on sale now!
D.Gray-man
SHONEN JUMP ADVANCED
Story & Art by KATSURA HOSHINO
D.Gray-man™
$7.99
SHONEN JUMP ADVANCED
On sale at:
www.shonenjump.com
Also available at your local bookstore and comic store.
RATED T+ FOR OLDER TEEN
ratings.viz.com
viz media
D.GRAY-MAN © 2004 by Katsura Hoshino/SHUEISHA Inc.

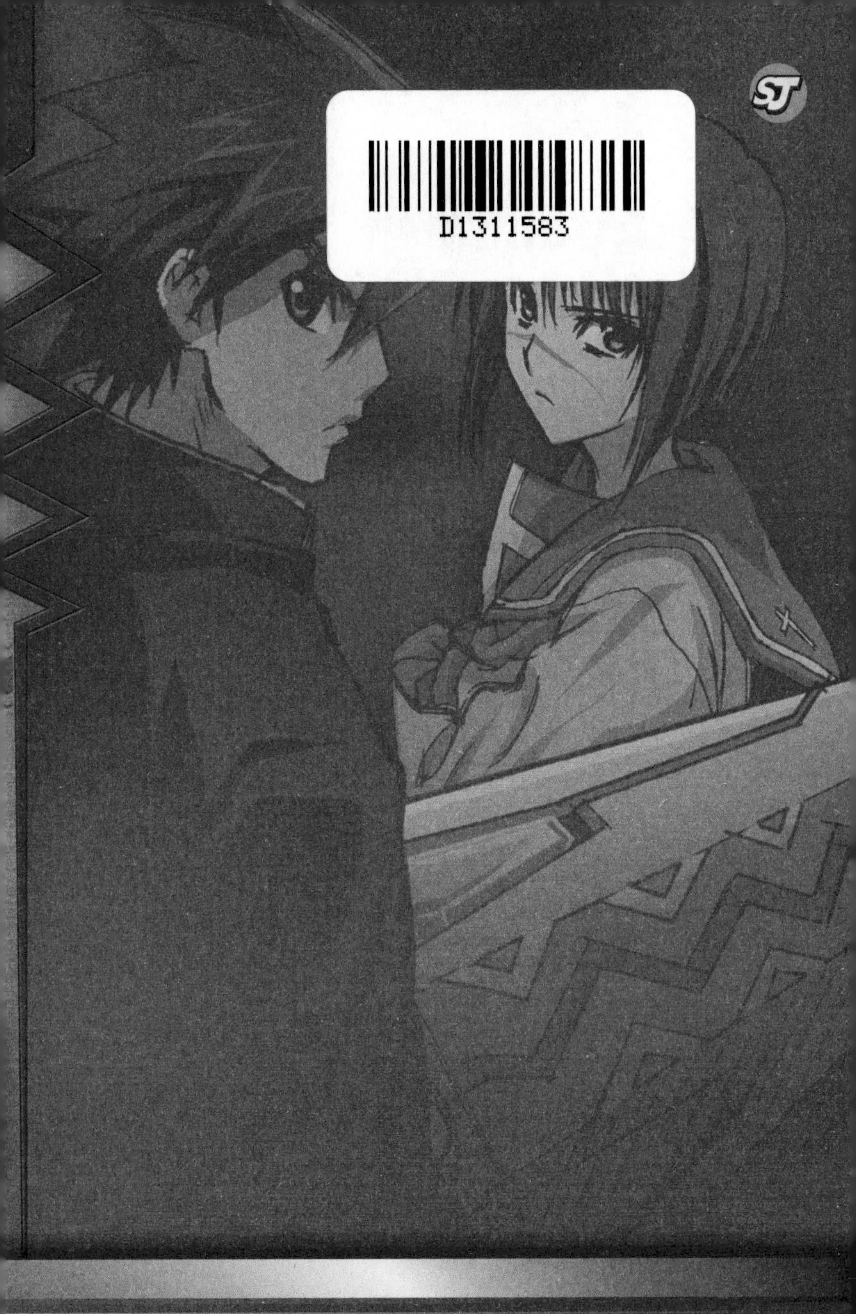

www.viz.com